Europeanisation as violence

Manchester University Press

Europeanisation as violence

Souths and Easts as method

Edited by

Kolar Aparna, Daria Krivonos
and Elisa Pascucci

MANCHESTER UNIVERSITY PRESS

Copyright © Manchester University Press 2025

While copyright in the volume as a whole is vested in Manchester University Press, copyright in individual chapters belongs to their respective authors, and no chapter may be reproduced wholly or in part without the express permission in writing of both author and publisher.

This electronic version has been made freely available under a Creative Commons (CC BY-NC-ND) licence, thanks to the support of the University of Helsinki, which permits non-commercial use, distribution and reproduction provided the author(s) and Manchester University Press are fully cited and no modifications or adaptations are made. Details of the licence can be viewed at https://creativecommons.org/licenses/by-nc-nd/4.0/deed.en

Published by Manchester University Press
Oxford Road, Manchester, M13 9PL

www.manchesteruniversitypress.co.uk

British Library Cataloguing-in-Publication Data
A catalogue record for this book is available from the British Library

ISBN 978 1 5261 7472 7 hardback

First published 2025

The publisher has no responsibility for the persistence or accuracy of URLs for any external or third-party internet websites referred to in this book, and does not guarantee that any content on such websites is, or will remain, accurate or appropriate.

Typeset by Newgen Publishing UK

Contents

List of figures	vii
Foreword by Manuela Boatcă	viii
Acknowledgements	xv
Introduction: Europeanisation as violence: Souths and Easts as method – Daria Krivonos, Kolar Aparna and Elisa Pascucci	1

Part I: Europeanisation as infrastructural violence and colonial asymmetries

1 Europeanisation and infrastructural violence in South East Europe – Senka Neuman Stanivuković	33
2 Europeanisation, border violence, counterinsurgency: expanded geographies and reconnected histories across the Sahelo-Sahara and the Mediterranean – Hassan Ould Moctar	51
3 A battleground for French and Russian imperialism: how Chad's (post)socialist and (post-)colonial present is shaping its political future – Kelma Manatouma	68
4 The making of 'the bread basket of Europe': from the Dutch East India Company to the East Company in Ukraine and grain in the Soviet Union – Daria Krivonos and Kolar Aparna	82

Part II: Europeanisation as slow violence and stratified subalternities

5 No alternative but Europeanisation: slow violence and critical imaginaries in/from/with South East Europe – Maria-Adriana Deiana and Katarina Kušić	101

6 Hierarchising heritage: bordering Europe and stratified
 subalternities in the Easts and Souths of Europe
 – Alexandra Oancă   120
7 The good, the bad and the ugly European: racial Eastern
 Europeanisation and stratified (sub)alter(n)ities – Ana Ivasiuc   142

Part III: Europeanisation as epistemic dispossession

8 The trauma of the key beyond dominant narratives:
 navigating epistemic and structural violence in Yemen's
 historical landscape – Saba Hamzah   163
9 From singular to plural: how to write the story
 of a Roma actress – Mihaela Drăgan   184

Part IV: Border epistemologies of Europeanisation

10 Patterns of coloniality within the innovation economy: talent
 attraction and the converging racialising processes
 of migration administration – Olivia Maury   195
11 'Keep your clients because I quit': An ethnodrama
 of creolising research with Roma women – Ioana Țîștea   212
12 Swimming with the coelacanth into the black holes
 of Breslau/Wrocław, the Eastern Polish Kresy
 and Madagascar – Olivier Kramsch   230

Afterword: Souths, Easts and the politics of dissent
at this colonial conjuncture – Prem Kumar Rajaram   248

Index   259

List of figures

3.1	Map of Chad	69
8.1	Wooden lock with keys, Tropen Museum/Wereld Museum, Amsterdam	163
8.2	Wooden lock with keys, Tropen Museum/Wereld Museum, Amsterdam	165
8.3	An old notebook that I found in the notebooks section in a supermarket during my research stay in Doha	165
8.4	Ghaiman, the home	169
8.5	Ghaiman, the old gate	170
8.6	Asad Alkamel foot on a stone on a building in Ghaiman	171
8.7	My mother's aunt, my Western grandmother: Atika Hamdan	173
8.8	Excavated gold heads, gift from Yemen at the coronation of the British King. Sana'a, 1942	176
12.1	The German Reich, 1920–37	232
12.2	Kresy	236
12.3	Reconstruction of a West Indian Ocean coelacanth: 'archaique, lourd, gras et gluant' (Millot, cited in Coppens, 1988: 122–23)	240

Foreword

Manuela Boatcă

During his speech at the inauguration of the European Diplomatic Academy in Bruges in October 2022, EU foreign policy chief Josep Borrell infamously pitted Europe against the non-European world in unmistakably racist colonial terms. Europe, Borrell declared live on camera, 'is a garden' in which everything works, 'the best combination of political freedom, economic prosperity and social cohesion that humankind has been able to build' (Borrell, 2022). At the same time, Borrell went on, directly addressing the rector of the College of Europe in Bruges and former Vice-President of the European Commission, Federica Mogherini – 'the rest of the world – and you know very well, Federica – is a jungle and the jungle could invade the garden' (Borrell, 2022). While walls built around the nice little garden could never be high enough to protect it, he suggested, the gardeners – that is, Europeans – could prevent the invasion by going to the 'jungle' – by being 'much more engaged with the rest of the world' (Borrell, 2022).

Almost seventy years after the publication of Aimé Césaire's 'Discourse on Colonialism' (1955), Borrell's speech unwittingly but clearly echoed the Martinican writer and politician's famous synthesis of Europe's violent history and its roots in long-standing colonial politics: For Césaire, the violence perpetrated by the Nazis during the Second World War only differed from other national politics in Europe by 'having applied to Europe colonialist procedures which until then had been applied only to non-European peoples' (Césaire, [1955] 2001: 36). The continuities and parallels between European colonial rule and latter-day racial politics in the metropoles that Césaire pointed to would soon thereafter be addressed by scholars across the colonial world and their allies in Europe – from Frantz Fanon and Jean-Paul Sartre to Hannah Arendt, Ambalavaner Sivanandan or Edward Said.

The public outcry that followed the broadcasting of Borrell's speech and the apology he soon issued as a result do not change the imagined geography that his framing evoked. As a Catalan politician who holds both Spanish and Argentinean citizenship thanks to his family's immigration to

Argentina, where his father was born, Borrell was acquainted with Europe's South and its internal hierarchies and was well aware of the long history of emigration from Europe to its (former) colonies. He nevertheless chose to place himself, his Italian colleague Mogherini and the European project as a whole firmly within an unmarked notion of Europe. This notion not only conflates Europe with the European Union project but also conveniently rids the latter of any – historical or present – connections to its Eurafrican beginnings, its ongoing control of non-European territories from the Caribbean to the Indian Ocean, and its political, military and economic interventions in non-European affairs. Indeed, Borrell's plea for increased engagement with 'the rest of the world' is a call for more, not fewer, such interventions. He thus provides only the most recent instance in a long line of colonial and racist imaginaries of Europeanisation as violence.

Starting instead, as this volume does, from the largely unacknowledged minor of global social theory – Europe's external and internal Souths and Easts, their overlapping territories and entangled histories of violence – is a radical endeavour and an urgent one. It addresses, both directly and indirectly, a specific dimension of several recent calls to place Europeanisation in the *longue durée* and trace it back to global structures (Böröcz, 2009; Hansen and Jonsson, 2014; Nicolaïdis et al., 2014). Such initiatives have paved the way for making the histories and legacies of colonialism and its manifest violences the point of departure of notions of Europeanisation; and they have offered lenses that reveal the European prosecution, extermination, enslavement, racialisation and evangelisation of Europe's internal and external Others as central to processes of Europeanisation. Against this background of colonial and imperial violence, Europeanisation has been shown to have been multifaceted. Europeanisation was just as much colonisation, enslavement and the plantation economy since the sixteenth century as it was the attempt at Eurafrican 'integration' and 'interdependence' in the mid-twentieth century. The term 'Europeanisation' also describes just as much the uneven and asymmetrical 'Eastern' Enlargement of the European Union at the beginning of the twenty-first century as it captures the colonial continuities that the dozens of extra-European territories still under the control of European states embody today (Santos and Boatcă, 2022). The present volume takes up this call for a fundamentally relational methodology at a specific juncture, and a rarely acknowledged one: the complementary but competing, the related but disavowed exclusion and racialisation of Europe's Souths and Easts, alongside their unequal inclusion and willing participation in violent projects of Europeanisation. Through theorising from across subalternities, Souths and Easts as a method reveals two often invisibilised outcomes of the violence of Europeanisation: the multiplicity of unequal Europes, or what the editors call the 'gradations of peripherality', and its rarely discussed counterpart, the interconnected complicity of Europe's East and South in Western coloniality and inter-imperiality. The subordinate imperial position prevented neither the 'decadent Europe' in the South nor 'epigonal Europe' in the East from harbouring imperial ambitions, embarking in active colonial exploits or partaking in the benefits of colonialism. Instead, decadent and epigonal Europes played joint, yet distinct, roles as accomplices of coloniality (Boatcă, 2013, 2021). While the South of Europe had declined from hegemony by the end of the seventeenth century, and the East of Europe never attained it, the two shared an economically and politically semiperipheral position in the capitalist world economy. As such, they oscillated between imperial nostalgia and the aspiration to Europeanness as defined from the self-proclaimed 'heroic Europe' of the hegemonic West. As perpetual candidates to Europeanisation on these Occidentalist terms, scholars, travellers and entrepreneurs from these 'other' Europes advanced Orientalist projects and migrated in high numbers to Europe's overseas colonies (Schär and Toivanen, 2024). They upheld notions of European whiteness and perpetuated racial colonial tropes even while being periodically defined out of whiteness themselves. If Borrell's family migrated from Spain to Argentina, theirs was a trajectory that millions of Southern and Eastern Europeans embarked upon at the end of the nineteenth century and the beginning of the twentieth, when Argentina and Brazil alone received more than one-fifth of all European migrants (Museo de la Inmigración, 2024). The Brazilian government was particularly active in explicitly recruiting European settlers with a view to 'whitening' its predominantly Black and mestizo population, so it even subsidised travel to Brazil for Eastern and Southern European immigrants for the purpose. The unprecedented surge in the number of (potential) settlers led the Hungarian government to ban immigration to Brazil altogether at the end of 1900 and the Spanish government to temporarily prohibit Brazilian subsidies for settlers in the early 1910s (Klein, 1992). Yet politics of 'whitening' through European migration were pursued across the Americas, from Central America and the Caribbean to Argentina, Colombia, Venezuela and Peru. In relinking these entangled histories of global Souths and Easts, the goal of the present volume is neither to unilaterally assign nor to finally exonerate either decadent or epigonal Europes from responsibility but to reveal the fundamental, long-standing historical relationality between the Souths and the Easts as a basis for what the editors envisage as 'common, coalitional, anti-racist and anti-imperial politics'.

One of the most salient examples that binds together the global South and East geographies with the violence of Europeanisation is the historical and present experience of the Roma. Not incidentally, it is a recurrent topic in this volume and a number of its dimensions are addressed at length in several chapters. How does Roma history belong to both the South and the East – and does this provide us with a fundamentally relational method? After eighteenth-century European ethnographies of the Roma traced their origin back to India, linguists took up the link between India and Europe as a way of including the Roma in a 'European family'. Yet insisting on the start of the Romani migration in India rather served as a way to Orientalise the Roma as a group (Parvulescu and Boatcă, 2022). At the same time, the five hundred years of enslavement of the Roma on the territory of today's Romania at the hands of the state, the local nobility and the Orthodox Church reinforced both the Orientalisation of the Roma as a group and that of the European East as the West's Other. While the West first initiated and greatly expanded transatlantic slavery, it later abolished it and gradually declared it incompatible with the principle of liberty on French or British soil. What Aparna, Krivonos and Pascucci call the 'fractured teleology of EUropean progress' thus hails back and relates to heroic Europe's older claims to an unbroken linear development towards enlightened politics (the only tragic and uncharacteristic exception to which is considered to have been the Holocaust). In contrast, the Romanian provinces, in which Roma slavery was legal until 1856 and which paid tribute to the Ottoman Empire up to the end of the nineteenth century, appeared as permanently less enlightened, civilised, free and ultimately less European – indeed, as a despotic Orient. As Talal Asad pointed out with respect to Muslims, the other group frequently defined in terms of its Asian origins and written out of Europeanness as a result: 'the "myth of Europe" defines the extent of its own solidarity. "The myth of Europe" does not simply suppress the collective memories of violence within Europe; the resurrection of those memories strengthens that myth' (Asad, 2002: 212). In turn, the violence imputed to Europe's Others is not a past lesson that has been or could be overcome through civilising efforts but an irredeemable essence that forever prevents access to (full) Europeanness. Unlike Muslims, who were perpetually viewed through the lens of the threat to Christendom that Islam represented throughout its history, but on the other hand just like Muslims, who have been present *in* Europe for centuries, the Roma are also still not considered *of* Europe (Asad, 2002; El-Tayeb, 2011). Nor are Muslims or Roma part of Europe's reckoning with either racism or enslavement, which routinely restricts European racism temporally to the Holocaust, conflating racism with antisemitism; and relegates enslavement spatially to Africa and the Americas, equating enslavement with Western Europe's transatlantic trade. A fundamentally relational method that connects the Souths and Easts that Romani European history encapsulates thus fulfils a double function: it prevents the Roma from repeatedly falling through these temporal and spatial cracks in Europe's politics of memory (Costache, 2020; Furtună and Turcitu, 2021); and it exposes the integral role that slavery kept playing on the European continent until the mid-nineteenth century through the violently racial institution that was Romani enslavement, which also included significant numbers of Muslim Roma (Achim, 2023).

In terms of this history's reverberations in the present, at stake is the larger question of when migration stops being the permanent background against which one's belonging, citizenship and Europeanness are being measured. Those to which migration is ascribed by default, such as Muslims and Roma, are thereby constantly left on the margins of all the above norms, including citizenship, and mostly defined out of whiteness. The assumption that certain individuals or groups have (recently) migrated, whether or not they ever actually did, has been theorised as 'migratism' – a form of racism when directed at those racialised as non-white (Tudor, 2023). The 800 years since the Romani migration into Europe still do not warrant their acknowledgment as *Romani Europeans* today, indeed that very designation is unthinkable, to echo Michel Rolph Trouillot's term for the Haitian Revolution (Trouillot, 1995). Conversely, as Asad notes, even though European Muslims 'may not have migrated to Europe from Asia, they cannot claim a Europeanness – as the inhabitants of Christian Europe can' (Asad, 2002: 213). The recurrent interpellation of Muslims, Roma and Black Europeans as migrants instead of citizens is thus not only an instance of migratism but reveals that their unequal citizenship status in Europe is only a late moment in a long history of being at the margins of different regimes of belonging that long predated the emergence of citizenship as an institution but are being reinforced through it.

Both migration and citizenship rely on constructed and often brutally policed borders. Here, too, the connection between the various violent impositions on the Souths and the Easts is more than apparent. While more than half of the borders of the world outside of Europe have been drawn by distant powers, and the vast majority of them resulted from British and French imperial intervention alone, most of today's borders in Central and Eastern Europe have been drafted by West European imperial states as part of the dissolution and reorganisation of local empires (Böröcz and Sarkar, 2005: 161). As expressions of the influence of successive hegemons and of competing colonial and imperial states, Europe's current borders thus 'at once protect and threaten its unity, define its authority, and engage with external powers that have entered its domain. The "inside" cannot contain the "outside", violent cultures cannot inhabit a civil one, Europe cannot contain non-Europe' (Asad, 2002: 219). Importantly, borders also function as bargaining currency in the process of continually enlisting the South and East of Europe in complicity with Western coloniality and imperiality, as Aparna, Krivonos and Pascucci remind us. The process of 'Eastern enlargement' required new members states to become the easternmost guardians of EU borders – or, in Borrell's imagery, its (new) gardeners. At the same time, the promise of eventual EU membership in an as yet uncertain future continues to tether the remaining Eastern European states to border policing functions against those racialised as non-European or non-white. When defined unilaterally from positions of power, Europeanisation is therefore but a fleeting prospect with moving goalposts. The framing of Russia's full-scale invasion of Ukraine in the Western media and politics as 'war in the midst of Europe' propelled Ukraine to the centre of notions of Europeanisation and, later, EU access negotiations, while, as this volume's editors point out, detention centres built with EU funding for non-Europeans fleeing war and poverty were operating on Ukrainian territory. Even as the EU proclaimed solidarity with Ukrainian refugees, Ukrainian Roma and African students fleeing Ukraine faced racial discrimination both at the Ukrainian border and upon arrival in the EU. Meanwhile, many Ukrainians, regardless of their qualifications, joined the ranks of the Eastern European seasonal agricultural workers in the West whose insufficient protection, mistreatment and overexploitation had made numerous headlines since the start of the COVID-19 pandemic. That refugees from Belarus, Syria or Palestine were not and still are not offered the same choice runs the risk of remaining incomprehensible and of continuing to prompt convenient images of peaceful gardens and unruly jungles. Unless, that is, all the Souths and Easts that have been an integral part of constructing and maintaining Europeanisation as violence are consistently deployed as a method of unthinking and dismantling it.

References

Achim, V. (2023) 'Slavery in southeastern Europe', in Pargas, D. A. and Schiel, J. (eds) *The Palgrave Handbook of Global Slavery throughout History*. Basingstoke: Palgrave Macmillan, pp. 535–52.
Asad, T. (2002) 'Muslims and European identity: can Europe represent Islam?', in Pagden, A. (ed.) *The Idea of Europe: From Antiquity to the European Union*. Cambridge: Cambridge University Press, pp. 210–27.
Boatcă, M (2013) 'Multiple Europes and the politics of difference within', *Worlds and Knowledges Otherwise*, 3(3). https://globalstudies.trinity.duke.edu/sites/globalstudies.trinity.duke.edu/files/documents/v3d3_Boatca2.pdf (accessed 19 February 2024).
Boatcă, M. (2021) 'Thinking Europe otherwise: lessons from the Caribbean', *Current Sociology*, 69(3), 389–414.
Böröcz, J. (2009) *The European Union and Global Social Change: A Critical Geopolitical-Economic Analysis*. London: Routledge.
Böröcz, J. and Sarkar, M. (2005) 'What is the EU', *International Sociology*, 20(2), 153–73.

Borrell, J. (2022) 'EU's foreign policy chief Josep Borrell calls Europe "a garden" and the rest of the world "a jungle"'. www.youtube.com/watch?v=-MncHLS51uM (accessed 17 February 2024).

Césaire, A. ([1955] 2001) *Discourse on Colonialism*. New York: New York University Press.

Hansen, P. and Jonsson, S. (2014) *Eurafrica: The Untold History of European Integration and Colonialism*. London: Bloomsbury Academic.

Costache, I. (2020) 'A roundtable on ideas of race, ideologies of racism: Roma rights in Europe during the #BLM Moment', *EuropeNow: A Journal of Research and Art*. www.europenowjournal.org/2021/04/01/a-roundtable-on-ideas-of-race-ideologies-of-racism-roma-rights-in-europe-during-the-blm-moment/ (accessed 21 February 2024).

El-Tayeb, F. (2011) *European Others: Queering Ethnicity in Postnational Europe*. Minneapolis, MN: University of Minnesota Press.

Furtună, A. and Turcitu, V. (2021) 'Roma slavery and the places of memory', Album of Social History. https://eriac.org/wp-content/uploads/2022/12/Furtuna-Adrian-Nicolae-Turcitu-Victor-Claudiu-2021–Roma-Slavery-and-the-Places-of-Memory-Album-of-Social-History.-Dykhta-Publishing-House-107–pp..pdf (accessed 22 February 2024).

Klein, H. S. (1992) 'The social and economic integration of Spanish immigrants in Brazil', *Journal of Social History*, 25, 505–29.

Museo de la Inmigración (2024) 'El Camino de los Inmigrantes'. www.argentina.gob.ar/interior/migraciones/museo/el-camino-de-los-inmigrantes (accessed 19 February 2024).

Nicolaïdis, K., Sèbe, B. and Maas, G. (eds) (2014) *Echoes of Empire: Memory, Identity and Colonial Legacies*. London: Bloomsbury.

Parvulescu, A. and Boatcă, M. (2022) *Creolizing the Modern: Transylvania across Empires*. Ithaca, NY: Cornell University Press.

Santos, F. and Boatcă, M. (2022) 'Europeanisation as global entanglement', in Büttner, S., Eigmüller, M. and Worschech, S. (eds) *Sociology of Europeanization*. Berlin: De Gruyter Oldenbourg, pp. 105–32. https://doi.org/10.1515/9783110673630–005.

Schär, B. and Toivanen, M. (eds) (2024) *Integration and Collaborative Imperialism in Modern Europe: At the Margins of Empire, 1800–1950*. London: Bloomsbury Academic.

Trouillot, M. (1995) *Silencing the Past: Power and the Production of History*. Boston: Beacon Press.

Tudor, A. (2023) 'Ascriptions of migration: racism, migratism and Brexit', *European Journal of Cultural Studies*, 26(2), 230–48.

Acknowledgements

This edited volume and the workshop from which it took shape would not have been possible without the team of administrative and research assistants that we were privileged to have at the University of Helsinki. Thank you so much Tuija von der Pütten, Viljami Salo, Laura-Helena Suominen, Visa Tuomela, Hanna Lucina Rudloff, Yasmine Murr and Fernando Oliveira Di Prinzio.

Our special thanks to Kate Sotejeff-Wilson for her timely language edits and close reading of the whole volume.

We are indebted to each of the contributors for their powerful work. We are also thankful to Imad Sayrafi for our exchanges, and we hope that our paths will cross in the future.

We are especially grateful to Manuela Boatcă, Kasia Narkowicz, Nandita Sharma and Prem Kumar Rajaram for their openness to think with us and bringing their critical comments with grace.

All editors have contributed equally to this work.

The Academy of Finland funded Centre of Excellence in Law, Identity and the European Narratives (funding decision numbers 336678 and 353311) funded work on this book. A KONE Foundation general grant (202102017) contributed to support the final writing and editing stages.

Introduction: Europeanisation as violence: Souths and Easts as method

Daria Krivonos, Kolar Aparna and Elisa Pascucci

We started work on this edited volume thinking together through the forms of mundane, often invisible violence that Europeanisation – not least as development aid, cultural cooperation and border externalisation – takes across the so-called Global South and Eastern Europe. We are completing it in the context of the intensification of Israel's decades-long war of elimination against Palestine and Palestinians, through the 2023 vicious bombardment and ground invasion of Gaza. As we write, the violence of this war is as openly genocidal (Segal, 2023) as it is mystified, and even justified. Those who resist it or even just denounce it from afar often face fierce repression. As academics based in Europe, while writing this Introduction, we have listened to the calls for action from Palestinian colleagues (Birzeit University Open Letter, 2023) and witnessed violence and censorship against pro-Palestine movements on our own campuses (Duong-Pedica, 2023). We cannot but contrast such repression with the unconditional support of Ukraine expressed by European powers and cultural and academic institutions after the country's full-scale invasion in 2022, a support that made legible regions that were otherwise illegible, reframed Ukraine as Europe and scripted its invasion as part of the 'tragedy on European soil' today (Boatcă et al., 2022). Once again, borders compound the total violence of genocide and determine who is counted as human while gradations of Europeanness – or complete exclusion from it – demarcate one's worthiness for refugee protection. At the same time, violence, as Palestine shows, operates not only through spectacular and high-intensity manifestations but also through the routinised, the slow and the silenced: from interceptions at the checkpoints and the expansion of settlements to the bureaucratic violence of waiting, humanitarianism, NGOisation (nongovernmental organisation) of resistance and epistemic dispossession, to name just some examples covered in this volume. Violence continues to creep when the news outlets are less (if ever) interested in showing footage of some wars, and solidarity fatigue leaves even the 'deserving refugees' to infrastructures that were never meant to support them. This becomes visible in the case of Ukrainian refugees, first celebrated as 'fellow Europeans' and then largely abandoned to precarious and individualised structures of remaking life (Taylor, 2023). Imperial borders distinguish between 'relatively European, relatively civilised' bodies and 'non-European, not-yet civilised others' fleeing wars and resisting occupation (Bayoumi, 2023). It is at the razor edges that separate these bodies that we situate this volume.

Rather than flattening difference and romanticising solidarities across subalternities, we urge for a relational lens which is attentive to the processes producing these separations. Souths and Easts as method (henceforth, S&E as method) is aware of the overlapping territories and entangled histories (Said, 1993) of violence through Europeanisation. S&E as method is about building theory from lived experiences and entanglements otherwise viewed as minor to global social theory (Bhambra, 2016; Boatcă, 2021; Bhambra et al., 2024). This becomes particularly urgent as we write from the moment when ideological camps fail to see and take seriously multiple forms of imperialism unfolding and accelerating beyond mere 'spheres of influence'. S&E as method moves away from these ideological camps that condemn some imperialisms while normalising, supporting and complying with others. We speak when pitting differently racialised groups against each other easily becomes a quick move to address questions of structural dispossession. While S&E as method starts with blatantly racist politics of solidarity in Europe, it refuses to see differently racialised subjects as mere competitors for scarce resources and invites us to build common ground for coalitional, anti-racist and anti-imperial politics.[1]

We thus begin introducing this collection through a reflection on the location of our bodies, the geohistories that have intersected to bring them into being and the politics of the encounter that – through the neoliberal conditions of the contemporary academy – have made our writing possible. This is necessary to keep our writing embodied and engaged, to write, as Stefan Ouma and Saumya Premchander (2022) urge us to do, non-metaphorically. We strive for a writing that does not simply 'evoke' the violence, the 'represent and destroy' (Melamed, 2011: ix–50, 179–218) of Europeanisation, but remains close to the materiality of their production and contestation. Inter-referencing is for us an inter-referencing of material histories of violence and survival in the interstices of peripheral worlds (Valencia, 2018). We do not approach Souths and Easts as geographical metaphors but as the material conditions that determine our locations and relations. Rather than a fixed cartography of material inequalities demarcating a clear 'Global North', 'Global South' and East/West, however, Souths and Easts refers to an orientation that is fundamentally relational. As such, it is about speaking, listening and sensing across subalternities to build epistemic perspectives relevant to de-imperialising social theory. It builds on and yet deviates from world systems approaches, by adopting something akin to subaltern feminist geopolitics (Spivak, 1988; Sharp, 2011; Cole, 2018) that inter-reference situated knowledges. Rather than a purely political economy perspective of fixed geographies of inequalities, regions emerge and shape-shift from the material, temporal sensorialities of Europeanisation as violence.

As we write, our bodies are immersed in the 'reverberations' (Navaro et al., 2021) of violence that are behind the Nordic welfare state and its foothold in European Union (EU) sanctioned market capitalism. Seemingly suspended, violence is highly racially distributed in this orderly landscape that is nationalistic and penal (Baker, 2018). Sheltered and protected, our bodies benefit from the resonances of violence that excludes other bodies from membership to foster our 'free movement' across EU space. At the same time, as scholars writing from the Russian–Finnish borderlands, we are not speaking from the Anglophone centres of academic knowledge production. Like most of the contributors to this volume, we are also not speaking from the dominant tongues of the national space where we work, while English remains a language that the migrant/colonised subject needs to learn in order to live and work in the precarious contexts of global academia. We are speaking from this triple bind – of market capitalism, academic precarity and lingua franca – which hinders us, as migrant women, from holding space (Cairo, 2021) in everyday institutional life. Our writing is structured by the health conditions this triple bind creates, often individually suffered while quickly swept away under the banner of resilience and exceptionalised as 'times of crisis' (see also Burlyuk and Rahbari, 2023). To us, this violence also works through patriarchal academic spaces of white feminism aiming for selective 'inclusion' of some bodies. Our migrancy as editors is shaped through processes part of the ongoing and longer imperial and colonial histories of the Soviet Union, Finland, Netherlands, Britain, Italy and (the post-independent state of) India, involving subaltern positions as well as privileges. We wish to make space for the silences and inter-generational traumas passed on in turning our bodies into edifices of fear. Our entangled biographies are influenced by the Soviet Union and members of the Non-Aligned Movement, alongside the major and peripheral empires and colonial histories that we carry in our movement as knowledge migrants to Finland.

Finland is marked by multiple fissures in the process of becoming and claiming its place as part of European nations and the shifting geohistorical and geopolitical alliances this involves (actively using concepts of West and North against East and South) that situate the politics of location from where we write (Raudaskoski, 2018; Kuusisto, 2021; Väätänen, 2021). Rather than claiming our globality, we position our thinking from these shifting and fractured borderlands to follow processes of Europeanisation as violence. We are completing this volume when Finland has joined NATO in the aftermath of Russia's full-scale attack on Ukraine, started building a border fence and temporarily closed its border with Russia entirely in late 2023, thus breaching asylum seekers' right to submit asylum applications at the EU border. The latter is driven by the Moscow's alleged channelling of asylum seekers to the border with Finland, a situation that has been commonly referred to as 'hybrid warfare' by both the media and academics. What very recently used to be ridiculed and laughed at as 'Trump exceptionalism' or an odd prerogative of 'illiberal East European states' is now normalised in a country that boasts with achievements in (white liberal) feminism and equality indexes in the global news outlets. Of course, the two developments are not and have never been a contradiction. Those of us who have mobilised around migrant struggles for over a decade (Aparna et al. 2022; Cantat et al., 2022) can hardly be surprised that life-seekers search for new routes to the EU when all other passages have been closed, heavily policed and militarised. We write from the moment when the vague and callous language of 'hybrid warfare' (Eberle and Daniel, 2022) overpowered obligations under international refugee and human rights law – however colonial its origins are and however corrupted the trust in it is among members of oppressed communities. In short, we are writing in a moment in which the liberal apparatus of Europeanisation is unravelling and its core underpinnings – racism, colonialism, militarisation, civilisational anxiety – are being unleashed.

Fractured teleology of EUropean progress

In *The Wretched of the Earth*, Fanon (1965: 312) writes that 'Europe now lives at such a mad, reckless pace that she is running headlong into the abyss'. This abyss is reflected today in an understanding of the failure of the teleological narratives of 'European' progress that is shared across Souths and Easts. Europe appears as the colonial echo chamber of a world in which, in the words of anthropologist Ghassan Hage (2021: 1), 'the very things that were the basis of modern expansion and development are now the drivers of contraction and dissolution'. *Postcolonial* Europe's legitimacy as a promoter of capitalist development and liberal rights outside it – through the donor power of conditional aid (Kiratli, 2021) – is shattered by humanitarian racism, even among technocratic elites stemming from the so-called Global South (Pascucci, 2019, 2023; Majumdar, 2020; Bian, 2022). This racism fractures the promise that one day, one can finally be allowed into Western modernity if only one follows the rules of structural adjustment policies, the World Bank, International Monetary Fund (IMF), European Bank for Reconstruction and Development (EBRD), shock doctrine, democratisation and transition to capitalism (Yurchenko, 2018; Dooley, 2019). Some economists proclaiming Central East European 'transition' to capitalism a success have elided and ignored the fact that the transition coincided with 'the worst recorded peacetime population decline in history' (Ghodsee and Orenstein, 2021: 67). According to some estimates, the average postsocialist country saw a population decline of 8.22 per cent from 1989 to 2017 (Ghodsee and Orenstein, 2021: 67). If it used to be the 'exotic other' denied coeval status with the West, the catching-up temporality in the East has also robbed the region of the ability to imagine alternative futures seeing the critics of dispossession as outdated and lazy *homo sovieticus* (Fabian, 1983: 31–4; Kušić et al., 2019: 11; Yurchenko, 2018).

Today, this perpetual denial that Souths and Easts are coeval becomes palpable in the position of labour migrants in the EU. In 2021, the top ten nationalities that got a residence permit based on work in the EU were citizens of Ukraine, Morocco, India, Syria, Brazil, Belarus, Venezuela, Russia, China and Turkey (Eurostat, 2021). This list makes clear how for many subjects across Easts and Souths, the only chance to join Western modernity is to become a (labour) migrant – considering that getting a residence permit itself and being documented becomes a relative privilege that is not accessible to many. This inevitably means that for some bodies to be available for exploitation other bodies are made abject. Under the conditions of racial capitalism, there has never been a universal disembodied 'worker' figure, because the production of difference has always operated *within* the proletariat. For instance, while the introduction of labour contracts for 'coolies' seemingly produced 'free and voluntary' movement within the British Empire, it needs to be seen as continued expropriation of lands and peoples, alongside processes of *becoming white* of working populations in the metropole.

We situate such historical processes of production of differential values attached to life, and freedom of movement as far from liberatory (Mongia, 2018; Sharma, 2020), but central to producing abjection, death (Valencia and Pluecker, 2018; Mbembe, 2019; Weheliye, 2014) and gradations of whiteness and its others. Subjects racialised as (white) 'Eastern European' are brought in and out of the service of the capitalist order and come to be located at varying distances from both anti-Black, anti-Roma and anti-Muslim racism *and* hegemonic whiteness (Krivonos, 2023; see also Ivasiuc, this volume), what one might call gradations of peripherality. What is now celebrated as a generous and unprecedented decision to grant temporary protection to Ukrainian refugees in the EU – indeed, a privilege compared to people fleeing other wars – includes little more than the right to join low-paid labour markets, at the time of writing with the future of this precarious 'temporary protection' remaining unknown (Odynets, 2022). As through histories and ongoing violence from the Russian Empire to the Occupied Territories of Palestine, what is sold as humanitarian assistance today is also an instrument to turn displaced people into agents in global racial capitalism, as they become integrated into raced labour markets (Talhami, 2003; Easton-Calabria, 2015; Rajaram, 2018; Tilley and Shilliam, 2018; Bhagat, 2022; Krivonos, 2023). We witness this moment neither as dividing unequally dis/placed subjects in competition for victimhood, nor as uniting as raceless, genderless proletariats against capitalism. Instead, we turn the gaze to the production of distances and proximities across boundaries of life and death.

On race and doubt

As Boatcă argues, Europe is not an 'unmarked category' (Boatcă, 2021) nor a clear fixed entity, and it is fundamentally shaped by the others integral to its societies. What does it mean then to look for alternatives to the teleological narratives of Europe today, in times of accelerating colonialism, nationalism, racism and nativism? When Aimé Césaire wakes up in an island village in Yugoslavia on a visit to his friend Petar Guberina during the summer of 1935 and finds out that the island is named Martinska, he writes *Notebook of a Return to My Native Land.* He feels that he has found his homeland in a third space that is neither France nor Martinique, unleashing a new poetic imagination. It is this not knowing what emerges and the unleashing of new imaginations from conversations of Souths and Easts as method that we want to hold on to, keenly aware that we are writing in another space and time when the Soviet project no longer provides the alternative that it did during the mid-twentieth century to diasporic anti-colonial scholars and political leaders like Césaire. Selected travellers and short-term residents sympathetic to the Soviet regime such as W. E. B. Du Bois, who were searching for an alternative to capitalist modernity, were used by the Soviet press to claim that, unlike in the capitalist West, the socialist states had overcome racism. In fact, state socialism perpetuated ideas of whiteness not only through its own civilising mission but also by claiming to be 'better' white people, the ones who left ideas of race behind (Mark, 2022). In other words, Eastern Europeans' commitment to an anti-colonial internationalism had rendered them the better kind of white. But the inability to engage with the colonial, imperial and racial politics of the Russian Empire/Soviet Union/Russian Federation still haunts some contemporary scholarly work where race and imperialism are only perceived as an issue for Western empires.[2] Following some important previous work, we see Eastern Europe more broadly as a geography within the colonial global economy, which has historically been connected to the benefits of global white supremacy through trade and exchange of goods (Todorova, 2021; Balogun, 2022).

When searching for alternatives to Europeanisation, considering the lessons of uneasiness around race and what Charles Mills (2007) called white ignorance becomes urgent. S&E as method helps us see the 'intertwined ends of the racialised Eurocentric modern ideologies that set the terms of our imaginations' (Todorova, 2021: 74). In her inspiring book on gender and race in socialist Bulgaria, Miglena Todorova warns us against a snap return and over-attachment to supposedly raceless socialist-era internationalist solidarity. While striving to build solidarities with women from decolonising states, the 'socialist female subject' often failed to explore their own complicity with local forms of racial violence (Todorova, 2021: 68–72). Todorova shows how socialist initiatives to 'reform' Roma and Muslim women in Bulgaria evoked and reproduced the gendered and raced tropes of technologies used by European and Russian/Soviet empires to subdue colonised populations.[3] Locating what she calls 'socialist racialism', European colonialism and the project of racial whiteness under one framework of analysis allows Todorova to examine the interlinked forms of violence tied to Eurocentric racial projects in locations that are typically considered rival. Todorova's critique not only points to the interlinked processes of racialisation where white socialist women racialise Roma and Muslim women but also shows the dismissal of socialist forms of feminism and a patronising understanding of socialism in the West. As Teresa Kulawik (2019: 16) puts it, 'the postsocialist space was turned into a feminist frontier: the Western view posited that "We already have what they are missing"'.

Following Da Silva (2007), we ask: why is there still no ethical rage against racial violence despite these histories of conversations, critique and resistance? Da Silva reminds us that the modern racialised subject was not radically transformed in postmodern thought, but also that anti-colonial, anti-racist and anti-capitalist nationalist movements that embraced the path of self-determination inevitably took on the 'project of producing and interpreting crafts that communicate their particular sociohistoricist trajectories as subaltern travellers on the road to transparency' (Da Silva, 2007: xxxiii). This production of cultural difference through transparency via arts and crafts partially also dogged the cultural exchanges in international socialism and connects to Todorova's insight on complicity to racial violence within one's own localities. In this volume, we take up Da Silva's call to trace the economic–juridical architectures of colonial/racial violence.

Here we enact a politics of doubt in inter-referencing relations beyond the historical path to self-determination and transparency of the racialised subaltern other. We build on Todorova's postsocialist doubt, and Minh-ha's exercise in 'multipolar reflecting reflection' (Minh-ha, 1989: 22) that emerges not from a single looking-glass but from a shattered mirror (Oancă in this volume). The shattered mirror in this case symbolises doubt within capitalism and state socialism but also within anti-racist, anti-colonial, anti-capitalist movements that make transparent the racial subaltern other or become appropriated, pacified or coopted. A doubt that rejects the idea that there is somewhere to progress towards and instead reassesses futurity itself (Valencia, 2018). Doubt allows us to face violence without embracing optimism, resilience, hybridity and cultural difference. We stay with the (epistemic and kinetic) violence producing these uneven terrains and positionalities in the process of Europeanisation presented as the only viable alternative and the synonym of "development" (Deiana and Kušić, this volume). We urge for a political project that is able to sense multiple levels of violence and geohistories of stratification simultaneously producing differential value to labour and life/death to eventually open political horizons without the Space Time of Europe (Da Silva, 2014; Aparna et al., 2020).[4]

Inter-referencing violence across Souths and Easts: connections and dissonances

The scholarly imagination dividing the world into separate regions approached under the rubric of 'area studies' has been reluctant to inter-reference Souths and Easts. However, capitalist and colonial powers have sometimes been quick to transfer, circulate and recycle forms of violence from one region to another. For instance, the 'loss of markets' (areas that later became Indonesia) of the Dutch East Indies to Japan in early 1940s made colonial administrators turn to extraction of lands in what is today parts of Ukraine (Krivonos and Aparna, this volume). Rather than solely an expansion of the German Reich, this was in fact also a national project of creating 'living space' for Dutch farmers alongside bringing 'Western culture' (Künzel, 2015: 92) to the East through the Dutch East Company.

These geographical imaginaries mark the histories of European violence in their most glaring and devastating recent manifestations. Historiographies of the Holocaust have contested liberal narratives after the Second World War that consider Nazi Germany's extermination machine an abhorrent rupture along the journey of Europe's celebrated civilisational path. They have argued instead for reading such violence as built through the colonial mould forged especially by Kaiser Wilhelm II's armies, sent to West Africa 'to destroy native rebels who had put themselves in the path of Germany's racial destiny' (Olusoga and Erichsen, 2010: 17). Violent fantasies of racial 'Easts' are not absent in this trajectory. In 1941, Adolf Hitler famously claimed that Slavs should be treated 'like colonial people', in a striking illustration of the convergences of Nazi racism with nineteenth- and twentieth-century colonialism (see also Connelly, 1999). A convergence that, as David Olusoga and Casper Erichsen (2010) observe, was certainly not lost to the generations of Nazis that had lived through the Kaiser's colonial genocide of Herero and Namaqua people.

The temporalities of colonialism and Nazi racial violence, which Europe's liberal institutions have relentlessly tried to relegate to the past, reverberate through the present of Europe's external and internal Souths. Palestine's ongoing *nakba* – the Arabic word for the 'catastrophe' of occupation and forced displacement – is the acknowledged product of the encounter of these forms of violence. This encounter took place in Zionist settler nationalism, but also in its liberal justifications from Sir Mark Sykes (a Zionist enthusiast who is commonly credited with first using the term 'Middle East') to the post-Oslo 'NGOisation' of the Occupied Territories (Bashir and Goldberg, 2018, Khoury, E., 2018; Khoury, N. 2018). Anti-Roma violence, structural and state-sanctioned, shows us an underacknowledged aspect of racial modernity that the Nazis elevated to a 'final solution'. This volume addresses the present of the colonial and racist imaginaries of Souths and Easts in relations within and beyond European geographies, including the aforementioned occupied Palestine and Roma communities. It asks, what are the material conditions and social relations of production at work in making ideas and practices of 'Europeanisation' today? It explores how relationalities of violence within EU heritage, built environment, security and migration control regimes, aid apparatuses and infrastructure projects, among others, produce gradations of Souths and Easts.

The last three decades of the twentieth century have seen these relationalities of violence work particularly through fiscal and developmental discipline. Structural adjustment funds and neoliberal reforms named the Washington Consensus were first 'tested' in Latin America in the 1980s and exported to Eastern Europe ten years later to 'help' transition to the market economy. Neoliberal reforms advised by the EBRD and the IMF allowed easy market penetration for transnational capital, as in Latin America and Africa (Easterly, 2006: 25). As political economist Yulia Yurchenko, citing the former Secretary General of European Roundtable of Industrialists, writes, 'the demise of the Soviet Union was as if they have discovered a new South East Asia on the (EU) doorstep' (Yurchenko, 2018: 92). Even though the people of East European countries were largely white, the Western lenders perceived the loans as 'missionary gifts for their Eastern counterparts' (Easterly, 2006: 75).

The thread that connects dispossession across Souths and Easts became visible again through the impact of the 2008 financial crisis on the peripheral economies of the EU monetary union (Dooley, 2019). Rather than a failure to integrate, it has been argued that it is the attempt to follow the rules of the projects of European financial integration that contributed to the Eurozone crisis (Dooley, 2019). By the early 2010s, as Greece was forced to seek financial assistance from the IMF and EU and other Southern European countries barely averted the same fate, historical anti-Irish and anti-Mediterranean racism re-emerged in the framing of the EU 'South' as financially reckless and lazy. The racial framings that underpin the architecture of the so-called Eurozone reflect the structural 'interaction between race, (neo)colonialism and capitalist development' in the institutional architecture of the Union (Van Vossole, 2016: 2). Debt and dispossessive loans place strict control on social spending, all at the cost of working-class households expelled to reproduce their lives through migration. The post-2014 war economy of Ukraine has diverted resources away from the public sector to fulfil the conditionalities attached to international financial institutions (IFIs) part of its 'pro-European trajectory' (Lyubchenko, 2022). This is why, as Ukrainian trade unionists and activists argue, post-war reconstruction of Ukraine should take place through debt cancellation, protection of labour rights, spending on public services and environmental protection – not cutting back on social expenditure as a condition for IMF and IFI loan agreements (Farbar and Rowley, 2023).

The colonial state is the basis not just of the liberal institutions of EU member states but of the very European Economic Community (Mamdani, 2020). From its foundation with the Treaty of Rome, the 'European' project is informed by a conception of European territory based on colonial cartographies and marked by a preoccupation with extending and renovating colonial management (Grovogui, 1996; Hansen and Jonsson, 2014: 7–8). In contemporary contexts of violent occupation (such as Palestine) where EU aid controversially merges state-building with peacebuilding, the Union's language 'mirrors the colonial prose of counter-insurgency' (Sen, 2022: 219). The supremacist, civilisationist ethos of 'Euniversalism' shapes the Union's external relations, enlargement, integration and policy harmonisation (Nicolaïdis, 2015), further complicating distinctions between Europe's inside and outside (Ould Moctar, this volume). The language of gender equality, diversity and inclusion characterising Europeanisation processes in Eastern and Southern peripheries entrench femo- and homonationalist structures (Bilić, 2016; Rexhepi, 2022; Slootmaeckers, 2023), including the emerging 'gender-critical' trends, which leave trans subjects caught 'between non-existence and normativisation' (Kamenou, 2020: 147).[5]

The violence of Europeanisation is also lived in the requirement to expel illegalised subjects from Europe's Eastern borders if one is to join the 'European family'. Southern and Eastern states and EU citizens, while framed as backward, unproductive and imprudent, are yet part of what Piro Rexhepi (2022) has recently termed 'white enclosures', a move of walling whiteness which takes place in the locations which seem to be outsiders to global coloniality and whiteness. This includes fulfilling the requirement to defend EU borders and maintain white supremacy on a local and global scale. This membership in a globally gated white enclosure, however precarious it may be, is a reminder of complicity of Eastern and Southern Europe in Western imperiality, something that can easily slip in the attempts to designate all Souths and Easts as equal victims of Western racism and racialisation. That some wars get more visibility and marked as more proximate to or 'on' European soil is part of the post-war European integration project in which shared histories of Europeanness are disconnected from the colonial state. This implies that the so-called 'Eastern enlargement' was conditional upon making accession states the Eastern guardians of the EU borders to prevent irregular migration while publicly condemning some of these same states for their failure to stand to human rights. The EU invested in fortifying its new Eastern borders (European Commission, 2015). EU direct involvement in state-building in the Balkans and the promise of 'eventual EU membership' become an inventive and a tool for EU border strengthening policies and turned those just outside the EU borders into the 'policemen of Europe' (Follis, 2012; Rexhepi, 2018; Sayyid, 2018). In Ukraine, three detention centres were constructed with EU funding since the mid-2000s as a condition for liberalising a visa-free regime for Ukrainian citizens part of the EU Eastern Partnership programme (Tsymbalyuk, 2023). Visa-free entry to the EU that allowed millions of Ukrainian nationals to flee Russian invasion was thus conditional upon making Ukraine into an EU border guard, keeping those fleeing other wars and poverty from reaching safety. These detention facilities have continued operating during the full-scale war (Human Rights Watch, 2022).

Amidst the Poland–Belarus border 'crisis' in the summer and autumn of 2021, many Polish pro-refugee activists claimed that Poland should embrace 'European values and open the borders to asylum seekers from the Middle East and African continent' (Fallon, 2021). But what would this mean if 'European values' are the cause of, not the solution to, border violence? What if European migration governance creates a violent space not despite but precisely because of its commitment to the liberal politics that historically have constructed the exclusionary 'human' figure as white? (Wynter, 2003).

The description of right-wing and far-right governments and formations as 'Eurosceptic' negates Europe's history of constituting itself as a white gated community – the very value these governments and groups are committed to. While appropriating the language of postcolonial victimhood and promising a better future through the nationalist narrative of 'sovereignty' vis-à-vis the West, right-wing formations in Eastern Europe precisely reproduce the essentialist, racist and civilisational narratives on which the Western project of modernity is built.

These 'new EU' states find it easier to adopt a quasi-anti-colonial discourse than to reckon with their own histories of racial subjugation of Roma, Muslims and Jews, as well as their colonial fantasies and material practices beyond the European continent (Mogilner, 2013; Ureña Valerio, 2019; Balogun, 2022). Claudia Snochowska-Gonzalez (2012) warns us by asking why the discourse of the postcolonial – inspired by Marxist critique and post-structural theory – found fertile ground among right-wing parties in Eastern Europe and turned into an aberration of nationalism. The right-wing parties' cry 'we are not a colony of Brussels' is far from a call for solidarity with the South; in fact, being compared to people in the current and former colonies by decreasing their own Europeanness is the last thing they want to do (Zarycki, 2014; Kalmar, 2022). In the end, their discourse of 'we are not a colony' is amplified by 'we have never been colonisers', which allows them to claim membership in Western modernity without the cost of recognising Europe's colonial past (Kalmar, 2022). To continue with the analysis in Claudia Snochowska-Gonzalez (2012: 716), insisting on Poland being a colonial victim of Soviet imperialism negates the country's present comfortable position in the world of global capital and at the heart of EU's immigration control and 'relieves it of its responsibility for participation in modern acts of (neo)imperialism and (neo)colonialism'.

This is why we are cautious to draw quick analogies between the postcolonial and the postsocialist. Such analogies anesthetise the racial realignment of Europe's East with Europe's project of modernity/coloniality and border violence. With the growing interest in exploring the 'shades of whiteness' among East European scholars living in Western Europe or solely focusing on Europe there is a danger to further silence the voices of those who have little to no access to these circuits of academic knowledge production shaped at the intersections of multiple regimes (see Hamzah, Ivasiuc, Dragana, Țîștea, this volume). The instrumentalisation of postcolonial identity by authoritarian and conservative actors makes visible the transnationality of racist, Islamophobic and anti-feminist discourses across Souths and Easts and beyond the Western core (Zhang, 2023).

As Nandita Sharma (2020) points out, in the postcolonial world order, formerly colonised states embracing the language of decolonisation soon adopted the language of national sovereignty. She argues that national self-determination predetermines hostility to migrants and enforcement of immigration controls. We join her call to follow these continuities while being attentive to the uneven borderscapes (Rajaram and Grundy-Warr,

2007) within the EU's supranational space. With Rahul Rao (2020), we share concerns and scepticism regarding the returns to the scene of the colonial, such as in analysing homophobia in formerly colonised states. As he warns us, the colonial may become an alibi of the postcolonial state for its perpetuation of anti-queer laws. Rao (2020: 9) calls us to look at 'shifts in power where formerly colonised states become colonial in their own right'.

S&E as method is then neither a reductive exercise of simply comparing forms of violence across Easts and Souths, nor is it aiming at flattening the differences *within* Easts and Souths. Our interest here is in examining stratified subalternities without subsuming one experience under another, as there is no South and no East in itself. Rather than comparing or simply 'bringing to dialogue' historical formations of Easts and Souths, we address both connections and dissonances in tracing these shifts in power while striving to build theory from situated knowledges.

Europeanisation as violence: Souths and Easts as method

We approach Europeanisation as an unfolding of historical processes of varying temporalities and genealogies of violence around questions of labour, race, gender, infrastructure, borders, settler expansion and differential value of exploitable lives and deaths, all of which produce relational geographies (Souths and Easts) that are not always evident and visible. We see this unfolding as the convergence of two simultaneous logics: the civilisational narrative of white supremacy, imperialism and developmentalism; the reinforcement of nation-state apparatuses; and their scalar transformation through the supranational project of the EU. While some have argued that the EU should be regarded as an imperial project (Behr and Stivachtis, 2015), and while we concur that the colonial roots of European institutions need exposing, we also question the prevalent liberal discourse that sees the EU as a project to create peace by overcoming nationalisms in a transborder Europe. Rather, our contributions, particularly on border epistemologies of Europeanisation, expose the EU integration project as an expansion and intensification of the exclusionary logic of national citizenship and uneven hierarchies of border enforcement.

We are not the first to draw connections between Souths and Easts. 'Thinking between the posts' and 'postcolonial and postsocialist dialogues' (Chari and Verdery, 2009; Suchland, 2011; Tlostanova, 2012; Dialoguing Posts Network, 2019; Kulawik and Kravchenko, 2020; Koobak et al., 2021; Kumar and Narkowicz, 2021) have been important frameworks for thinking about the histories and geographies of the 'postcolonial' and the 'postsocialist', state socialism and racial capitalism. Also, what has been recently theorised as 'alternative globalisations' recovers forgotten histories of 'Second–Third World' internationalism (Mark et al., 2020: 14). The convention that Western capitalism was the exclusive drive of globalisation produced a distorted view of postcolonial and postsocialist states as isolated from global connections until capitalism took over in the 1980s and 1990s (Mark et al., 2020). This work is a reminder that although often disregarded as simply instrumental in gaining positive recognition for socialism (Subotić and Vučetić, 2019), Eastern European expressions of solidarity with the decolonising world, especially across oppressed groups, fuelled grassroot social engagements that imagined other worlds from shared struggles against global inequality, racism, colonialism and imperialism (Karkov and Valiavicharska, 2018; Mark and Slobodian, 2018; Subotić and Vučetić, 2019; Djagalov, 2020; Rexhepi, 2022).

Unlike the project of 'postcolonial and postsocialist dialogues', we do not see postcolonialism and postsocialism as grand theoretical frameworks that might prescribe conditions of multiple coalitions. East European scholars inspired by postcolonial and decolonial thinking about Eastern Europe have almost exclusively animated these dialogues, often without duly recognising the region's active complicity within the reproduction of European violence (Menon et al., 2021). By engaging with the East, which has been until recently absent from the dominant 'Anglophone core of postcolonial theory' focused on the Global South, we resist the temptation to offer any grand theory of 'postness'.

In body-writing (Minh-ha, 1989: 36) the sensory and temporal dimensions of Europeanisation as violence, we call for S&E as method. We do not claim belonging to a clearly demarcated region or imaginary territory. We make space for this alter-geography by striving not to resolve tensions or hide ambivalences around locations, positionalities and the effects of political action and academic critique. We take up Chen's call, building on Yoshimi's work, for inter-referencing (Chen, 2010: 225). This inter-referencing is a call to locate violence at points of reference across, between and against empires. Junyoung Verónica Kim calls for Asia–Latin America as method, to create a space of 'dissensus, contradiction and cacophony' (Kim, 2017: 111). However, unlike Kim, we do not seek to decouple 'the global' from the South, given that what is South is also shifting in relation to inter-imperial designs, of which 'the global' are part.

Resisting a colonial aspiration to know the world in its totality, which would simply pluralise Europeanisation or re-signify imperial vocabularies, we gesture towards a politics of 'radically non-global knowledge production' (Palat Narayanan, 2022: 526). Writing across relational locations of knowledge production, we resist the temptation to become 'global' and 'globally relevant' by pluralising knowledges from outside the epistemic centre.

To borrow from Nipesh Palat Narayanan, if 'global' means becoming a concern of the metropole, then S&E as method is not globally relevant. To redirect Anca Parvulescu's more recent 'Eastern Europe as method', S&E as method is an invitation for scholars to build situated knowledges without needing theoretical mediation from the centres like Paris, Vienna or New York. By situating ourselves in the multiple cracks of knowledge production in the Easts and Souths we want to sidestep the Western metropole as a concern and a point of reference. By refusing to become 'globally relevant', we want to disavow the epistemic boundary between those who 'know' and those who 'experience'. We inter-reference collective self-reflexive accounts of the 'economies of writing' (Dufty-Jones et al., 2022) deriving from our respective academic and embodied positionalities. To do this, we script relational bibliographies from experiences of entangled legacies of violence, exilic existence and hierarchies of broken heritage with open boats (Glissant, 1997: 4). Inter-referencing Souths and Easts is a method that closely traces the material, corporeal and affective constituents of the 'collective undoing' and enduring struggles precipitated by the violence of Europeanisation. In this volume, we strive to unsettle the temporal and spatial dualities at work in Europe's many 'posts': postcolonial and postsocialist, the dichotomy between colonial past and present, the perilous static demarcations between 'inside' and 'outside' (Glissant, 1997).

Throughout these relational geographies of Europeanisation, violence is a pervasive concept. In the words of Eric A. Stanley (2021: 9), we strive for 'a method for considering violence as a generalised field of knowledge that maintains this collective undoing, lived as personal tragedy, of those lost to modernity'. Thinking with Fanon, Stanley (2021: 9, 16) sees violence as an atmosphere that captures the 'plastic totality of colonialism': such atmospheric force is what 'holds us to the world' yet its 'consistency must be fundamentally disturbed if we are to survive'. Violence, these writers remind us, is not a univocal terrain, and its trajectory can be multifarious. It is at times a tactic of escape, or communal endurance or residual protection of the conditions for living and flourishing.

Our collective work in this volume shows us how violence is at times the unforceful 'inclusion' imposed by states through social policies or strategies of geopolitical integration in the EU space (Deiana and Kušić; Stanivuković; Maury; Oancă, in this volume) and at other times the deceptive tools of strategic ignorance and isolation (Hamzah, in this volume). In other instances, violence appears as the 'organised abandonment' (Gilmore, 2011) and wounded attachments (Brown, 2020: 52–76) resulting from neoliberal reform through the expansion of the EU common market (Țîștea; Ivasiuc, in this volume). Often, it is the kinetic military violence of border enforcement and counter-insurgency, and its financial and administrative infrastructures ingrained in development and humanitarian interventions (Ould Moctar; Manatouma, in this volume). As the chapters show, through these multiple manifestations, the violence of Europe as a narrative of modernity, an intellectual project and an identity is often embedded in infrastructures, built environments and embodied encounters.

We strive to comprehend these materialities, supported by writers about the atmospheres, reverberations and remnants of political violence. Yael Navaro and coauthors (2021) infuse sensuous and political life into new materialisms, offering timely resistance to the temptation to efface violence in academic theorising. Their writing shows us how to remain attentive to matter – in the form of infrastructures, landscapes and more-than-human vitalities – without dissolving maiming, abandonment, suffering and death into 'a vitalist flow of becoming' that is nothing more than an exercise in 'intellectual detachment'. Instead, they offer an imaginary for thinking violence through sensory and temporal dimensions, through 'roaring' and 'murmuring', through ruins and echoes. Violence is experienced as 'continuation rather than eruption' (Wilkinson and Ortega-Alcázar, 2019: 156; Lisle, 2021) in a series of what Elizabeth Povinelli calls 'quasi-events', which can nonetheless entail brutality and contestation, kinetic force and resistance (Povinelli, 2011: 13; Lisle, 2021). This durability of violence allows us to connect entangled timelines and situated knowledges that counter-map topographies of Europeanisation in four inter-related sections as infrastructural violence and colonial asymmetries, production of stratified subalternities, epistemic dispossession and border epistemologies.

The collection

Representation – perhaps especially academic representation – entails violence. Doubt allows the chapter authors to contribute to this collection without flattening our positionalities and fixing the regions we speak from. Together, we respond to the total violence and racialised gradations of 'territories of conflict' produced in geopolitical vocabularies as within or outside 'European soil'. We refuse to add to a repertoire of traumatic spectacles for educated yet 'innocent' audiences. Rather, we are companions in writing from the subject position of those for whom such 'scenes' are not new nor surprising, but we remain determined to work through the ongoing and uneventful to counter this violence. The chapters we introduce below create space for doubtful and lively inter-referencing, by attuning to the material and sensuous disruptions of Europeanisation as violence in four inter-related sections. The structure we outline stems from the thematic and epistemological engagement of the chapters and foregrounds the multifaceted connections between the contributions. It explores the potentials and limitations of Souths and Easts as method that the volume launches.

The contributions in the first section, titled 'Europeanisation as infrastructural violence and colonial asymmetries', theorise Europeanisation as kinetic violence, as part of shifting geopolitical and geohistorical terrains of extraction, expulsion, expropriation, occupation and death. The chapters explore these geographies of violence in relation to the making of Eurafrican and Eastern European spaces. In doing so, they render the inter-referencing between Europe's inside and outside legible and concrete, material and embodied. Aparna and Krivonos's chapter follows imperial projects of the Soviet Union and German and Dutch loss of colonies in Indonesia and East Africa with the shift of gaze towards conquering Ukraine to meet food insecurities around grain. This is read in the context of Russia's full-scale invasion of Ukraine and the consequent blockade of Ukrainian grain in the country's ports, whose consequences threaten Europe's African and Asian Souths but also Europe itself. Centring the role of Ukrainian land and labour in feeding the world, they link seemingly disparate projects of socialist and capitalist accumulation, as well as Europe's East and former overseas colonies part of today's so-called Global South. They call for opening up political horizons that build on these historical relationalities of the extraction of labour and the appropriation of land by both Western and Soviet imperial projects through direct violence against the peasantry to reimagine and situate current day power asymmetries around refugeehood and agricultural migrant labour feeding Europe and the world.

While land and agricultural resources are central in Aparna and Krivonos's chapter, Senka Neuman Stanivuković explores violence in the built environment. In her chapter, infrastructural interventions bring 'material and economic connectivity' and 'transit speed' to the very peripheral spaces where violence against asylum seekers trying to reach Europe is enacted. Like heritage policies in Spain and Romania (see Part II), the EU's connectivity agenda in the Western Balkans and the extension of the so-called European corridor network produce South East Europe as a space of waiting, one which yet enables violent expulsion, containment and neglect of bodies produced as migrant others. Writing about a still scarcely explored 'modernisation' agenda, Neuman Stanivuković shows how financial and administrative infrastructures, such as grants awarded by the EU pre-accession instrument and similar tools of geopolitical government through development, reshape the built environment. She urges us to think the durability of spatialised and material violence together with atmospheric and movable violence. She shows us how in the EU today, infrastructures are going through a 'renaissance, fuelled largely by the interests of finance capital, smart city tech companies, logistics and extractive industries' (Cowen, 2020: 481) linked to global supply chains of kinetic war.

Writing about the roarings of border violence in the Sahel and Mediterranean, Hassan Ould Moctar also engages the spatial politics of the EU's 'inside' and 'outside'. The chapter conceptualises the mass violence and death that mark both the Mediterranean and the Sahelo-Sahara regions as manifestations of a collapse in European hegemony over what has historically been a colonial backyard and postcolonial sphere of geopolitical influence. Ould Moctar draws on an extraordinarily deep ethnographic engagement with EU officials and actors navigating lethal governmental interventions at the structural intersection between EU migration control efforts in the Mediterranean and an international counter-insurgency campaign in the Sahel. He weaves an expanded geography and reconnected history of the Mediterranean and Sahelo-Sahara in the *longue durée* to speculate political horizons under the waning arc of European hegemony.

A similarly rigorous engagement with the spaces and subjects of his writing marks Kelma Manatouma's chapter on the imperial rivalries between Russia and France in the territories of Chad and the Central African Republic. Russia emerges here as an 'object of fantasy' that is militarised, imperial and, in the context of French colonial pasts and presents, infused with anti-colonial revanchism. The chapter explores diachronic asymmetries in imperial and colonial powers' relations with the African postcolonial state, from Soviet cooperation in the fields of culture and technical education to the role of Russia in shaping the protests against the rule of Transitional Military Council in 2021–22. Manatouma offers important reflections on the broader geopolitical imaginaries – as well as fears and ghosts – that animate Russia's military, economic and political engagement with the African state amidst France's declining hegemony.

In the second part, 'Europeanisation as slow violence and stratified subalternities', South East Europe emerges as a space that complicates the geographies of inter-referencing. In exposing the colonial gaze that the EU projects on its unequal inside, the chapters highlight processes of graded racialisation and nested orientalisms (Bakić-Hayden, 1995). Maria-Adriana Deiana and Katarina Kušić relate to us the murmurs of slow violence as experienced, theorised and felt from South East Europe. Their work traces aggressively normative EU interventions implemented in youth politics, civil society, cultural production and land politics in the post-Yugoslav space. The authors unsettle the theoretical landscape of 'slow violence', as put forward in critical geography and international relations (Nixon, 2011: 45–67). They do so by resolutely starting from and staying 'in the middle' (Lisle, 2021:436): centring the writers' embodied positionalities to theorise from within sites that are both 'marginal and pivotal' to EU security politics.

Showing how the definitions of multiculturalism adopted in EU-funded heritage projects impact across Spain and Romania, Alexandra Oancă weaves a sophisticated tale of borders and 'gradients of Europeanness'. Andalusia, Spain and Transylvania, Romania, are respectively constructed as 'domestic Orient' and 'domestic Occident' in EU-sanctioned policies to preserve historical urban forms and built environments. In Oancă's powerful argument, interventions that render Islamic heritage 'hygienically' EU-proofed – what she calls European heritage-making – are intrinsically racialised, classed and gendered. She argues that 'multicultural monoculturalism' is epistemically violent: inter-religious conviviality is represented through heritage at the expense of the actual religious rights of Muslims and other minoritised people, while valorising Saxon settler colonialism and German heritage that places Romanian, Hungarian and Roma heritage in a 'not-yet-European' position. Like Ivasiuc, she argues for a relational lens in situating Transylvania's and Andalusia's position between empires and nation-building projects, what she calls 'mirrored postcolonialities' in exploring the distorted image of Europeanisation reflected to us in such heritage-making practices in the EU.

Ana Ivasiuc looks at the failure of 'integration' interventions that 'fix' Western, Southern and Eastern European identities through the government of a 'quintessentially European' minority, the Roma people. Her chapter builds on her previous work on the 'securitisation of Eastern European identities in the relational construction of (sub)alter(n)ities in Western Europe', as well as on autoethnographic reflections on her own navigations as a racialised subject in the city of Rome. Her chapter gifts us with a gripping tale of the formal and informal policing of Eastern European migrants in a Southern European metropolis. Three intensely racialised figures populate the sprawling peripheries of Rome: the Good Western European, invested with a sort of *mission civilisatrice* towards the migrants whose labour she exploits; the Bad Eastern European, violent and untrustworthy; and the Ugly Roma, often policed through sanitising interventions that involve displacement and erase specific built environments. She urges us to treat these three figures as situated within contrapuntal dynamics and to examine their effects within knowledge/power assemblages uniting seemingly disparate sites of violence.

The chapters in the third part entitled 'Europeanisation as epistemic dispossession' foreground the deceptive politics of European white saviourism and their violent material repercussions. Poet–scholar Saba Hamzah interrogates the selective documentation of Yemen in historical written records marked by silences and absences. She presents a sensorial poetic language deeply situated in the personal to entangle the structural and epistemic violence of heritage and heritage-making. She follows the emotions and hidden knowledges evoked in her encounters with 'a key' and 'a lock' as symbolic of silences in written historical records. Far from romanticising oral histories, she takes us on a journey to heritage sites past and present, here and there, public and domestic, reflecting on stories circulating in everyday rural life in Yemen. She invites us to sense these stories as shaped by dominant narratives while nevertheless remaining sites for reclaiming the right to narrate. In doing so, she brings attention to strategic ignorance and isolation used as tools of control by various ruling regimes, from the Imamate to European imperial powers, whose repercussions perpetuate the ongoing war in Yemen.

In the concluding chapter to this part, like Hamzah, actress and playwright Mihaela Drăgan reflects on the stories that legitimise the domination and dehumanisation of Roma people, reflecting on her experience as a Romani artist. She takes issue with the public and media perception of her persona as a poor 'Roma girl from Cândești village' who miraculously made it, showing how, in Romania's neoliberal precarity economy, individual success is the only allowed – if partial – escape from the violence of anti-Roma racism. Her work with the autonomous theatre collective Giuvlipen is a challenge to the racial violence of this economy but most importantly a path paved for future generations of Roma actresses. Her collective is a practice and call for shifting the place of Roma actresses from performing for the 'white tears' of non-Roma audiences to one of reinventing themselves from a queer feminist practice to 'imagine a future where we stop the historical cycle of oppression against us' (Drăgan, 2019).

The fourth and final part, 'Border epistemologies of Europeanisation', builds on the authors' work on exile, mobilities and migrancy to explore the violence of nation-building in the making of EU's European space. The chapters explore the ramifications of this violence as the geographies of 'temporal borders entrenched in colonial duress' (Maury, the volume). Olivia Maury looks at patterns of coloniality within the innovation economy's treatment of migrant labour in Helsinki. The chapter introduces us to a labour market in which student migrants from across the EU's Eastern borders and the 'Global South' are socially, legally and administratively sorted through the lexicon of talent, entrepreneurialism and competition. The chapter exposes this shiny market as an assemblage that rearticulates a dark colonial ordering of the present. Maury's contribution thus expands the inter-referencing of violence across and beyond the European space through an engagement with critical sociologies of the knowledge economy.

The many Souths and Easts of Europe and the obscure 'inside' of EU colonisation recur in the chapter by Ioana Țîștea, who confronts us with the forced inclusion of Roma groups within the EU. Through the form of the ethnodrama, her chapter exposes racialised, classed and gendered hierarchies reproduced in state-sanctioned public policies. At the same time, Țîștea dissects her own problematic position as an Eastern European white researcher in the role of non-Roma 'Roma expert' silencing the resistant, divergent and creative agencies of Roma women, confronting white ignorance. The doors that become violent traps (Gosset et al., 2017) of social and cultural interventions aimed at Roma 'integration' reveal Finland, and the other Nordic countries, as no exception to the violence of Europeanisation. We are thus reminded of how, in Finland, whiteness and Europeanness are constructed largely on racism against the indigenous Sámi and the Roma people, while the country's outsider status to colonialism and racism is carefully manufactured through national branding.[6]

In the last chapter, we return to the contemporary violent core of border enforcement in inter-imperial and nation-building spaces after the Second World War. Olivier Kramsch attempts to stitch together the post-war 'Recovered Territories' of Western Poland, retrieved after the mass expulsion of ethnic Germans from the region, the so-called Kresy (Borderlands, encompassing Eastern Poland, Western Belarus and Ukraine) and, finally, the South Indian Ocean island of Madagascar. He describes his method as spatial accidents of biography. The chapter juxtaposes two myths. The first is Poland's Eastern borderlands, conceived as either a site of nostalgic longing for a lost arcadia or a territory of benevolent colonisation towards less developed Belarussian and Ukrainian Other. The second is Madagascar as a site capable of solving Poland's 'Jewish question'. The simultaneous interplay of these myths, he argues, produces a nationalising border and an external frontier dynamic whose subterranean rumblings continue to inform our lived present, as witnessed most recently in the selective closures enacted by the Polish state at the Polish–Belarussian border.

We invite the reader to journey through the chapters. Our hope is that this volume brings closer the fleeting horizons emerging from the ruins of empires and nation states.

Notes

1 Some recent examples include 'Ukrainian letter of solidarity with the Palestinian people', Spilne. https://commons.com.ua/en/ukrayinskij-list-solidarnosti/; Srećko Horvat, Paul Stubbs and Dubravka Sekulić (2023) Against the 'Denkverbot': If you cancel Palestine, cancel us. www.aljazeera.com/opinions/2023/11/1/against-the-denkverbot-if-you-cancel-palestine-cancel-us

2 For important intervention on race and postsocialism, see Baker, 2018: 11; Balogun, 2022: 1–8; Kassymbekova and Chokobaeva, 2021: 483–503; Rexhepi, 2022.

3 Some of the technologies of assimilating Roma and Muslim women into socialist modernity included unveiling, boarding schools and separation from the families. See Todorova, 2021: 152.
4 Europe here signifies the World of Space and Time shaped by Western philosophical tradition and shaping the Subject of progress, see Da Silva, 2014.
5 On Europeanisation and sexual politics, see also Ayoub, 2016: 21–52; 158–98.
6 Finland's historically precarious position on the East/West divide led to concerns about the country's proximity to Russia, international representation and projections as part of the Eastern hemisphere. Against this risky backdrop, Finland's belonging to European cultural heritage and the West had to be highlighted. The hierarchies produced by scientific racism in the nineteenth and twentieth centuries assigned Finns a status of non-white and non-European 'Mongolian race', which led some Finnish anthropologists and sociologists to get involved in forceful counter-arguments to prove that Finns were white and racially unrelated to Mongolians. The Sámi continue to be subjected to direct processes of colonisation through theft of land, extraction of natural resources and industrialisation, as well as assimilation and separation. A nuanced understanding of colonialism and racism in the Nordic region must thus include the continued colonisation of the Arctic. See Andersen et al., 2015; Alemanji and Mafi, 2018; Keskinen, 2019; Seikkula, 2019.

References

Alemanji, A. A. and Mafi, B. (2018) 'Antiracism education? A study of an antiracism workshop in Finland', *Scandinavian Journal of Educational Research*, 62(2), 186–99.
Andersen, A., Hvenegård-Lassen, K. and Knobblock, I. (2015) 'Feminism in postcolonial Nordic spaces', *Nordic Journal of Feminist and Gender Research*, 23(4), 239–45.
Aparna, K., Kande, O., Schapendonk, J. and Kramsch, O. (2020) 'Europe is no longer Europe: montaging borderlands of help for a radical politics of place', *Nordic Journal of Migration Research*, 10(4), 10–25.
Aparna, K., Kramsch, O. and Kande, O. (2022) 'Where are the refugees? The paradox of asylum in everyday institutional life in the modern academy and the space-time banalities of exception', in Cantat, C., Cook, I. M. and Rajaram, P. K. (eds) *Opening Up the University: Teaching and Learning with Refugees*. Oxford: Berghahn Books, pp. 247–59.
Ayoub, P. M. (2016) *When States Come Out: Europe's Sexual Minorities and the Politics of Visibility*. Cambridge: Cambridge University Press.
Baker, V. (2018) *Nordic Nationalism and Penal Order: Walling the Welfare State*. London: Routledge.
Bakić-Hayden, M. (1995) 'Nesting orientalisms: the case of former Yugoslavia', *Slavic Review*, 54(4), 917–31. https://doi.org/10.2307/2501399.
Balogun, B. (2022) 'Eastern Europe: The "other" geographies in the colonial global economy', *Area*, 00, 1–8. https://doi.org/10.1111/area.12792.
Bashir, B. and Goldberg, A. (2018) 'Introduction: the Holocaust and the Nakba: a new syntax of history, memory, and political thought', in Bashir, B. and

Goldberg, A. (eds) *The Holocaust and the Nakba: A New Grammar of Trauma and History*. New York: Columbia University Press, pp. 20–70.

Bayoumi, M. (2023) 'They are "civilised" and "look like us": the racist coverage of Ukraine', *Guardian*, 2 March 2022. www.theguardian.com/commentisfree/2022/mar/02/civilised-european-look-like-us-racist-coverage-ukraine (accessed 29 February 2024).

Behr, H. and Stivachtis, Y. (2015) 'European Union: an empire in new clothes?', in Behr, H. and Stivachtis, Y. (eds) *Revisiting the European Union as Empire*. London: Routledge, pp. 1–16.

Bhagat, A. (2022) 'Governing refugees in raced markets: displacement and disposability from Europe's frontier to the streets of Paris', *Review of International Political Economy*, 29(3), 955–78.

Bhambra, G. K. (2016) 'Postcolonial reflections on sociology', *Sociology*, 50(5), 960–6. https://doi.org/10.1177/0038038516647683.

Bhambra, G. K., Mayblin, L. and Kathryn, M. (2024) *The Sage Handbook of Global Sociology*. London: Sage.

Bian, J. (2022) 'The racialization of expertise and professional non-equivalence in the humanitarian workplace', *Journal of International Humanitarian Action*, 7(3). https://doi.org/10.1186/s41018-021-00112-9.

Bilić, B. and Biliâc, B. (2016) *LGBT Activism and Europeanisation in the Post-Yugoslav Space*. Basingstoke: Palgrave Macmillan.

Birzeit University. (15 October 2023) 'Do not be silent about genocide' [Open Letter]. www.birzeit.edu/sites/default/files/upload/open_letter_from_birzeit_university_-final.pdf (accessed 23 December 2023).

Boatcă, M. (2021) 'Thinking Europe otherwise: lessons from the Caribbean', *Current Sociology*, 69(3), 389–414.

Boatcă, M., Plakhotnik, O., Krivonos, D., Böröcz, J., Tichindeleanu, O. and Seegel, S. (2022) 'Unequal Europes at war: placing Ukraine, (re)placing Eastern Europe', German Sociological Association roundtable. www.soziologie.de/aktuell/news/unequal-europes-at-war-placing-ukraine-replacing-eastern-europe (accessed 4 April 2022).

Brown, W. (2020) *States of Injury: Power and Freedom in Late Modernity*. Princeton, NJ: Princeton University Press.

Burlyuk, O. and Rahbari, L. (eds) (2023) *Migrant Academics' Narratives of Precarity and Resilience in Europe*. Cambridge: Open Book Publishers.

Cairo, A. (2021) *Holding Space: A Storytelling Approach to Diversity and Inclusion*. Amsterdam: Aminata Cairo Consultancy.

Cantat, C., Cook, I. M. and Rajaram, P. K. (2022) 'Introduction', in Cantat, C., Cook, I. M. and Rajaram, P. K. (eds) *Opening Up the University: Teaching and Learning with Refugees*. Oxford: Berghahn Books, pp. 1–30.

Chari, S. and Verdery, K. (2009) 'Thinking between the posts: postcolonialism, postsocialism, and ethnography after the Cold War', *Comparative Studies in Society and History*, 51(1), 6–34.

Chen, K. H. (2010) *Asia as Method: Toward Deimperialization*. Durham, NC: Duke University Press.

Cole, Juan R. I. (2018) 'Between the postcolonial and the Middle East: writing the subaltern in the Arab world', in Ball, Anna and Mattar, Karim (eds) *The Edinburgh Companion to the Postcolonial Middle East*. Edinburgh: Edinburgh University Press, pp. 81–96.

Connelly, J. (1999) 'Nazis and Slavs: from racial theory to racist practice', *Central European History*, 32(1), 1–33.
Cowen, D. (2020) 'Following the infrastructures of empire: notes on cities, settler colonialism, and method', *Urban Geography*, 41(4), 469–86.
Da Silva, D. F. (2007) *Toward a Global Idea of Race*. Minneapolis, MN: University of Minnesota Press.
Da Silva, D. F. (2014) 'Toward a Black feminist poethics: the quest(ion) of blackness toward the end of the world', *The Black Scholar*, 44(2), 81–97.
Dialoguing Posts Network (2019) *CfP 'Decolonial Methods, Peripheral Selves: The Migrant Figure between (South)East European and Global South Entanglements'*. https://dialoguingposts.wordpress.com/ (accessed 13 May 2022).
Djagalov, R. (2020) *From Internationalism to Postcolonialism: Literature and Cinema between the Second and the Third Worlds*. Montreal: McGill-Queen's University Press.
Dooley, N. (2019) *The European Periphery and the Eurozone Crisis: Capitalist Diversity and Europeanisation*. London: Routledge.
Drăgan. M. (2019) 'Roma futurism manifesto'. https://giuvlipen.com/en/roma-futurism/ (accessed 3 August 2023).
Dufty-Jones, R., Gibson, C. and Trevor B. (2022) 'Writing economies and economies of writing', *Environment and Planning A: Economy and Space*, 54(2), 370–81.
Duong-Pedica, A. (2023) 'Suffocating the academic and student solidarity movement for Palestinian liberation in Finnish higher education, Raster'. https://raster.fi/2023/12/04/suffocating-the-academic-and-student-solidarity-movement-for-palestinian-liberation-in-finnish-higher-education/ (accessed 23 December 2023).
Easterly, W. (2006) *The White Man's Burden*. New York: Penguin Press.
Easton-Calabria, E. E. (2015) 'From bottom-up to top-down: the 'pre-history' of refugee livelihoods assistance from 1919 to 1979', *Journal of Refugee Studies*, 28(3), 412–36.
Eberle, J, and Daniel, J. (2022) 'Anxiety geopolitics: hybrid warfare, civilisational geopolitics, and the Janus-faced politics of anxiety', *Political Geography*, 92, 102502.
European Commission. (2015) *A Symbolic Place for Europe: EU to Invest Over €78 Million in the Border Region of Austria and Hungary*. https://ec.europa.eu/regional_policy/en/newsroom/news/2015/07/a-symbolic-place-for-europe-eu-to-invest-over-eur78–million-in-the-border-region-of-austria-and-hungary (accessed 1 July 2022).
Eurostat. (2021) *Residence Permits: Statistics on First Permits Issued During the Year*. www.ec.europa.eu/eurostat/statistics-explained/index.php?title=Residence_permits_-_statistics_on_first_permits_issued_during_the_year&oldid=507019#Remunerated_activities (accessed 2 June 2022).
Fabian J. (1983) *Time and the Other: How Anthropology Makes Its Object*. New York: Columbia University Press.
Fallon, K. (2021) 'Poland-Belarus: humanitarian fears grow as child reportedly dies', *Aljazeera*, 12 November. www.aljazeera.com/news/2021/11/12/poland-belarus-humanitarian-fears-grow-as-child-reportedly-dies (accessed 8 June 2022).
Fanon, F. [1961] (1965, 1991) *The Wretched of the Earth*. Translated from the French by Constance Farrington. New York: Grove Weidenfeld.
Farbar, K., and Rowley, T. (2023) 'Ukraine's social welfare system shrinks as cost of war rises.' OpenDemocracy. www.opendemocracy.net/en/odr/ukraine-social-policy-reform-imf/ (accessed 29 February 2024).

Follis, K. S. (2012) *Building Fortress Europe: The Polish–Ukrainian Frontier*. Philadelphia, PA: University of Pennsylvania Press.
Ghodsee, K. and Orenstein, M. A. (2021) *Taking Stock of Shock: Social Consequences of the 1989 Revolutions*. New York: Oxford University Press.
Gilmore, R. W. (2011) 'What is to be done?', *American Quarterly*, 63(2), 245–65.
Glissant, É. (1997) *Poetics of Relation*. Ann Arbor, MI: The University of Michigan Press.
Gossett, R., Stanley, E. A. and Burton, J. (2017) 'Known unknowns: an introduction to Trap Door', in Gossett, R., Stanley, E. A. and Burton, J. (eds) *Trap Door: Trans Cultural Production and the Politics of Visibility* Cambridge, MA: MIT Press, pp. xv–xxvi.
Grovogui, S. (1996) *Sovereigns, Quasi Sovereigns, and Africans*. Minneapolis, MN: University of Minnesota Press.
Hage, G. (2021) 'Introduction: states of decay', in Hage, G. (ed.) *Decay*. Durham, NC: Duke University Press, pp. 1–16.
Hansen, P. and Jonsson, S. (2014) *Eurafrica: The Untold History of European Migration and Colonialism*. London: Bloomsbury.
Human Rights Watch (2022) 'Migrants, asylum seekers locked up in Ukraine', 4 April 2022, www.hrw.org/news/2022/04/04/migrants-asylum-seekers-locked-ukraine (accessed 29 February 2024).
Kalmar, I. (2022) *White But Not Quite: Central Europe's Illiberal Revolt*. Bristol: Bristol University Press.
Kamenou, N. (2020) 'When one doesn't even exist': Europeanisation, trans* subjectivities and agency in Cyprus', *Sexualities*, 24(1–2), 131–53.
Karkov, N. R. and Valiavicharska, Z. (2018) 'Rethinking East-European socialism: Notes toward an anti-capitalist decolonial methodology', *Interventions*, 20(6), 785–813.
Kassymbekova, B. and Chokobaeva, A. (2021) 'On writing Soviet history of Central Asia: frameworks, challenges, prospects', *Central Asian Survey*, 40(4), 483–503.
Keskinen, S. (2019) 'The "crisis" of white hegemony, neonationalist femininities and antiracist feminism', *Women's Studies International Forum*, 68, 157–63.
Khoury, E. (2018) 'Foreword', in Bashir, B. and Goldberg, A. (eds) *The Holocaust and the Nakba: A New Grammar of Trauma and History*. New York: Columbia University Press, pp. 10–20.
Khoury, N. (2018) 'Holocaust/Nakba and the counterpublic of memory', in Bashir, B. and Goldberg, A. (eds) *The Holocaust and the Nakba: A New Grammar of Trauma and History*. New York: Columbia University Press, pp. 153–73.
Kim, J. V. (2017) 'Asia–Latin America as method: the global south project and the dislocation of the West', *Verge: Studies in Global Asias*, 3(2), 97–117.
Kiratli, O. S. (2021) 'Politicization of aiding others: the impact of migration on European public opinion of development aid', *Journal of Common Market Studies*, 59(1), 53–71.
Koobak, R., Tlostanova, M. and Thapar-Björkert, S. (2021) 'Introduction: uneasy affinities between the postcolonial and the postsocialist', in Koobak, R., Tlostanova, M. and Thapar-Björkert, S. (eds) *Postcolonial and Postsocialist Dialogues: Intersections, Opacities, Challenges in Feminist Theorizing and Practice*. London and New York: Routledge, pp. 1–10.
Krivonos, D. (2023) 'Racial capitalism and the production of racial difference in Europe: young post-Soviet migrants in Helsinki and Warsaw', *Journal of Ethnic and Migration Studies*, 49(6), 1500–16. doi: 10.1080/1369183X.2022.2154911.

Kulawik, T. (2019) 'Introduction: European borderlands and topographies of transnational feminism', in Kulawik, T. and Kravchenko, Z. (eds) *Borderlands in European Gender Studies: Beyond the East–West Frontier*. London: Routledge, pp. 1–38.

Kulawik, T. and Kravchenko, Z. (2020) *Borderlands in European Gender Studies: Beyond the East–West Frontier*. London: Routledge.

Kumar, M. and Narkowicz, K. (2021) 'Postcolonial-postsocialist decolonial investigations: a programmatic overture', *Artha Journal of Social Sciences*, 20(2), v–xii.

Künzel, V. F. D. (2015) *Hitler's Brudervolk: The Dutch and the Colonization of Occupied Eastern Europe, 1939–1945*. New York and London: Routledge.

Kušić, K., Lottholz, P. and Manolova, P. (2019) 'From dialogue to practice: pathways towards decoloniality in Southeast Europe', *DVersia, Decolonial Theory and Practice in Southeast Europe*, 3, 6–30.

Kuusisto, A. (2021) 'Finland, the European Union, and the strategies of the Northern region', in Laine, J. P., Liikanen, I. and Scott, J. W. (eds) *Remapping Security on Europe's Northern Borders*. London: Routledge, pp. 138–58.

Lisle, D. (2021) 'A speculative lexicon of entanglement', *Millennium*, 49(3), 435–61.

Lyubchenko, O. (2022) 'Neoliberal reconstruction of Ukraine: a social reproduction analysis', *Gender Studies*, 26(1), 21–48.

Majumdar, A. (2020) 'Bearing witness inside MSF', *The New Humanitarian*, 18 August, www.thenewhumanitarian.org/opinion/first-person/2020/08/18/MSF-Amsterdam-aid-institutional-racism (accessed 1 June 2022).

Mamdani, M. (2020) *Neither Settler nor Native: The Making and Unmaking of Permanent Minorities*. Cambridge, MA: Harvard University Press.

Mark, J. (2022) 'Race', in Mark, J. and Betts, P. (eds) *Socialism Goes Global: The Soviet Union and Eastern Europe in the Age of Decolonization*. New York: Oxford University Press, pp. 221–54.

Mark, J. and Slobodian Q. (2018) 'Eastern Europe in the global history of decolonization', in Thomas, M. and Thompson, A. S. (eds) *The Oxford Handbook of the Ends of Empire*. Oxford: Oxford University Press, pp. 351–72.

Mark, J., Kalinovsky, A. and Marung, S. (2020) 'Introduction', in Mark, J., Kalinovsky, A. and Marung, S. (eds) *Alternative Globalizations Eastern Europe and the Postcolonial World*. Bloomington, IN: Indiana University Press, pp. 1–34.

Mbembe, A. (2019) *Necropolitics*. Durham, NC: Duke University Press.

Melamed, J. (2011) *Represent and Destroy: Rationalizing Violence in the New Racial Capitalism*. Minneapolis, MN: University of Minnesota Press.

Menon, N., Thapar-Björkert, S. and Tlostanova, M. (2021) 'Anti-colonial struggles, postcolonial subversions: an interview with Nivedita Menon', in Koobak, R., Tlostanova, M. and Thapar-Björkert, S. (eds) *Postcolonial and Postsocialist Dialogues*. London and New York: Routledge, pp. 109–20.

Mills, C. (2007) 'White ignorance', in Sullivan, S. and Tuana, N. (eds) *Race and Epistemologies of Ignorance*. New York: State Univesity of New York Press, pp. 26–31.

Minh-ha, T. T. (1989) *Woman, Native, Other: Writing Postcoloniality and Feminism*. Bloomington, IN: Indiana University Press.

Mongia, R. (2018) *Indian Migration and Empire: A Colonial Genealogy of the Modern State*. Durham and London: Duke University Press.

Mogilner, M. (2013) *Homo Imperii: A History of Physical Anthropology in Russia*. Lincoln, NE: University of Nebraska Press.

Navaro, Y., Biner, Z. Ö., von Bieberstein, A. and Altuğ, S. (2021) 'Introduction: reverberations of violence across time and space', in Navaro, Y. and Biner, Z. Ö., von Bieberstein, A. and Altuğ, S. (eds) *Reverberations: Violence Across Time and Space*. Philadelphia, PA: University of Pennsylvania Press, pp. 1–32.

Nicolaidis, K. (2015) 'Southern barbarians? A post-colonial critique of EUniversalism', in Nicolaïdis, K., Sèbe, B. and Maas, G. (eds) *Echoes of Empire: Memory, Identity and Colonial Legacies*. London: I. B. Tauris, pp. 247–64.

Nixon, R. (2011) *Slow Violence and the Environmentalism of the Poor*. Cambridge, MA, and London: Harvard University Press.

Odynets, S. (2022) 'Ukrainian refugees in Scandinavia, or how to talk about migration without talking about it', *Topos*, 2022(2), 31–6. https://doi.org/10.24412/1815-0047-2022-2-31-36.

Olusoga, D. and Erichsen, C. W. (2010) *The Kaiser's Holocaust: Germany's Forgotten Genocide and the Colonial Roots of Nazism*. London: Faber and Faber.

Ouma, S. and Premchander S. (2022) 'Labour, efficiency, critique: writing the plantation into the technological present-future', *Environment and Planning A: Economy and Space*, 54(2), 413–21.

Palat Narayanan, N. (2022) 'Dislocating urban theory: learning with food-vending practices in Colombo and Delhi', *Antipode*, 54(2), 526–44.

Pascucci, E. (2019) 'The local labour building the international community: precarious work within humanitarian spaces', *Environment and Planning A: Economy and Space*, 51(3), 743–60.

Pascucci, E. (2023) 'Labour', in Mitchell, K. and Pallister-Wilkins, P. (eds) *The Routledge Handbook of Critical Philanthropy and Humanitarianism*. London: Routledge, pp. 50–8.

Povinelli, E. A. (2011) *Economies of Abandonment: Social Belonging and Endurance in Late Liberalism*. Durham, NC, and London: Duke University Press.

Rajaram, P. K. (2018) 'Refugees as surplus population: race, migration and capitalist value regimes', *New Political Economy*, 23(5), 627–39.

Rajaram, P. K. and Grundy-Warr, C. (eds) (2007) *Borderscapes: Hidden Geographies and Politics at Territory's Edge*. Minneapolis, MN: University of Minnesota Press.

Rao, R. (2022) *Out of Time: The Queer Politics of Postcoloniality*. New York: Oxford University Press.

Raudaskoski, M. (2018) 'From "between" to Europe: remapping Finland in the post-Cold War Europe', in Laine, J., Liikanen, I. and Scott, J. W. (eds) *Post-Cold War Borders: Reframing Political Space in Eastern Europe*. Abingdon and New York: Routledge, pp. 188–206.

Rexhepi, P. (2018) 'Arab others at European borders: racializing religion and refugees along the Balkan Route', *Ethnic and Racial Studies*, 41(12), 2215–34.

Rexhepi, P. (2022) *White Enclosures: Racial Capitalism and Coloniality along the Balkan Route*. Durham, NC: Duke University Press.

Said, E. (1993) *Culture and Imperialism*. New York: Knopf.

Sayyid, S. (2018) 'Islamophobia and the Europeanness of the other Europe', *Patterns of Prejudice*, 52(5), 420–35.

Seikkula, M. (2019) 'Adapting to post-racialism? Definitions of racism in non-governmental organization advocacy that mainstreams anti-racism', *European Journal of Cultural Studies*, 22(1), 95–109.

Segal, R. (2023) 'A textbook case of genocide', 13 October 2023. https://jewishcurrents.org/a-textbook-case-of-genocide (accessed 2 January 2024).

Sen, S. (2022) 'The colonial roots of counter-insurgencies in international politics', *International Affairs*, 98(1), 209–23.

Sharma, N. (2020) *Home Rule: National Sovereignty and the Separation of Natives and Migrants*. Durham, NC: Duke University Press.

Sharp, J. (2011) 'Subaltern geopolitics: introduction', *Geoforum*, 42(3), 271–73.

Slootmaeckers, K. (2023) *Coming in: Sexual Politics and EU Accession in Serbia*. Manchester: Manchester University Press.

Snochowska-Gonzalez, C. (2012) 'Post-colonial Poland: on an unavoidable misuse', *East European Politics and Societies*, 26(4), 708–23.

Stanley, E. A. (2021) *Atmospheres of Violence: Structuring Antagonism and the Trans/Queer Ungovernable*. Durham, NC: Duke University Press.

Spivak, G. C. (1988) 'Can the subaltern speak?', in Nelson, C. and Grossberg, L. (eds) *Marxism and the Interpretation of Culture*. Urbana, IL: University of Illinois Press, pp. 271–316.

Subotić, J. and Vučetić, S. (2019) 'Performing solidarity: whiteness and status-seeking in the non-aligned world', *Journal of international Relations and Development*, 22(3), 722–43.

Suchland, J. (2011) 'Is postsocialism transnational?', *Signs: Journal of Women in Culture and Society*, 36(4), 837–62.

Talhami, G. H. (2003) *Palestinian Refugees: Pawns to Political Actors*. New York: Nova Science Publishers.

Taylor, D. (2023) 'Ukrainian refugee families in UK four times as likely to end up homeless', www.theguardian.com/world/2023/nov/21/ukrainian-refugee-families-in-uk-at-risk-of-homelessness-this-winter (accessed 20 February 2024).

Tilley, L. and Shilliam, R. (2018) 'Raced markets: an introduction', *New Political Economy*, 23(5), 534–43.

Tlostanova, M. (2012) Postsocialist ≠ postcolonial? On post-Soviet imaginary and global coloniality. *Journal of Postcolonial Writing*, 48(2), 130–142. https://doi.org/10.1080/17449855.2012.658244.

Todorova, M. S. (2021) *Unequal Under Socialism: Race, Women, and Transnationalism in Bulgaria*. Toronto: University of Toronto Press.

Tsymbalyuk, D. (2023) 'Ukraine and the traps of proximity to European and Russian Slavic whiteness', *The Funambulist*, 48, 66–71.

Ureña Valerio, L. A. (2019) *Colonial Fantasies, Imperial Realities: Race Science and the Making of Polishness on the Fringes of the German Empire, 1840–1920*. Athens, OH: Ohio University Press.

Väätänen, V. (2021) 'Securing anticipatory geographies: Finland's Arctic strategy and the geopolitics of international competitiveness', *Geopolitics*, 26(2), 615–38.

Valencia, S. and Pluecker, J. (2018) *Gore Capitalism*. Cambridge, MA: MIT Press.

Van Vossole, J. (2016) 'Framing PIGS: patterns of racism and neocolonialism in the Euro crisis', *Patterns of Prejudice*, 50(1), 1–20.

Weheliye, A. G. (2014) *Habeas Viscus: Racializing Assemblages, Biopolitics, and Black Feminist Theories of the Human*. Durham, NC, and London: Duke University Press.

Wilkinson, E. and Ortega-Alcázar, I. (2019) 'The right to be weary? Endurance and exhaustion in austere times', *Transactions of the Institute of British Geographers*, 44(1), 155–67.

Wynter, S. (2003) 'Unsettling the Coloniality of being/power/truth/freedom: towards the human, after man, its overrepresentation: an argument', *CR: The New Centennial Review*, 3(3), 257–337.

Yurchenko, Y. (2018) *Ukraine and the Empire of Capital: From Marketization to Armed Conflict*. London: Pluto Press.

Zarycki, T. (2014) *Ideologies of Eastness in Central and Eastern Europe*. London: Routledge.

Zhang, C. (2023) 'Postcolonial nationalism and the global right', *Geoforum*, 144, 103824. https://doi.org/10.1016/j.geoforum.2023.103824.

Part I

Europeanisation as infrastructural violence and colonial asymmetries

1

Europeanisation and infrastructural violence in South East Europe

Senka Neuman Stanivuković

In the spring of 2018, after efforts of migrants to move through South East Europe (SEE) were halted and rerouted from Serbia and Hungary to Bosnia and Herzegovina (BiH), a convoy of five buses carrying some 300 people found itself stranded by political and administrative complexities of BiH's post-conflict, postsocialist and pre-European contexts. These buses were to relocate people from informal shelters and open spaces in Sarajevo to Salakovac, one of the country's two official state-managed reception centres (RSE, 2018). Salakovac is located only a few kilometres away from Mostar in the Herzegovina-Neretva canton, which was predominantly governed by a party representing ethnic Croats. Local authorities have decided to contest the relocation decision as a centrally imposed act and an unconstitutional violation of their powers. They argued that the central government politicises and weaponises migrants to destabilise regions populated by ethnic Croats (N1, 2018). Accordingly, soon after the buses left Sarajevo and tried to cross into the Herzegovina-Neretva canton, they were stopped by local police. The central government responded that the stoppage of buses is an attempt to destabilise the state, reinstall internal borders and separate territories with a Croatian ethnic majority from the rest of the country (N1, 2018).

After hours-long negotiations, the migrants were finally admitted to the centre, but were separated from a few families from Kosovo, Northern Macedonia and other parts of Bosnia and Herzegovina that were housed there for already a long time. The Salakovac centre emerged as a refugee camp in the 1990s. It continued to operate despite of governmental promises to provide refugees and internally displaced people with better and more permanent housing, with these plans fully abandoned when BiH became more visible as part of the so-called Western Balkan route in 2018. In sharp contrast to the highly politicised arrival of migrants to Salakovac, the fact that many of them left the camp only a few days or weeks after in an attempt to reach southern and northern borders with Croatia was barely noticed (RSE, 2020).

The migrants' mobilities make clear that the bus blockade is embedded in – and must be read also in the context of – the European migration regime. Their stay in the Sarajevo informal camp, their organised relocation to Salakovac, their time spent in the camp together but separate from other refugee families and finally their departure towards borders with EU member states is entangled with how Europeanisation constitutes SEE as adjacent to the EU. Mobility struggles and regimes that try to control them must be considered together with spaces that migrants inhabit. As our reading of migration is largely focused on mobilities and transformations, we tend to disregard how these struggles are entangled with physical, political and economic violence of spaces that migrants come from, stay or end up in. Majstorović (2022) develops a related argument to critique how the 'people on the move' category obscures empirical realities of inequality across different geographies and silences underlying questions about who gets to move, where and how. Hence, vehicles, routes, infrastructures and geographies assembled by migration are routed in specific spaces that migrants inhabit and are contingent upon local processes. I argue that research should think together different forms of violence that are made possible by Europeanisation and show how violence that stems from the EU's infrastructural investments in SEE is entangled with open and covert violence of the EU's migration regime.

As addressed in the Introduction to this volume, relational encounters of Souths and Easts act as a method that helps ask how Europeanisation entangles and reproduces different forms of violence. The move towards thinking together violence experienced by migrants and spaces that they inhabit adds a layer to the complex workings of Europeanisation, as shown in this volume. Ould Moctar interprets the mass violence of the EU's border externalisation in the Sahel as resulting from the gradual breakdown of the region's spatial positioning as Europe's extreme periphery. Oancă brings the discussion directly to how Europeanisation produces uneven geographies of gradient Europeanness, which enables the rationalisation and marginalisation of Roma and Muslim communities in semi-peripheral spaces of Europe's South and South East.

In this chapter, I echo the need to think together durability of spatialised and material violence on the one hand and atmospheric and movable violence on the other, through the analytical lens of infrastructures. Infrastructures are complex systems (Harvey et al., 2018). They can assemble and maintain different apparatuses of harm. Infrastructures are also contradictory. They appear durable but are fragile, uncertain and defined by continuous disruptions (Howe et al., 2016). Infrastructures promise connectivity and mobility yet concurrently cause disconnection and exclusion. They rest on modernist visions of improved futures but can disperse and alter harm over time.

Precisely because of their complex and contradictory nature, infrastructures are a relevant lens through which to study how fluid assemblages of violence are embedded in harm that persists over space and time.

I start this chapter by showing how the analytical lens of infrastructures exposes Europeanisation as violence: infrastructural Europeanisation makes violence possible by rendering certain spaces as transitional and adjacent to Europe. I then move to two exploratory case studies. The first case shows how imaginaries of the future that arise from the EU's promises of connectivity and technopolitical assemblages of the European transport corridor system expose Europeanisation as a violent promise and produce SEE as a space of waiting.[1] The second case draws from the analysis of the EU's infrastructural investments in SEE to show how roads, highways, paths and railway tracks work in conjunction with the spatialised abjection of SEE and become mouldable as potentially violent.

Europeanisation and infrastructural violence in South East Europe

The proposed argument that Europeanisation should be studied through the lens of infrastructural violence rests on the broader realisation that SEE's political and societal impasse is an actively created condition. Particularly anthropological explorations of SEE's postsocialist and post-conflict transformations have shown that promises of transition to democracy and market economy carry and legitimise extractive and exploitative practices by different apparatuses that have managed this transition. Writing from different locations and across different themes, authors have established material and ideational connections between ethnonationalism, deindustrialisation and extraction and destruction of natural resources on the one hand and postsocialist democratisation and market liberalisation reforms on the other (Donias, 2002; Kurtović and Hromadžić, 2017).

Europeanisation's linear and teleological narratives of a move to democracy, peace and market economy with related promises of EU membership obscure forms of structural violence endured by populations as only malfunctions of transition. Hence, Europeanisation is complicit in the production of vulnerabilities and the violence of postsocialist transitions. Accession negotiations have provided a normative basis and techniques for measuring the extent of transition. As such, the promise of EU accession in conjunction with the so-called enlargement methodology offers a framework for governing transition. Enlargement captures transition as a practice of (self)improvement through different regulatory schemes, programmes, projects, vocabularies or material infrastructure. The promise of Europe and European integration adopts a function of an imagined end goal of transition and the EU's institutional order becomes a benchmark for evaluating progress in the transition process. This is why in the context of SEE, transition and Europeanisation are entangled and thus should be analysed and critiqued together.

On the one hand, Europeanisation and the promise of EU accession order and institutionalise post-socialist transitions to liberal democracy and market economy. On the other hand, SEE serves in EU integration as an imaginary counterfactual representation of what Europe would be like in the absence of integration: disunited, stagnant and always potentially violent. It is precisely this potentiality of the Balkans to become Europe and Europe to become the Balkans that is at stake in Europeanisation. The transitioning SEE as 'not-yet' or 'not-quite' Europe continuously unsettles Europe's boundaries, while it underpins the integration process.

Infrastructural violence brings an additional dimension through which one can explore the complicity of Europeanisation in the production of violence in so-called transition contexts. This refers to instances when infrastructural development and promises of connectivity become central tools of Europeanisation and mechanisms of measuring progress in transition. Next to disconnection and displacement as relatively visible consequences of infrastructural development, more complex forms of resource exploitation, environmental degradation or marginalisation can be inscribed into infrastructural systems (Rodgers and O'Neill, 2012). Built or anticipated infrastructures can be sites of abnegation of responsibility (Appel, 2012).

Significant work has been done to connect infrastructural Europeanism to colonial and postcolonial violence (Cupers, 2021). The afterlives of colonial infrastructures structure contemporary injustices in complex relations between, for instance, the EU's regulatory or standardisation schemes and development programmes, extractive violence, labour exploitation, expulsion or displacement, across geographies and temporalities. Authors have examined colonial rationalities inscribed into infrastructural development projects in East and North Africa, colonial afterlives of European border infrastructure, or explored linkages between infrastructural promises of green future in Europe and extractive violence in the Global South (Pasture, 2018; Enns and Bersaglio, 2020; Dunlap and Laratte, 2022).

The semi-peripheral position of SEE further obscures the complicity of Europeanisation in infrastructural violence. Global historical processes reproduce the borderline position of SEE as concurrently empowered and dominated by Europeanisation. This means that institutional Europeanisation through accession or quasi-accession frameworks in SEE or Eastern Europe is entangled with the regions' histories as arenas of imperial and colonial power. To this end, Doyle discusses inter-imperiality and Boatcă and Parvulescu (2020) call on their colleagues to render legible sites and subjectivities that emerge from the intersection of power and exploitation hierarchies, to show how Europeanisation silences the entanglement of violence and integration by differentiating between non-Europe and emerging Europe. As resource extraction, oppression or exploitation become identified as predicaments of SEE's postsocialist backwardness and almost-Europeanness, it becomes more difficult to link these forms of violence to European integration.

I assume that infrastructures create uneven effects on spaces and communities within and outside of the EU. As some spaces become sites of connectivity, others are excluded, neglected or made abject. In SEE, infrastructural Europeanism is entangled with violence also in contexts where legacies and contemporary patterns of subjugation and exploitation are complex, defined by contradictions and oftentimes diffused. Following Majstorović and Vučkovac (2022) on BiH's peripherality where promises of peace and state-building naturalise and coopt extractivism and interventionism, this analysis of the violence of infrastructural Europeanism in SEE furthers our grasp of when, for whom, under what conditions and why infrastructures become violent.

The tension between integration and connectivity is particularly visible in the EU's infrastructural investments in SEE, which have underpinned post-conflict and postsocialist transformations and been legitimised by the region's aspirations for EU membership. On the one hand, Europeanisation and the promise of becoming European materialise in infrastructures as visions of an improved future. Foreign investments are carried by economic and moral desires for improvement. On the other hand, connectivity solidifies the region's peripheral relations with the EU and its indeterminate not-yet and not-quite Europeanness.

Europeanisation inscribes the ambiguity of the decaying past and unfulfilled futures into infrastructural projects. This creates a space of possibility for infrastructural violence. Europeanisation is built on and overwrites the decaying socialist road, housing or energy systems while reproducing uncertainties of protracted transition. Infrastructures become objects co-constituted by fragile hopes, anticipation, doubt and waiting.

The EU's initial infrastructural development efforts in SEE were tied to post-conflict reconciliation. Restitution and repair of homes were expected to enable a safe return of displaced people to normal life (European Commission, 2001). Yet Jensen (2007) points out that a reductionist framing of a home as private property by the EU's and World Bank's reconstruction efforts created tension. Because a return to normal life and employment was deeply embedded in pre-war memories of the Yugoslav modernisation project, restructuring resulted in a contradiction in which certainties associated with the Yugoslav infrastructure were erased and replaced with the uncertain and, in Jansen's words, 'forced transition' to liberal-democratic and market-oriented Europe (Jansen, 2007: 22). Similarly, Dalakoglou (2017) describes how the physical construction of a highway between Albania and Greece in the 2000s was conditioned by the metaphysical destruction of the communist regimes' infrastructure and materiality: the highway brought together local desires and anxieties about the future after socialism, yet sedimented the ambiguous and protracted positioning of the region as Europe's border-space.

Methodologically, I map a network of material, socio-political, institutional elements that are meshed together by infrastructures, to examine how their presence and absence enables different vulnerabilities and forms of violence in SEE. Accordingly, I 'follow infrastructures' to uncover how violence unfolds across multiple geographies and temporalities and to problematise forms of violence that have been made unseen by binaries that are inherent to Europeanisation, such as EU/non-EU or progress/decay. I draw from desk research on policies and project documentation; archival research; ten semi-structured interviews with EU and local policy-makers, project managers and activists; and two field visits to the region. I take the EU's Western Balkans Connectivity Agenda (CA) as an analytical starting point to map EU investments into transport infrastructures in SEE. The EU's infrastructural investments in the region have not begun with the CA as these go back to the post-war recovery programmes of the 1990s and were integrated in pre-accession instruments. Similarly, the EU's investments need to be examined in the context of broader efforts to globalise the Balkans, such as through Chinese and Turkish infrastructural projects. Yet, the CA signifies how Europeanisation activates infrastructures to shape and mediate hope and inclusion, but also dislocation, violence or abandonment. In studying the CA, I look at how discursive and material promises of transport and energy connectivity are conditioned by acquis-based EU regulatory schemes, project-planning frameworks and the material remains of other infrastructures. My aim is to situate Europeanisation in a complex network of policies, regulations and standards, project methodologies and materialities that support infrastructural investments.

The analysis opens the following questions. First, how are promises of connectivity producing SEE as a space of not only inclusion and incorporation, but also fragmentation, displacement and exploitation? Second, how are transport infrastructures – as material forms of the European project – entangled with the reproduction of existing and production of new vulnerabilities and forms of violence in SEE? These questions are answered in two exploratory cases that problematise Europeanisation in terms of infrastructural violence of waiting, abjection and exploitation.

Europeanisation is about waiting in line

In the first exploratory case study, I show how promises of a European future become captured by the technopolitical temporalities of extending the CA and the related extension of the European transport corridor network (TEN-T) to SEE. Infrastructural connectivity makes EU membership both anticipated and doubted and affirms the position of SEE as a space of waiting for the EU. I suggest that Europeanisation works as a violent promise of accession, which is always in potential and locks countries into a state of protracted waiting. This chronic waiting is a technique of control. It is also a violent practice since it exposes those who wait to oppression by the temporary impasse and to practices of self-denigration (Jeffrey, 2008). I follow this line of argumentation to illustrate that infrastructures order Europeanisation as a sustained and open-ended meantime, which accelerates and normalises systemic precarisation, exploitation and marginalisation.

Chronic waiting for EU membership hurts the acceding countries because it locks them into a permanent state of transitioning where a distant promise of Europe appears as the only telos of the transition process (see also Deiana and Kušić, in this volume). Concurrently, the temporal impasse of protracted accession is filled with project timetables, financial planning, construction and bureaucratic rhythms, deadlines of infrastructural projects and near-term promises of connectivity. More specifically, the EU's infrastructural projects fill the empty time of transition with promises of improvement and connectivity in the near future and create an illusion that Europeanisation is an achievable and tangible goal. Goals of infrastructural connectivity help the EU to multiply reform initiatives outside of the direct EU accession framework, while SEE countries are made responsible for their own self-improvement in anticipation of distant membership.

The EU's investments in SEE's transport infrastructures and extension of the TEN-T to the region became politically visible in 2015 with the introduction of the CA. The CA was incorporated into the new platform for intergovernmental support of SEE's regional integration and relations with the EU, also known as the Berlin Process. The Berlin Process and goals of infrastructural connectivity came as a response to an enlargement impasse and as an attempt to maintain Europeanisation at times when the promise and prospect of EU membership became increasingly questioned and doubted in the region.

The CA has positioned connectivity and discourses, practices and materialities of infrastructural development as core elements of the EU's involvement in SEE. From 2015 to 2020, the CA has channelled into infrastructural development EUR 3.7 billion of grants and loans. Following the end of the Berlin Process in 2020, infrastructural investments were continued as core programmes of the EU's Economic and Investment Plan for the Western Balkans.

Apart from building new or restoring the existing transport network, the CA has asked the involved countries to adopt their policies and technical standards to EU legalisation. As part of this so-called soft connectivity, countries have reformed their institutional organisation, policies, regulation and standards related to transport networks, competition and procurement to EU norms and rules. This includes transport sustainability and safety measures, road maintenance schemes or simplification of cross-border procedures. Additionally, the EU has supported the formation of regional bodies such as the Transport Community that mimic European transport integration on a regional level. The actual planning and construction of roads and maintenance of the road network was managed as a part of the extension of the TEN-T corridors to SEE.

The analysis of discourses and practices related to infrastructural connectivity and the extension of the TEN-T shows how Europeanisation operates through the mesh of promises of progress on the one hand and temporalities of chronic waiting on the other. The created structure of concurrently promised, awaited and doubted futures is not a neutral condition. The voluntary ethos of the EU accession process and participation in the infrastructural development projects are driven by rationalities of progress and self-improvement. At the same time conditions of chronic waiting, which are inscribed into Europeanisation, open space for domination, control and oppression.

The way Europeanisation utilises infrastructures to manipulate time becomes clear when we observe how projects like the CA and other related infrastructural investments place SEE in a state of uncertainty, outside the realms of the present and the future.

Infrastructural development abstracts and suspends the EU accession process into the time of concurrent doubting and anticipating EU membership, which is then inhabited by connectivity as a tangible and concrete response for this period of the meantime. In the EU's political discourse, infrastructural projects were defined as an effective way to use the time between today and tomorrow, while waiting for enlargement. In the 2018 address to the political leaders of SEE, the then-president of the European Council, Donald Tusk, described connectivity as 'a way to use the time between today and tomorrow more effectively than before' (European Council, 2018). Similar references to the CA as a programme for the accession meantime have reappeared in many policy discourses (TCF, 2019). When asked to explain political motivation for the introduction of the CA, interviewed EU officials and experts have explained that connectivity offers tangible results while the region is waiting for the uncertain enlargement (Interview 1, Interview 5).

On the policy level, EU investments in roads and railways are no longer positioned exclusively as a reform carrot in preparing countries for EU membership but became a goal in their own right carried by promises of improved infrastructural connectivity, economic growth, improved employment prospects and more stable neighbourly relations (European Commission, 2015: 3). This is mostly achieved through the differentiation between what is described as immediate and tangible results of infrastructural development on the one hand and the abstractness and potentiality of EU membership on the other. Interviewed European and national policy-makers described connectivity as 'a measure that brings visible and fast results to communities … unlike the accession process' (Interview 5, Interview 8). They have almost exclusively defined connectivity as a tangible and real goal in opposition to the uncertainties and ambiguities of the EU's enlargement policy, although they clearly struggled to provide an exact definition of connectivity.

Furthermore, the CA and the extension of the TEN-T organise Europeanisation as a project system with time-bound goals, defined project phases and funding schedules, and temporalities of road or railway construction and maintenance. The logic of infrastructural projects renders narratives and promises of EU membership abstract in exchange for promises of socio-economic improvement through very specific and quantifiable result indicators. Grant applicants are asked to motivate the projects' compliance with the EU's legal system, but this compliance is defined as a technical rather than political matter and it is placed outside the field of accession (WBIF, 2021: 5). Project funding mechanisms enable the EU to impact sensitive questions such as public procurement regulations in a depoliticised way. In a relatable vein, even the politically troublesome goals of furthering regional integration in SEE are rendered technical and achievable through project-based interventions. Temporalities of projects that are organised as a linear move across different project phases with pre-defined and measurable goals provide an additional sense of Europeanisation as a time-bound and achievable process. This is at odds with ground realities since construction works are marked by significant delays and many of the projects fail before they even move to the implementation stage (Interview 10).

The positioning of infrastructural development as time spent in anticipation of EU accession is adopted by domestic political discourses and processes. Whereas in their rhetoric, national politicians inscribe into the new highways and railways grand narratives of state development and a globally connected Balkans, they have referred to infrastructural development as an activity for the meantime before EU accession (TCF, 2019). In the same sentence, these elites would highlight the necessity of the EU's regional presence while framing infrastructural investments by China or Turkey as a needed answer to the protracted accession process (Interview 10). Direct investments and loans for highways, railways or mining infrastructure have been framed as a way of ensuring the region's development while waiting for EU membership (TCF, 2019).

The infrastructural boom in SEE should therefore be seen not only as a tool in the geopolitical balancing between the EU and China but also as having a temporal dimension because it reproduces the country's not-yet EU status. CA- and TEN-T-related investments in SEE reproduce the image of SEE as a laboratory of infrastructural development at the periphery of Europe. It is a place where state desires for growth through infrastructural expansions entangle EU-funded projects with the Belt and Road Initiative investments. SEE's indeterminate status makes the region an attractive node in global supply chains, which is a perspective that helps us see the EU's and Chinese infrastructural investments as entangled rather than mutually competing. Additionally, SEE's indeterminacy vis-à-vis the EU makes possible regulatory flexibility in terms of environmental or labour standards and dependency on unfavourable loans from, for instance, the China Eximbank (Rogelja, 2020). Chinese state-owned construction companies participate in and have won EU funding bids.

Accordingly, Europeanisation through infrastructural investments creates transportation zones that appear – discursively and at times materially – separate from other infrastructures and from the socio-political conditions in which these other infrastructures emerge. Framed as a tangible promise of European connectivity, the extension of the EU's corridor network to SEE and related procurement and environmental regulations create roads and railways as transitory zones that connect Western Europe to the East Mediterranean but also integrate the European corridor network with global supply chains. Even though the EU's infrastructural development projects reproduce the region's indeterminacy, the consequently established transport corridors appear as Europeanised enclaves that signify development and order and are detached from the deteriorating local transport networks or the violence of land disposition, environmental contamination or labour exploitation.

Europeanisation as infrastructural abjection

In the second case study, I show how promises of connectivity and the EU's infrastructural investments and regulation are entangled with the production of spaces of transit, suspended mobility or abjection. The link between accession-driven Europeanisation and national legislative, regulatory and infrastructural frameworks that control, contain and pre-empt migration to the EU has been widely documented and well analysed (Isakjee et al., 2020).

Through the lens of connectivity and infrastructural violence, it is possible to map a wide infrastructural landscape of camps, routes, zones and frontiers that enable violence. This mapping shows how the spectacularised violence of border 'push-back', but also the slower violence of neglect and abandonment is made possible by the absence and presence of particular infrastructures.

Through the analytical lens of infrastructures, it is possible to see how spatialised production of SEE as Europe's abject self enables violence towards migrants. Following Ferguson (2001), who adapted Kristeva's work on abjection to describe how globalisation and promises of modernisation produce a complex state of being expelled and discarded from the emerging new order, I argue that Europeanisation can be read as a process and practice of abjection. European integration erases histories and experiences of Eastern Europe and reproduces the region as a less civilised, more violent, more nationalistic, more homophobic and more unstable image of Western Europe (Gržinić, 2014). Identification of the EU with peace, integration, stability and progress constructs the SEE as its threatening antithesis; a violent, disintegrated and backward version of the European *self* (Vukasović, 2020). The dissolution of Yugoslavia, war violence, postsocialist deindustrialisation and neoliberalisation, or growth of ethnonationalism in post-Yugoslav countries were critical not only for foreign and security policy in the EU, but for the EU's self-identification as a peace and stability project. In this collective identity, SEE performs the ambiguous temporal position of the past that the EU has overcome and the threatening future that the EU could become in the absence of integration. Europeanisation constructs SEE as its *abject self*, an indeterminate entity that continuously unsettles Europe's boundaries, yet underpins the essence of the integration process.

The infrastructural lens problematises spatialised and materialised effects of the construction of SEE as Europe's abject *self*. Put differently, infrastructures operate as technopolitical vehicles of this abjection. Infrastructural interventions, while not directly designed to be harmful, produce SEE as an abject space in which they create conditions of possibility for violence (Rodgers, 2012). These conditions are created in many ways. Abject spaces are marginalised, neglected and become visible only as a troubling factor in the established order. Abject spaces obscure boundaries of what is seen as normatively acceptable. Those that inhabit these spaces are marginalised, neglected and governed by an interplay of regimes of visibility and invisibility.

The techno-politics of border control are an example of violence made possible by spatialised forms of abjection. Borders as infrastructures assemble different policies, practices, discourses and materialities that are intended to exclude particular groups of people, which can have severe humanitarian consequences and directly violate human rights (Dijstelbloem, 2021). Violence inherent to the externalisation of the EU's border and migration control ranges from direct physical violence at border crossings through systemic police practices of 'push-back' to structural violence that arises from the restriction of movement by controlling migration routes and migrants' abandonment in precarious living conditions in camps, reception facilities and informal housing (Davies et al., 2017; Isakjee et al., 2020). Whereas violent and illegal 'push-back' is a direct consequence of border infrastructures, infrastructural harm and violence can be indirect. Camps or informal settlements exclude, contain and abandon those seeking refuge. Control of roads, railway tracks or ports can do the same. These networked infrastructures of mobility control bring together policies, technologies and standards, discourses, vehicles, materiality of transport routes and the environment in which they are embedded (Xiang and Lindquist, 2014).

Infrastructures intersect and mediate different forms of abjection. Hromadžić (2019) describes how violence related to Bosnian industrial decay gains a material form in infrastructural ruins of socialist buildings and intertwined with violence against migrants that now inhabit these places. These infrastructural ruins become a site of non-linear, converging violence of postsocialist, post-war transformations and violence toward migrants. 'Push-out', 'push-back' and violence connected to separation and abandonment of those seeking refuge across SEE is conditioned by the production and infrastructural territorialisation of SEE as abject space. The abjection of SEE makes it possible for the EU to displace its border and migration violence to the region.

How materialised and spatialised abjection of SEE performs a critical role in the violence of the EU's migration and border regime becomes visible in the formalisation and de-formalisation of the Balkan route. Trakilović (2019) analyses political discourses on the so-called opening of the Balkan route and suggests that both migrants and the region remain abject configurations in the dominant European imaginary. EU attempts to control, manage, monitor and curb migration through the formalisation and de-formalisation of the Balkan corridor are sustained by the dual abjection of migrants and SEE. While migrants are represented as culturally different, deviant and threatening to the essence of Europe, SEE becomes a peripheralised space of externalised violence that encroaches upon the EU's order. Hence, Frontex's naming and spatialisation of the corridor as the 'Western Balkans' is not benign, not only because it renders migration routes controllable but also because it situates these routes in the spatial imaginary of Balkans as Europe's abject self.

The infrastructural lens distances us from the formalisation of the Balkan corridor in summer 2015 and enables us to problematise how EU migration management works through the complex dynamics of abjection. The common imaginary of the Balkan corridor as people walking on dirt roads or sleeping at train stations obscures the complex transport infrastructure that was assembled by migrants in SEE (Hameršak et al., 2020). Frontex's discourses and practices on the route create an imaginary of a coherent political and infrastructural formation that makes possible an onward migratory trajectory to Europe. Description of the route as 'one of the main migratory paths into Europe' and related monitoring of illegalised border crossings formalises and controls migration connections and routes, while obscuring how EU infrastructural politics in SEE mould migratory movements from and through the region (Frontex – Western Balkans Route).

Investments in SEE's transport infrastructure are not direct tools of the EU's migration control regime. The EU adopts membership and financial conditionality to externalise its border and migration regime to SEE through strengthened police capacities, border surveillance and information sharing, and alignment of national asylum systems with the EU's legal order. Frontex's status agreements with Albania, Serbia and Montenegro deploy border-police corps to these countries and enhance digital border management infrastructures in the region through pre-accession financial and technical assistance packages (IPA) and border management funding. Financial assistance and the alignment of national laws and policies with EU rules and norms is also used to reestablish, repair and sustain a widespread infrastructure of migrant reception and detention centres in SEE. In contrast to these legislative and financial measures through which the EU externalises its migration and border management regime to SEE, direct causalities between the EU goals of infrastructural connectivity and the extension of the TEN-T to SEE and violence against migrants are hard to demonstrate. Instead of harming migrants directly, EU interventions in the region's transport infrastructure construct SEE as an abject space where the atmosphere of migrant violence is rendered adequate, maintained and normalised.

Thus, roads, highways, paths or railway tracks are not predetermined sites and tools of violence as such, but – in conjunction with the abjection of SEE – are mouldable to become violent in different forms and functions (Dijstelbloem and Walters, 2021). To better understand the heterogenous ways in which the construction of SEE as an abject space transforms transport infrastructures as potential tools of violence towards migrants, one needs to study the EU's infrastructural investments in conjunction with the externalisation of its border and migration regime to the region.

The EU transforms SEE's transport infrastructures as potential tools in differentiating between desired and undesired mobilities. Efforts to align border-crossing procedures and create Joint Border Crossing Points within SEE illustrate this. Abject ambiguity of SEE as Europe's unwanted *self* manifests in the region's integration into the European corridor system but as its unstable and insecure part. Connectivity targets of more efficient border crossings or reduced wait and clearance times are linked to European security needs. Accordingly, regulation, standards and investments in material and digital infrastructures of border crossings position roads or railways as potential tools in border and migration control. Although investments in transport infrastructure are not directly subordinate to the EU's migration and border regime, the EU's technical assistance documentation inscribes security needs (differentiating between 'legitimate' and 'irregular' mobilities) in the design, operation and management of border-crossing facilities.

Furthermore, the abjection of SEE as a disorderly space that is within Europe but also inferior to it is reproduced through infrastructural differentiation of the region between spaces of connection and disconnection. As SEE is constituted as adjacent to Europe in infrastructural terms, movement becomes governed through the concurrent formalisation and visibility of particular highways and railways as zones of transit, while other infrastructures are de-formalised and disconnected as zones of irregularised mobility, forced waiting and violence. The so-called opening of the Balkan route and its consequent suspension and rerouting is a good case in point for how SEE becomes reproduced as a dual space of connections and disconnections, where mobility is governed through an interplay of regularised and irregularised infrastructures. Kasparek and Hess (2021) have described what is now an iconic image of an organised transit corridor of railway and highway routes through SEE, which in 2015 marked the so-called opening of the Balkan route. Frontex's visual mapping and policy representations of migrant struggles in SEE construct an imaginary of linear movement across official border checkpoints and supported by the established transport network (Frontex – Migratory Map). These transport networks correspond to infrastructures that are currently being incorporated into the TEN-T network. Highways and railway tracks that were used by migrants to move from Thessaloniki to Belgrade and then Budapest in 2015 are now governed as an extension of the European corridor network and the EU's connectivity ambitions in SEE. Yet, declared aims to boost circulation of people and goods in Europe by repairing existing and building new infrastructures stand in sharp contrast to how the TEN-T network is made a tool of migration containment and violence after the so-called suspension of the Balkan route. Activist structures have continuously reported on people dying after being hit by a train as they walk along the railway tracks. Moreover, train stations and highway service stations are sites of 'push-back' and other forms of violent assault on migrants.

Simultaneously to the migratory movement being rerouted away from Greece and Northern Macedonia and through Serbia and Croatia to Hungary,

Austria and Western Europe along Corridor X, official and self-organised camps emerged in the Una-Sana canton at the Bosnian-Herzegovian border with Croatia. This region is disconnected from the TEN-T and any major transit routes to Western Europe. Moreover, housing infrastructures for migrants in Serbia were reorganised to contain mobility within the region. Mitrović and Vilenica (2021) has already pointed out that a topology of state and non-state housing structures for migrants transforms SEE into a borderscape. An assemblage of camps across the region that differ in their status and degree of permanence operates as an infrastructure of control. A complex network of camps, abandoned and ruining post-industrial complexes and walking paths, operates through mobility control and containment with concurrent practices of violent 'push-back' and hospitality. This complex infrastructural web works as a tool of disconnection and neglect as migrants are forced to move within the region, yet prevented from escaping from it.

Conclusion

In this chapter, I showed that Europeanisation and future promises of a liberal, transborder and post-national Europe not only obscure different forms of violence but also make violence possible. The analytical lens of infrastructures, as complex and contradictory systems, helps us make sense of Europeanisation as an entanglement of enduring, spatialised harm on the one hand and disperse, atmospheric harm on the other.

This violence can be subtle. It works through practices of exclusion from the futures that ought to be. While infrastructures transmit promises of political stability and economic growth associated to EU membership, they render improvement as always just out of reach. The combination of the very tangible visualisation of what progress and Europeanness ought to look like with chronic exclusion from it through the abstraction of EU membership perspective, creates conditions of violence. Infrastructural development operates as a trap because the region and its populations are written out of the European order and concurrently made to believe that the hardship of transition is a needed precursor to future prosperity (Stengers, 2015).

This violence can be normalised. It works through the production of SEE as an indeterminate space of abjection where the distinction between order and disorder, normalcy and rupture is blurred. Accordingly, infrastructures such as roads, highways or railway tracks can operate as zones of connectivity, improvement and mobility and keep the EU detached from responsibility for violence in SEE. The very same infrastructures can be activated as tools of disconnection, marginalisation and neglect, enabling open and covert violence against migrants.

Interviews

Interview 1. Transport Community. (25 November 2020).
Interview 2. Transport Community. (30 November 2020).
Interview 3. Delegation of the European Union to Bosnia and Herzegovina. (28 January 2021).
Interview 4. DG MOVE. (2 February 2021).
Interview 5. DG NEAR. (8 March 2021).
Interview 6. Delegation of the European Union to Kosovo. (18 March 2021).
Interview 7. Interview with an NGO representative in Serbia. (19 March 2021).
Interview 8. Vlada Republike Srbije. (25 March 2021).
Interview 9. Delegation of the European Union to Serbia. (26 March 2021).
Interview 10. European Investment Bank. (2 April 2021).

Note

1 I am thankful to Elisa Pascucci for this conceptualisation.

References

Appel, H. C. (2012) 'Walls and white elephants: oil extraction, responsibility, and infrastructural violence in Equatorial Guinea', *Ethnography*, 13(4), 439–65.
Boatcă, M. and Parvulescu, A. (2020) 'Creolizing Transylvania: notes on coloniality and inter-imperiality', *History of the Present*, 10(1), 9–27.
Cupers, K. (2021) 'Editorial: coloniality of infrastructures', *E-flux Architecture* (September 2021), 1–6.
Dalakoglou, D. (2017) *The Road: An Ethnography of (Im)mobility, Space, and Cross-border Infrastructures in the Balkans*. Manchester: Manchester University Press.
Davies, T., Isakjee, A. and Dhesi, S. (2017) 'Violent inaction: the necropolitical experience of refugees in Europe', *Antipode*, 49(5), 1263–84.
Dijstelbloem, H. and Walters, W. (2021) 'Atmospheric border politics: the morphology of migration and solidarity practices in Europe', *Geopolitics*, 26(2), 497–520.
Donais, T. (2002) 'The politics of privatization in post-Dayton Bosnia', *Southeast European Politics*, 3(1), 3–19.
Dunlap, A. and Laratte, L. (2022) 'European Green Deal necropolitics: exploring "green" energy transition, degrowth & infrastructural colonization', *Political Geography*, 97, 1–17.
Enns, C. and Bersaglio, B. (2020) 'On the coloniality of "new" mega-infrastructure projects in East Africa', *Antipode* 52(1), 101–23.
European Commission (2001) *Bosnia and Herzegovina CARDS Additional Support programme 2001*. https://neighbourhood-enlargement.ec.europa.eu/system/files/2018-12/bosnia_additional_support_programme_en.pdf (accessed 15 August 2024).

European Commission (2015) *Connectivity Agenda Co-financing of Investment Projects in the Western Balkans*. www.wbif.eu/storage/app/media/Library/6.%20Connectivity%20Agenda/27.%20Vienna-Info-Pack-Final.pdf (accessed 1 June 2022).
European Council (2018) *EU–Western Balkans Summit in Sofia*. www.consilium.europa.eu/en/meetings/international-summit/2018/05/17/ (accessed 15 August 2024).
Ferguson, J. (2001) 'Global disconnect: abjection and the aftermath of modernism', in Javier, J., Rosaldo, I. and Rosaldo, R. (eds) *The Anthropology of Globalization*. New York: Blackwell, pp. 136–53.
Gržinić, M. (2014) 'Europe's colonialism, decoloniality, and racism', in Broeck, S. and Junker C. (eds) *Postcoloniality Decoloniality-Black Critique: Joints and Fissures*. Frankfurt/New York: Campus Verlag, pp. 129–46.
Hameršak, M., Hess, S., Speer, M. and Mitrović, M. S. (2020) 'The forging of the Balkan route: Contextualizing the border regime in the EU periphery', *Movement: Journal for Critical Migration and Border Regime Studies*, 5(1), 1–12.
Harvey, P. (2018) 'Infrastructures in and out of time: The promise of roads in contemporary Peru', in Anand, N., Gupta, A. and Appel, H. (eds) *The Promise of Infrastructure*. Durham, NC: Duke University Press, pp. 80–101.
Hess, S. and Kasparek, B. (2021) 'Historicizing the Balkan route: governing migration through mobility', in Walters, W., Heller, C. and Pezzani, L. (eds) *Viapolitics*. Durham, NC: Duke University Press, pp. 183–208.
Howe, C. et al. (2016) 'Paradoxical infrastructures: ruins, retrofit, and risk', *Science, Technology, & Human Values*, 41(3), 547–65.
Hromadžić, A. (2019) 'Uninvited citizens: violence, spatiality and urban ruination in postwar and postsocialist Bosnia and Herzegovina', *Third World Thematics: A TWQ Journal*, 4(2–3), 114–36.
Isakjee, A. et al. (2020) 'Liberal violence and the racial borders of the European Union', *Antipode*, 52(6), 1751–73.
Jansen, S. (2007) 'Troubled locations: return, the life course, and transformations of "home" in Bosnia-Herzegovina', *Focaal*, 49, 15–30.
Jeffrey, C. (2008) 'Waiting', *Environment and Planning D: Society and Space*, 26(6), 954–58.
Kurtović, L. and Hromadžić, A. (2017) 'Cannibal states, empty bellies: protest, history and political imagination in post-Dayton Bosnia', *Critique of Anthropology*, 37(3), 262–96.
Majstorović, D. and Vučkovac, Z (2022) 'Bosnia and Herzegovina after the transition: forever postwar, postsocialist and peripheral?', in Gagyi, A. and Slačálek, O. (eds) *The Political Economy of Eastern Europe 30 Years into the 'Transition'*. Cham: Palgrave Macmillan, pp. 81–96.
Mitrović, M. S. and Vilenica, A. (2021) 'Enforcing and disrupting circular movement in an EU Borderscape: Housingscaping in Serbia', in Dadusc, D., Grazioli, M., and Martinez, M. A. (eds) *Resisting Citizenship*. Abingdon: Routledge, pp. 20–38.
'N1 – Migranti stigli u izbjeglicki kamp Salakovac u BiH' *N1 BiH*, 18 May 2018. https://n1info.hr/regija/a303327–migranti-stigli-u-izbjeglicki-kamp-salakovac-u-bih/ (accessed 10 October 2022).
Pasture, P. (2018) 'The EC/EU between the art of forgetting and the palimpsest of empire', *European Review*, 26(3), 545–81.

Rodgers, D. (2012) 'Haussmannization in the tropics: abject urbanism and infrastructural violence in Nicaragua', *Ethnography*, 13(4), 413–38.

Rodgers, D. and O'Neill, B. (2012) 'Infrastructural violence: Introduction to the special issue', *Ethnography*, 13(4), 401–12.

'RSE – Migrantski kamp u centru Sarajeva' (2018) *Radio Slobodna Evropa* (10 May 2018). www.slobodnaevropa.org/a/migranti-sarajevo/29219213.html (accessed 3 October 2022).

'RSE – Tjeraju nas iz Sarajeva, Banjaluke, Velike Kladuše i Bihaća, nigdje nas neće' (2020), *Radio Slobodna Evropa* (24 August 2020). www.slobodnaevropa.org/a/tjeraju-nas-iz-sarajeva-banjaluke-velike-kladu%C5%A1e-i-biha%C4%87a-nigdje-nas-ne%C4%87e-/30800128.html (accessed 10 October 2022).

Rogelja, I. (2020) 'Concrete and coal: China's infrastructural assemblages in the Balkans', *Political Geography*, 81, 102202.

Stengers, I. (2015) 'Accepting the reality of Gaia: a fundamental shift?', in *The Anthropocene and the Global Environmental Crisis*. London: Routledge, pp. 134–44.

TCF (2019) 'Connectivity agenda and structural weaknesses of EU candidate countries', *Cooperation and Development Institute*, pp.1–55.

Trakilović, M. (2019) 'On this path to Europe – the symbolic role of the "Balkan corridor" in the European migration debate', in Buikema, R., Buyse, A. and Robben, A. C. G. M. (eds) *Cultures, Citizenship and Human Rights*. Abingdon: Routledge, pp. 49–63.

Vukasović, D. M. (2020) *Constructing a (EU)ropean Identity, the Balkans and the Western Balkans as the Other*. Belgrade: Institute for Political Studies.

WBIF (2021) 'How to fill in the WBIF grant application form for investment grants – guidelines for applicants', *WBIF*, pp. 1–55. https://wbif.eu/storage/app/media/Library/11.Funding/WBIF%20INV%20GAF%20Guidelines_Jan%202021.pdf (accessed 3 June 2022).

Xiang, B. and Lindquist, J. (2014) 'Migration infrastructure', *International Migration Review*, 48, 122–48.

2

Europeanisation, border violence, counterinsurgency: expanded geographies and reconnected histories across the Sahelo-Sahara and the Mediterranean

Hassan Ould Moctar

In the southern Mauritanian border town of Rosso, two young men from Mali recounted to me scattered and violent trajectories of mobility. Spanning two macro-regions and encompassing a range of lethal governmental interventions, their stories lie at a structural intersection between European Union (EU) migration control efforts in the Mediterranean and an international counterinsurgency campaign in the Sahel. Soro,[1] from the central Malian region of Mopti, first left his home in 2006 for Libya. From there he eventually made his way to Algeria, before attempting to cross the Mediterranean from the port city of Oran. He was intercepted by the Algerian coast guard and abandoned by security forces in Algeria's southern desert borderlands, where he made an arduous crossing on foot into Niger. He then made his way back to Libya, from where he hoped to reach Italy, before instead reluctantly participating in an IOM 'voluntary return' programme. His companion in Rosso, Ali Bakar, was from the Malian region of Timbuktu. His trajectory also commenced in Libya, where he worked with his brother in a Turkish-owned factory. Following the collapse of the Libyan state after the 2011 NATO intervention, his brother made the Mediterranean crossing to Italy before settling in Malta. Ali Bakar fled in the opposite direction, eventually settling in Mauritania in 2017. This remained a preferable option to returning home to Timbuktu where, in his words, 'everything had been ruined' since the war with the jihadists broke out in 2012. Soro, too, spoke of ongoing 'problems with the jihadists' in his home region of Mopti, which has been equally drenched in insecurity since becoming the hotspot of an international counterinsurgency campaign in 2015 (Cold-Ravnkilde and Ba, 2022).

While varying in degrees of European causal responsibility, each of these experiences of direct violence bear an asymmetry reminiscent of the colonial era, which saw a process of pacification and liberalisation within the

European metropole alongside mass violence in the colonies (Lal, 2005: 221). Insofar as they follow from the removal of barriers to free movement in Europe and the process of European integration more generally, EU migration control policies in the Mediterranean and military intervention and stabilisation missions in the Sahel together uphold this colonial asymmetry.[2] There are, however, instructive distinctions to be drawn between past and present. Having been born of a moment in which the formal colonial order was dying amidst strident hopes and efforts to keep it alive (Hansen and Jonsson, 2014), the EU is today instead charged with upholding its remnants, which nonetheless continue to hold powerful material weight and ideological sway. Indeed, once Eurocentric conceits are absorbed, as Samir Amin (1988: 107) once observed, 'it becomes impossible to contemplate any other future for the world than its progressive Europeanisation'.

At the same time, it is becoming ever clearer that the progressive Europeanisation of the world is a material and cultural impossibility. What happens when these two facts – the hegemony of European teleology and the impossibility of its concrete realisation – come into conflict? Put differently, if, as Fanon (2004: 58) has it, 'Europe is literally the creation of the Third World', what happens when this exploitative and entrenched link begins to become undone? In this chapter, I conceptualise the mass violence, death and instability that mark both the Mediterranean and the Sahelo-Sahara regions as manifestations of a collapse in European hegemony over what has historically been a colonial backyard and postcolonial sphere of geopolitical influence. While bearing all the morbid symptoms by which Antonio Gramsci once famously characterised such periods of interregnum, this juncture creates openings to view what is typically obscured in times of unchallenged hegemony.

In this chapter, I attempt to grasp two elements of this opening. The first concerns an expanded geography of the Sahelo-Sahara and the Mediterranean, and the second, a reconnected history of these two regions. The former means working against a tendency, rife within EU policy documents and beyond, to reproduce a colonial geography that treats the Mediterranean and the Sahelo-Sahara as distinct and discretely bounded entities.[3] It does so by contextualising Ali Bakar's and Soro's experiences of violence within these two zones, tracing experiential and spatial connections between them, and showing each to be framed by European military and security interventions. The second element reconnects some of the histories that Ida Danewid (2017) has argued to be disconnected by white liberal interventions in the Mediterranean.[4] This work of reconnection here involves relaying the precolonial co-constitution of these two regions, and the gradual shift toward asymmetry generated by the emergence of a new world-systemic centre in the Atlantic at the turn of the fifteenth century.

The era of European hegemony which followed transformed the Mediterranean into a centre–periphery boundary of this new world system (Amin, 1988), while the Sahelo-Sahara region was degenerated into its extreme periphery (Idrissa, 2021).

In light of this expanded geography and reconnected history, contemporary border violence in the Mediterranean and political violence in the Sahel each appear to be not only 'a late consequence of Europe's violent encounter with the Global South' (Danewid, 2017: 1679); they are also a symptom of the breakdown in Europe's exclusive dominance over the Global South. In other words, they are the brutal manifestation of a distinction drawn by Achille Mbembe (2021) between 'primitive Eurocentrism' and 'late Eurocentrism': 'where primitive Eurocentrism sought to establish European conquest and domination of the world, the late Eurocentrism of the twenty-first century seeks to justify the battening down of Europe on itself, its withdrawal from the world'.

Of course, in situating contemporary dynamics in the Sahel and Mediterranean within a longue durée characterised by European conquest and dominance, there is a risk of overstating 'foreign interveners' allegedly 'exceptional' power to shape political dynamics at will' (Raineri, 2021: 17). This risk is all the more pronounced at a juncture arguably defined by a decline in influence of such historic hegemons. But for this very reason, it is necessary to dissect the historic genesis of this flailing power projection, for it is within such moments that cracks and continuities become more apparent. From this vantage point, the contemporary juncture appears not as an outright continuation of this trajectory of European supremacy, but rather a manifestation of its secular decline.

Before proceeding, a word on terminology is in order, and in particular on how 'violence' is understood. While I primarily discuss violence of a direct and physical nature here, I do not deny the realities of structural and epistemic violence (Galtung, 1969; Bourdieu and Wacquant, 2004), nor that border regimes in general contribute to these indirect forms of violence (cf. Davies, Isakjee and Obradovic-Wochnik, 2022). Less still do I want to imply that the following discussion is somehow removed from these multi-layered structures of violence. For academic representation itself entails violence. This is arguably all the more the case when life experience is not only represented academically, but reproduced in multiple academic fora. On this point, elsewhere I discuss different elements of Ali Bakar's and Soro's life experience in Rosso (Ould Moctar, 2022). For this reason, a sense of doubt underpins the following discussion, as it involves not just the violence of academic representation, but also risks that of reproduction. But there may be a productive aspect to this dilemma: doubt 'allows the chapter authors to contribute to this collection without flattening our positionalities and fixing the regions we speak from' (see Introduction to this volume). It is in this spirit that I hope to mobilise my own doubt about harnessing the violence of academic repetition to this chapter. Whether or not it succeeds is for readers to judge.

An expanded geography of violence

Of the many recent moments of spatial connection between the Mediterranean and the Sahelo-Sahara, the 2011 uprisings in North Africa stand out for their strikingly centrifugal effects. As many critical migration scholars have observed (Tazzioli, 2014; Hess and Kasparek, 2017), the 2011 uprising in Tunisia involved a social movement in both senses of the phrase: a revolutionary movement aimed at upending the rule of Zine El Abidine Ben Ali, and a physical northward movement of people toward Europe. The latter was no less revolutionary than the former, but its end result was less decisive. Indeed, while the challenge to the EU border regime in the Mediterranean continued to mount post-2011, culminating in the mass arrivals during the 'summer of migration' of 2015, the years since have seen a move toward a broader and deeper externalisation of migration management responsibilities outside the EU (Gabrielli, 2016). This can be seen in the 2015 launch of the EU Emergency Trust Fund (EUTF) for Africa, and in deepening cooperation between Frontex (the European Border and Coast Guard) and the Libyan Coast Guard from 2017 (Stierl, 2019). This shift toward externalisation was further consolidated over the course of the COVID-19 pandemic, consigning untold numbers to death, containment and abandonment in the Mediterranean (Stierl and Dadusc, 2021).

The aftermath of the 2011 uprisings also rippled southward, laying a foundation for the Sahelian counterinsurgency campaign in which Ali Bakar's and Soro's lives are equally caught up. As revolutionary fervour spread from Tunisia to Libya, dynamics took a violent turn, in the form of armed resistance from below and a NATO-led military intervention from above. Together, these resulted in the toppling of authoritarian pillar of stability Muamar Al-Qadhafi in October 2011. Three months later, galvanised by an influx of weapons and combatants, a long-term Tuareg insurgency in northern Mali relaunched its independence struggle. Having been primarily orchestrated through a tactical and at times uneasy alliance between the secular Mouvement national de libération de l'Azawad (MNLA movement) and local jihadist outfit Ansar Ad-Din, the insurgency shifted in the ideological direction of the latter as it expanded southward to take the regions of Gao, Kidal and Timbuktu (Thurston, 2020: 127).[5] All of this compounded a simmering sense of disillusionment within the Malian armed forces, which found expression in a military coup in March 2012. Just under a year later, with the jihadist insurgency advancing south and political disarray reigning in the capital of Bamako, Mali's beleaguered interim head of government called on France under Francois Hollande to intervene.

What began as Operation Serval in January 2013 was a geographically and tactically restricted intervention aimed at stemming the southward jihadist advance, an objective that was achieved in a matter of months. This was, however, but the forerunner to a much more ambitious counterinsurgency campaign. Rebranded in 2014 as Operation Barkhane, the operational aim evolved from stemming and dispersing a southward advance to the much more elusive goal of quashing jihadist activity across the Sahel. As such, it became more firmly anchored within the ideological hubris and self-perpetuating mechanisms of the US Global War on Terror (cf. Keen, 2006). Increasing its troop deployment to 4,000, Barkhane spread its operational wings outward from its initial Malian locations of Timbuktu, Gao and Bamako to Njammena (Chad), Ougadougou (Burkina Faso) and Niamey (Niger), with a view to extending counter-terrorist operations across this Sahelo-Saharan space.

The counterinsurgency effort acquired further international dimensions in 2013 with the deployment of the UN stabilisation mission in Mali (MINUSMA), and with the 2014 launch of the G5 Sahel, a regional security cooperation framework consisting of Mali, Mauritania, Chad, Niger and Burkina Faso. Intended to endow Sahelian states with greater ownership over the regional securitisation drive, the G5 Sahel has nonetheless continued to reflect EU security interests and priorities (Venturi, 2017; Lopez-Lucia, 2020). These interests were given direct expression in 2020, when the EU deployed a military mission to Mali dubbed the Takuba Taskforce. Under French command, it accompanied Malian armed forces in counterinsurgency operations until it was discontinued in June 2022, along with the winding down of Operation Barkhane, for reasons that will be detailed shortly.

Collectively, these diverse interventions amount to what Bruno Charbonneau (2021) has termed a regime of counterinsurgency governance in the Sahel. While the roots of this regime of counterinsurgency governance are many, they include the southward ripple effects of the 2011 uprisings, which also spurred the movements across the Mediterranean that permanently reconfigured EU external border policy from 2015 onward.

If there is indeed an expanded geography connecting the Mediterranean and the Sahelo-Sahara regions, one of its core features is thus a fusion between the wars on migration and on violent extremism. Given its flexible and informal nature, the EUTF has been key to this structural crossover. Indeed, the inclusion of stabilisation within the EUTF's mandate expands its sphere of concern to include projects concerning territorial integrity and the control of illicit flows in general (Raineri and Strazzari, 2019: 550). One such project is the Rapid Action Groups – Surveillance and Intervention in the Sahel (GAR-SI), which are flexible and mobile security units trained for the purpose of addressing cross-border security issues such as trafficking and terrorism (Delegation de l'union europeenne en Mauritanie, 2016). Another example is an EUTF-financed support programme for the G5 Sahel, operated by the French technical cooperation operator Civipol[6] and staffed by European security experts based in the G5 Sahel permanent secretariat in Nouakchott.[7] Speaking of a database being piloted within G5 Sahel member states, a member of this support programme gave succinct expression to the structural overlap embodied in the EUTF: the idea is 'a database that details everything: immigration, human trafficking, drug trafficking, weapons trafficking, terrorism. Everything'.[8] At origin an emergency initiative to tackle the perceived root causes of 'irregular migration' to Europe, the EU Trust Fund and, by extension, the EU border regime have thus merged with the regime of counterinsurgency governance in the Sahel.

As Ali Bakar's and Soro's experiences suggest, however, this merger has generated little improvement in the security situation across the region, not least in Soro's home region of Mopti. After becoming the locus of the international counterinsurgency campaign in 2015, Mopti saw a sharp spike in jihadist activity and intercommunal violence (Cold-Ravnkilde and Ba, 2022: 18). This is in part because French counterinsurgency doctrine relies upon a reductive and blinkered understanding of what drives recruitment to jihadist groups, which are, as Nathaniel Powell (2022) has argued, best understood as rural insurgencies against state forces who often bear the largest share of responsibility for civilian deaths. To this ignorance must be added a strong dose of arrogance, as was made clear in French President Emmanuel Macron's summoning of Sahelian heads of state to a summit in Pau in January 2020. Disconcerted by a marked increase in visible anti-French sentiment across the region, he urged them to demonstrate their commitment to the goals of the counterinsurgency campaign (Yvan, 2020: 901). They duly obeyed, and Sahelian security forces subsequently embarked upon a spate of extrajudicial killings, leading to another spike in civilian fatalities in the region in 2020, further inflaming the grievances that drive recruitment to jihadist groups (Nsaibia, 2020). Extremist violence in the Sahel is, in other words, coproduced by the regime of counterinsurgency governance that is formally aimed at stemming it.

Meanwhile, in the years since the 2015 'summer of migration' and the subsequent deepening of the externalisation drive, the trajectory of the border regime in the Mediterranean has taken an equally macabre turn. As successful arrivals dropped from over 1 million in 2015 to just under 400,000 one year later (UNHCR, 2022), the death toll climbed in the opposite direction, from 4,055 drowned in the Mediterranean in 2015 to 5,136 in 2016 (IOM, 2022). Even when these numbers came back down in 2017 and 2018, however, the proportion of deaths out of total arrivals continued to mount (Kouvelakis, 2018: 19), from one death for every 42 arrivals in the first six months of 2017 to one death for every eighteen arrivals in the first six months of 2018 (Guardian, 2018). In recent years, the Atlantic Route to the Canary Islands has come to epitomise this tendency, with the Alarm Phone Network (2021) estimating the death rate on this route to be have been as high as one for every twelve arrivals on the Canary Islands in 2021. Moreover, as deaths at sea have dropped in absolute numbers, the volume of torture, enslavement and deaths in EU-supported Libyan detention centres has risen commensurately (cf. Heyden, 2022).

The fusion between the wars on migration and on terrorism within this expanded geography is thus characterised by a vicious feedback loop between military and security interventions, on the one hand, and the suffering and death of the displaced and dispossessed on the other.[9] Having experienced first-hand the interceptions, detentions and abandonment that pepper the EU's Mediterranean border, as well as the extremist violence that is coproduced by the regime of counterinsurgency governance in the Sahel, Ali Bakar and Soro are together testament to this expanded geography of violence. The preceding contextualisation of their life experiences will have hopefully provided grounds for viewing each of these regions in terms of a differentiated but contiguous geographic whole, marked by non-linear trajectories of violence and suffering that are reproduced by militarised interventions nominally aimed at alleviating them.

While the EU's multilateral oversight is crucial to this expanded geography of violence, there are important delegations of responsibility at bilateral level. Spain, for its part, has acted as pioneer of externalised migration governance on the West Mediterranean and Atlantic Routes, which served as an early laboratory for many of the strategies of externalisation implemented post-2015 (Carrera, 2007; Casas-Cortes, Cobarrubias and Pickles, 2014). France, in contrast, has spearheaded the counterinsurgency operation intended to neutralise jihadist activity in the Sahel, and as such has presided over the upsurge in civilian displacement and fatalities detailed above. Framing these maritime and terrestrial operations is the EU, whose backing takes both indirect and direct form: the former through funding and capacity building, and the latter through Frontex, in the case of migration control efforts, and the Takuba Taskforce, in the case of the counterinsurgency campaign in Mali.

Incidentally, this spatial division of labour between Spain and France mirrors a colonial-era agreement that carved up the northwest African coastline. According to this 1902 agreement, Spain obtained access to the marine resources off the Sahara's Atlantic coast, while France would gain control of the Saharan interior and the iron ore minerals that had been discovered by French researchers in 1935 (Antil, 2004). Forged in the era of formal colonialism, this spatial dispersal of labour lingers on today, in the form of a Spanish war against migration at sea and a French one against violent extremism inland. As financial and technical benefactor to each of these endeavours, the EU sits astride this colonially endowed spatial division of interests and responsibilities. There is, in other words, a long history to Europe's contemporary entanglement in the expanded geography of violence that has been detailed here. In the following section, I trace the historic origins of this European dominance of these two regions, to provide an explanatory frame for the unprecedented levels of violence presently engulfing them. From this longue-durée perspective, this death and violence is the expression of a breakdown in historically rooted European hegemony across this expanded geography.

Reconnected histories in the Mediterranean and the Sahelo-Sahara

In his monumental history of the Mediterranean in the late sixteenth century, Fernand Braudel (1992) described the Sahara as the 'second face of the Mediterranean', an observation that has since acquired something of a seminal status. As he and many other scholars have since shown (Horden, 2012; Scheele and McDougall, 2012; Kea, 2014), the histories of each of these regions indeed engulf and enfold one another, in a manner not unlike the ritual advance and retreat of waves and dunes that are so fundamental to the basic ecological rhythm of each zone. This macro-regional co-constitution is observable within diffuse geographic imaginaries of the Sahara and the Mediterranean, such as those of medieval Arab geographers for whom a neat conceptual symmetry could be discerned between the two zones. This was observable in the nature of the spatial expanse to be navigated – sea on the one hand, desert on the other; the means of transport by which this was achieved – ships at sea, camels on land; or the docking and rest points that served them – wells and oases on the one hand, port cities and islands, on the other (Horden, 2012: 30).

While necessarily reductive, these conceptual parallels have the advantage of retrieving the Sahara from the peripheral frontier zone status to which diffuse elements of European thought have long relegated it (McDougall, 2007a; Scheele and McDougall, 2012). Indeed, the Sahara has throughout much of modern history been a central conduit within the world economy (Austen, 2010). Having roughly spanned the fifth century BCE to the nineteenth century, the trans-Saharan caravan trade forged relations of trade and exchange not just laterally from the Nile Valley to the Sahelian oasis towns of Oulata and Timbuktu but also upward through the Sahara to North Africa's Mediterranean port cities. For this reason, economic exchange in the Mediterranean and beyond it appears irrevocably shaped by desert centres far removed from the coasts of North Africa, be this in the export of Saharan agricultural surpluses to Mediterranean emporia, or in the form of gold originating in the Gao Kingdom, in modern-day Mali, to be minted as coinage in Carthage and Alexandria (Kea, 2014: 429). This Saharan conditioning of the Mediterranean holds for its people well as its goods. Indeed, for Braudel, the movements of nomadic pastoralists from arid Saharan plains to Mediterranean coastal cities such as Oran during the dry season was one of the organic regional rhythms that earned the Sahara its status as second face of the Mediterranean (Braudel, 1992: 129).

These trans-Saharan processes that were so constitutive of the Mediterranean were also expressions of structures and relations that are *intra*-Saharan in character, with economic exploitation, labour relations and social structures each having an intensely local character (McDougall, 2012b). Indeed, by the nineteenth century, the vast geographic area spanning from Southern Morocco to Timbuktu and Niger had become an integrated and contiguous trading bloc in which goods and people circulated (McDougall, 2012a). This precolonial history of intra-Saharan social formation is, furthermore, deeply dynamic. While colonial ethnographers tended to assume stasis to be the rule underlying social identity, rank and structures, the reality was more fluid, with social formations being repeatedly transformed and upended by emigration, marriage alliances and revolutionary struggle (Curtin, 1971; Cleaveland, 2002). In other words, the Sahara and its peoples have historically not only conditioned social processes and structures on the Mediterranean; they have also been autonomously and dynamically generative of their own internal economic, ecological and social relations.

With the gradual rise of European supremacy from the late fifteenth century, the long-distance co-constitution between the Mediterranean and the Sahara would remain unbroken, but its dynamics shifted in a decidedly more asymmetric direction. A comprehensive overview of this shift is of course beyond the scope of this chapter. But in broad and therefore reductive terms, the emergence of the Atlantic as a new centre of exchange within a nascent world capitalist system undergirded this newfound asymmetry (Amin and Girvan, 1973). Given the socially destructive nature of the primary export commodity that was channelled through this new world-systemic centre, this shift represented a gradual but qualitative break with the nature of exchange that prevailed between the Mediterranean and the Sahara in previous epochs. For many of the Sahara's inhabitants, this took the form of a loss of autonomy over the management of local ecological resources and political structures relative to preceding eras (McDougall, 2012b: 87). Of course, intra- and trans-Saharan trade persisted, as did Saharan autonomy in the face of a new European economic and military presence on the coasts of West Africa (McDougall, 2007b). But in net terms, the gradual diminishment of trans-Saharan commerce and exchange in favour of coastal exports shifted the balance of the world system decisively towards an era of unprecedented European dominance.

The dawn of this epoch was of course materially characterised by mass enslavement and exploitation, but it acquired an important symbolic dimension which cloaked this violent material base. As Samir Amin (1988) has shown, the exploitative and violent foundations of the world capitalist system came to be masked and justified by an intellectual project that fabricated a European civilisation which was purported to have emerged seamlessly from Greek and Roman Antiquity. The Mediterranean is vital to the erasures and omissions entailed in this intellectual project:

> The new European culture reconstructs itself around a myth that creates an opposition between an alleged European geographical continuity and the world to the south of the Mediterranean, which forms the new centre/periphery boundary. The whole of Eurocentrism lies in this mythic construct. (Amin, 1988: 11)

Having been a centre of gravity for trade and exchange in its own right, the Mediterranean would thus henceforth act as a new centre–periphery boundary following a reorientation of the embryonic world capitalist system toward the Atlantic.

While now forming the economic boundary between the centre and periphery of this world system, the Mediterranean also acts as the ideological screen onto which this system projects its own imagined past. In other words, the Eurocentric intellectual project took what was a novel spatial split between the worlds north and south of the Mediterranean, and falsely projected it backwards into history (Amin, 1988: 93). This backward projection has since been taken up and disseminated by a slew of actors with diverse and even contradictory stakes in the modern capitalist system:

> from the works of apologists for the French colonial conquest to the speeches of Mussolini to the textbooks still in use throughout Europe, this North-South cleavage is presented as permanent, self-evident and inscribed in geography (and therefore – by implicit false deduction – in history). (Amin, 1988: 93)

If a sharp delineation runs through Amin's work between the material and the ideational – between base and superstructure – the Mediterranean border is the site in which the two coalesce. It is at the same time the mediating zone between the economic core and the periphery and the source of the myth that justifies the very existence of this spatial bifurcation.

Beyond this novel spatial boundary lies the West African Sahel, whose colonial peripheralisation equally holds material and symbolic dimensions. While the under-development of the region long preceded the nineteenth century (cf. Rodney, 1972), it reached its zenith at this time with the inland colonisation of West Africa (Amin, 1995). This was expressed in the Sahelian interior's new politico-economic status as a strategic but economically lean wedge between the settler colonies of North Africa and the coastal export hubs of West Africa. As with the newfound centre–periphery boundary role of the Mediterranean, this material role had its Eurocentric ideological counterpart. 'In the world that the West created', Rahmane Idrissa (2021: 10) observes in a discussion of the historic roots of the Sahel's contemporary crisis, 'the Sahel is an extreme periphery, one whose very name is meant to reify it into a remote, stultifying land where only dire things happen' (cf. Bonnecase and Brachet, 2013). While the shift to formal political independence did little to alter the material and symbolic peripheralisation of the Sahelo-Saharan interior, the actors charged with managing and mitigating its social consequences traded a colonial garb for an international developmental one (Mann, 2015; Idrissa, 2021: 18).

This is why, while the region today remains a hub of trade and exchange, these flows are often governed at an international level as illicit objects of security intervention. Accordingly, they become the target of the EU-funded projects detailed in the previous section, which are aimed at documenting these flows so that they may be safely contained within the Sahelian periphery (cf. Duffield, 2010). This is the implied logic underpinning such EUTF-funded initiatives as the West Africa Police Information System and the G5 Sahel Security Cooperation Platform (cf. Gorman and Chauzal, 2018; Frowd, 2021; Stambøl, 2021). In imposing gradated categories of risk and danger upon the Sahel, information platforms of this kind aid in cordoning off vast portions of the region, thereby reproducing the spatial segregation associated with Sahelian peripherality (Andersson, 2019).

For people like Ali Bakar and Soro who inhabit these risk categories, the consequence of subverting them by attempting to cross the Mediterranean can all too often be violence and death. But in the history being recounted here, these macabre outcomes force a question upon us: what does it mean when a site of such symbolic importance to the myth of European civilisational superiority as the Mediterranean is today the deadliest border-zone in the world? In light of Amin's critique of the Eurocentric intellectual project, a triple convergence can be discerned at the EU's southern border, namely between the world system's historic birth, its Eurocentric narrative of civilisational superiority and the unprecedented degree of death and suffering that has materialised in this zone today. Far from its original role as the moral source of European world-systemic dominance, the Mediterranean centre–periphery boundary is today a site where this Eurocentric narrative has been utterly detached from its material reality.

If the civilisational conceits of the world system's Eurocentric superstructure are thus coming apart in the Mediterranean, events in the Sahelian periphery offer some tentative insight into the form this growing rupture may take. In recent years, a wave of social mobilisations, military coups and unprecedented shifts in geopolitical alliances have swept the West African Sahel. While social mobilisations in West Africa have long been driven by liberalism's failed promises to the region (Sylla, 2014), this most recent bout of revolt and unrest has for the first time been accompanied by a concrete decline in Western hegemony (cf. Niang, 2022). In August 2020, after months of popular protests, Malian President Ibrahim Keita was ousted in a military coup. Shortly afterward, it was announced that Operation Barkhane would be gradually wound down, with the EU's Takuba Taskforce soon following suit (Euractiv, 2022). Nine months later, in May 2021, yet another coup in Mali quashed hopes that these were just blips in the otherwise smooth proceedings of the regime of counterinsurgency governance. Such delusions were definitively shattered with Mali's withdrawal from the G5 Sahel a year later. Meanwhile, a coup in Burkina Faso in January 2022 was preceded by months of popular protest against the French counterinsurgency and the inability of domestic forces to quell insecurity. Much like in Mali, this was followed by another military coup just eight months later.

In each of these contexts, anti-French and pro-Russian sentiments have proliferated, with protests against symbols of French authority being accompanied by official moves to minimise France's military, diplomatic and media presence in the region. At the same time, ever more explicit overtures are being made to Russia, which in the region's imaginary fulfils a collective desire for a degree of yet-to-be realised autonomy from the former coloniser (see Manatouma, this volume, for how this plays out in Chad). Whether any of this translates to a move out of peripherality, or a mere shift in its form and orientation, these developments nonetheless amount to substantial shift in the colonially endowed world-systemic order of things.

Conclusion

Across the Sahelo-Sahara and Mediterranean, the long-term arc of European hegemony is waning. The expanded geography of violence that was detailed in the first part of this chapter is one important expression of this decline, but the preceding discussion shows that it gives rise to social revolt and shifts in geopolitical alliances. I conclude with two important qualifiers to this claim.

The first is that a decline in European hegemony across the Mediterranean and the Sahel does not signify European withdrawal from these regions. On the contrary, it could well mean an intensified and more cynically militarised approach to the region.[10] Glimmers of such an approach can be seen in the moves to deploy Frontex risk analysis cells and liaison officers in Senegal and Mauritania (Statewatch, 2022), and in a proposed EU military expansion in the Sahel, framed largely in terms of countering Russian influence in the region (Rettman, 2022). Second, and relatedly, this world-systemic shift carries no intrinsically progressive character. Indeed, notwithstanding the rearrangement in security partners, the Malian state has upheld the tradition of massacring civilians in the name of counter-terror operations, with up to 300 civilians reportedly being killed by armed forces and their Russian partners in Moura, Mopti, at the end of March 2022 (UN News, 2022). Furthermore, for those like Soro and Ali Bakar who continue to flee these atrocities, there is little likelihood of EU external border policy in the Mediterranean autonomously changing tack in the near future.

This juncture does, however, carry opportunities, which may or may not be capitalised upon. When viewed along the timescale detailed in the second half of this chapter, these could result in intra and trans-Saharan trade and exchange taking a less pathologically criminalised and securitised form than at present. In this light, the era of late Eurocentrism may eventually prove James McDougall (2012b: 75) correct in his observation that 'the "closure" of the desert corridor in the early twentieth century might now look more like a brief parenthesis in a longer, continuous history than like a final and defining death knell'. Meanwhile, the conversion of the Mediterranean into a mass grave may appear in retrospect a bleak curtain call before an era of less lethal and illegalised circulation between both shores of the sea. Beyond such speculations, what is clear is that the 'understanding of the failure of the teleological narratives of "European" progress' (see Introduction to this volume), has manifested with potency in the Sahel. As a result, its expanded geography encompasses not just the Mediterranean but also the broader Souths and Easts across which this understanding is shared.

Notes

1. All names of individuals in this piece are pseudonyms. I discuss elements of Ali Bakar and Soro's experiences in Rosso elsewhere (Ould Moctar, 2022).
2. As detailed later, the French counterinsurgency initiative, Operation Barkhane, is operationally distinct from the EU training and capacity building missions in the Sahel (such as EUTM Mali, EUCAP Sahel and EUCAP Niger). But there have been areas of shared responsibility and direction, as in the EU military mission in Mali, the Takuba Taskforce, which was under French military command.

3 The EU Trust Fund for Africa, for instance, divides the African continent into three distinct zones of project implementation: the Sahel and Lake Chad region, the Horn of Africa and North Africa.
4 For more on Eurocentrism and disconnected histories, see Gurminder Bhambra, 2007.
5 This occurred through the incorporation of Al-Qaeda in the Islamic Maghreb and the Movement for Unity and Jihad in West Africa. Having long been embedded in smuggling and militant activities in northern Mali, these regional jihadist insurgencies increasingly side-lined the MNLA as the rebellion moved south.
6 For an analysis of the colonial logics of commodified mobility control and state-private partnerships sustained by Civipol, see Stambøl and Jegen, 2022.
7 Interview with G5 Sahel support programme staff, Nouakchott, May 2018
8 Interview with G5 Sahel support programme staff, Nouakchott, May 2018.
9 For further theorisation of feedback loops generated by such war systems, see Keen and Andersson, 2018.
10 I am grateful to Nandita Sharma for the suggestion that these developments reflect intensification as much as decline.

References

Alarm Phone (2021) 'Shocking number of deaths, but also growing struggles on the ground: Western Mediterranean Regional Analysis'. https://alarmphone.org/en/2021/01/29/shocking-number-of-deaths-but-also-growing-struggles-on-the-ground/#atlantic (accessed 9 July 2021).
Amin, S. (1988) *Eurocentrism*. New York: Monthly Review Press.
Amin, S. (1995) 'Migrations in contemporary Africa: a retrospective view', in Baker, J. and Akin Aina, T. (eds) *The Migration Experience in Africa*. Uppsala: Nordiska Afrikainstitutet, pp. 29–40.
Amin, S. and Girvan, C. (1973) 'Underdevelopment and dependence in Black Africa: their historical origins and contemporary forms', *Social and Economic Studies*, 22(1), 177–96.
Andersson, R. (2019) *No Go World: How Fear Is Redrawing Our Maps and Infecting our Politics*. Berkeley, CA: University of California Press.
Antil, A. (2004) 'Découpage colonial et création des frontières: le cas des frontières sahariennes et maliennes de la Mauritanie', in Salem, Z. A. (ed.) *Les Trajectoires d'un État-Frontier: espace, évolution politique et transformations sociales en Mauritanie*. Dakar: Conseil pour le développement de la recherche en sciences sociales en Afrique, pp. 46–65.
Austen, R. (2010) *Trans-Saharan Africa in World History*. Oxford: Oxford University Press.
Bhambra, G. (2007) *Rethinking Modernity: Postcolonialism and the Sociological Imagination*. New York: Palgrave Macmillan.
Bonnecase, V. and Brachet, J. (2013) 'Les "crises sahéliennes" entre perceptions locales et gestions internationales', *Politique africaine*, 130(2), 5. doi: 10.3917/polaf.130.0005.
Bourdieu, P. and Wacquant, L. (2004) 'Symbolic violence', in Scheper-Hughes, N. and Bourgois, P. (eds) *Violence in War and Peace: An Anthology*. Oxford: Blackwell, pp. 272–74.

Braudel, F. (1992) *The Mediterranean and the Mediterranean World in the Age of Philip II*. 2nd edn. London: HarperCollins.

Carrera, S. (2007) 'The EU border management strategy: FRONTEX and the challenges of irregular immigration in the Canary Islands', *Centre for European Policy Studies*, (261). doi: www.ceps.eu.

Casas-Cortes, M., Cobarrubias, S. and Pickles, J. (2014) '"Good neighbours make good fences": seahorse operations, border externalization and extra-territoriality', *European Urban and Regional Studies*, 23(3), 231–51.

Charbonneau, B. (2021) 'Counter-insurgency governance in the Sahel', *International Affairs*, 97(6), 1805–23. doi: 10.1093/ia/iiab182.

Cleaveland, T. (2002) *Becoming Walata: A History of Saharan Social Formation and Transformation*. Portsmouth: Heinemann.

Cold-Ravnkilde, S. M. and Ba, B. (2022) 'Unpacking "new climate wars": actors and drivers of conflict in the Sahel', *Danish Institute for International Studies*, 4.

Curtin, P. D. (1971) 'Jihad in West Africa: early phases and inter-relations in Mauritania and Senegal', *Journal of African History*, 12(1), 11–24. doi: 10.1017/S0021853700000049.

Danewid, I. (2017) 'White innocence in the Black Mediterranean: hospitality and the erasure of history', *Third World Quarterly*, 38(7), 1674–89. doi: 10.1080/01436597.2017.1331123.

Davies, T., Isakjee, A. and Obradovic-Wochnik, J. (2022) 'Epistemic borderwork: violent pushbacks, refugees, and the politics of knowledge at the EU border', *Annals of the American Association of Geographers*, 0(0), 1–20. doi: 10.1080/24694452.2022.2077167.

Delegation de l'union europeenne en Mauritanie (2016) 'Groupe d'Action Rapide de Surveillance et d'Interventions au Sahel (GAR-SI Sahel) – Fonds Fiduciaire d'Urgence de l'UE en faveur de l'Afrique (FFUE)', p. 2.

Duffield, M. (2010) 'The liberal way of development and the development-security impasse: exploring the global life-chance divide', *Security Dialogue*, 41(1), 53–76. doi: 10.1177/0967010609357042.

Euractiv (2022) 'EU's Takuba anti-terror force quits junta-controlled Mali'. www.euractiv.com/section/global-europe/news/eus-takuba-anti-terror-force-quits-junta-controlled-mali/ (accessed 19 January 2023).

Fanon, F. (2004) *The Wretched of the Earth*. New York: Grove Press.

Frowd, P. M. (2021) 'Borderwork creep in West Africa's Sahel', *Geopolitics*, 00(00), 1–21. doi: 10.1080/14650045.2021.1901082.

Gabrielli, L. (2016) 'Multilevel inter-regional governance of mobility between Africa and Europe: towards a deeper and broader externalisation', *Grup de Recerca Interdisciplinari en Immigració*, (30). www.sipri.org/commentary/topical-backgrounder/2018/establishing-regional-security-architecture-sahel (accessed 5 July 2018).

Galtung, J. (1969) 'Violence, peace and peace research', *Journal of Peace Research*, 6(3), 167–91.

Guardian (2018) 'Sharp rise in proportion of migrants dying in Mediterranean, says UN'. www.theguardian.com/world/2018/sep/03/sharp-rise-in-proportion-of-migrants-dying-in-mediterranean-says-un (accessed 28 February 2024).

Gorman, Z. and Chauzal, G. (2018) 'Establishing a regional security architecture in the Sahel', *Stockholm International Peace Research Institute*.

Hansen, P. and Jonsson, S. (2014) *Eurafrica: The Untold History of European Integration and Colonialism*. London: Bloomsbury Publishing.

Hess, S. and Kasparek, B. (2017) 'De- and restabilising Schengen: the European border regime after the summer of migration', *Cuadernos Europeos de Deusto*, (56), 47–77. doi: 10.18543/ced-56-2017pp47-77.
Heyden, S. (2022) *My Fourth Time, We Drowned*. London: Harper Collins.
Horden, P. (2012) 'Situations both alike? Connectivity, the Mediterranean, the Sahara', in McDougall, J. and Scheele, J. (eds) *Saharan Frontiers*. Bloomington: Indiana University Press, pp. 25–38.
Idrissa, R. (2021) 'The Sahel: a cognitive mapping', *New Left Review*, 132, 5–39.
IOM (2022) *Missing Migrants Project*. https://missingmigrants.iom.int/region/mediterranean (accessed 17 May 2022).
Kea, R. A. (2014) 'The Mediterranean and Africa', in Horden, P. and Kinoshita, S. (eds) *A Companion to Mediterranean History*. Hoboken: Wiley Blackwell, pp. 425–40. doi: 10.1002/9781118519356.ch27.
Keen, D. (2006) *Endless War? Hidden Functions of the War on Terror*. London: Pluto Press.
Keen, D. and Andersson, R. (2018) 'Double games: success, failure and the relocation of risk in fighting terror, drugs and migration', *Political Geography*, 67(April), 100–10. doi: 10.1016/j.polgeo.2018.09.008.
Kouvelakis, S. (2018) 'Borderland: Greece and the EU's Southern question', *New Left Review*, 5–33.
Lal, V. (2005) 'The concentration camp and development: the pasts and future of genocide', *Patterns of Prejudice*, 39(2), 220–43. doi: 10.1080/00313220500106451.
Lopez-Lucia, E. (2020) 'A tale of regional transformation: from political community to security regions the politics of security and regionalism in West Africa', *Political Geography*, 82(July), 102256. doi: 10.1016/j.polgeo.2020.102256.
Mann, G. (2015) *From Empires to NGO's in the West African Sahel: The Road to Nongovernmentality*. Cambridge: Cambridge University Press.
Mbembe, A. (2021) 'Notes on late Eurocentrism', *Critical Inquiry*. https://critinq.wordpress.com/2021/07/01/notes-on-late-eurocentrism/ (accessed 28 May 2022).
McDougall, E. A. (2007a) 'Constructing emptiness: Islam, violence and terror in the historical making of the Sahara', *Journal of Contemporary African Studies*, 25(1), 17–30. doi: 10.1080/02589000601157022.
McDougall, E. A. (2007b) 'The caravel and the caravan: reconsidering received wisdom in the sixteenth-century Sahara', in Mancall, P. (ed.) *The Atlantic World and Virgina: 1550–1624*. Chapel Hill: University of North Carolina Press, pp. 143–69.
McDougall, E. A. (2012a) 'On being Saharan', *Saharan Frontiers: Space and Mobility in Northwest Africa*, (March), 39–57.
McDougall, J. (2012b) 'Frontiers and borderlands in Saharan/world history', in Scheele, J. and McDougall, J. (eds) *Saharan Frontiers: Space and Mobility in Northwest Africa*. Bloomington: Indiana University Press, pp. 73–92.
Niang, A. (2022) 'Coups, insurgency and imperialism in Africa: review of African political economy' (blog). https://roape.net/2022/03/08/coups-insurgency-and-imperialism-in-africa/ (accessed 17 May 2022).
Nsaibia, H. (2020) 'State atrocities in the Sahel: the impetus for counterinsurgency results if fueling government attacks on civilians', *Armed Conflict Location & Event Data Project*. https://acleddata.com/2020/05/20/state-atrocities-in-the-sahel-the-impetus-for-counter-insurgency-results-is-fueling-government-attacks-on-civilians/ (accessed 9 May 2022).

Ould Moctar, H. (2022) 'The constitutive outside: EU border externalisation, regional histories, and social dynamics in the Senegal River Valley', *Geoforum*, (September). doi: 10.1016/j.geoforum.2022.09.009.
Powell, N. (2022) 'Why France failed in Mali, war on the rocks'. https://warontherocks.com/2022/02/why-france-failed-in-mali/ (accessed 23 May 2022).
Raineri, L. (2021) 'The bioeconomy of Sahel borders: informal practices of revenue and data extraction', *Geopolitics*, 00(00), 1–22. doi: 10.1080/14650045.2020.1868439.
Raineri, L. and Strazzari, F. (2019) '(B)ordering hybrid security? EU Stabilisation practices in the Sahara-Sahel region', *Ethnopolitics*, 18(5), 544–59. doi: 10.1080/17449057.2019.1640509.
Rettman, A. (2022) 'New EU military missions in West Africa to counter Russia', EU Observer. https://euobserver.com/world/155068 (accessed 19 November 2022).
Rodney, W. (1972) *How Europe Underdeveloped Africa*. Cape Town: Pambazuka Press.
Scheele, J. and McDougall, J. (2012) 'Introduction: time and space in the Sahara', in McDougall, J. and Scheele, J. (eds) *Saharan Frontiers*. Bloomington: Indiana University Press, pp. 1–24.
Stambøl, E. M. (2021) 'Borders as penal transplants: control of territory, mobility and illegality in West Africa', *Theoretical Criminology*, 25(3), 474–92. doi: 10.1177/1362480621995457.
Stambøl, E. M. and Jegen, L. (2022) 'Colonial continuities and the commodification of mobility policing', in Lemberg-Pedersen, M. et al. (eds) *Postcoloniality and Forced Migration*. Bristol University Press, pp. 76–92. doi: 10.2307/j.ctv2tjdgxr.10.
Statewatch (2022) 'Plan for Frontex to deploy "vessels, surveillance equipment, and carry out operational tasks" in Senegal and Mauritania'. www.statewatch.org/news/2022/july/eu-tracking-the-pact-plan-for-frontex-to-deploy-vessels-surveillance-equipment-and-carry-out-operational-tasks-in-senegal-and-mauritania/ (accessed 19 November 2022).
Stierl, M. (2019) 'Migrants calling us in distress from the Mediterranean returned to Libya by deadly "refoulement" industry', *The Conversation*, pp. 1–5.
Stierl, M. and Dadusc, D. (2021) 'The "Covid excuse": EUropean border violence in the Mediterranean Sea', *Ethnic and Racial Studies*, 0(0), 1–22. doi: 10.1080/01419870.2021.1977367.
Sylla, N. S. (2014) *Liberalism and Its Discontents: Social Movements in West Africa*. Edited by N. S. Sylla. Dakar: Rosa Luxember Foundation, Dakar.
Tazzioli, M. (2014) *Spaces of Governmentality: Autonomous Migration and the Arab Uprisings*. London: Rowman & Littlefield Publishers.
Thurston, A. (2020) *Jihadists of North Africa and the Sahel*. Cambridge: Cambridge University Press.
UN News (2022) 'Mali: UN expert calls for independent probe into Moura massacre'. https://news.un.org/en/story/2022/04/1115702 (accessed 19 January 2023).
UNHCR (2022) 'Operational data portal: Mediterranean situation'. https://data2.unhcr.org/en/situations/mediterranean (accessed 28 February 2024).
Venturi, B. (2017) *The EU and the Sahel: A Laboratory of Experimentation for the Security–Migration–Development Nexus*. IAI Working Papers. Rome: Istituto Affari Internazionali.
Yvan, G. (2020) 'The bitter harvest of French interventionism in the Sahel', *International Affairs*, 96(4), 895–911. doi: 10.1093/ia/iiaa094.

3

A battleground for French and Russian imperialism: how Chad's (post-)socialist and (post-)colonial present is shaping its political future

Kelma Manatouma

Imperialism as a system of domination by one state over the population of another territory is an ancient method of subjugation. While the words used – imperialism, colonialism and neocolonialism – have evolved in line with political and social changes in societies, the method remains founded on domination. Africa was a prized area of conquest (Coquery-Vidrovitch, 2016) and competition between the European great powers from the period of the slave trade through to colonisation, and these rivalries did not end with the independence of African states, which has accentuated the divisions between Western countries. 'Who owns Africa?' asks the title of a book edited by US researcher Bekeh Utietiang Ukelina (2022) which examines this conquest of the African continent. Today, both the European powers and 'emerging' economies are turning to Africa to establish diplomatic relations with a view to securing natural resources and making geostrategic gains. During the period of anti-colonial struggle, Russia was one of a number of states that established contacts with African leaders, in the name of socialist ideologies and in order to combat Western domination (Mark and Betts, 2022). This African–Soviet relationship, founded on the idea of liberating dominated peoples, was strengthened after independence by cultural and economic cooperation between the countries of the Soviet Union and the new African states (Blum et al., 2021). While these diplomatic relations cooled following the collapse of the Soviet Union in 1989, since the early 2010s, Russia's presence in Africa has become a key concern in African and international current affairs.

Chad, with its location in central Africa and total area of 1,284,000 km², links the countries of the Mediterranean to the equatorial region (Figure 3.1), and is the object of intense competition between its former

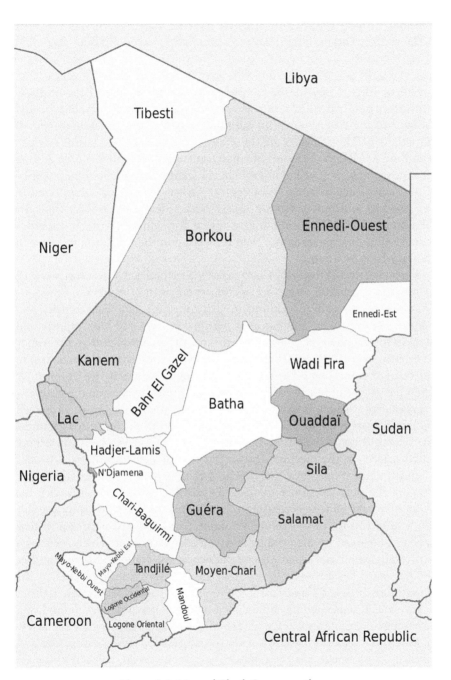

Figure 3.1 Map of Chad. Source: author

colonial power, France and Russia. During the protests on 14 May 2021 against the military takeover, protesters waved Russian flags and appealed to Russia as an anti-colonial power to counter France. Chad is central to the political tensions that have developed since the death of its president Idriss Déby in 2021, in the wake of the failure of the political transition planned by the late president's son. This rivalry has turned Chad into a battleground for multiple interests and different forms of imperialism. The presence of the Wagner Group in the Central African Republic (CAR), to the south of Chad, is causing growing concern among European, and in particular French, diplomats about the expansion of Russia's presence in this part of central Africa. This rivalry is reflected in the rhetoric and military build-up on both sides of the border between Chad and the CAR. Competing forms of Russian and French imperialism are thus emerging via the Wagner Group in the CAR and the French military base in Chad.

France's colonial ties with Chad make it a pivotal actor in security terms, as it has had a military base in the country since 1939. Russia, meanwhile, is attempting to gain a foothold in Chad through political, security and community networks, and has thus become an object of both fantasy and anxiety for Chadian and international actors as an alternative to the legacy of French colonial power. The historical legacy of international socialism in the form of cultural and economic cooperation with the Soviet Union since 1966 has played a decisive role in enhancing Russia's image on the political, economic and academic fronts. In this chapter, I analyse the protests against the French presence in Chad and the pro-Russian movement. I examine the Franco-Russian rivalry via the rhetoric of the two countries concerning Chad, based on the protests against the rule of the Transitional Military Council, and explore how the effects of these competing imperialisms are shaping the political future of Chad in terms of its relationship with the Western world and its increasingly demanding youth. I begin by providing a brief history of the colonial conquest of Chad; an imperialism that was accompanied by the establishment of a military base which remains a powerful symbol of French neocolonialism in the country. I then consider the historical ties between Russia and Chad before finally turning to the oppositions between Chadian actors over French and Russian imperialism. France and Russia each have their own national actors who are mobilising to support their interests in Chad. The aim is to demonstrate how the imperialist rivalry between these two countries impacts on the dissemination and circulation of violence in the political, economic, social, cultural and even aesthetic spheres.

A brief history of France's colonial conquest of Chad

Chad's current borders were established by agreements between France, Germany and Great Britain in 1894, 1898 and 1899. After the Berlin Conference the territories of Chad were handed over to France in their entirety. Some historians (Bouquet, 1992) argue that the conquest of Chad was motivated by the desire to own Lake Chad, due to its strategic position at the centre of four different regions (Cameroon, Nigeria, Niger and Chad). After several exploratory missions, France continued to face resistance from the local peoples, most notably the slave trader and warlord Rabih. He had ruled over the Baguirmi and Bornu regions for many years, establishing the capital of his empire at Dikwa, reorganising his army and forging new alliances with other Arab countries in order to launch other operations. To establish sole control over these territories, France realised it would have to decisively destroy its main enemy's fighting capability. The French government thus sent in three columns – the Joalland-Meynier mission from Niger, the Foureau-Lamy mission from the Congo and the Gentil mission – which joined forces at the confluence of the Logone and Chari rivers. The French forces met Rabih as he was preparing an attack on the Wadai and were supported by hunters and soldiers from the Baguirmi empire, which had been repeatedly attacked by Rabih.

The battle took place on 22 April 1900 in Kousséri, a small town in the far north of Cameroon, and following Rabih's decisive defeat, on 5 September 1900 the president of the French Republic, Emile Loubet, signed a decree in Rambouillet creating a Military Territory of the Countries and Protectorates of Chad and annexing it to the territories of the French Congo and Dependencies. A French soldier, Major Lamy, was killed in the Battle of Kousséri, and following its victory France raised its flag and created an administrative post in a small Arab and Kotoko village at the confluence of the Logone and Chari rivers, calling it Fort Lamy in his memory. The French army's power was not yet fully secured by the post at Fort Lamy, since it continued to face resistance not only from the troops of Rabih, but also from the Sultan of Wadai and adherents of the Senussi religious order in the north. The Military Territory of Chad became a *circonscription* in 1902, with a civil administrator responsible for its political and financial management. Four years later, another decree on 11 February 1906 created the colony of Oubangi-Chari-Chad, under the authority of a lieutenant-governor based in Bangui. It should be noted that the territory of Chad was not fully under French occupation at this time, since most of the northern regions, in particular the Wadai empire, remained hostile to France until 1911.

When the Federation of French Equatorial Africa (AEF) was established in 1910, the territory of Chad became part of this entity. On 12 April 1916 the territory of Chad was separated from Oubangi-Chari and given colony status under a lieutenant-governor, with support from a governing board and a military administration. As Pierre Hugot describes it, until the 1960s, Chad remained a territory of 'majors' (Ngothé Gatta, 1985). The administration of the Borkou-Ennedi-Tibesti region remained in place until 1964, when the region was handed over to Chadian civil administrators, four years after the country's independence in 1960.

After a period of improvisation during the military conquest and the early years of occupation, on 5 October 1910 Governor General Merlin introduced a territorial division system for the AEF, with local administrators. In 1947 these territorial subdivisions were named districts and came under the direct administration of the Governor General in Brazzaville until the Defferre Reform Act of 1956. Alongside the colonial administration, there was a local administration, led by traditional chiefs by social group. This introduced the oral-based local administration to a paper-based culture for the first time. But this new practice ran into obstacles, first because of a lack of fluency in French, and second because of unfamiliarity with this administrative culture. These difficulties were resolved when the first Chadian senior administrators were trained up in the 1940s. In order to pacify the conquered territory, the colonial administration turned a number of large villages into military posts. Roads were laid to link the villages to other regions, and the administration then grouped these villages into cantons and *circonscriptions*.

The long history of the French military base

The French military base is north of Chad's capital city, N'Djamena, and was built in 1939 as an operational site for the air force before becoming permanent in 1986 during the Libyan occupation of the Aouzou Strip. It occupies a huge space next to Hassan Djamous International Airport, the military camp and the general headquarters of the Chadian army. It was the base for Operation Épervier during the Libya–Chad war, and then in 2014 became the headquarters for Operation Barkhane, France's military counter-terrorism campaign in the Sahel, with more than 4,000 soldiers stationed there. Although it was built outside N'Djamena, it has been gradually integrated into the city's urban fabric due to urbanisation of the surrounding neighbourhoods and provides employment for young people in the first arrondissement and other parts of the capital city. It has a well-known health facility that provides basic care in surgery and other areas of medicine. In addition to the N'Djamena site, the French army has small operational units in Abéché and in Faya. Senka Neuman Stanivuković (in this volume) shows how infrastructure constitutes an important component of violence. In *Brutalisme,* Achille Mbembé (2020) analyses how architecture is a tool of power in contemporary societies. In relation to infrastructure, European imperialism through French colonisation in Chad has manifested itself not only in political and economic terms but also in an architectural sense, via transformation of the inhabitants' living spaces. In Chadian society, space (physical, social, cultural …) constitutes a place of social, economic and cultural life, but with the presence of the colonial administration certain sacred places were turned into military camps or construction sites for the offices of colonial administrators. This constituted a form of violence against the country's people, who lost their places of worship.

Chad's political and security history has been partly shaped by the French military presence. Its political leaders, from François Tombalbaye to Idriss Déby, have all obtained the support of this base to varying degrees. In the early years of independence, it provided key support to the Chadian army to counter the rebellion by the Front for the National Liberation of Chad (FROLINAT), which emerged in the north of the country in 1966 (Balmond, 2019). While he was in power, Déby received support from the base to combat incursions by various rebel groups in 2006, 2008 and most recently in 2019. In 'Que fait l'armée française au Tchad?', French researcher Marielle Debos (2019) reveals the important role played by the French army in protecting Déby's regime by supplying intelligence. The perception of the French military base is also fuelled by wild ideas and rumours about the role of the French army in Chad. Since the early 2000s, it has been a focus for criticism of Déby's political governance and the military transition. In *France's Wars in Chad: Military Intervention and Decolonization in Africa*, Nathaniel K. Powell (2021), a historian at Lancaster University, analyses the wars in Chad from the early years of its independence through to the 1980s and the authoritarian rule of president Hissène Habré. In Powell's view, France, the former colonial power, was a witness to these wars and to the collapse of the Chadian state from the outset of independence. France's military interventions thus provide an insight into the interplay between the actors involved in the conflicts in Chad, on both the Chadian and French sides. But, as Powell asks in his book, why has Chad been the only state to experience multiple political and military crises? The post-colonial Chadian state remains weakened by war and the perpetuation of domination via a new form of cooperation between the French state and its former colonies. The Chadian state typically uses the resources of the French state to defend itself against its internal and external enemies (Powell, 2021). France's current position in Chad is partly the result of its colonial heritage and the dissemination of its power in the economic, political, academic, cultural and military spheres. In economic terms, France has considerable influence, since

Chad's currency exchanges are still dominated by the colonial currency, the CFA franc (Nubukpo, 2015), which was created to facilitate trade between the French colonial empire and its colonies, and over sixty years after independence remains a currency of exchange in West and Central Africa. African intellectuals and activists have criticised the colonial ties between the CFA franc and France, but this has had little impact on the policies of the countries that share this currency. The Chadian economy uses the CFA franc of the Central African Economic and Monetary Community, the institution responsible for monetary policy across the six Central African countries of Cameroon, Congo, Equatorial Guinea, CAR and Chad. In addition to this, the Chadian economy is dominated by major French corporations, including Total in fuel distribution, Canal Plus in television broadcasting, Vinci in public works and sugar refining, and numerous others across various sectors of the economy. As a result of its geographical position and the continuing ties between Chadian political leaders and their French counterparts, Chad is viewed as one of the last bastions of French power in Africa. President Emmanuel Macron's visit to attend Déby's funeral goes some way to demonstrating the importance of Chad in French security policy in Africa. With anti-French sentiment spreading in former French colonies such as the CAR, Mali, Burkina Faso and Senegal, Chad remains a bulwark against Russian expansion in Africa by way of 'FrançAfrique' (Borrel, Boukari-Yabara, Collombat and Deltombe, 2021) defined as a system of domination based on an asymmetrical strategic alliance between the French and African elites.

Russia: from the socialist legacy to a new interest in Chad

Chad, along with a number of other African countries (Arkhangelskaya, 2013), established contacts with the states of the Soviet Union in the name of the socialist alliances that prevailed at the time. These went back to 1946, when the Rassemblement Démocratique Africain (RDA), a party with ties to the French Communist Party, was founded in Bamako by Gabriel Lisette, a Chadian deputy of West Indian origin. After independence in 1960, the Chadian government signed an initial series of cooperation agreements with the Soviet Union: a cultural and scientific cooperation agreement in 1966, a trade agreement in 1967 and an air traffic agreement in 1974. The cultural cooperation agreement notably enabled Chad to send an annual batch of students to Russian universities for training in a number of fields. This cultural and scientific cooperation was strengthened in 1998, and in 2000 the two countries signed a further agreement on mutual recognition and equivalence of mutual recognition of qualifications. Through this cultural cooperation programme, the Russian Federation awards university scholarships to over a hundred Chadian students every year. These scholarships are a tool of political domination, since after their return home these students are known to be culturally and politically sympathetic to Russia. France also awards scholarships via its cooperation scheme, providing funding for several Chadian students and civil servants to study at French universities every year. This is a very important channel of soft power for these countries. In 2007, the Chadian foreign minister made a trip to Russia to renew contacts in various areas of cooperation, and Mikhail Margelov, Russia's international affairs minister, visited N'Djamena for the same purpose. Chad and Russia continued to maintain a strong relationship until the visit made by foreign minister Chérif Mahamat Zene, following a period of turmoil in the wake of Déby's death.

Although long-standing, the Russian presence in Chad is not as visible as that of its former colonial power. Russia's resurgence reflects a broader trend of economic and military cooperation, notably in the conquest of Africa (Kalika, 2019). In terms of military cooperation, it is important to note that Chad's long period of war has been primarily waged with Russian-made military equipment. The Russian ambassador to Chad, Vladimir Sokolenko, recently told journalists from the Russian press agency that 80 per cent of Chad's military equipment originated in Russia (Sputnik, 2023), a statistic that contradicts the popular image among activists and politicians of Chad being under the thumb of France. Russia's lead in defence contracts is due to the relative ease of buying military equipment on the Russian market compared to in France. Chad's minister delegate to the presidency in charge of national defence visited Russia to attend the MAKS-2015 international aerospace exhibition, and during this trip held talks with his Russian counterpart on military cooperation between the two countries. Sokolenko also reported that:

> Moscow and N'Djamena are considering setting up an intergovernmental commission on economic cooperation in order to boost trade. Russian companies could be involved in the extraction of mineral resources such as gold, diamonds, uranium, rare metals and oil. Russian pharmaceuticals, antiviral vaccines and medical equipment are also in demand. Russia is also training specialists [...]. Several hundred Chadian students are studying at Russian institutions. As a third of Chad's law enforcement officers are female, Russia has offered a special training course for female peacekeepers. (Sputnik, 2023)

Chad–Russia relations are developing in the context of international tensions between Russia and the West over the Ukraine crisis and the incursion of the Wagner Group into areas usually regarded as France's preserve.

For several years, Russia has enjoyed good relations with Chad's neighbours: Libya, where it supported Colonel Gaddafi; Sudan, which has a Russian military base on its territory; Cameroon, with which it has signed a defence agreement; Nigeria, which received an official visit from President Dmitry Medvedev in 2009; and now the CAR, where the Wagner Group of Russian mercenaries is supporting the government in its fight against the rebels. Chad is currently becoming a focus of competition between Russia and France. Such competition is evident not only at the national level, but also within international institutions, notably the United Nations General Assembly where Chad voted in favour of the resolution condemning Russia's intervention in Ukraine. In the view of observers of Chadian politics, Chad's vote against Russia was steered by France's support of the transitional government. The security of Chad is also dependent on that of its neighbours, especially to the south of the country, where the Wagner Group is very active in the CAR. During his official visit to Russia, Chad's foreign minister reaffirmed his desire to maintain close ties with Russia. Meanwhile, a media war is raging between France and Russia. During Macron's visit to N'Djamena to attend Déby's funeral, he declared that 'France will never let anyone threaten Chad's stability and integrity'.[1] This was a veiled reference to Russia, on the basis of unverified reports that rebels' assassination of the Chadian president was supported by Russian military resources via the Wagner Group in Libya. At present, there is no evidence that the Front for Change and Concord (FACT), the rebel group that killed President Déby, received such support from Russia or the Wagner Group. The Libya-based Chadian rebels have an indirect connection to Russia through the Wagner Group mercenaries, who have supported Field Marshal Haftar, the leader of a rebel faction fighting against the transitional government in Tripoli (Teurtrie, 2021), and reportedly obtained military resources through this connection, in order to enable them to fight alongside Haftar's forces against the authorities in Tripoli. But amid the international upheaval resulting from the war in Ukraine and Russia's increasingly offensive diplomacy, France, which considers Chad to remain its bailiwick, sees Russia's offensive via the Wagner Group as a serious threat.

It is important to note, however, that the Franco-Russian competition in Chad represents a new neocolonial logic. While France sees Chad as its preserve, and Russia is led by a nationalist discourse, both are looking for ways to spread their influence. To achieve this, these countries need actors in Chad who support their actions, as the following analysis of the alliances forged between Chadian actors shows.

Franco-Russian rivalry and alliances between the Chadian actors

The competition between France and Russia is also being played out through military operations. The debate about the presence of France's military base is increasingly raised in public by certain political and community activist leaders. While criticism of the base remains contained to the country's major cities – N'Djamena, Abéché and Faya – it is a strong feature of certain opposition political parties. The monopoly of social media platforms and the political instrumentalisation of these means of communication have resulted in young people and civil society seeing the base as a tool for the neocolonisation of Chad. The army, meanwhile, highlights its strategic importance in the fight against insecurity in the Sahel. The potential withdrawal of the military base has been discussed as part of the political dialogue during the transition, but this is unlikely to be a priority for Chad's political elites, since the base has been seen as a way for France to support the Déby regime previously, and now the Transitional Military Council. Opinions are divided between those who see the military base as a tool of neocolonial support for autocratic regimes and those who believe that it is necessary for intelligence purposes. The presence of French soldiers in Ati, in the centre of the country, has thus led to civil society organisations condemning the idea of a new military base being established there (Doukoundjé and Daoudou, 2022). Despite the denial of any such plans by the French embassy in Chad, on 14 May 2021 a demonstration was held by the Wakit Tama group, with a very clear message: to protest against French government interference in Chad's domestic affairs. The Wakit Tama coalition, whose name means 'the time has come' in local Chadian Arabic, is an alliance of opposition political parties and civil society groups and was set up to oppose Déby's candidacy in the 2021 presidential elections. It has been critical of the French authorities' position on the political transition in Chad, and its protest condemned France's unconditional support for the Transitional Military Council. This demonstration was unprecedented in Chad's political history, with densely packed crowds, consisting mainly of young people, chanting 'France bara' and 'France dégage' ('France out') in the streets of N'Djamena. The protest reflected a regional trend across various African countries, such as the CAR, Mali, Niger and Senegal, that is driven by numerous factors, including those beyond the national sphere. The protest condemned the French government's automatic support for the autocratic rule of the various regimes that have taken power in Chad but was also linked to the issue of the military base, with demonstrators holding up signs attacking the French army as a tool of support for the Transitional Military Council.

While Russia does not have a military presence on Chadian territory, it is present in the north of the CAR through the Wagner Group, all along Chad's southern border, and this presence is generating fear within the Chadian government and French diplomatic circles. On the night of 30 to 31 May 2021, several Chadian soldiers were executed following an assault by the CAR army on a border outpost with Wagner support, and Chad's government accused Russia of being behind the attack. In April 2023, a rebel group newly established in the Logone Oriental region carried out an attack in the Mbaibokoum prefecture, in which several people were killed. The group had previously issued a statement asking for Russia's help to lead a rebellion against the Chadian government, which it accused of being supported by France. Following this attack, the Chadian and French armies led a mission in southern Chad to help the population affected and to patrol the area in order to combat the rebels, who were believed to have support from the Wagner Group.

The tensions between France and Russia are reminiscent of the Cold War, and the conflict between Chad and Libya over the Aouzou Strip, a territory in the north of the country that was occupied by Muammar Gaddafi's government in the 1980s. In the resulting war Libya was supported by the Soviet Union and Chad by the West, France and the USA. We are now seeing competition between France and Russia as they seek new political, geostrategic and economic alliances. The colonial ties between Chad and France give the latter a major linguistic, cultural, political and economic advantage, unlike Russia, which draws on a nationalist and anti-colonialist repertoire. Russia does, however, have the support of a large share of Chad's young people, as demonstrated by the anti-French protests held in a number of African countries, including Chad. These protests have been organised by civil society organisations, some of whose members previously studied in Russia. These former Chadian students in Russia have set up a group called the Association of Former Chadian Students in the Former Soviet Union and the Russian Federation (AETUSFR). The group has around a hundred members, many of whom hold political and administrative posts in Chad, including the former foreign minister Chérif Mahamat Zene, presidential adviser Ali Abdel-Rahmane Haggar, the former minister Dr Hawa Outman Djame and many other leading figures in the political, economic and security spheres. While they do not all necessarily share the idea that France should exit Chad, this does provide a sense of the Russian network in the country. Significantly, the name of the group also appears on the Russian embassy website.

Franco-Russian rivalry in Chad is reflected not only in the commercial ties resulting from the sale of Russian military equipment but also in the cultural sympathies of former Chadian students who studied at Russian universities. France has a significant network of influence, thanks to its colonial ties with Chad. In addition to the military and economic influence discussed above, there is an extensive network of Chadian students who have studied in France. These alumni remain very close to France, which sometimes makes it easier for them to make connections in the economic, political, military, cultural and academic spheres. One stated that: 'I'm demonstrating because France wants to reimpose the Déby system on us' (2021 interview).

The Transformers political party refused to call on its activists to join the demonstration on 14 May, despite being a member of the Wakit Tama coalition. Party leader Succès Masra argued that Chad's political problems should be resolved by its own people, and that calling for a French exit from Chad was unacceptable. His position was criticised by some members of Wakit Tama, who saw him as a protégé of the French government. Members of the Association of Arabic-Speaking Intellectuals, who joined Wakit Tama during the demonstration, were also present. They took to the streets with banners and placards displaying slogans such as 'no to France', 'no to the French army' and 'France out'. Hissein Massar Hissein, a lecturer and researcher at the University of Roi Fayçal and a former minister and presidential adviser to Déby, also took part in the protest, sparking an intense debate in the national press (Tchadinfos, 2022).

The criticism of the French army in Chad is a consequence of France's support for dictatorial regimes and a lack of political opportunities, which have led certain political actors and a large proportion of young people to see France as one of the main causes of their problems. As one protester proclaimed: 'The Chadian people came out to demand the exit of the French army from Chad. Colonisation is over. Free Chad, France out. Long live the Chadian revolt' (Ousmane, 2022).

Despair among young people, due to a lack of jobs and economic and political opportunities, is being exploited by certain activists and foreign powers to deter the efforts of France and its allies to combat insecurity in the Sahel. Social media is flooded with propaganda against French military policy, as is the web radio station Réseau des citoyens, set up by a member of the Chadian diaspora in Canada, which is frequently highly critical of the French army's presence in Chad. During the protest on 14 May 2022, young people held up pro-Russian signs and banners. The lack of a political transition, and France's political directives, are fuelling this resentment, in the name of defending national sovereignty. Some political leaders and groups close to the government have called for support for the French army, such as the Coalition of Civil Society Organisations (CASAC), which held a demonstration on 6 March 2022 in support of France's presence in Chad. This coalition, which is close to the government, is led by the youth and sport minister, Mahmoud Ali Seid. According to a number of verbal sources, the vast majority of the demonstrators were young members of the Patriotic Salvation Movement (MPS), the party founded by former president Déby, and had been paid to take part. The head of CASAC was also the Director of Administrative and Financial Affairs to the Presidency of the Republic for several years. The former transitional prime minister, Albert Pahimi Padacké, sees the French army as an important source of intelligence, and this view is shared by certain officers in the Chadian army.

Chad is set to remain a battleground between France and Russia on the basis of political, geostrategic and economic interests, since both powers covet its extensive territory linking the Maghreb to Central Africa. As a colonial power, France is increasingly losing ground to new actors who are adopting very different strategies to conquer Chad. The clashes between European countries over the conquest of Chad are producing new forms of domination that also involve certain national actors. This Franco-Russian rivalry impacts on the violence experienced by the Chadian people in the context of European neocolonialism in Africa. The political, economic, social, cultural, aesthetic and architectural forms of this violence shape how Chadian society works as a whole.

Note

1 www.lemonde.fr/afrique/article/2021/04/23/l-apres-deby-au-tchad-un-test-pour-macron_6077768_3212.html (accessed 23 April 2021).

References

Arkhangelskaya, A. (2013) 'Le retour de Moscou en Afrique subsaharienne, entre héritage socialiste, le multilatéralisme et activisme politique', *Afrique contemporaine*, 4(248), 61–74.

Balmond, L. (2019) 'L'intervention de la France au Tchad en février', *Questions de Paix et Sécurité Européenne et Internationales*, 13, 245–55.

Blum, F., Kiriakou, H., Mourre, M., Basto, M., Guidi, P., Pauthier, C., Rillon, O. Roy, A. and Vezzadini, E. (eds) (2021) *Socialismes en Afrique*. Paris: Editions de la MSH.

Borrel, T., Boukari-Yabara, A., Collombat, B. and Deltombe, T. (eds) (2021) *L'empire qui ne veut pas mourir. Une histoire de la FrançAfrique*. Paris: Seuil.

Bouquet, C. (1992) *Tchad: Genèse d'un conflit*. Paris: L'Harmattan.

Coquery-Vidrovitch, C. (2016) *Histoire des villes d'Afrique noire: Des origines à la colonisation*. Paris: Albin Michel.

Debos, M. (2019) 'Que fait l'armée française au Tchad?' *Liberation*, 8 February 2019.

Doukoundjé, J. and Daoudou, O. B. (2022) 'Ati: la présence de l'armée française crée la polémique', *Ialtchad Presse*, 12 May 2022.

Kalika, A. (2019) 'Le grand retour de la Russie en Afrique', *Note de l'IFRI* no. 114.
Mark, J. and Betts, P. (eds) (2022) *Socialism Goes Global: The Soviet Union and Eastern Europe in the Age of Decolonization*. Oxford: Oxford University Press.
Mbembé, A. (2020) *Brutalisme*. Paris: La Découverte.
Ngothé Gatta, G. (1985) *Tchad. Guerre civile et désagrégation de l'État*. Paris: Présence Africaine.
Nubukpo, K. (2015) 'Le franc CFA, un frein à l'émergence des économies africaines?', *L'Économie politique*, 4(68), 71–9.
Ousmane, D. (2022) 'Manif de Wakit tamma: "France barra", scandent les manifestants', *Tchadinfos*, 14 May 2022.
Powell, N. K. (2021) *France's Wars in Chad: Military Intervention and Decolonization in Africa*. Cambridge: Cambridge University Press.
Sputnik (2023) 'Russie-Tchad: l'amitié, malgré un contexte difficile', *Sputnik Afrique*, 11 February 2023.
Tchadinfos (2022) 'Dr Hissein Massar Hissein, ex-conseiller du PCMT, est arrêté', *Tchadinfos*, 14 May 2022.
Teurtrie, D. (2021) *Russie: Le retour de la puissance*. Paris: Armand Colin.
Ukelina, B. U. (2022) *Who Owns Africa? Necolonialism, Investment, and the New Scramble*. Leuven: Leuven University Press.

4

The making of 'the bread basket of Europe': from the Dutch East India Company to the East Company in Ukraine and grain in the Soviet Union

Daria Krivonos and Kolar Aparna

The Russian Federation should allow grain and food to leave Odesa unharmed to feed a hungry world. (Thomas-Greenfield, 2022)

Lebensraum did not only mean the Ukraine and Poland to them. The Nazi dream also included the hills and valleys and plains at the foot of that snow-capped mountain in Africa. (Gurnah, 2021: 275)

Half of the population will be able to find work in industry. But the other half will have to find *Lebensraum* in the east. I myself have only one desire, that the first Netherlands settlement in the Ukraine be named New Emmen'. (van Emmen, 1943, quoted in Joesten, 1943: 338)

Recently, the countries of origin of migrant agricultural labour supply have shifted further east, e.g., to Balkan countries, Ukraine, and Southeast Asia. (Netherlands Labour Authority or NLA, 2019: 5, quoted in Siegmann et al., 2022: 25)

Troubling Ukrainian whiteness and competing victimhood narratives

It is raining outside, and we all huddle up in the warm room of a space for collective action in Helsinki. It is the ten-year anniversary of a collective initiative to run a space in the city for grassroots anti-capitalist actions, including no-border solidarity action and supporting asylum application processes. Different groups make short speeches. One of them is a poem read out by one of the no-border activists. Her first words are: 'If Afghanistan was Ukraine'. Every line of the poem begins with this line 'If Afghanistan was Ukraine', underlining that Ukrainian refugees are treated better than refugees from Afghanistan. It is making our Ukrainian friends extremely uncomfortable; those of us from countries outside the EU, people of colour, Russians, other East European migrants are uncomfortable too. What was this poem meant to do? It felt that it was meant to script the person reading it as the one shedding light on our unequal positions vis-à-vis the border regime. It felt that guilt was demanded from Ukrainians present there. It felt that anger was demanded from others present who were not from Ukraine. But what it did to us was sever the ties, friendships and relational conversations where anger and guilt could cohabit with the many other emotions forged among racialised groups gathering to navigate and contest border regimes. Just a few months before this event one of the authors of this chapter, Kolar Aparna, spoke to a friend in Nijmegen, the Netherlands, where she used to live and work. He was shocked by the number of mobilisations made for Ukrainians that we were unable to garner in the last seven years of work as a community of activists and volunteers supporting people awaiting their asylum decisions. There was an open bitterness to the situation. He seemed disillusioned with his own work.

We find this moment productive to trouble Ukrainian 'whiteness', while staying with the material violence and differential value given to Ukrainian refugees temporarily in the West vis-à-vis other life-seekers. How can we break these divisive vocabularies of solidarity in the selective and temporary attribution of whiteness to some subjects from Ukraine? The momentary selective embrace of Ukrainians as white hides the historical conditions of expropriation of land and labour of 'others of Europe' including Ukraine (Robinson, 1983; Da Silva, 2022). Across Souths and Easts (Aparna, Krivonos and Pascucci, Introduction, this volume), this is a moment to revisit the present power asymmetries in refugee solidarity and agricultural migrant labour in EU states.

In this chapter, we employ the methodological lens of reading across empires, empirically linking Ukrainian land and farming labour with overseas colonial projects and intra-European imperial rivalries (see also Parvulescu and Boatcă, 2022). We follow the projects of the Soviet, German and Dutch empires, relating the latter's loss of colonies in Indonesia and East Africa with the shift of gaze towards conquering Ukraine to meet food insecurities around grain. We make a plea for situating the present uneven geometries around famine, refugee migration and agricultural migrant labour feeding EU economies relationally rather than along nationalistic, imperial divisions and competing victimhoods of racialised groups. Our own migrant trajectories – from India to the Netherlands to Finland, and from across the Russian/Finnish borderlands with family histories in Ukraine – shape these inquiries to situate the present moment of displacement and selective embrace of Ukrainians in longer relational histories of expropriation of land and labour.

We start by situating the current moment, in which Ukrainian land and labour are a lifeline for global food security and Russia's invasion of Ukraine increases the threat of famine in low-income countries, to explore inter-imperial rivalries over this land and then connect Ukraine to Europe's overseas colonies. Empirically centring the role of Ukrainian land and labour in feeding the world allows us to link seemingly disparate projects of primitive socialist and capitalist accumulation, as well as Europe's East and overseas colonies part of today's so-called 'Global South' in providing 'Europe' with land and labour.

Ukrainian land and labour feeding the world

Russia's full-scale invasion of Ukraine in 2022 and blockade of Ukraine's Black Sea ports prompted an urgent question of food security globally, and especially in low-income countries. Before the war, half of the world's sunflower oil came from Ukraine, as well as almost a fifth of the world's barley, a sixth of its maize and an eighth of its wheat (European Council, 2023a). With its fertile soil and access to the global markets via Black Sea ports, Ukraine was known as a breadbasket since at least the nineteenth century (Plokhy, 2016). A dramatic drop in its exports as a result of Russia's attack led to a sharp increase in food prices globally and serious concerns over food security for millions of people. Some 90 per cent of Ukraine's wheat exports went to Africa and Asia between 2016 and 2021 (European Council, 2023b). Among the countries heavily dependent on cereals from Ukraine are Indonesia, Philippines, Bangladesh, Tunisia, Morocco and Egypt (European Council, 2022). The UN Black Sea grain initiative between Turkey, the UN and Russia was launched in July 2022 to allow the circulation of grain from Ukraine's Black Sea ports via the Bosphorus. Over 60 per cent of the wheat transported via the initiative reached 'developing countries' (European Council, 2023b), although the deal between Kyiv and Moscow remains precarious. As we finalised this chapter in summer 2023, Russia pulled out of the deal. The situation is aggravated by the fact that in April 2023, the EU reached an agreement to ban the import of Ukrainian grain to Poland, Slovakia, Hungary, Romania and Bulgaria in the aftermath of local farmers' protests against lowering prices, although it allowed the transit of grain. As the war continues, Ukrainian fields continue to be a battlefield with Ukrainian farmers threatened, machinery, barns and soil destroyed. Attacks on Ukrainian food security and farming are now examined as Russia's tool in the war and an aspect of its geopolitical strategy (Hall, 2023).

Two years before the invasion, in spring 2020 as the COVID-19 pandemic began and borders closed to prevent the spread of the virus, food security also featured as a key concern in EU public policy. EU agricultural economies rely heavily on foreign-born labour, including seasonal labour from Ukraine, which could not reach their workplaces in Western Europe or return to their homes in Eastern Europe and non-EU countries (Bejan and Boatcă, 2021; Szelewa and Polakowski, 2022). During the pandemic, Ukrainian seasonal workers, similarly to other migrants from Eastern Europe, were exceptionally allowed to travel as they were seen by many EU governments as disposable yet indispensable labour with little to no social protection amidst the global health emergency (Krivonos, 2020; see also Bejan and Boatcă, 2021). Recent debates underline that in searching for more compliant workers, Western employers have shifted their gaze further East, from EU member states to non-EU states like Ukraine, Georgia and Kyrgyzstan (Bejan and Boatcă, 2021; UK Home Office, 2023). These workers are more disposable due to their citizenship status and are more willing to pay for their own travel costs. The COVID-19 pandemic offers a retrospective angle on the racialisation of Ukrainian nationals from cheapened labour to somewhat white 'deserving' refugees, vis-à-vis bodies produced as 'non-white non-European' asylum-seekers in 2022 (Babakova et al., 2022). Even such a short leap back allows us to question simplistic and ahistorical accounts regarding Ukrainian 'whiteness', which continues to be seen in binary opposition to non-white non-European life-seekers.

These two examples side by side show not only the role of both Ukrainian labour and land in sustaining food security globally, but also the links between Ukrainian land and conditionally included labour vis-à-vis Europe's non-white others, who are expelled from EU borders altogether (see Kramsch and Ould Moctar in this volume). In this chapter, we further historicise food anxieties that found fertile soil in Ukraine making the land subject of inter-imperial rivalries of the Soviet, German and Dutch empires. We ask how this land is imagined as available, where, when and why?

Namely, we examine how Ukraine suddenly became a substitute for Dutch lost colonies in Indonesia, and how the Soviet project used grain coming from Ukraine for industrialisation. Our aim here is not to give a comprehensive historical account of inter-imperial rivalries of German/Dutch and Soviet regimes. Instead, we ask what geographical imaginaries lead the material conditions of extraction, occupation, conquest and displacement of land and labour in Ukraine. How is the body of the farmer in Ukraine positioned vis-à-vis bodies of German 'model farmers' occupying the land and the 'new' socialist peasantry in the Soviet Union? How can we situate the present unequal geographies of agricultural labour migration from Europe's former colonies and Eastern Europe in these historical processes of extraction of land and labour as part of modernisation and industrialisation? To examine these links, we engage with and expand a theoretical discussion on inter-imperiality.

Inter-imperiality and violence across geotemporalities of modernisation

The inter-imperial framework considers how empires interact and how these interactions have shaped the material and ideological conditions of oppression (Doyle, 2014). The object of inter-imperial analysis is often a single locale, as well as persons and polities existing precariously among empires (Doyle, 2014; Shih, 2016; Parvulescu and Boatcă, 2022). This approach makes it possible to perceive a historical heterogeneity of colonial and imperial experience that does not always align with 'classic Anglo-American' postcolonial discourse. We examine the space between European, non-European and Soviet imperial formations to analyse the power asymmetries of violence that produce the peasants and soil of Ukraine in relation to Europe's colonies and the farmers in Western Europe as white. We do so to situate the present unevenness in 'asylumscapes' (Aparna and Schapendonk, 2020) and agricultural migrant 'labourscapes' in EU states in such geohistories of modernisation. Our approach is similar to that of Ukrainian feminist scholars Maria Mayerchyk and Olga Plakhotnik (2021). They take a critical perspective on two imperial regimes that subjugate Ukraine: Russia treating Ukraine as its mere province and EUrope positioning Ukraine as a not-fully-modernised periphery in need of Europeanisation. Writing during Russia's full-scale attack on Ukraine, we do not equate imperial powers, as currently violence operates as a kinetic force that manifests in Russia's bombings alongside a selective embrace of 'European values'.

In conversation with the inter-imperiality frame (Doyle, 2014), we aim to move away from compartmentalising imperial projects into separate entities and from seeing them in isolation. We trace how different forms of imperialism and colonial projects co-constitute each other and shift geographic terrains depending on socio-political needs while sometimes recycling the same old tropes justifying the expropriation of new land and labour. We thus see colonialism as 'a project of transnational networks of collaborations and oppositions' (Ureña Valerio, 2019: 119). Similarly to Manuela Boatcă and Anca Parvulescu (2022: 127) in their inter-imperial analysis of Transylvania, we 'weave the experience of former colonies, imperial peripheries, and racialised populations into the analysis of past and current processes'. We follow the shape-shifting inter-imperial forms of violence that manifest in specific modes and at specific moments in producing Ukraine relationally to 'Europe's others' (Lim, 2022) that nevertheless continue under conditions of what Nandita Sharma (2020) calls the postcolonial world order in present border control modes of the EU.

We thus work against a double move which separates (1) external colonies and intra-European racialisation and (2) capitalist and socialist projects of development and industrialisation. First, to bring seemingly disconnected geographies of Europe's overseas colonies and intra-European racialisation into conversation, we draw on a body of scholarship which argues against an analytical distinction of racialisation within Europe and colonial rule beyond Europe's shores (Zimmerer, 2005; Robinson, 1983; Césaire, 1950). Writers in the Black radical tradition remind us that intra-European racism preceded and became a 'foundation' for the production of racial difference in the overseas colonies:

> English merchant capital (to cite an important example) incorporated African labour in precisely these terms, that is, the same terms through which it had earlier absorbed Irish labour' and 'the colonisation of Ireland had played a significant role in the development of English colonisation of the New World. (Robinson, 1983: 67)

Rather than a theory of diffusion of racism from core to periphery, Robinson and Césaire invite us to think of such relationalities as intimately entangled and as a 'boomerang effect'.

Second, by bringing the socialist project of modernisation and Western colonialism into conversation, we follow the relationalities of violence underpinning both these projects (Tlostanova, 2010; Todorova, 2021). We take cues from Miglena Todorova (2021) to examine the shared features of otherwise distinct projects of Western capitalism and state socialism. We examine collectivisation – the USSR's policy of transferring the ownership of private farmland to the state – as part of the violence of socialist modernisation. Despite the different ideological foundations, both Western and Soviet imperial projects extracted labour and appropriated land through violence against the Ukrainian peasantry. Both projects relied on ideas of progress and modernisation, the violence of which intersected in the exploitation of Ukrainian land and peasant bodies, to which we turn in our empirical sections below.

We structure our analysis not in a linear chronology but rather by focusing on two analytical threads: (1) the centrality of Ukrainian peasantry, their labour and bodies in the Soviet and Western imperial modernisation projects, and (2) the shift in Western colonial imaginaries from the East Indies to Eastern Europe.

Centring the peasant body: the Great Famine, production of Dutch peasant whiteness and 'lazy farmer' narratives

'Socialist industrialisation' meant a Soviet-type industrial revolution, a programme intended to bring revolutionary increase in industrial production (Plokhy, 2016: 246). The plan was to transform a traditional agricultural society into a modern industrial power, where the proletariat has replaced peasantry as the dominant class. To finance industrial development and build socialism in a predominantly peasant society, the ground for industrialisation had to be found from within, through agriculture and the peasantry (Klid and Motyl, 2012; Andriewsky, 2015; Plokhy, 2016; Goldman, 2022a). A way towards industrialisation 'would have to be found to extract a "surplus" from the peasant, which could be sold for the foreign currency needed to import machinery—and used to fill the bellies of a growing working class' (Snyder, 2010: 13; see also Andriewsky, 2015; Plokhy, 2016). Some scholars use the concept of 'primitive socialist accumulation', first introduced by the Soviet theorist Evgeny Preobrazhensky, to examine these means to industrialise the underdeveloped economy through extracting surplus from the peasantry (Cucu, 2022; Goldman, 2022b; Lebowitz, 2023). Primitive socialist accumulation was initially conceptualised as an alternative to the violence of the capitalist variant; yet, in practice, the Stalinist variant imposed major sacrifices on peasants whose labour was the main source of capital for state appropriation (Goldman, 2022a).

Ukraine, the second most populous Soviet republic, was seen as both a source of funds for industrialisation given its agricultural output reaching international markets, and a major area for investment in the Soviet Union given its industrial potential (Plokhy, 2016). This is why the Ukrainian peasantry was crucial to Moscow's economic plans, which relied on unrealistic grain-procurement quotas. Collectivisation hit hardest the grain-producing areas of the Soviet Union, the most productive of which was Ukraine. Throughout Ukraine, peasants rose up in resistance and collective action against collectivisation defending their property, families, beliefs and culture – arguably, one of the greatest demonstrations of popular resistance in the early years of the Soviet Union, which was often led by peasant women (Viola, 1996). Faced with their resistance to collectivisation, the authorities declared that peasants were hiding grain and put even higher quotas on both the collectivised peasantry and those who refused to join the collective farms. The new policy brought famine, and by 1933 death by starvation became a mass phenomenon. Tens of thousands of city dwellers starved to death. Yet the vast majority of the dead and dying in Soviet Ukraine were peasants, the very people whose labours had brought what bread there was to the cities (Plokhy, 2016: 33).

Failure to deliver grain was regarded as sabotaging the food supply to cities and hence the whole project of industrialisation. Peasant migrants entered and left cities in search of jobs and housing, with the state introducing mandatory internal passports for all urban inhabitants to become eligible for jobs and housing. Peasants did not receive passports and thus could not move to cities – a policy that fixed the rural population in place (Goldman, 2022a). The industrial 'leap forward' meant that the population of Soviet Ukraine, according to some estimates, fell from 29 to 26.5 million between 1926 and 1937 (Plokhy, 2016: 255), although a precise figure is difficult to establish because of problems with Soviet census materials, especially the 1937 and 1939 data (Andriewsky, 2015).

> The question of numbers—whether three million, six million, or more—is irrelevant to and a distraction from the far more important issues […] namely, the existential reality of the Holodomor, the enormous suffering that its victims experienced, and the genocidal nature of Stalin's assault on Ukrainian peasants. (Klid and Motyl, 2012: 3)

The Great Ukrainian Famine (Holodomor, in Ukrainian) is now recognised by Ukraine and a number of governments around the world as a genocide against the Ukrainian people. While famine also affected the North Caucasus, Kazakhstan and the lower Volga region, scholars argue that only in Ukraine did famine result from clear ethnonational policy, termination of the Ukrainisation policy and attack on Ukrainian culture (Klid and Motyl, 2012; Plokhy, 2016: 254). Resistance to grain acquisition was equated with nationalism, and Soviet party cadres explained the repressions in Soviet Ukraine as a response to Ukrainian nationalism and the threat of counter-revolution in the border region (Klid and Motyl, 2012). Famine worked not only as an economic tool but also as a political disciplining mechanism. As a result of famine, Stalin got a 'new' socialist peasantry. Those who survived it had learned that they could live only by joining the collective farms, which were taxed at a lower rate and were the only farms to receive governmental relief (Plokhy, 2016: 254).

Years later, Ukrainian peasantry became subject to another imperial project, this time coming from Western capitalist powers shifting their gaze from the lost overseas colonies in Africa and Indonesia. Rich Ukrainian soil and peasant labour were again central to the project of modernisation, expansion and acquisition. Ukrainian peasants were racialised as less 'white' than Dutch farmers in the imperial project of eastward expansion. Dutch farmers who had neither land nor farm within the Dutch metropolitan/national borders were incorporated into this eastward expansion. The occupation of East Ukraine through the Dutch East Company when the Netherlands were under Nazi German occupation (1941–44) was understood as a solution to the perpetual lack of land within their national borders. This move was accomplished through designating Ukrainian peasants as lazy, backward, unworthy of the rich soil they lived upon and unable to use the land productively (Künzel, 2015a). Referring to the 'natives' in Ukraine that Dutch farmers were to encounter in this Eastern expansion, Dutch East Company (Nederlandsche Oost Compagnie or NOC) pamphlets circulating in the Dutch metropole portrayed people in the Ukrainian lands as 'colonial others': different, inferior, untrustworthy and lazy (Künzel, 2015a: 139–41). The entire occupied area was considered to be in dire need of 'capable Dutch hands' and cultivation by advanced German machinery. The area was described through qualifications such as 'backward', 'wild', 'primitive' and 'lagging decades behind Western civilisation' – a condition believed to be driven by '(Judeo-)Bolshevism' (Künzel, 2015a: 142). The need to maintain distance towards locals was repeated in all the pamphlets. The head of the Dutch East Institute (Nederlands Ost Instituut or NOI) wrote the following to describe Ukrainians: 'Lazy like the Scythes, hardened like the Huns, skilled with arms like the Goths, tanned like the Indians, cruel like the Samaritans, lions they are, just as smart as the Turks and incredibly mean as the Tartars' (Künzel, 2015a: 147).

It is here that we draw connections between overseas colonial projects with intra-European hierarchies and imperial rivalries that unfold in Ukraine. Indeed, imperial consciousness played a central role in looking at Dutch/German Eastern expansion as a continuation of racialised labour hierarchies in the colonies. As historian Serhii Plokhy (2016: 272) points out, 'Hitler treated Ukrainians as European colonisers treated blacks and Asians in overseas colonies, asserting, "No German soldier will ever die for that n* people"'. What made the Nazi project of Ostland (Eastern expansion and colonisation) recruit 'model farmers' from the Netherlands, but also Norway and Denmark, was part of actively producing whiteness in relation to Ukrainians produced as non-white.

The German/Dutch settler project in Ukraine was not completely separated from the Soviet system of controlling peasants, and drew on the system of kolkhozes. The collectivisation of farms in the kolkhoz system meant that the farmer could not access the produce which ended up as profitable both for the Soviet and German/Dutch projects. As a leading German expert wrote in 1943: 'From the viewpoint of acquisition, the kolkhoz system appeared as ideal' mainly because the 'peasant does not get his hands on the agricultural commodities that his work produces' and 'the state keeps in their hands how much they want to give away to the village population' (Schiller, 1943, quoted in Lyautey and Elie, 2019: 102).

As Ukrainian peasants were seen as unworthy of their fertile land, Dutch peasants' settlement in Ukraine became the ground for their own claims to whiteness as a class. Whiteness has been historically constructed not only in relation to negatively racialised others but also in relation to the system of production, where members of the white working class were designated as degenerate, backward, lazy and dirty until they became fit enough to become the 'model farmer'. Not all farmers qualified as fit enough for participation in the land reclamation projects even within metropolitan Dutch lands. For instance, farmers were selected based on the criteria of social geographer Nicolaas ter Veen's Social Darwinist ideas 'on the basis of professional, educational, psychological and moral criteria' (van de Grift, 2015: 149). To NOC, Dutch volunteers represented the 'Germanic people' in the East, superior in physique, culture and morals. German/Dutch and Ukrainian peasants thus took different positions in relation to conditions of production, the state and the capital. Subjugated Dutch workers and peasants solidarised with the Dutch/German colonial power and the project of Dutch nationalism rather than along the lines of labour with Ukrainian peasants (see also Robinson, 1983). Yet, Dutch peasants' claims to whiteness were not fulfilled in the context of settlement policies in Ukraine as the project of peasant emigration largely failed. Despite supposed racial kinship with Germanic people that allowed settlement on Ukrainian land in the first place, Dutch peasants who were part of this mission not only had to go through the strict selection criteria but also eventually found themselves as forced labourers. Upon arrival, the first handful of Dutch settlers were shocked by the immense poverty of the area, and found themselves accommodated in barracks with the local population, short of clothes and with poor hygiene (Künzel, 2015a). In addition, contrary to the expectation of Dutch settlers bringing long-awaited civilisation to Ukraine, locals resisted their settlement.

Finally, the Nazis exploited Ukraine as a source not only of agricultural products but also forced labour in Germany itself. ' "Germany calls you! Go to beautiful Germany!" ran one ad in Kyiv newspaper. One poster, titled "The Wall Has Come Down", portrayed Ukrainians looking through an opening in the wall isolating the Soviet Union from Europe' (Plokhy, 2016: 273). The reality was different with 2.2 million young Ukrainians ending up as slave labourers in factories, farms or households, marked out by wearing an OST badge (Plokhy, 2016: 273–74).

By bringing socialist and capitalist forms of accumulation needed for the maintenance of imperial projects under one framework of analysis, we can see how both the modernisation of the Soviet economy and the accumulation of capital in Western empires that lost overseas colonies relied on the violence, expulsion and starvation of Ukrainian peasantry. (In this volume, see also Manatouma on inter-imperial rivalries between Russia and France and military infrastructural violence in Chad; Hamzah on epistemic and structural violence in inter-imperial relations between Western colonial missions and the anti-colonial, socialist-supported Imamate rule in Yemen).

Empirically anchoring the Ukrainian peasant body in inter-imperial rivalries illuminates how, to both imperial projects, the labour of peasants created the surplus to fuel industrialisation, 'progress' and food security (Goldman, 2022a).

Europe's many Easts: Ukraine as a substitute for overseas colonies

High Representative of the European Union for Foreign Affairs and Security Policy Josep Borrell described Russia's invasion in the following way: 'With the invasion of Ukraine, we witness the return of war and tragedy on European soil' (Borrell, 2022). The anxieties, especially cartographic anxieties underpinning this statement and centring the meaning of 'European soil' need to be seen part of historical anxieties projected onto these lands. Whether Ukrainian soil is European or not has been subject of ruling relations across Soviet and European empires alongside geographical imaginaries claiming civilisational divides. Samuel Huntington's 'velvet curtain of culture' also ran through Ukraine, assigning former Galicia to the West and the backwardness to the East. Historically, 'Eastern Europe' has had a precarious relationship with the geographical imaginaries of Europe (Boatcă, 2021), while the Soviet Union saw Ukraine as located in strategic Western borderlands of the empire. This historically unstable and shifting position becomes visible in the way in which 'Eastern Europe' became the substitute for the impossibility of colonial expansion for Germany and the Netherlands at the end of the First and Second World Wars (Plokhy, 2016: 259; Künzel, 2015a). The shift in gaze from a Europe of overseas colonies to a continental empire is an important geohistorical moment for the production of Ukraine as available for the expropriation of its people and lands, similar to the exploitation of land and labour in overseas colonies, such as the East Indies. The land was to be found outside the empires' metropolitan borders.

As Plokhy (2016: 260) points in relation to German 'Lebensraum' (living space) in Eastern Europe, 'the goal was to wipe out existing population all the way to Volga River and settle fertile lands, particularly those of Ukraine, with German colonists'. Already in the mid-nineteenth century, Ukraine accounted for 75 per cent of all exports of the Russian empire (Plokhy, 2016). Ukrainian grain filled the gap in the imperial budget when Siberian furs dropped and before Siberian gas and oil would become the major imperial export via Odessa. Odessa was the empire's main gateway to the markets of Europe, with railroads linking grain-producing areas to Black Sea ports and further to the Mediterranean Sea and rich European markets (Plokhy, 2016: 178–79). This fertile land with access to international markets via Black Sea ports became a lucrative alternative to German and Dutch lost colonies in the East Indies and Africa. The land for settlement and natural resources would turn Germany into a continental empire, 'whose links with its colonies the British navy could not disrupt' (Plokhy, 2016: 260). The 'overpopulation' of the East and Ukrainian grain was seen as crucial to feeding the Third Reich. The occupation of Ukraine came to be framed around a 'geopolitics of starvation' (Lyautey and Erie, 2019), where feeding German and Dutch metropole areas would rely on Ukraine as the granary of Europe, which went hand in hand with the starvation and deportation of its people. While the term is used in the context of German/Dutch imperial expansion (Lyautey and Erie, 2019), arguably the 'geopolitics of starvation' can be also used in the context of the Great Famine in Soviet Ukraine, where the project of modernisation went hand in hand with the starvation of the peasantry.

Losing its colonies, especially the East Indies, created anxieties in the Netherlands about loss of food supplies within the Dutch metropolitan borders. Hence, a shift in the gaze from one East to another. But what did shifting the colonial gaze from the East Indies to Eastern Europe entail? This not only meant modelling similar institutions used for colonial expansion (Nazi Germany's Ostministerium or Ministry for the East was said to be modelled on the British India Office, Zimmerer, 2005: 206) but also recruiting former colonists as the preferred settlers in the East of Europe, with their pioneer qualities seen as useful in the conquest of territories (Zimmerer, 2005: 214). By 1943, NOC was in charge of several properties in the occupied Eastern territories and took care of the Dutch volunteers employed in the area (Künzel, 2015a). 'Western culture had made its entrance' mentioned one of the top officials visiting Ukraine to assess the occupation (van Maasdijk, 1942, quoted in Künzel, 2015a: 92). In fact, for some, the Dutch East Indies worked as a point of reference for the occupied Eastern territories: Ukraine appeared as uncivilised and uncultivated, a farthest corner of Europe where they would bring culture, civilisation and economic growth (Künzel, 2015a). Imperial splendour lost in its overseas trade to Japan in 1942 (Künzel, 2015b: 14) was mainly understood to be revived by using similar modes of expropriation of Ukraine. Dutch settlers, including peasants, were considered a good fit for the endeavour of expansion to the East because of their national colonial heritage. Nazi Germany also used the expertise of planters from the Dutch East Indies to cultivate tobacco in Ukraine's Zhytomyr area (Miller, 2020).

The 'Ukrainian project' also drew on the South African model of settler colonialism (Künzel, 2015a: 140). While Eastern Europe was to substitute for the markets of the Vereenigde Oostindische Compagnie (VOC, The United East India Company), it was to become a destination for emigrant farmers. The recruits of NOC were seen as settlers and pioneers, a model which is different from one that only relies on colonised local labour. The publicity campaigns recruiting Dutch farmers to move eastwards of this frontier articulated this mission part of the legacy of 'historical treks' of

Dutch farmers outside its metropolitan borders. They were seen as 'descendants' of those Dutch 'pioneers' to the East and South who 'held up the good name of our descent' (Künzel, 2015a: 140).

Dutch recruits imagined Ukrainian land as rich, fertile, vast, empty and 'virgin'. As Rost van Toningen, secretary general of the Dutch central bank and leader of the Dutch East Company, described the lands after his first trip, 'enormous partly still virgin land, from Belarus via Ukraine to the Sea of Azov' (Künzel 2015a: 90). While this Eastern frontier was projected as lands 'waiting' to be occupied in NOC propaganda, as Künzel (2015a: 141) underlines, Ukraine 'fired the imagination: the mystic black earth of Ukraine could produce larger, better, and more crops than anywhere else in Europe' (Künzel 2015a: 142).

Dutch newspapers such as *Het Volk* praised the pioneers for restoring Ukraine as the granary of Europe. At the same time, the production of lack came to frame the occupation of the Eastern Front: it was argued that while the Netherlands lacked surplus land for its farmers, Ukrainian peasants lacked knowledge and civilisation that the NOC would bring to them. Given that the mission did not fully succeed with the Germans pushed to withdraw, for the Dutch, ultimately, Ukraine 'lacked historic, cultural, and financial ties with the Netherlands and, as such, appeared a foreign territory. The Indies, by contrast, constituted an intrinsic, indelible part of the Dutch empire, an overseas extension of the European Netherlands even' (Foray, 2012: 107).

The hunger for new land to feed the metropole brought colonial imaginaries, administration and practices from Europe's overseas East to a continental East, using similar tropes to justify settlement, extraction and exploitation. The shift from the VOC to the NOC was a shift from a European Netherlands to the Third Reich's Ostland plan, at the heart of which was the Ukrainian project. In its precarious position as an exploited part of the German or Dutch empire, Ukraine occupied that liminal space of an imperial battlefield, as the NOC was quickly dissolved and the Ostland plan terminated. Geotemporalities of lack, anxieties, proximity/distance and backwardness to metropolitan Europe produced this East in relation to Europe's overseas Easts. These geographies thus do not exist in isolation but must be seen as intimate to imperial technologies and uneven cartographies of violence (Souths and Easts as method).

Russia's 2022 invasion, competing refugeehoods and Ukrainian agricultural labour (once again)

We started this chapter with a reflection on the present moment of unequal mobilisation of solidarity with differently racialised life-seekers. Seen from the linear temporalities of queues of visa regimes, Afghanistan is Ukraine's past, given that with a Ukrainian passport one can now enter EU states for 90 days visa free in any 180–day period, while Afghanistan still has one of the most difficult passports to travel with visa free. We make a plea for moving beyond the hierarchies and binaries the EU is now producing within regimes of asylum support. We invert the gaze to flexible imaginations of imperial expansions and border power asymmetries of nation states part of the EU. We urge for staying with the violence of unequal regimes of border control and inter-imperial projects that produces what Ana Ivasiuc (in this volume) calls '(sub)alter(n)ity' 'to suggest the simultaneity and processuality of constructions of alterity that amount to stratified subalternities in the differential imagined moral landscapes'.

While postcolonial theory has importantly showed the role of colonialism, racism and enslavement as a ground for accumulation (e.g. where did the cotton for English factories come from?, Bhambra, 2007), this theoretical work does not always account for the flexibility of colonial imagination and inter-imperial formations. By analysing more than a single colonial power concurrently, we show how Soviet modernisation was built from the starvation of peasants, alongside the Dutch/German eastward expansion relying on the expropriation of Eastern European land and people. The 'model farmers' moving eastwards and joining the Ostplan became white in this imperial move and reproduced the colonial gaze that designated Ukrainians as lazy, degenerate, uncivilised and dirty – just as those from the maritime colonies (Alatas, 1977).

At times, Europe's multiple Easts have been thus produced as interconnected geographies within inter-imperial formations. By turning to historical accounts, we can see how overseas colonial territories are tied to the imaginaries of Ukraine as 'virgin' land, and how both the Soviet and Western projects depended on the exploitation of agricultural land and labour. At the same time, national economies of formally decolonised states competed unequally with Soviet agricultural economies, as the developmentalism of anti-colonial Soviet industrialisation structurally peripheralised these states (Burton, Mark and Marung, 2022: 80–1). This peripheralisation underpins the present-day geopolitics of food security and dependence on Ukrainian grain.

Our intention here is not to lump together different experiences of racialised bodies, as we do recognise Ukrainian citizens' privilege of crossing EU borders and gaining access to international protection. EU state institutions' blatantly unequal and racist geopolitical mobilisations ease the barriers to some life-seekers, leaving others to die. Yet, we wish to highlight how this relative privilege can be conditional to inclusion as cheapened migrant labour. In the aftermath of Russia's 2022 invasion, information desks for Ukrainian refugees at Warsaw railway station had posters advertising work in the Dutch farms – as one author of this chapter, Daria Krivonos observed during her fieldwork in May 2022. Ukrainian workers would receive housing (so workers' housing became dependent on their jobs, spouses had to work in the same farm and children were not accommodated) and pay 12.61 euros per hour. After asking for information about this work, a Ukrainian woman said: 'This pay is only good for breathing in the Netherlands'. Ukrainian refugee workers labouring in agriculture continue to produce surplus and food for EU economies that 'stand with Ukraine'; at the same time, other life-seekers are expelled from the EU. Yet, Russian bombing continues to displace Ukrainians to seek life in EU states and become 'integrated' in these precarious labour markets.

Today, Ukrainian land continues to be seen as offering unlimited possibilities for the growth of Dutch agricultural expertise. The website of the Dutch Ministry of Agriculture, Nature and Food (Anon, 2022) reads:

> Ukraine offers the Dutch companies the possibility to scale up. The average Dutch farm is up to 100 hectares with limited possibility to grow. Ukraine has good soil, diverse climate, efficient logistics and unlimited opportunities for farmers and companies which are ready to deal with local risks and challenges, which we of course understand.

These histories of famine, expropriation of lands and peoples must be traced relationally to identify the gradations of subalternities they produce as part of inter-imperial relations and to show where political horizons to undo systems of oppression have and could emerge. We hope that this chapter stimulates conversations in this direction.

References

Alatas, S. H. (1977) *The Myth of the Lazy Native: A Study of the Image of the Malays, Filipinos and Javanese from the 16th to the 20th Century and Its Function in the Ideology of Colonial Capitalism.* New York: Routledge.

Andriewsky, O. (2015) 'Towards a decentred history: the study of the Holodomor and Ukrainian historiography', *East/West: Journal of Ukrainian Studies*, 2(1), 18–52.

Anon (2022) 'FRUITful cooperation Ukraine and The Netherlands', *Ministerie van Landbouw, Natuur en Voedselkwaliteit.* www.agroberichtenbuitenland.nl/actueel/nieuws/2022/08/18/ukraine-and-the-netherlands-fruitful-cooperation (accessed 27 February 2023).

Aparna, K. and Schapendonk, J. (2020) 'Shifting itineraries of asylum hospitality: towards a process geographical approach of guest-host relations', *Geoforum*, 116, 226–34.

Babakova, O., Fiałkowska, K., Kindler, M. and Zessin-Jurek, L. (2022) 'Who is a "true" refugee? On the limits of Polish hospitality', *CMR Spotlight*, 6(41), 1–15.

Bejan, R. and Boatcă, M. (2021) 'Migrant workers' safety concerns should be a pandemic priority', *Verfassungsblog: On Matters Constitutional* (blog). 28 April. https://verfassungsblog.de/migrant-workers-safety-concerns-should-be-a-pandemic-priority/ (accessed 20 June 2023).

Bhambra, G. (2007) *Rethinking Modernity: Postcolonialism and the Sociological Imagination*. Basingstoke: Palgrave.
Boatcă, M. (2021) 'Thinking Europe otherwise: lessons from the Caribbean', *Current Sociology*, 69(3), 389–414.
Borrell, J. (2022) *The Future of Europe Is Being Defined Now*. EEAS: The Diplomatic Service of the European Union. www.eeas.europa.eu/eeas/future-europe-being-defined-now-0_en (accessed 3 April 2023).
Burton, E., Mark, J. and Marung, S. (2022) 'Development', in Mark, J. and Betts, P. (eds) *Socialism Goes Global: The Soviet Union and Eastern Europe in the Age of Decolonization*. Oxford: Oxford University Press, pp. 75–114.
Césaire, A. (1950 [1972]) *Discourse on Colonialism*, trans. J. Pinkham. New York: Monthly Review Press.
Cucu, A.-S. (2022) 'Socialist accumulation and its "primitives" in Romania', *International Review of Social History*, 67(2), 251–74. doi:10.1017/S002085902200030X.
Da Silva, D. F. (2022) *Unpayable Debt*. London: Sternberg Press.
Doyle, L. (2014) 'Inter-imperiality', *Interventions*, 16(2), 159–96.
European Council (2022) 'Infographic: how the Russian invasion of Ukraine has further aggravated the global food crisis'. www.consilium.europa.eu/en/infographics/how-the-russian-invasion-of-ukraine-has-further-aggravated-the-global-food-crisis/ (accessed 5 April 2023).
European Council (2023a) 'Food for the world: what EU countries are doing to mitigate the impact of Russia's war'. www.consilium.europa.eu/en/food-for-the-world-eu-countries-mitigate-impact-russia-war/ (accessed 5 April 2023).
European Council (2023b) 'Food security and affordability'. www.consilium.europa.eu/en/policies/food-security-and-affordability/ (accessed 5 April 2023).
Foray, J. L. (2012) *Visions of Empire in the Nazi-occupied Netherlands*. Cambridge: Cambridge University Press.
Goldman, W. (2022a) 'Blood on the red banner: primitive accumulation in the world's first socialist state', *International Review of Social History*, 67(2), 211–29.
Goldman, W. (2022b) 'Introduction: primitive accumulation and socialism', *International Review of Social History*, 67(2), 195–209. doi:10.1017/S0020859022000098
van de Grift, L. (2015) 'Introduction: theories and practices of internal colonization: the cultivation of lands and people in the age of modern territory', *International Journal for History, Culture and Modernity*, 3(2), 139–58.
Gurnah, A. (2021) *Afterlives*. London: Bloomsbury.
Hall, D. (2023) 'Russia's invasion of Ukraine and critical agrarian studies', *The Journal of Peasant Studies*, 50(1), 26–46.
Joesten, J. (1943) 'Hitler's fiasco in the Ukraine', *Foreign Affairs*, 21(2), 331–9. https://doi.org/10.2307/20029229.
Klid, B. and Motyl, A. J. (2012) *Holodomor Reader: A Sourcebook on the Famine of 1932–1933 in Ukraine*. Toronto: Canadian Institute for Ukrainian Studies Press.
Krivonos, D. (2020) 'Ukrainian farm workers and Finland's regular army of labour', *Raster* (blog). https://raster.fi/2020/04/30/ukrainian-farm-workers-and-finlands-regular-army-of-labour/ (accessed 5 April 2023).
Künzel, G. V. F. D. (2015a) *Hitler's Brudervolk: The Dutch and the Colonization of Occupied Eastern Europe, 1939–1945*. London: Routledge.
Künzel, G. V. F. D. (2015b) 'National concerns and international collaboration: the Dutch and the Germanization of Nazi occupied Eastern Europe', *Segle XX. Revista catalana d'història*, (8), 1–21.

Lebowitz, M. A. (2023) '"Primitive socialist accumulation": Then and now', *Socialism and Democracy*, 36(3), 1–13.
Lim, J. H. (2022) *Global Easts: Remembering, Imagining, Mobilizing*. New York: Columbia University Press.
Lyautey, M. and Elie, M. (2019) 'German agricultural occupation of France and Ukraine, 1940–1944', *Comparativ. Zeitschrift für Globalgeschichte und vergleichende Gesellschaftsforschung*, 29(3), 86–117.
Mayerchyk, M. and Plakhotnik, O. (2021) 'Uneventful feminist protest in post-Maidan Ukraine: nation and colonialism revisited', in Koobak, R., Tlostanova, M. and Thapar-Björkert, S. (eds) *Postcolonial and Postsocialist Dialogues: Intersections, Opacities, Challenges in Feminist Theorizing and Practice*. London: Routledge, pp. 121–37.
Miller, M. (2020) 'When East met East: Dutch East Indies planters and the Ukraine project (1942–1944)', *Central European History*, 53(3), 613–35.
Parvulescu, A. and Boatcă, M. (2022) *Creolizing the Modern: Transylvania across Empires*. Ithaca, NY and London: Cornell University Press.
Plokhy, S. (2016) *The Gates of Europe: A History of Ukraine*. London: Penguin Books.
Robinson, C. (1983) *Black Marxism: The Making of the Black Radical Tradition*. Chapel Hill, NC: University of North Carolina Press.
Sharma, N. (2020) *Home Rule: National Sovereignty and the Separation of Natives and Migrants*. Durham, NC: Duke University Press.
Shih, S. (2016) 'Race and relation: the global sixties in the South of the South', *Comparative Literature*, 68(2), 141–54. https://doi.org/10.1215/00104124-3507922.
Siegmann, K. A., Quaedvlieg, J. and Williams, T. (2022) 'Migrant labour in Dutch agriculture: regulated precarity', *European Journal of Migration and Law*, 24(2), 217–40.
Snyder, T. (2010) *Bloodlands: Europe between Hitler and Stalin*. London: Bodley Head
Szelewa, D. and Polakowski, M. (2022) 'European solidarity and "free movement of labour" during the pandemic: exposing the contradictions amid east–west migration', *Comparative European Politics*, 20, 238–56.
Thomas-Greenfield, L. (2022) 'Remarks by Ambassador Linda Thomas-Greenfield at a UN Security Council Briefing on Ukraine'. https://usun.usmission.gov/remarks-by-ambassador-linda-thomas-greenfield-at-a-un-security-council-briefing-on-ukraine-2/ (accessed 1 April 2023).
Todorova, M. (2021) *Unequal Under Socialism: Race, Women, and Transnationalism in Bulgaria*. Toronto: University of Toronto Press.
UK Home Office (2023) 'National statistics: summary of latest statistics. Published 23 February 2023'. www.gov.uk/government/statistics/immigration-system-statistics-year-ending-december-2022/summary-of-latest-statistics (accessed 29 March 2023).
Ureña Valerio, L. (2019) *Colonial Fantasies, Imperial Realities: Race Science and the Making of Polishness on the Fringes of the German Empire, 1840–1920*. Athens, Ohio: Ohio University Press.
Viola, L. (1996) *Peasant Rebels Under Stalin: Collectivization and the Culture of Peasant Resistance*. New York: Oxford University Press.
Zimmerer, J. (2005) 'The birth of the Ostland out of the spirit of colonialism: a postcolonial perspective on the Nazi policy of conquest and extermination', *Patterns of Prejudice*, 39(2), 197–219.

Part II

Europeanisation as slow violence and stratified subalternities

5

No alternative but Europeanisation: slow violence and critical imaginaries in/from/with South East Europe

Maria-Adriana Deiana and Katarina Kušić

Since the end of the Cold War, the post-Yugoslav region has figured prominently in international politics and research as a space of international intervention. Framed as a space in transition from socialism to market economy, from war to peace, and from non-alignment to Europeanisation, the region has been a target for a wide array of material and ideological interventions. These interventions have, essentially, cemented the region as both a pivotal and a marginal site in the so-called European geopolitical imagination. To varying degrees across the post-Yugoslav space, the EU has been at the forefront of such projects involving state-building and peace-building initiatives, support for civil society building and gender equality, cultural diplomacy, market deregulation and different forms of border security and cross-border cooperation.

Critical scholars have long questioned the aggressive promotion of the EU *mission civilisatrice* that projects the EU as normative political trajectory and ideal of community for the post-Yugoslav space and South East Europe (SEE) more broadly (e.g. Horvat and Štiks, 2012; Majstorović, Vučkovac and Pepić, 2015; Kušić, Lottholz and Manolova, 2019). Crucially, this literature spotlights the different forms of epistemic violence through which Europeanisation proceeds in different, yet interconnected, ways: as a part of 'transition' narratives, as a never-ending return to Europe and in the making of region as a 'case study' and/or testing ground for theories and policies made elsewhere. In this chapter, we propose to think about these processes as forms of slow violence intrinsic to Europeanisation, and we highlight how this literature can be useful for understanding processes and building solidarities in the many spaces where Europeanisation as violence unfolds. We are inspired by the work of Rob Nixon (2011) who coined the term 'slow violence' to understand the environmental harm of invisible and extended processed. In the context of East Europe, Alexander Vorbrugg (2022) expanded it to capture the slow deterioration and abandonment that, instead of spectacular dispossession, marks the postsocialist transition in Russia. In a slightly different vein, we also consider the slow and violent reworkings of political and academic frameworks quietly but dramatically reshaped under the weight of Europe. Here the work of Lauren Berlant on the concept of crisis ordinariness also infuses our thinking (Berlant, 2011).

As scholars with different personal and academic entanglements in the post-Yugoslav space, we have both grappled with these issues in our own research and collective academic engagements. Our paths have crossed through our involvement in the British International Studies Association's (BISA) working group on SEE, a collective created to bring together scholars in UK higher education with an interest in spotlighting the significance of the region for international studies and geopolitics. The working group has offered an opportunity to engage in much needed (self-)critical reflections on existing scholarship on/about the region, not understood through essentialist lenses but rather as a productive epistemic location entangled in connected global processes of marginalisation, racialisation and coloniality. Even though paradoxically situated behind a visa regime that often makes it inaccessible to scholars and activists from the region, it has successfully brought together ongoing efforts to theorise international studies from a plurality of positions and move beyond Eurocentrism.[1]

The working group has contributed to developing dialogues across postcolonial/decolonial studies and the insights emerging from the region. This includes engaging the ambivalent legacies of postsocialism, which have been long marginalised by the overwhelming focus on studying the post-Yugoslav space through the value-laden prism of nationalism, ethnic conflict and post-conflict solutions. We agree with the editors of this volume that postcolonial and postsocialist dialogues should not imply two distinct geohistorical processes and academic trajectories. Even though such framings have often remained in distinct academic circles, the power of the dialogue comes precisely from thinking them together (Chari and Verdery, 2009; Karkov and Valiavicharska, 2018).

These conversations are particularly significant in the field that we inhabit: International Relations (IR). Thinking between the posts complicates post-Cold War narratives framed through the triumphalist emergence of international liberalism as the dominant solution for a more ethical and peaceful international order. Instead, this way of thinking explores the ambivalent, interlocking efforts to make socialism a relic of history and join the self-transformative journey to progress, modernity and liberalism, yet hold on to socialism's promises, political bonds and systems of sociability. Just as the postcolonial is not simply a temporal designation, post-Cold war implies attention to the ongoing contentions, reverberations and attachments to socialism as an archive of lived experiences that might offer possible alternatives to this triumphalist view, while demanding critical interrogation of its own investments in colonial modernity. Additionally, thinking between the posts, as Sharad Chari and Katherine Verdery (2009) invite us to do, is helpful to situate the region in wider analyses about the nested colonial legacies and racialised formations at the core of European modernity. Crucially for this chapter, thinking between posts enables us to capture this complex historicity, nested hierarchies and transnational reverberations that are irremediably discounted and erased with the emergence of Europeanisation as the region's only viable alternative.

In the following, we take stock of these developments to posit the post-Yugoslav space, and SEE more broadly, as a productive vantage point for understanding the multifarious forms of violence through which Europeanisation proceeds around the world. In the next section we trace the contours of these critical dialogues, discussing contributions that help us interrogate the workings of Europeanisation as materialised and felt in the region. After a reflection on our own positionalities, we outline our own engagement in making sense of 'Europeanisation as violence'. Katarina's research on the Europeanisation of agricultural governance in Serbia highlights how civilisational explanations were used to diagnose problems (having similarities with countries in the Global South) and diagnose solutions (becoming more European). These ambivalent dynamics also emerge in Maria-Adriana's research on the Sarajevo Film Festival wherein efforts to Europeanise the Balkans, cinematic narratives that both reproduce and challenge balkanising understandings of the region, and powerful critical and imaginative interventions on Europe that dispel its relegation to the EU's dysfunctional periphery intersect. We conclude the piece outlining some reflections on the potential of mobilising Souths and Easts as method informed by situated knowledges and parallel connections.

Mapping the field: from object of study to Yugosplaining

The ruins of the teleological narratives that guided – and in many cases still guide – both international engagement with the post-Yugoslav region and local politics are now exposed. While, in the early days of 'transition', anthropologists were tasked with deconstructing the linear narratives of democratisation and market transition (re)produced in political science, IR and economics, today we see a wider interdisciplinary literature taking these narratives to task. As our research testifies, the region's structural position vis-à-vis Europe is increasingly understood, not only in hierarchies of representation as a balkanised and forever balkanising internal other, but also as a site of exploitation of labour and resources, and a space of violent bordering of the EU.

We identify three significantly interrelated threads in the scholarship that critically interrogate existing frameworks of analysis and disrupt knowledge production of the region merely as object of study.

A space of intervention and Europeanisation

Given its prominent role in the post-Yugoslav space, understanding the multifarious practices and effects of Europeanisation has been at the centre of critical scholarship on the region. In the past two decades, the EU has been increasingly involved in preventing conflict and promoting peace and security outside its borders. However, its shifting configurations, as a geopolitical space and a global security actor, have been shaped by inherent tensions between consolidating bordering tendencies and aspirations for increased cooperation among EU member states and its neighbourhood. Artificially renamed the 'western Balkans', the post-Yugoslav space has been a key target of such security policies and practices. When investigating this international involvement, thus, we must bear in mind that a differentiated process of EU accession in the post-Yugoslav region overlaps with projects of state-building and post-war reconstruction largely driven by the rhetoric of EU enlargement and peace-building, but arguably aiming at stabilising the region in the interest of EU security.

To capture this complexity, Vjosa Musliu (2021: 5) provides a useful working definition of Europeanisation as 'a set of practices and projects that are in turn used to building particular states and societies that are amenable to European governance, as well as liberal and open economics'. We suggest that the effects of this seemingly benign logic for the region are ambivalent, producing a politics of complicity, attachment, impasse and in some cases material dispossession. On one level, as Musliu (2021: 3) observes, Europeanisation has become 'infinitely amorphous, vague in referent and ambiguous in usage'. At the same time, precisely as Europeanisation has become 'everything and nothing', the task of today's critical scholarship is to unpack its concrete manifestations (see Neuman Stanivuković in this volume). Musliu (2021: 3) does this by investigating the everyday performances of Europe, thus studying Europe and Europeanisation 'as a way of life, other than as a global logic imposing itself in peripheries'. We share Musliu's urgency to move away from seeing the effects of the EU as restricted to the formal accession process – conditionalities, the screening and opening of individual chapters of the *acquis communautaire*, the technical cooperation that socialises national elites, etc. – and instead investigate it as a 'project, a process', questioning 'what Europe represents in and for the region' (Musliu, 2021: 4–5).

One illuminating broadening of how we understand the 'effects' of EU/ international involvement in post-war reconstruction in the region comes from Daniela Lai (2020) in her work on socioeconomic justice in Bosnia and Herzegovina (BiH). In her work with peripheral (outside of Sarajevo) communities in BiH, Lai shows how a limiting understanding of transitional justice – introduced and operationalised by EU and international agencies – made ethnicity the crux of BiH justice. This makes it nearly impossible to recognise socioeconomic violence that transpired before, during and after the war in BiH, and leaves it essentially unaddressed. Europeanisation of justice here has meant conceptually emptying the concept and the process of any socioeconomic content. Also, it has meant the empirical bypassing of socialist experiences that provide the reference point and comparison against which the economic suffering of Yugoslav (post)war period is understood.

But Europeanisation also operates in frames much wider than EU membership and international interventions. Piro Rexhepi (2023) has, for example, shown how the inclusion of BiH in Europe requires a particular 'Europeanisation' of Islam in the Balkans. This recasting depends on using whiteness to differentiate it from its Arabic other, and stands in stark contrast with Muslim activists' world-making in the 1970s and 1980s that launched a global critique of socialism and capitalism rooted in Pan-Islamism.

Our own research testifies that the workings of Europeanisation must be understood as an assemblage of policies, institutional, bureaucratic and b/ ordering processes, everyday practices, structures of feeling and a specific aesthetics. These different modes of Europeanisation (re)configure the region through multifaceted internal hierarchies, while also continuously (re)producing hierarchies between local and global politics. Musliu (2021) shows how the revival of Tirana as a 'European city' proceeded through balkanising and orientalising images. These images, captured in the mayor's exclamation that 'Tirana will not be Calcutta' have a twofold effect (see Oancă in this volume). First, they cast both Albania and countries in the East/South as inferior in the global political economy of value. Here, Albanians are not simply victims of Balkanist discourses but active agents of their perpetuation: they see themselves and others through the same lens. Second, these images once again reify the myth of Europe as a space devoid of inequality, violence and suffering. As Böröcz (2006) put it, Europe becomes the exclusive location of goodness unavailable to SEE without tutelage and subordination. Such statements, and the emerging scholarship making sense of it, is tasked with moving beyond understanding racism and whiteness not only as 'imports' into the South East and East Europe (as spaces until then supposedly excluded from formation of global coloniality), instead locating the region as an active (re)producer of global racial hierarchies – an issue we return to in the next section.

Global entanglements

These intersections of multiple hierarchies make the positionality of the Balkans at times difficult to comprehend and articulate. Writing from a decolonial perspective, Piro Rexhepi (Gržinić, Kancler and Rexhepi, 2020: 18) summarises it well: 'the (post)socialist world still cannot resolve its (geo)political position of being in pact and proximity of Euro-American coloniality or its product and defying periphery'. Similarly, Manuela Boatcă (2013: 7) described the Balkans as the 'epigonal Europe': a semi-peripheral reproducer of modernity with the attitude of aspiration and main role of accomplice. It is not so easy to translate this understanding in research practice.

One area where it has been done exceptionally well is in the emerging study of race and racialisation in SEE (Bjelić, 2018; Baker, 2018a; Rexhepi, 2023). Catherine Baker's (2018b: 29) work has investigated 'how global racial formations have been adapted and translated into, across and through the Yugoslav region'. The Yugoslav region is thus recast as 'deeply embedded in transnational racialised imaginations and therefore a global history of coloniality' (Baker, 2018b: 4). Sunnie Rucker-Chang (2019) has similarly recognised 'various forms of Blackness in Yugoslav space' – from Afro-Albanian communities in Montenegro to students arriving from the Global South and Romani communities. This diversity, she argues, 'open[s] possibilities for a localised understanding of how Blackness functions as a result of and beyond the global colour line' (Rucker-Chang, 2019).

These global racial formations, and racism as their expression, did not enter the region with the dawn of postsocialism. Piro Rexhepi has shown how the 1980s Yugoslav Islamophobia (culminating in the imprisonment of twelve activists of Young Muslims in Sarajevo) was a particular product of a global understanding of Islam as a security threat, and the very local history of anti-Muslim feelings and structures in pre-socialist and socialist Yugoslavia. Importantly, he also excavates the different world-making that these activists were engaged in. Instead of distancing from the East – like in the proclamation of 'Tirana will not be Calcutta' – activists like Melika Salihbegović and Alija Izetbegović connected their own struggles in Yugoslavia with the transatlantic slave trade and colonial conquest in order to critique both capitalist and socialist ideas of humanity, civilisation and development (Rexhepi, 2023: 50).

Global entanglements have also been the focus of research on Yugoslav socialism, and specifically the Non-Aligned Movement (NAM) as one of its key institutions. Paul Stubbs (2021: 133) argues for a decolonial historiography of NAM that would first 'bring Yugoslavia back into global social relations' – a move against erasure – but he also points to the need for 'decentring this positionality and ensuring that other sites of analysis and struggle, and the relations between them, are taken into consideration'. In other words, an argument for salvaging Yugoslav agency from the weight of Eurocentrism needs to be paired with a focus on 'other-than-EU' global entanglements of this position. This not only counters silences in the historical record but also helps recover solidarities and politics that can be used to imagine different futures (Stubbs, 2019; 2023). Yet, these East–West solidarities were not exempt from the racial hierarchies in which they operated. Scholars have excavated the racial investments that ran alongside non-aligned solidarities in Yugoslav projects of modernisation (Subotić and Vučetić, 2017; Karkov and Valiavicharska, 2018).

The deeply ambivalent position of the region – constantly understood through narratives of civilisational backwardness, and often even racialised as 'off white', while remaining deeply invested in projects of whiteness and coloniality – can also be seen as a productive: a space where the complexities of Europeanisation as violence can be explored beyond the binaries of North/South. This intersectional thinking is crucial for making sense of current practices of EU bordering and security that make the post-Yugoslav countries, especially Croatia, the new enforcers of racialised and militarised EU borders. One of the effects of Europeanisation imaginaries has been the severing of global connections in favour of relations to and with EUrope as the centre point of political and research imaginations. The examples provided here show the value of scholarship that de-centres Europe while not ignoring its power.

The politics of knowledge production

While the empirical entanglements with Europe and its racial and civilisational hierarchies have been researched and conceptualised extensively, a parallel research programme investigates the hierarchies of knowledge production. This is not surprising given that the region has served, especially within IR, as a showcase for theories and laboratory for methods devised elsewhere (Kušić 2021; see also Zinaić, 2016). Underpinning this scholarship is the aim to position the region as analytically productive, for both conceptual development and for understanding the current global moment. This was the goal of a series titled Yugosplaining the World, published in 2020 on the Disorder of Things blog (Hozić, Subotić, Vučetić, 2020). The series emerged as a way of 'talking back' to the hordes of experts from the West. 'Westernsplaining' interpreted the horrors of the 1990s and their reverberations as isolated from world history and somehow uniquely 'Balkan'. In a moment where, yet again, the world at large is unravelling under the weight of nationalism and nativism, the texts illustrate powerful analyses precisely from the Yugoslav experience. Instead of Westernsplaining the Balkans, the authors Yugosplain global politics to show that the Balkans are not an isolated case of disorder, but an epistemic place from whence global politics can be productively studied.[2]

The project of 'talking back' has explicitly shaped academic publications. The collection published on the blog of the BISA SEE working group[3] reflects on the materialities of inequality in knowledge production, whether in collaborations with regional researches whose working conditions are dramatically difficult compared to higher education in the Global North (Majstorović, 2022), or in research conducted by researchers from the Global North without language and area studies training (Piersma, 2022). These discussions expanded the growing sophisticated reflections on methods and approaches used to understand the Yugoslav region (Radeljić and González-Villa, 2021). Gëzim Visoka and Vjosa Musliu's (2019) edited volume, for example, brings together Kosovar scholars to articulate local critiques of state-building in Kosovo. Dženeta Karabegović and Adna Karamehić-Oates (2023) similarly bring Bosnian diaspora together to examine their contributions to the development of Bosnian studies. And finally, the collective project Yugoslawomen+ critically reflects on knowledge production and coloniality from the perspective of SEE migrants working within the contradictions and hopes of critical IR scholarship in the Global North (see Yugoslawomen+ Collective, 2021).

Brought together by a critical reflection on ways of studying and theorising from the post-Yugoslav region, these interventions uncover the everyday violence of Europeanisation in the Balkans and point to larger frameworks that prevent better understanding that violence. They ponder moving away from the Eurocentrism that constantly pulls post-Yugoslav scholarship towards the EU as the most important, and often only relevant relation. And they critically reflect on the ways in which knowledge production is embodied in positions of migration. Within these themes, the knowledge produced in and about the region connects to the burning questions that also face other spaces of Europeanisation.

Locating our bodies, writing and research

Our own positionalities and diverse stakes in writing about/with/in the post-Yugoslav region highlight many of the points reviewed above. Moreover, they also account for the materiality and relationality of our own writing encounters – one of the explicit goals of this edited volume.

Katarina

Growing up in the 1990s and 2000s in Croatia, I was/am very much a product of both transition thinking and Europe as a structure of feeling. It is, of course, difficult to evaluate the person we once were, but when I think of myself as a teenager and young adult, I think of teleological optimism: we were children of transition who were to make everything better. I started university in 2007, eight years after the death of Franjo Tuđman and six years before Croatia joined the EU. I had won a scholarship to a private US university in Dubrovnik where we studied business, economics and management with the explicit goal of becoming new – meaning more transparent and less corrupt – regional business leaders. It was a motley crew of relatively wealthy students from all over the region and many second and third generation migrants who wanted to try 'coming back' but were either intimidated by or unable to follow degrees in Bosnian/Croatian/Montenegrin/Serbian. At the end of my studies, I stayed to work in the Dubrovnik tourism industry, where I was exposed to both political and affective economies of international tourism. It was a system that opened the world from the small alleyways of Dubrovnik Old Town, in rituals that both rewarded and exploited the many young and old bodies propelling the Croatian tourism machine.

I bring this background in to show you why, when I was applying to study IR at the Central European University (CEU), I wrote in the application letter that I feel 'the international' and 'Europe' all around me. The date of Croatia's accession was set shortly after my graduation and the bureaucratic aspects of EU membership were increasingly conflated with Europe and international politics. I was not interested in the bureaucracy of EU membership, but I was curious about how Europe and 'the international' live in romantic relationships, decisions about jobs, ways of imagining the future and frameworks through which we understand pasts. Today, I also ask how they live in the methodological and analytical tools we use to study SEE.

It is then not surprising that my PhD research and the ensuing monograph (Kušić, forthcoming) pursued the discursive and material embodiments of international intervention. I studied youth non-formal education and agricultural production in Serbia as sites shaped by Europeanisation, state-building and post-war reconstruction. Through ethnographic research, I hoped to see how these concepts play out in everyday life, but I also wanted to make that everyday life epistemically productive. This was a process of discovery: while I was introduced to postcolonial theory while studying at CEU in Budapest, studying and teaching in the UK exposed me to reverberations of colonial empires: in classrooms where students insisted the railways in India brought 'development', and in conversations with colleagues thinking through colonial wounds in the Americas, South Asia and Palestine. My own conversations with postcolonial and decolonial thought thus led me to ask not only what concepts tell us about everyday life, but how experiences of everyday life force us to rethink concepts – making the Balkans not only a space of gathering 'data', but also of building theory.

The Europeanisation of agricultural policy implies the simultaneous transformation of three distinct subjects: the public servants who are expected to transform the state along neoliberal lines; the agricultural workers themselves who are led to become entrepreneurs more responsive to the market; and the civil society that is supposed to participate in and mediate between the two. Specific images of 'Balkan backwardness' inspire these programmes – both within contemporary EU approaches and in longer historical developments. Yet their effects are not only representational. They further 'projectivise' politics, limiting what is thought as possible in political action and the tools available for getting there; they discriminate against small producers in a way that posits the resulting inequalities as a 'natural' order of progress; and they help the brain drain that makes it impossible for the public sector to keep employees from the consultancies of the private sector.

Agriculture also helped me dislocate international intervention, a concept and sub-field of IR where Balkan subjects are over-represented (Kušić, 2021). Following the concerns of my interlocutors led me to the politics of agricultural land. Even though land policy is not directly in the realm of EU accession, the foreign direct investment in land is a particular logic of government that moves alongside Europeanisation. Such an empirical widening also expands the period under inquiry – to understand how agricultural land moves, we need to bring together Ottoman governing systems, socialist experiments in ownership and economic democracy, the violence of post-socialist transition and the EU Common Agricultural Policy and the markets it powerfully shapes. There is a global element to these processes: the notorious investments from the United Arab Emirates, for example, are rightly criticised for their lack of transparency and the poorly investigated effects of privatising and selling huge swathes of agricultural land (Kušić and Lazić, 2022). At the same time, those investments are framed in racialised discourses of 'Arab arrival' which foreclose critiques based on the consequences, rather than the origin, of these investments, and further remove from discussion the very domestic processes and actors that drive the unfair concentration of land.

In thinking about Europeanisation and 'the international' to which it supposedly leads – as shaping my personal trajectory and an object of my research – the challenge for me has always been to expand postcolonial understandings of SEE's position in relation to Europe into more global understanding of that position in wider structures of coloniality. And for this, I have the multiple generations of East–South dialogues in and about the Yugoslav space to thank. While I work to think from the minutiae of human experience – first in intervention and now in relation to land and agriculture – my involvements in collaborative projects and networks bring to fore the global and ambivalent entanglements of Yugoslav socialism and capitalism with coloniality and global racial hierarchies.

Maria-Adriana

To some extent the logic of optimism and progress through learning English and Europeanisation that Katarina describes resonates with me. Having grown up in Sardinia, Italy's insular periphery, the promises of mobility, progress and escape through programmes like Erasmus were particularly seductive for our generation. While other friends had chosen 'cosmopolitan' cities such as Paris or Madrid, I took a somewhat different path, choosing another peripheral destination, Northern Ireland, where I later returned and I am now currently based as a researcher and educator. Thinking about and 'feeling' Europeanisation from Italy's 'backward' and underdeveloped South echoes the developmental narratives of accession used for the enlargement, although privileged through the EU membership afforded to those holding an Italian passport. This claim to Europeanness goes hand in hand with Italy's refusal to acknowledge its own postcolonial condition and history of colonial violence which, lest we forget, was instrumental in cementing Italy's positioning within white, European modernity given the ambiguous, racialised in-betweenness of its southern regions and populations (Pesarini, 2021). Such refusal is mirrored not only in Italy's racist citizenship policies and culture but also in its eager embrace of and complicity in the deadly policing and externalisation of EU external borders.

Currently, I find myself writing about the violence of Europeanisation from Northern Ireland, another peripheral 'problem space' where peace 'failures' and silences about Empire collide with the reverberations and contentions of Brexit that have made critical engagements with EUrope, well, complicated. In this chapter, we write about no alternative but Europeanisation as experienced, felt and theorised in/from/with SEE. Yet, from where I write, the space for thinking critically about EUrope has become narrower as the EU has emerged as the 'sensible' alternative to a Brexit driven by British exceptionalism, nationalism and racism. Just as in the post-Yugoslav region, the mantra of 'no alternative but Europeanisation' looms large from this other semi-periphery where progressive politics and imaginaries are firmly 'stuck' towards EU membership, irrespective of evidence of its deadly and slow violent effects. This juncture makes a 'connected sociologies approach built on postcolonial and decolonial critiques' (Bhambra, 2015), as well as a commitment to thinking between posts, even more urgent to understand these global entanglements and interrogate our complicated investments in Europeanisation and its violence more deeply.

In terms of locating my writing and thinking in relation to SEE, I became interested in the post-Yugoslav region most explicitly through my academic training, as well as through indirect personal histories and attachments that inevitably inflect our research interests. Growing up in in the 1980s, Yugoslavia felt somewhat close to home for us, not necessarily in a strict geographical sense, but more importantly ideologically, through my family's political attachment to socialist internationalism. Yugoslavia had represented the last bastion of hope, a familial-political utopia that a fairer version of socialism could exist. I now know that watching its dissolution, worriedly yet safely, on our television screens ignited the first glimpses of a feminist curiosity about women in war, whose stories ever so present in the often sensationalist reportages during the Yugoslav wars nevertheless quickly fell from view once the world, we, stopped caring about the Balkans. These are some of personal/political threads that, years later, led me to awkwardly enter and inhabit the discipline we call IR initially with an interest in developing a feminist exploration of the promises of peace in Bosnia and Herzegovina centred around women's diverse experiences and fragile, yet stubborn, individual/collective imaginations for life and peace otherwise (Deiana, 2018). It is through this research that I became attuned to the cruel promises of resolution through international intervention and to attachments to a Europeanness that for places like Bosnia remains ambivalent and foreclosed. The process also prompted me to interrogate romanticised attachment to socialism and its legacy as political alternative which I had also reproduced.

On one level, my own research trajectory mirrors patterns that have been highlighted in critical literature: of international researchers who flock to sites of armed conflict to conduct fieldwork, write publications as 'experts'. However self-reflexive, critical of the logics of expertise and attentive to the politics of knowledge production emerging from scholars in/from the region, this ambivalent, fractured imbrication in the neoliberal hierarchies of international academic research remains an inescapable component of my positionality. At the same time, I view my work not in isolation, but rather as an opportunity to engage in collective critical conversations about deepening, widening and transforming dominant analytical frameworks that rely on the construction of BiH and the post-Yugoslav region as a space that fails to live up to normative narratives of success, progress and ultimately modernity. It is precisely this ongoing dialogue, grounded in the multiple knowledges emerging from the region, that can help us subvert such narratives of the international, revealing violence and toxicity as foundational to seemingly benign normative imaginaries.

In my own research, this has entailed troubling the perennial relegation of Bosnia and Herzegovina to a contained space wherein the frame of conflict, belatedness and failure irremediably structures how we narrate local histories, agencies and subjectivities. Working at the intersection of EU border politics, security and peace-building, I became interested in unpacking how constructions of Bosnia as a site of endemic failure are intertwined with investments in the elusive and cruel promises[4] of EU futurity, but also with broader anxieties about European identity, borders and security, as well as the future of EU as a peace and security actor.[5] These entanglements became perhaps more visible in 2015 when the region became one of the epicentres of the so-called EU refugee crisis as a route of 'illegal' migration and, again, labelled a threat to EU stability. Both in academic and media discourse, explanations of the intensification of border and security regimes in response to refugee influx, nationalist sentiments and fear of security threats centred around the idea of the EU facing multiple crises, exceptional crisis, besetting its institutions, borders and sense of community. However, taking seriously the complex positionality and historicity of Bosnia, as a space that has long been targeted by the logic and bordering practices of peacebuilding through Europeanisation, throws in sharp relief the self-referential narrative of exceptionality and crisis.

Rather than an aberration or crisis-response, such forms of violence are foundational to narratives that 'anchor' the EU's identity as political project and security 'actor'. Interrogating EU practices of peace and security from the vantage point of Bosnia and Herzegovina reveals the paralysing effects of investing in the promises of Europeanisation as constant deferral. Producing Bosnia as (perennial) candidate, made to 'patiently wait in the ante-chamber of modernity' (Kušić, Lottholz and Manolova, 2019: 17), the seemingly linear, coherent and progressive cartography of EU b/ordering obscures its complex historicity shaped as much by interlocking postsocialist and postconflict legacies as by the transnational circuits of violence foundational to EUrope. Crucially, at this juncture we can observe how manifestations of Europeanisation as violence work through differentiated registers against the EU's variously defined 'Others', whether they are framed as racialised threats that might cross EU external borders or 'balkanised' targets in need of civilisation, connectivity and development. Indeed, a continuum exists from the brutality of border police, tear gas, barbed wire and diabolical living conditions experienced by those who attempt, and often tragically fail in, crossing the Balkan route to the curtailing of alternatives and slow violence in the promises of progress through Europeanisation. As Neuman

Stanivuković (this volume) also shows, it is precisely the construction of the SEE region as an abject space trapped and invested in the logic of EU futurity that makes such different, yet interconnected, forms of violence possible. As she powerfully illustrates, seemingly mundane infrastructure projects (i.e. roads, highways, railway) mobilised in the promise of development and connectivity operate as tools that relieve Europe from its responsibility for violence in the region, while also enabling structural violence against migrants.

In a similar vein to Neuman Stanivuković and Musliu (2021), rather than examining the workings of Europeanisation in the institutional domain, I have explored lesser-known sites by focusing on how EU narratives of peace and security entered the 2015 edition of the Sarajevo Film Festival where film makers and festival organisers 'flirted' with performances of Europeanness, but also created an opportunity to raise critical questions about EU border politics through the medium of cinema. As echoes of conflict histories and imaginaries of the region and the contemporary militarised spectacle of EU border security reverberated, the festival became a productive entry point to explore, through films from/about the region, what is at stake for communities and spaces perennially constructed through narratives of failure in this marginal, yet often pivotal space for the EU geopolitical imagination.

Focusing on two documentary films presented at the festival that both engaged with histories of conflict and loss, as well as with the ambivalent position of the region, I posited these cinematic imaginaries as powerful epistemological interventions.[6] They cast a critical eye on narratives of crisis and exception mobilised to frame current EU border politics by confronting the viewer with the deadening effects of the seemingly benign logic of EU peace and security, and their duress. Through an aesthetics of disorderly memories and complex border imaginaries the documentaries recentred 'local' histories of loss and failure, but also endurance and survival in compromised conditions of existence from the perspective of communities conceived as 'Other'. Activating peripheral connections between the plight of communities in the post-Yugoslav space and those seeking refuge against the EU militarised border enabled by the political context of their screening, the films offered a source of inspiration in articulating more complicatedly human stories of war, failure and displacement, gesturing to commonalities and fragile solidarities as alternatives that are constantly under erasure in narratives that seek to secure Europe as a singular, coherent and, ultimately, exclusive space.

At the time of conducting this research in 2015, the peripheral connections activated at the Sarajevo Film Festival and through the films' imaginaries mirrored solidarity movements led by citizens in support of those on the move along the Balkan route. Since then, however, such fragile solidarities have been severely compromised by both the intensification of the EU security regime that increasingly sees the region as the violent buffer zone for policing its borders with the complicity of local elites, and overt forms of racism in the region that target refugee communities in spite of a 'shared' experience of marginalisation. As we point out earlier, it is indeed crucial to interrogate the region not simply as a 'victim' of the failed promises of Europeanisation, but as deeply entangled in its foundational logics of racialised b/order violence.

Conclusion

In this chapter, we sought to highlight the epistemic potential of the post-Yugoslav space for thinking about the many facets of Europeanisation as violence. We have illustrated how, from this vantage point, Europeanisation engenders a complex set of affective registers and material effects that 'entrap' the region in a never-ending transition towards the cruel promises of Europeanisation. Whether through investing in the alluring promises of agricultural modernisation, or in the performances of Europeanness in the region's most famous film festival, we have termed this affective/material impasse as slow violence. Echoing other chapters in this volume, attending to Europeanisation as slow violence is particularly productive to capture the region's ambivalent positioning as both the Balkan other in need of EU intervention, supervision, connectivity and containment, and its accomplice in racialised logics of spectacular and everyday violence at the core of the European project and its b/ordering.

At the same time, through the rich intellectual dialogues that underpin scholarship radiating from it, we spotlight the post-Yugoslav space as a site of critical imaginaries and alternative solidarities, mobilised through creative interventions in the aesthetics and politics of the region, through social movements that challenge the violence of Europeanisation. We have argued that, situating the region in wider epistemological frames shaped by intersecting postcolonial, postsocialist and post-conflict legacies, these critical dialogues enable us to complicate dominant parameters that, particularly in IR, continue to frame the post-Yugoslav space as an object of intervention. The long-standing engagement of scholars studying how this space has been imagined and intervened in provides a wide range of tools, expertise and experiences useful for thinking about the global entanglements of Europe. While this broad literature might have blind spots and limitations, many of which have been criticised in the past decade, it also provides a productive basis for developing both conceptual analyses and political solidarities with peripheries North and South that are sites of Europeanisation as violence.

As we think about this ongoing conceptual and methodological endeavour, our task is to broaden our frameworks in ways that do not limit our focus to the Balkans' relations with the EU but conceptualise the region through its global entanglements with the politics of race and Empire. Crucially this entails an effort to move beyond considering the region as an innocent victim or bystander, to explore the reproduction of modernity's violent logics within the Balkans. Doing so will not only sharpen our attention to local hierarchies (including race, class and gender) that are often obscured by the focus on Balkan–EU relations, but it can also help explore the political potential of Souths and Easts as method more fully. In conversation with the other contributors to this volume, we see our research as part of collective efforts to interrogate of Europeanisation as violence from multiple positionings, activating alliances across seemingly unrelated histories and struggles.

Notes

1 For example, the group helped fund the 2017 Belgrade workshop 'Dialoguing "between the posts:" Post-socialist and post-/decolonial perspectives on domination, hierarchy and resistance in South-Eastern Europe' (see Karkov et. al., 2017).
2 The curators were also aware of the trappings of 'Yugo' as a category. In discussing the series with the editors, Vjosa Musliu described how this category, when experienced from the *inside*, 'is bound to alienate, silence and limit subjects and subjectivities' (Hozić, Subotić and Vučetić, 2020). In translation, there were not many 'Albanians, Jews, Roma, Slovenians, Macedonians' in the list of authors, an absence that reflects Balkan politics and Yugoslavia's contradictory history (Hozić, Subotić and Vučetić, 2020). It should also be noted that an earlier effort to bring together the 'post-Yugoslav academic diaspora' was published in the journal *Reč* (Jović, 2003).
3 It is based on a panel organised by Katarina Kušić and Elena Stavrevska at BISA 2021 conference. Stavrevska, E. Kušić, K., Kaczmarska, K. and Piersma, M. 2021. '/ Within / Without: Strategies and possibilities for cultivating knowledge with the Global East [Roundtable]'. *BISA 2021 conference – Forget International Studies?* London (online), 21–23 June 2021.
4 I use this term here with reference to Berlant's *Cruel Optimism* (2011) as a way of capturing both the affective mechanisms that binds the region to ideas of Europeanness (whiteness and progress), as well as the material consequences that investing in this (im)possible promise engenders.
5 To do so I interweaved post-colonial and decolonial analyses of the region with another theoretical approach that has long been concerned with failure: queer scholarship (Deiana, 2020).
6 Jasmila Žbanić's *One Day in Sarajevo* (2015) and Vladimr Tomic's *Flotel Europa* (2015).

References

Baker, C. (2018a) 'Postcoloniality without race? Racial exceptionalism and southeast European cultural studies', *Interventions*, 20(6), 759–84. https://doi.org/10.1080/1369801X.2018.1492954.

Baker, C. (2018b) *Race and the Yugoslav Region: Postsocialist, Post-Conflict, Postcolonial?* Manchester: Manchester University Press.

Berlant, L. G. (2011) *Cruel Optimism*. Durham, NC: Duke University Press.

Bhambra, G. K. (2015) 'A "connected sociologies" approach to global sociology', *ISA The Futures We Want: Global Sociology and the Struggles for a Better World*, 21 September 2015 [online]. https://futureswewant.net/gurminder-bhambra-connected-sociologies/ (accessed 14 May 2023).

Bjelić, D. I. (2018) 'Toward a genealogy of the Balkan discourses on race', *Interventions*, 20(6), 906–29. https://doi.org/10.1080/1369801X.2018.1492955.

Boatcă, M. (2013) 'Multiple Europes and the politics of difference within', *Worlds & Knowledges Otherwise*, 3(3). https://globalstudies.trinity.duke.edu/sites/globalstudies.trinity.duke.edu/files/documents/v3d3_Boatca2.pdf (accessed 14 May 2023).

Böröcz, J. (2006) 'Goodness is elsewhere: the rule of European difference', *Comparative Studies in Society and History*, 48(1), 110–38.

Chari, S. and Verdery, K. (2009) 'Thinking between the posts: postcolonialism, postsocialism, and ethnography after the Cold War'. *Comparative Studies in Society and History*, 51(1), 6–34. https://doi.org/10.1017/S0010417509000024.

Deiana, M.-A. (2018) *Gender and Citizenship: Promises of Peace in Post-Dayton Bosnia-Herzegovina*. London: Palgrave Macmillan. https://doi.org/10.1057/978-1-137-59378-8.

Deiana, M.-A. (2020) 'Undoing EU security through the art of failure: cinematic imaginations in/from the post-Yugoslav space', *Critical Studies on Security*, latest articles, 1–16. https://doi.org/10.1080/21624887.2020.1799645.

Gržinić, M., Kancler, T. and Rexhepi, P. (2020) 'Decolonial encounters and the geopolitics of racial capitalism', *Feminist Critique: East European Journal of Feminist and Queer Studies*, (3), 13–38.

Horvat, S. and Štiks, I. (eds) (2012) 'Welcome to the desert of transition! Post-Socialism, the European Union, and a new left in the Balkans', *Monthly Review*, 63(10), 38.

Hozić, A., Subotić, J. and Vučetić, S. (2020) 'Yugosplaining the world', Disorder of Things (2 July 2020). https://thedisorderofthings.com/2020/07/02/yugosplaining-the-world-%E2%80%AF/ (accessed 14 May 2023).

Jović, D. (2003) 'Nova generacija: Postjugoslovenska akademska dijaspora', *Reč*, 16(70), 24–32.

Karabegović, D. and Karamehić-Oates, A. (2023) *Bosnian Studies: Perspectives from an Emerging Field*. Columbia, MO: University of Missouri Press.

Karkov, N., Kušić, K., Lottholz, P. and Manolova, P. (2017) 'Workshop report: dialoguing "between the posts", developing critiques of coloniality, modernity and neoliberal capitalism in (and beyond) South-Eastern Europe', *Dialoguing Posts Network*, 9 November 2017. https://dialoguingposts.wordpress.com/2017/11/09/workshop-report-dialoguing-between-the-posts-developing-critiques-of-coloniality-modernity-and-neoliberal-capitalism-in-and-beyond-south-eastern-europe/ (accessed 14 May 2023).

Karkov, N. R. and Valiavicharska, Z. (2018) 'Rethinking East-European socialism: notes toward an anti-capitalist decolonial methodology', *Interventions*, 20(6), 785–813. https://doi.org/10.1080/1369801X.2018.1515647.

Kušić, K. (2021) 'Balkan subjects in intervention literature: the politics of over-representation and reconstruction', *Journal of International Relations and Development*, 24(4). 910–31. https://doi.org/10.1057/s41268-021-00235-x.

Kušić, K. and Lazić, S. (2022) 'Land on the move: inequality and consolidation of agricultural land in Serbia', *LeftEast* (11 March 2022). https://lefteast.org/land-on-the-move-inequality-and-consolidation-of-agricultural-land-in-serbia/. (accessed 14 May 2023).

Kušić, K., Lottholz, P. and Manolova, P. (eds) (2019) *Decolonial Theory and Practice in Southeast Europe*. Sofia: dVersia.

Lai, D. (2020) *Socioeconomic Justice: International Intervention and Transition in Post-War Bosnia and Herzegovina*. Cambridge and New York: Cambridge University Press.

Majstorović, D. (2022) 'Doing epistemic decolonisation in Bosnia: peripheral selves', *BISA South East Europe (SEE)*, 10 March 2022 [online]. www.bisa.ac.uk/members/working-groups/seewg/articles/doing-epistemic-decolonisation-bosnia-peripheral-selves (accessed 14 May 2023).

Majstorović, D., Vučkovac, Z. and Pepić, A. (2015) 'From Dayton to Brussels via Tuzla: post-2014 Economic Restructuring as Europeanization Discourse/Practice in Bosnia and Herzegovina', *Southeast European and Black Sea Studies*, 15(4), 661–82. https://doi.org/10.1080/14683857.2015.1126093.

Musliu, V. (2021) *Europeanization and Statebuilding as Everyday Practices: Performing Europe in the Western Balkans*. London: Routledge. https://doi.org/10.4324/9780429343469.

Nixon, R. (2011) *Slow Violence and the Environmentalism of the Poor*. Cambridge, MA: Harvard University Press.

Pesarini, A. (2021) 'When the Mediterranean "became" Black: diasporic hopes and (post)colonial traumas', in Proglio, G., Hawthorne, C., Danewid, I., Khalil Saucier, P., Grimaldi, G., Pesarini, A., Raeymaekers, T., Grechi, G. and Gerrand, V. (eds) *The Black Mediterranean: Bodies, Borders and Citizenship*. London: Palgrave Macmillan, pp. 31–55.

Piersma, M. (2022) 'Academic knowledge production in "home" institutions: a call for material positionality in research on Bosnia and Herzegovina', *BISA South East Europe (SEE)*. www.bisa.ac.uk/members/working-groups/seewg/articles/academic-knowledge-production-home-institutions-call-material (accessed 14 May 2023).

Radeljić, B. and González-Villa, C. (eds) (2021) *Researching Yugoslavia and Its Aftermath: Sources, Prejudices and Alternative Solutions*. Cham, Switzerland: Springer International Publishing. https://doi.org/10.1007/978-3-030-70343-1.

Rexhepi, P. (2023) *White Enclosures: Racial Capitalism and Coloniality along the Balkan Route*. Durham, NC: Duke University Press.

Rucker-Chang, S. (2019) 'Mapping Blackness in Yugoslavia and post-Yugoslav space', *Black Perspectives – African American Intellectual History Society* (blog). 17 July. www.aaihs.org/mapping-blackness-in-yugoslavia-and-post-yugoslav-space/ (accessed 14 May 2023).

Stubbs, P. (2019) 'Socialist Yugoslavia and the antinomies of the non-aligned movement', *LeftEast* (17 June 2019). www.criticatac.ro/lefteast/yugoslavia-antinomies-non-aligned-movement/ (accessed 14 May 2023).

Stubbs, P. (2021) 'Yugocentrism and the study of the non-aligned movement: towards a decolonial historiography', *History in Flux*, 3(3), 133–55. https://doi.org/10.32728/flux.2021.3.6.

Stubbs, P. (ed.) (2023) *Socialist Yugoslavia and the Non-Aligned Movement: Social, Cultural, Political, and Economic Imaginaries*. Montreal: McGill-Queen's University Press.

Subotić, J. and Vučetić, S. (2017) 'Performing solidarity: whiteness and status-seeking in the non-aligned world', *Journal of International Relations and Development*, 22(3), 722–743. https://doi.org/10.1057/s41268-017-0112-2.

Visoka, G. and Musliu, V. (eds) (2019) *Unravelling Liberal Interventionism: Local Critiques of Statebuilding in Kosovo*. Abingdon: Routledge.

Vorbrugg, A. (2022) 'Ethnographies of slow violence: epistemological alliances in fieldwork and narrating ruins', *Environment and Planning C: Politics and Space*, 40(2). 447–462. https://doi.org/10.1177/2399654419881660.

Yugoslawomen+ Collective (2021) 'The Yugoslawomen+ Collective since 2019'. https://yugoslawomenplus.net/ (accessed 14 May 2023).

Žbanić, J. (2015) *One Day in Sarajevo*. Sarajevo: Deblokada.

Zinaić, R. (2016) 'The scope of violence: Elizabeth Dauphinée and the neoliberal moment', *The Slavonic and East European Review*, 94(3), 401–30. https://doi.org/10.5699/slaveasteurorev2.94.3.0401.

6

Hierarchising heritage: bordering Europe and stratified subalternities in the Easts and Souths of Europe

Alexandra Oancă

Introduction: Beyond the unmarked category of Europe

Culture and heritage have figured prominently in European politics, policies and interventions. Starting with the 1980s, programmes such as the European City/Capital of Culture and later the European Heritage Label were explicitly designed to spur Europeanisation, although cultural legacies and de facto initiatives existed. In EU attempts to construct a unified European community and to maintain cultural hegemony and domination, culture and heritage are not only entangled with different forms of violence but foundational and infrastructural to violence.

During my research on EU-supported cultural interventions, I came across a series of comics and political cartoons published by the European Cultural Foundation (2014) that attempt to understand citizenship and the issues facing Europe. I was equally impressed by their critical perspectives on 'Fortress Europe', immigration and enlargement, and disturbed by the b/ordering and narratives that were sometimes reproduced. The comic *The European Dream* by Iranian cartoonist Ali Divandari represents the heavy toll of longing for and belonging to Europe: it shows an overly eager goldfish – meaning all 'those non-Europeans' or 'almost-Europeans' – going full force and colliding into a mirror with stars, leaving the fish dazed, confused and bloody among the shards of the European dream. Another comic, *The Gap* by Turkish cartoonist Halit Kurtulmus Aytoslu, was striking in its criticism of the gap between Fortress Europe and surrounding countries. The cartoon represents Europe as surrounded by a sharp fence that a couple of men attempt to climb over to throw letters in the closed voting box at the centre of EUrope. A child and two women in traditional Islamic clothing are also drawn outside the EU fence. Moreover, whereas EUrope is represented as a uniform place designated through its blue flag with stars, its 'outside' is marked by the presence of mosques, minarets, pyramids and a distant bridge. The underlying assumption of the cartoon is that the migrant, the veiled woman and the mosque are only present outside of the EU: these are representative of 'the rest' and do not belong in Europe, even though they long for it.

As Manuela Boatcă (2019, 2020) argues, 'Europe' is neither an 'unmarked category', nor a homogenous geo-historical entity with stable borders and a clearly defined space. However, the critique of Fortress Europe represents it as a uniform, undifferentiated, homogenous entity, united 'against all "those" non-Europeans' (Said, 1978: 7). It is associated with a particular heritage and religious and racial make-up, predicated on internal homogeneity and on the absence of Muslims and Islam. In these representations, Islam is represented as an outsider to EUrope, in conjunction with orientalised articulations of urban forms. Heritage, racialisation and bordering go hand in hand in this representation, defining and redefining the stratifications of belonging.

The analytical lens of heritage and heritage-making is particularly productive, as heritage is a significant bordering practice through which Europeanisation operates, in conjunction with other b/ordering practices and forms of violence. EUrope has actively engaged in bordering practices and the continuous making and unmaking of borders and boundaries through its policies (Oancă, 2015; Vos 2011, 2017; Dimitrovova and Kramsch, 2017), including through heritage and cultural policies that rearrange and sanitise Europe's borders and internal hierarchies based on their proximity to an ideal of Westernness and Western European history. In this chapter, I centre the violence of European heritage-making, including cultural interventions – such as the European Capital of Culture – that have been infrastructural to violence via their production of stratified subalternities, rankings of non-Europeanness and non-Westernness, and affective registers of stratified longings and belongings.

Theorising Europeanisation as violence captures a multifaceted and multiscalar process: it ranges from forms of structural, epistemic and slow violence within the institutions, laws and technocratic apparatuses promoted by EUropean powers, from the physical and material violence of European politics in EU-sanctioned border enforcement and border externalisation (Ould Moctar, this volume) to symbolic violence and stratifications (Ivasiuc, this volume). The violence of borders, migration management, military and humanitarian interventions feature significantly in critical accounts of EUrope's engagements with the postcolonial and postsocialist worlds. Concurrently, epistemic, material and slow violence of interventions attempt to b/order Europe from without and from within. Neuman Stanivuković (this volume) explores how infrastructural

Europeanisation operates through promises conditioned on altered behaviour while rendering certain spaces as abject and transitional to Europe, heightening border control and exclusion. Looking at Europeanisation as slow violence in the post-Yugoslav space allows Deiana and Kušić (this volume) to capture the region's ambivalent positioning as both Europe's other and Europe's border guard. From hard and fast to soft and slow violence, and back again, theorising Europeanisation allows us to think relationally about how Europe is bordered both through physical border enforcement and through affective registers and imaginaries of culture, heritage and history. Heritage-making functions as a 'softer', 'slower', insidious bordering practice but is no less effective than border control and externalisation in maintaining inequalities and asymmetrical relations of power.

Looking at Europe from the 'margins' in a relational manner from its Souths and Easts (hereafter, S&E), from Córdoba (Andalusia, Spain) and from Sibiu (Transylvania, Romania), I seek to illuminate the violence of Europeanisation and heritage-making processes. My aim in this chapter is to highlight the production of stratified subalternities and the very conditions upon which one is allowed – or not – into the 'European family'. Different forms of violence, bodies, histories and territories are entangled in Europeanisation. The cities of Andalusia and Transylvania are mirror images – mirrored postcolonialities – of each other and can be seen as useful case studies to grasp how heritage-making and b/ordering are performed. While Spanish historiography and symbolic geographies ended up establishing Al-Andalus (Andalusia) as a 'domestic Orient' of Spain (Fernández Parrilla, 2018; Venegas, 2018), the towns of Saxon colonial settlers in Transylvania (Siebenbürgen) function as a 'domestic Occident' of Romania. In the mirror, these postcolonialities show that Europeanisation produces uneven geographies of stratified subalternities through heritage (including within urban territories) and this enables the disavowal and/or adverse incorporation of Roma and Muslim communities in Europe's S&E.

Thus, in the following, I reflect on the 'inventory' of traces that Europeanisation deposited in me (Said, 1978: 25) and on the spaces made available through my positionality. Then, I conceptualise European heritage-making as violence, locating my mirrored cases in this approach. After that, I analyse dialogically EU-supported initiatives such as the European City/Capital of Culture (ECoC) across Sibiu and Córdoba: in one section on the politics and practices of selection, valuation and racialised overevaluation of ethnicities and histories perceived as close to Westernness, and another section on how European heritage-making processes overemphasises peace and conceals past and present violences.

Mirror, mirror on the wall: Unlearning the cruel optimism of Europeanisation

To enable an alter-geography of heritage initiatives across the South and East of Europe, in what follows I do not aim to either fix the regions I speak about/with/from, nor to hide or flatten my embodied positionality and the affect of academic critique. However, listing categories of identity and belonging (such as Romanian, woman, precarious anthropologist, neurodivergent, based in Belgium) is not enough to subvert epistemic authority nor to illuminate how the personal shapes research. For Gabriel Dattatreyan (2014: 155), the dangers of 'laundry lists' is that anthropologists 'potentially reify categorical markings, such as race, class, ethnicity etc., and thereby limit the heuristic possibilities of self-reflexivity'. This demands that we attune ourselves to how our shifting positionalities and social relations shape the research process and (im)mobilise access to particular spaces of Europeanisation.

South and East are not precise geographical locations but shattered 'fleshscapes' (Weheliye, 2014) and wounded 'bodyminds' (Schalk, 2018) that allow us to problematise Europeanisation as violence and to connect its many locations, territories and histories. 'After all, only the wearer knows where the shoe pinches' (Doharty, 2020: 556), potentially giving access to forms of situated knowledge. As such, my choice to start this chapter with the figure of the overeager-to-wounded fish represented in the comic *European Dream* by Divandari was motivated both by my argument and the affective politics of location. My own navigations of Western Europe and academia as a subject racialised and gendered as an 'Eastern European woman' left me too dazed, confused and wounded among the shards of the European dream, still unlearning its 'cruel optimism' (Berlant, 2011). I am speaking as a woman of the border who has 'one foot in and one foot out' of the academy (Behar, 1996: 162), from bodyminds wounded by the triple bind of academic precarity, market capitalism and lingua franca, and often marked as deficient or unproductive compared to the white Western male ideal of the successful academic. As a Romanian diasporic scholar currently based in Western Europe, I found Europeanisation marked by shifting, relational class and racial markers, and by growing disillusionment, doubts and wounds associated with postsocialist transition and the academic market.

The logic of optimism associated with Europeanisation described by Katarina Kušić (this volume) resonates with me, and probably with other of Central East Europe (CEE) diasporic scholars of our generation. Born shortly before 1989, I grew up in Galați, Eastern Romania, in the 1990s and 2000s, shaped by the (failed) promises and (cruel) optimism of both the transition to capitalism and the return to Europe. Growing up in Galați, a major industrial city during socialism, allowed – or forced – me to see up close and personal the devastating effects of privatisation on major local industries in 1999–2002 and generally of the shock therapy promoted by the International Monetary Fund in postsocialist Romania. This led to a collapse of the local economy and pushed many to migrate, particularly to Spain, Italy and Germany; however, the aspiring middle-class position of my parents remained stable and protected me from the brunt of both postsocialist shock therapy and transnational migration. The privatisation of Galaţi's major steel plant and its devastating local effects later became the focus of my BA thesis in sociology at the University of Bucharest.

Moving as a young woman from an Eastern city in the historical region of Moldova to Bucharest, and then to Budapest and Sibiu to pursue graduate studies and research at the Central European University, involved a significant reckoning with Romanian and Hungarian brands of racism, sexism and exclusion, more particularly with nesting orientalisms and self-colonising practices through which 'people subverted their own (Orientalised/Balkanised) identities by orientalising one another' (Velickovic, 2012: 166). This legacy of nesting orientalisms meant that discrimination was 'always directed at those who were on the next rung down geographically and economically' (Velickovic, 2012: 166). So, in Romania, this is directed at Moldovan Romanians and Romanians of Roma ethnicity, particularly vis-à-vis the capital and Transylvania, its 'domestic Occident'. This gradation of nested 'Orients' refers to a tendency of each region to view the territories to its South and East as inferior.

My biography and migration experience involved both shifting class privileges and subaltern positions, including experiences of being subject to nested orientalisms and racial Europeanisation. As Çankaya and Mepschen (2019) argue, ethnographers, too, are subject to racial Europeanisation during research, and are involved in the relational production of whiteness in research settings. Moreover, positionality is relational and can shift between places and times: in Sibiu, Transylvania, that meant a reckoning with a Romanian brand of nested orientalism vis-à-vis Moldova, while in Córdoba that meant navigating research as a 'Romanian migrant woman' in a region with significant immigration of Romanians in agriculture, construction and services. For some of my interlocutors, my ability to be there to study 'up (professional) Spaniards' and not pick strawberries somewhere in Andalusia made me a curiosity and an exception. As Ana Ivasiuc would put it, even though passing as white, I was embodying a racialised figure: the 'Good Western Eastern European' migrant since 'racialised middle-class people are often more easily accepted in "polite" society than some members of the white working class' (Çankaya and Mepschen, 2019: 629). I was able to pass and to navigate those research spaces due to the embodiment of this racialised figure, my middle-class background and affiliation with a Hungarian university. As a researcher that mirrored, or attempted to mirror, the classed and racialised performance of most of my white interlocutors, they felt comfortable sometimes making 'polite' utterances with classist, racist undertones, assuming that I thought or should think the same.

Both in academic and policy-making spaces, including during research in Córdoba and Brussels, I often wondered 'what to wear for whiteness' and self-policed my appearance and behaviour, aware that the bodies of Eastern European women are read 'not as "quite" white/western' and 'perceived as sexually excessive and in need of toning down' (Krivonos and Diatlova, 2020: 116). This implied studying and carefully enacting a particular type of upper middle-class whiteness and toned-down femininity through dress, talk or behaviour, that would not bar my access by default to people, places and meetings. It was of course an imperfect performance with plenty of slippages and moments when 'a certain body posture, a single word or an [...] item of clothing can betray one's status in society' (Çankaya and Mepschen, 2019: 630), though those slippages are too numerous to analyse here.

Despite this, there were spaces of Europeanisation that became available to me through my shifting positionality, spaces that scholars of colour and/or from working-class backgrounds might not be granted access to (Khosravi, 2021). Although 'studying up' Europeanisation has the potential to turn the gaze on spaces of power, it also carries the danger of re/racialising knowledge production and academic labour by limiting 'studying up' and access to powerful institutions to researchers that can perform (Western) Europeanness and a middle-class habitus. Access to white powerful individuals and organisations was sometimes limited or barred, but my right to 'study up' was not contested by my interlocutors in the way discussed by Yildiz (2020). For anthropologists, more routinely interested in studying 'down', there's an uncanniness in researching with/about interlocutors that mirror back at you different versions of your own life and professional trajectory. Thus, it is important to remain reflexive on both the privileges and subaltern positions underpinned in turning the gaze on violent processes of Europeanisation as white Eastern European women, often employed in Western and Northern institutions.

Without projecting my own wounds or competing for woundedness or victimhood, in this chapter I centre doubt about the promises and cruel optimism of Europeanisation, post-socialist transition and EU enlargement to the S&E of Europe. That doubt can connect our own wounds in a relational way: for the stratified subalternities of EUrope, either adversely incorporated or downright excluded for which full, uncomplicated belonging is out of reach, the shards of the so-called European dream appear as the actual unifying characteristics of Europeanisation. Instead of romanticising solidarities across subalternities or flattening difference (between Sibiu and Córdoba, between marginalised communities, between Europe's many gradations of otherness), I attend to the uneven processes that produce these gradations.

In the trenches and mirrors of Europe's b/ordering: Conceptualising European heritage-making as violence

Spurred by feelings of cultural superiority, exceptionalism and its *mission civilisatrice*, culture and heritage have long been seen as one of the markers of Western Europe vis-à-vis its past and present others. Assertions of Europe as 'cultural superpower in the world' continue to be made by EU officials (Mogherini, 2018). As an approach, creolising Europe contests this cultural superiority and the centring of Europe as 'a geographically, culturally, religiously, and racially coherent entity' (Parvulescu and Boatcă, 2022: 4). Moreover, if heritage and culture were 'conceived originally as an entity with fixed boundaries marking off insiders against outsiders, we need to ask who set these borders and who now guards the ramparts' (Wolf, 1999: 67). Specific policies and societal norms are implemented to strengthen cultural identification with Europe among its citizens, so that they can become 'European' or 'more European' (Sassatelli, 2009; Lähdesmäki, 2012). But what are the hegemonic understandings of 'European heritage' and Europeanness? Beyond the official rhetoric of 'united in diversity', what counts and does not count as 'European culture' or 'European heritage'? What are the epistemic and material practices that attempt to shape and reshape 'European heritage' from without and from within? Who upholds the stratification? How are the various rankings of non-Westernness and stratified subalternities upheld? These are some of the questions that structure this section on the place of heritage and cultural interventions within Europeanisation.

In the early stages of the European project, culture and heritage were strongly embedded in its imaginaries and narratives but not targeted through official policies or initiatives. Europeanisation has been narrated as a benevolent, post-war peace project in which political and economic unification functioned as both antidote and deterrent to future conflicts. Enlargement beyond the original the 'original' six member states (Belgium, France, Germany, Italy, Luxembourg and the Netherlands) and towards the S&E has often been portrayed as progress and as a technical-juridical matter that goes uncontested. Critical scholars, particularly from decolonial, postcolonial and postsocialist perspectives, have long questioned both the positive, linear narratives of enlargement and 'transitology' and the sanitised history of EUrope, particularly its othering practices and its occlusion of EU's colonial history and legacies (Hansen, 2002; Hansen and Jonsson, 2011, 2014; Velickovic, 2012; Kuus, 2004, 2014; Bhambra, 2016; Buettner, 2016; Boatcă, 2019). Dimier and McGeever (2006, 2014) argue that European integration functioned as a recycling ground for European empires, and that former colonial agents, particularly French and Belgian, were integrated within its emerging development aid architecture. For these authors, post-war European integration emerged as an attempt to rescue crumbling empires after decolonisation and to sublimate imperialism and colonialism into a more politically acceptable project during a rapidly advancing process of decolonisation.

I am analysing Europeanisation and enlargement towards the S&E not as a triumphant story of the cosmopolitan, linear expansion of the idea of Europe nor as 'the return to Europe' but as a redirection and reframing by which European nations were able to sublimate colonial and imperial legacies and 'learned to redirect their ambition from without to within' (Nicolaïdis, Sèbe and Maas, 2015: 288), towards accelerated processes of extraction, b/ordering and uneven development[1] in the S&E of Europe. Thus, enlargement has been one of the toolkits of neoliberal capitalism and 'empire(s) at home', through which EUrope has 'continually constructed its own exclusive boundary – and transgressed it' (Asad, 2003: 170). This made the EU into an intercontinental institutional formation that extends beyond Europe to North Africa, South America, the Caribbean and the Pacific (Boatcă, 2019), as enlargement included countries with diverse colonial and imperial histories and with semi/peripheral positions, with countries of CEE and Southern Europe being placed in a perpetual catching-up position in relation to Western Europe.

The 1980s was the decade of the so-called Mediterranean enlargement and the (adverse) incorporation of post-dictatorship Greece (1981) and Spain and Portugal (1986) into the fold (after the initial rejection of Francoist Spain's application in 1964). In this decade, 'culturalist' approaches became part of the toolbox of European integration. Spain, and particularly Andalusia, is positioned as a place that was 'orientalizing (and colonizing) at the same time it was orientalized' due to its Islamic heritage and Francoist dictatorship, a 'situation that created (and still creates) many disorientations' (Fernández Parrilla, 2018: 229) for postcolonial and decolonial perspectives.

Then, the EU enlargement extended East to postsocialist countries in 2004 and 2007, with Romania joining in 2007. This led to the inclusion of regions with inter-imperial conditions, uniquely positioned at the intersection of and across a variety of empires (Ottoman, Russian, Austro-Hungarian, Habsburg), such as Transylvania (Parvulescu and Boatcă, 2022), that had gone through socialist state-building projects (including technologies of ethnic homogenisation and assimilation into socialist modernity) and postsocialist, neoliberal transformations. Thus, (orientalised) Andalusia and (inter-imperial) Transylvania complicate both the models of orientalism and colonialism that critics have developed for Europe's Norths and Wests.

Particularly, the accession of CEE and Southern European countries has been narrated as civilisational and saturated by Eurocentric, orientalist discourses on European identity. Civilising narratives, moral paternalism, conditionality and asymmetrical relationships have been part and parcel of Europeanisation. Despite significant differences between S&E Europe and former European colonies, Western dominant representations bear uncanny similarities: they are cast as incomplete, as 'not yet', or as 'not fully' white/European/developed, kept in perpetual waiting and incompleteness (see Deiana and Kušić, in this volume for the post-Yugoslav space). Without subsuming one experience under another, countering these narratives allows for productive alliances between postsocialism and postcolonialism to make sense of the ways in which this incompleteness is gradated, stratified and refracted in the mirrors, gates and trenches of Europe's b/ordering.

As such, enlargement did not imply a simple 'dissolution of Europe's "Other" and its assimilation into the "Self"' but also 'the redefinition and the renegotiation of the very "Self"' (Tzifakis, 2007, 13). It did not involve just a reproduction of earlier 'gradients of Europe' and symbolic geographies (see Figure 1, Lévy, 1977), but a more striking exclusion of non-EU European territories from symbolic imaginaries together with a redrawing and sanitation of territories within the EU. Europeanisation is a sanitation and reorganisation of 'Souths within Souths', 'Wests within Easts' and 'Easts within Wests', based on EU membership, their proximity to Western ideals, histories and indicators of economic development (see Figure 2, EU regions, Lambrechts, 2019). Lambrechts (2019) discusses how the EU, nation states and even local authorities have redrawn their borders and reorganised their territories according to a less developed-more developed axis, to attract EU funding to the former.

While both Spain and Romania are seen as 'margins' of contemporary Europe, not least because of their economic positions and post-dictatorship and respectively postsocialist histories, the regions of Andalusia and Transylvania are mirror images of each other across 'core' European metropoles, the Iron Curtain and capitalist structures. Although Spain has been a colonial power and a major country for Romanian immigration after the 1990s, Andalusia (Al-Andalus) is represented as a 'domestic Orient' of Spain and Europe due to uneven development and its legacies of Islamic past (Fernández Parrilla, 2018), while Sibiu and other towns of Saxon colonial settlers in the region of Transylvania (Siebenbürgen) are seen as a 'domestic Occident' of Romania. In Eurostat statistics,[2] both Transylvania and Andalusia are placed in 'the red': they are labelled as less developed regions with a respective GDP of 60–67 per cent and 68 per cent of the EU average. While Transylvania is in a more advantageous position than the rest of Romania, Andalusia is in a disadvantaged position vis-à-vis most of Spain's autonomous communities. Moreover, Andalusia has been orientalised and fetishised both within Spain and Europe. In contrast, Transylvania has been perceived as the embodiment of a higher culture within Romanian territories. Like looking in a mirror, what was right appears to be left. These are places that modulate across imperial nostalgia, aspirations to Europeanness and racial capitalist structures. Their mirrored postcolonialities show that being (partially) labelled as European heritage depends on the disavowal and marginalisation of European others.

Hierarchising heritage: The politics and practices of valuation and selection

As heritage has long been associated with positive and productive values, critical heritage studies increasingly deal with dark, difficult, dissonant and negative heritage and its legacies of violence, particularly heritage associated with wars, genocides, colonialism and dictatorship; this approach also problematises the politics and dissent of 'regular' heritage processes (Macdonald, 2009; González-Ruibal, 2015). Moreover, heritage has been shaped by nation states and increasingly by European institutions and connected to the making of state power and dominant identities. As Ashworth and Tunbridge (1996: 21) mention, '(a)ll heritage is someone's heritage and therefore logically not someone else's: the original meaning of an inheritance (from which "heritage" derives) implies the existence of disinheritance and by extension any creation of heritage from the past disinherits someone completely or partially, actively or potentially'. Heritage and cultural interventions are powerful precisely because they are curated and can be harmonised with the objectives of Europeanisation, from 'integrated rehabilitation' to leaving the (socialist and Francoist) past behind (Kirshenblatt-Gimblett, 2004; Vos, 2011). These authorised interventions are expected to bring about Europeanisation in its margins: to dissolve Europe's 'others' and assimilate them into the European 'family'. Looking at what historical urban forms and built environments are selected and preserved in these territories allow us to see what and whose heritage is selected and preserved. This is an important question, particularly as these valuations and choices are embedded within relations of powers, and within postcolonial and postsocialist legacies and asymmetries. To achieve this, in this section I focus on the politics of selection and on the presuppositions and resonances embedded in selection processes in the European Capital of Culture policy, for Sibiu and Córdoba.

In the 1980s, in synchronicity with the accession of post-dictatorship Southern European countries, 'culturalist' approaches became part of the toolbox of European integration (Shore, 2000; Sassatelli, 2009; Lähdesmäki, 2011, 2012). Cultural policies were considered necessary for the integration and identity-building of members states not just through economy and politics but also through culture. The ECoC was established in 1985, after the proposal of the Greek minister of culture (Melina Mercouri), and it was imagined as a top-down tool meant 'to bring the peoples of the Member States closer together' through culture, more precisely through a programme in which cities celebrate their status as cultural centres of Europe (EC, 1985). It is considered a success and a 'brand' of the European Union, as it became a dominant policy paradigm for how 'European' culture, memory and heritage can be articulated, promoted and sold in cities.

To create cultural coherence and promote a sense of belonging and awareness of the common history, culture and value of EUrope, the EU cultural policy-makers made choices. The first two cities which held the title were chosen as Athens and Florence both to reassert the European identity of post-dictatorship Greece and to assert the existence of a historical link between Greek and Roman antiquity and the contemporary European project. from which EUrope draws its cultural identity and hegemony from Romantic perceptions of a Europe that started with the Greek and Roman empires. The next ECoC cities were Amsterdam, Berlin and Paris. Further, for 1992 the Spanish authorities lobbied for the title of ECoC for Madrid in order to coincide with the Barcelona Olympic Games, the Expo in Seville (Andalusia) and the unabashed celebrations of the 'Fifth Centenary of the discovery of America'. It bears noting that 1492 was not just the year of Columbus's voyages to the Americas but also the completion of the Christian Reconquest (Reconquista), the end of Muslim Rule in Andalusia (711–1492) and the expulsion of Jews from Spanish territories. In their ECoC application, the Spanish authorities 'showcased a new Spain eager to cast off its inferiority complex as a European backwater' (Venegas, 2018: 6). Through these synchronous mega-events and brazen celebrations of colonial history and conquest, Spanish officials were hoping to mark 1992 as its triumphant return to democratic and capitalist Europe. Thus, colonial heritage was still authorised and promoted as one of the markers of the 'new' EUrope, continuing to provide legitimacy to celebratory, positive discourse of colonialism for European citizens.

After EU enlargements to the S&E, 'modernisation' and 'Europeanisation' appeared as the main aims of the ECoC programme, alongside rationales of economic development via culture. Sibiu's tenure as ECoC coincided with Romania's accession to the EU in 2007, heralded as the 'return to Europe'. In the 2000s, Sibiu gained leverage and competitive advantage over other Romanian cities, due to its Saxon/German 'heritage' and the (disproven) myth of common linguistic origins with Luxembourg. After lobbying initiatives, Luxembourg officials invited Sibiu to jointly apply in 2004 for the 2007 title. Romanian and Luxembourg officials motivated these decisions on the founding myths of the city of Sibiu by German/Saxon colonisers and on historical, architectural and linguistic links. Although the thesis of common linguistic origins between the Luxembourg language and the language spoken by the Saxons of Transylvania was disproved in 1905, it still holds importance in public discourse (Oancă, 2010). The myth of common origins persisted because it provided historical weight to a micro-state, Luxembourg, and a connection to Western Europe to a small Eastern European city, Sibiu. While Sibiu's application jumped the queue vis-à-vis other CEE cities that could only apply after 2009, it was applauded as aiming 'at the higher goal of acquainting and bringing closer Western and Eastern Europe as cornerstone of European integration', but conditionally approved with a clause meant 'to safeguard the high standard of the ECoC event' (selection panel cited in Oancă, 2010: 55). Just like the restrictive clauses of Romania's enlargement, Sibiu was partially and adversely integrated within the ECoC family in 2007.

Sibiu's title as ECoC in 2007 put forward a multicultural and multi-ethnic history of the city in which Romanians, Saxons/Germans, Hungarians and Roma supposedly lived together peacefully. It emphasised the German heritage of the city and the contribution made by Saxon colonial settlers to the city's heritage at the expense of other heritage or urban forms. The history of the multicultural city was put forward although Transylvanian Saxons currently amount to less than 2 per cent of Sibiu's population (96 per cent Romanians). Contemporary Sibiu and Transylvania have been characterised as performing 'Saxonness without Saxons', 'Germanicity without Germans', 'Philo-Germanism without Germans' (Cercel, 2015), or multiculturalism without multiculturalism.

As such, although local authorities formally promoted a multicultural image of a 'City of Cultures', Sibiu's ECoC was underpinned by a hierarchisation of ethnicities and heritages with Saxons/Germans at the top. I call this process 'multicultural monoculturalism' to emphasise the promotion of a historical multiculturalism and to contest the dominant 'unity in diversity', multicultural discourses of EUrope.

Sibiu was always used in association with the German name of the city, Hermannstadt, and it ascribed a positive value to the settler colonisation process undertaken by German Saxons in the twelfth century, when at the behest of the Magyar King Géza II, settlers from different German-speaking regions, such as the Mosel region, Flanders and Luxembourg, were invited to defend Transylvania's border area and to colonise the *presumably deserted territory* newly conquered by the Hungarian Crown. As Cristian Cercel (2012: 83) argues, '(t)heir migration to Eastern Europe is historically part of the so-called Deutsche Ostsiedlung, German colonization towards East [...], a quintessential process in view of the subsequent shaping of German identity in the Central and Eastern parts of the European continent'. As the settlements urbanised, privileges were given to German settlers.

These practices of valuing German heritage in 'return to Europe' narratives have been noticed in other postsocialist and post-communist cities, such as Kaliningrad/Königsberg (Sezneva, 2000, 2012) and Wrocław/Breslau (Halauniova, 2021). Halauniova and Sezneva (2021) argue that ascribing aesthetic value is not simply a matter of taste divorced from the social order. Rather, practices of valuation are reflective of its complexity and inequalities. In Sibiu, valuing German heritage implied ascribing an aesthetic stigma to socialist architecture and devaluing and vilifying socialist history. The aesthetic binary opposition between 'Romanian socialist/ugly' and 'German/beautiful' worked together with a binary between socialist and pre- or postsocialist histories.

Thus, Romania and Sibiu signalled Europeanisation and 'return to Europe' through the valorisation of Saxon settler colonialism and German heritage and embedded in nesting orientalism. It was presented as the meeting point of European civilisations, with Sibiu acting as the 'easternmost European city' since the seventeenth century. Yet, presenting Sibiu as the gateway to the West and placing it 'at the border of "Central Europe" practically "de-orientalizes" it, while at the same time ascribes an "Oriental" identity to everything lying east and south of it' (Cercel, 2015: 821). The perception of Saxonness as 'embodiment of a higher culture and symbol of civilisation' has been accompanied by a perception of the Romanian/Wallachian other as Balkan/oriental, which reinforce stereotypes of the Balkans as the uncivilised, backward region on the 'other' side of the Carpathians (Cercel, 2012).

Both Sibiu and Córdoba put forward applications as multicultural, multiconfessional cities (that emphasised certain ethnicities and religions): Sibiu as 'City of Culture. City of Cultures', Córdoba as 'the city of the three cultures'. However, as mirrored postcolonialities, these strategies were received differently. While it was strategic to bet on the 'occident' within Sibiu, the domestic Occident of Romania, it proved unsuccessful to emphasise the 'orient' within Córdoba, the domestic orient of Spain (even though Islamic legacy is already adversely incorporated within post-Francoist Spain).

As Sibiu was (conditionally) included in the ECoC family in 2007, in 2016 Córdoba was not; Islamic heritage was devalued in a competitive bidding process for the ECoC title. Córdoba put forward an image of 'the city of the three cultures' premised on the so-called Paradigm of Córdoba, religious coexistence between Christianity, Islam and Judaism inspired by the Al-Andalus past, although Christianity is the majoritarian religion in Córdoba (and Sibiu). Córdoba became a contentious place through which Islam, usually one of Europe's others, is marked as European and reintroduced as part of local, national and European cultural interventions (Arigita, 2013). However, this new narrative about Europe regarding Islam was rejected. As one interlocutor underlined,

> very conservative decisions were taken in the candidacy … They stayed with the safe. The mosque does not fail, patrimony does not fail, the three cultures cannot fail. It was a model of culture about exhibitions, heritage, and tourism; they did not dare to leave the past behind and propose a truly innovative project. (interview)

Jury members and cultural professionals underscored that the candidacy was stuck in the lost Islamic splendour of Al-Andalus past and that it was not 'modern' or 'forward-thinking' enough. For Merve Kayikci (2020), representing Islam as a tradition of splendour and bliss further places Islam and Muslims in an immemorial past and writes them as the other civilisation. Both local and European heritage-making evacuated and reduced the legacies of Spain's and Europe's Islamic past to its architectural gems, at the expense of contemporary religious and cultural practices. While the supporters and detractors of the candidacy embraced and respectively rejected the aesthetic valuation of Islam, they both rejected its morality, norms and religious practices.

This process showed an ambivalent incorporation of a quintessential Andalusian identity, premised on Al-Andalus heritage and the exotic valuation of Roma heritage, particularly of flamenco. Within (post)Francoist Spain, perceptions of Islamic heritage and the Afro-Moorish past have fluctuated between the denial and acceptance. José Luis Venegas (2018: 13) argues that Moorish Andalusia as Spain's orient was a characterisation made by Western European Romantic writers of the nineteenth century, and that the Spaniards internalised these orientalised stereotypes to resist their colonial identifications which they 'saw alternatively and contradictorily as a marker of identity and a despised self-image'. To complicate matters, Andalusia's shifting engagements with oriental otherness were used as a justification of colonial intervention in Morocco, as a hinderance to Europeanisation and as marker of cultural authenticity in tourism. During the developmentalism of the 1960s, tourism and agriculture were prioritised in the South-East and Mediterranean coast of Spain, including in Andalusia, through an exotic valuation of Romani folklore, customs and flamenco dancers and of Islamic heritage as flashy promotion for international tourism and propaganda during Franco's regime (Pack, 2006; see also Drăgan, in this volume). After the end of Franco's regime in 1975, institutional efforts were made 'to free Andalusia from folkloric connotations, not only in Spain, but in Europe and the world' (Venegas, 2018: 16), and to free them from Franco's heritage-making.

The way the markers of Córdoba's identity was narrated for the ECoC – and then rejected – is emblematic of a reluctance within post-Francoist Spain and Europe to fully value Islamic heritage as part of Europe (Fadil, 2019, 2022). Whereas Córdoba's candidacy was embedded within debates on whether Islam was an integral part of Spanish/European history and identity or an impediment to its development, Sibiu's tenure as ECoC never had to debate the importance of Saxon settler colonialism and German heritage for Romanian and European history. These mirrored postcolonialities show the stratified subalternities, valuations and hierarchies made within European heritage-making. Within its modus operandi of multicultural monoculturalism, ethnicities, histories and places are valorised and marked as (almost or not-quite) 'European', depending on their proximity to an ideal of Western European heritage and history, while others (such as Muslims and Roma) are excluded from those narratives, or adversely incorporated.

European heritage-making as violence: the concealment of past and present violences

The previous section shows that the violence of European heritage-making comes from its racialised, stratified politics of valuation and selection in the Easts and Souths of Europe. So, on the one hand, 'multicultural monoculturalism' selects and hierarchises, while overvaluing ethnicities perceived as close to Westernness, and on the other hand, it overemphasises peace and conceals the violence of multicultural societies and heritage-making processes. Only a partial analysis of these past and present violences is offered.

As Maria Cardeira da Silva (2012: 68) discusses, in cities which laud themselves as 'the city of three cultures' like Sibiu and Córdoba, it is all too 'easy to insist on the notions of diversity and conviviality, which really only conceal and aestheticize a succession of historical events' and frequently hides moments of conflict and 'multiculturalist' policies of segregation. Churches that become mosques or synagogues – or mosques or synagogues that become churches like the Mezquita of Córdoba – 'reflect the presences of different religious groups at different times' (Cardeira da Silva, 2012: 68), but the synthetic and uncritical argument is that of a timeless fusion of a common past, in which conflict and inequalities are concealed.

Historical facts are much more complicated than what is promoted in relation to multiculturalism, coexistence and conviviality (Arigita, 2009, 2013; Venegas, 2018). The Mosque–Cathedral of Córdoba (also known as the Great Mosque or Mezquita of Córdoba) has been promoted as a symbol of conviviality and religious coexistence, especially during the ECoC bid. Built for Islamic worship beginning in the eighth century and reconstructed as a Catholic church in the thirteenth century, the temple became a symbol of the restoration of the Catholic faith after the Reconquista in Córdoba and the later expulsion of Jews and Muslims from Iberia. In 1998, its name was changed in tourist brochures to the 'Cathedral (former Mosque)' of Córdoba. At the height of the ECoC bid, the Catholic Church banned Muslim prayer in the building in 2004, and renamed it as Córdoba Cathedral, removing the word 'mosque' altogether in 2010. A backlash and a local campaign caused the church to restore the 'Mosque–Cathedral' name, yet only in 2016, long before Córdoba's loss of the ECoC competition. While today, the monument's hybrid nature is reflected in its name, the Mosque–Cathedral is supervised by the local diocese and only Christians are allowed to worship there (with security guards monitoring and forbidding Muslims praying). As such, for contemporary Córdoba, the Mezquita belongs exclusively to Spanish Christians, despite historical conviviality and the fantasies of a multicultural, multi-confessional past. Moreover, Córdoba signalled Europeanisation and 'its European dimension' through the historical conviviality of three religions (Christianity, Islam and Judaism), at the expense of contemporary non-conviviality and present-day campaigns made by Spanish Muslims since the 2000s to allow inter-confessional prayer in the Mezquita and other historical mosques.

Similarly, historical facts are much more complicated than what was promoted in Sibiu's multicultural narrative. Transylvania was indeed a multi-ethnic, multi-confessional and multi-lingual region but one characterised by deep fractures and inequalities, as brilliantly analysed by Parvulescu and Boatcă (2022). During socialism, Sibiu and its Saxon historical quarter was not demolished but went through disinvestment and ethnic homogenisation, including through the emigration of German settlers, industrialisation and the construction of satellite, self-sufficient neighbourhoods in the peripheries of the city. Thus, the Saxon historical quarter of Sibiu became a relatively isolated and underprivileged urban area, characterised by neglect and urban poverty.

Overvaluing Saxon heritage hid moments of conflict within settler colonisation and its aftermaths, while vilifying the socialist period. In 'the model city of Europeanism' in the year of Romania's integration in EUrope (as Klaus Iohannis called it), this overvaluation of German heritage involved valuation of an 'ethnic and racial field' when ethnic Romanians were second-class citizens and 'where anti-Jewish and anti-Romani sentiments were produced relationally, through the stereotypical comparison of the two groups' (Parvulescu and Boatcă, 2022: 61). This heritage-making process has wide ranging effects, particularly its influence over regional and national electoral politics, its consolidation of the uneven development of Sibiu and Transylvania, and the racialised gentrification of city centre.

At the local level, institutions that did not fit the perception of urban German heritage as the embodiment of a higher culture – such as the ASTRA open-air museum of Romanian rural and peasant life, including Roma artefacts and lives – were disadvantaged within Sibiu's ECoC programme. Furthermore, promoting German and pre-twentieth-century architecture as the most representative of European heritage contributed to the state-led gentrification of the historical quarter of Sibiu and the displacement of Roma and/or working-class inhabitants. For public officials, these inhabitants 'live in horrible conditions; they do not value these buildings, they do not know' (interview). As such, they justified the racial sanitisation and emptying of the city centre with dehumanising animal metaphors usually associated with discriminated groups. Moreover, the costs of renovating historical buildings, in conjunction with an increase in tourism and heritage initiatives, led to an increase of tourists, prices, rents and noise levels and a population decline in the city centre. The German Society for Technical Cooperation (GTZ) started renovating in 2000 and spearheaded gentrification with its projects of regeneration, renovating 'a house here, another there in order to induce competition among neighbours' (interview). Finally, the actors and institutions which benefited the most from the investments in cultural distinctiveness and Saxon heritage which produced monopoly rents in the centre were 'the Evangelical Lutheran Church, the Orthodox Church, the Catholic Church and some really important people; all of them own almost 70% of the centre of Sibiu' (Gicu cited in Oancă, 2010: 59). Most strikingly, the Democratic Forum of Germans in Romania made considerable advances in the region, and Klaus Iohannis, the former mayor of Sibiu (2000–14) became the current president of Romania (2014–present). The ethnic and racial valuation attached to Saxons and to heritage-making processes undoubtedly contributed to this success.

Conclusion

If heritage can function as 'a mirror that society holds up to itself, to reflect upon and understand itself as it undergoes change, and furthermore to manage this social change' (Lafrenz Samuels cited in Fryer, 2023: 424), what is the distorted image of Europeanisation that it is reflected back at us? In this chapter, I highlighted that Europeanisation actively excludes and adversely incorporates ethnicities, histories and places in its heritage-making processes.

To reinscribe Europeanness, both Sibiu and Córdoba put forward a multicultural, multi-ethnic and peaceful history of the city that evacuated past and present violences, while hierarchising ethnicities, histories and places from not-quite to almost 'European', depending on their proximity to an ideal of Westernness. Sibiu, seen as the 'domestic Occident' of Romania, signalled Europeanisation and 'return to Europe' through the valorisation of Saxon settler colonialism and German heritage at the expense of Romanian, Hungarian and Roma heritage, again placing the latter groups in a 'not-yet-European' position. Córdoba, seen as the 'domestic Orient' of Spain, attempted (unsuccessfully) to signal 'its European dimension' through the historical conviviality of three religions (Christianity, Islam and Judaism), at the expense of present-day campaigns made by Spanish Muslims to allow inter-confessional prayer in historical mosques. Moreover, these processes are emblematic of a reluctance within post-Francoist Spain and Europe to fully value Islamic heritage as part of the European family. As such, the violence of Europeanisation is premised not just on the reproduction of older symbolic geographies but on a further stratification of these stratified subalternities across territories and histories (a reorganisation of Souths within Souths, Wests within Easts and Easts within Wests) and even bodies (such the stratifications of the good-bad-ugly Eastern Europeans discussed by Ivasiuc).

Dealing with mirrored postcolonialities across the Souths and Easts of Europe has epistemic potential, particularly with Transylvania's and Andalusia's in-between status: between orientalising and being orientalised, asymmetrically integrated within empires and colonial powers, and within nation building. In considering these disorientations, I have argued here that (orientalised) Andalusia and (inter-imperial) Transylvania complicate the models of both orientalism and colonialism that critics have developed for Western colonial powers. Spain's shifting engagements with Andalusia's otherness could better be accounted through 'nesting orientalisms' (Bakić-Hayden, 1995), an approach more common in CEE. A detailed relational engagement both with Andalusia's and Transylvania's 'inter-imperial creolization' and legacies (Parvulescu and Boatcă, 2022) would be a necessary contribution to understanding complex geohistories of Europeanisation as violence.

Notes

1 These processes of subordination, both before and during the European project, have been conceptualised in a variety of ways – such as 'internal colonialism', 'domestic colonialism' and the turn inward to colony, 'intra-European colonization', Arneil, 2017; Głowacka-Grajper, 2018 – however, a comprehensive analysis of their advantages and limits is beyond the scope of this chapter.

2 Eurostat statistics and the creation of the Nomenclature of territorial units for statistics (the NUTS classifications) have been instrumental for the stratification of subalternities and b/ordering of Europe. The drive towards quantification and the poetics and politics of EU statistics would demand a separate analysis.

References

Arigita, E. (2009) 'Spain – the Al-Andalus legacy', in Hansen, S., Mesoy, A. and Kardas T. (eds) *The Borders of Islam: Exploring Samuel Huntingtons's Faultlines*. London: Hurst and Columbia University Press, pp. 223–34.
Arigita, E. (2013) 'The 'Cordoba paradigm': memory and silence around Europe's Islamic past', in Peter, F., Dornhof, S. and Arigita, E. (eds) *Islam and the Politics of Culture in Europe: Memory, Aesthetics, Art*. New York: Colombia University Press, pp. 21–40.
Arneil, B. (2017) *Domestic Colonies: The Turn Inward to Colony. Domestic Colonies: The Turn Inward to Colony*. Oxford: Oxford University Press.
Asad, T. (2003) *Formations of the Secular: Christianity, Islam, Modernity*. Stanford: Stanford University Press.
Bakić-Hayden, M. (1995) 'Nesting orientalisms: the case of former Yugoslavia', *Slavic Review*, 54(4), 917–31. https://doi.org/10.2307/2501399.
Behar, R. (1996) *The Vulnerable Observer: Anthropology That Breaks Your Heart*. Boston, MA: Beacon Press.
Berlant, L. (2011) *Cruel Optimism*. Durham, NC: Duke University Press.
Bhambra, G. K. (2016) 'Whither Europe? Postcolonial versus neocolonial cosmopolitanism', *Interventions*, 18(2), 187–202. https://doi.org/10.1080/1369801X.2015.1106964.
Boatcă, M. (2019) 'Forgotten Europes: rethinking regional entanglements from the Caribbean', in Cairo, H. and Bringel, B. (eds) *Critical Geopolitics and Regional (Re)Configurations*. London: Routledge, pp. 96–116.
Boatcă, M. (2020) 'Thinking Europe otherwise: lessons from the Caribbean', *Current Sociology*, 69(3), 389–414. https://doi.org/10.1177/0011392120931139.
Buettner, E. (2016) *Europe after Empire: Decolonization, Society, and Culture. Europe After Empire: Decolonization, Society, and Culture*. Cambridge: Cambridge University Press.
Çankaya, S. and Paul, M. (2019) 'Facing racism: discomfort, innocence and the liberal peripheralisation of race in the Netherlands', *Social Anthropology* 27(4), 626–40. https://doi.org/10.1111/1469-8676.12699.
Cardeira da Silva, M. (2012) 'Castles abroad: nations, culture and cosmopolitanisms in African heritage sites of Portuguese origin', in Bendix, R. (ed.) *Heritage Regime and the State: Nomination, Implementation, Regulation*. Gottingen: Institute of Cultural Anthropology/European Ethnology, pp. 61–78.
Cercel, C. (2012) 'Transylvanian Saxon symbolic geographies', *Civilisations*, 60(2), 83–101. https://doi.org/10.4000/civilisations.3019.
Cercel, C. (2015) 'Philo-Germanism without Germans in Romania after 1989', *East European Politics and Societies*, 29(4), 811–30. https://doi.org/10.1177/0888325414550360.
Dattatreyan, E. G. (2014) 'Diasporic sincerity: tales from a 'returnee' researcher', *Identities*, 21(2), 152–67. https://doi.org/10.1080/1070289X.2013.854722.

Dimier, V. (2014) *The Invention of a European Development Aid Bureaucracy: Recycling Empire*. Basingstoke: Palgrave Macmillan.

Dimier, V. and McGeever M. (2006) 'Diplomats without a flag: the institutionalization of the delegations of the commission in African, Caribbean and Pacific countries', *JCMS: Journal of Common Market Studies*, 44(3), 483–505. https://doi.org/10.1111/j.1468-5965.2006.00632.x.

Dimitrovova, B. and Kramsch T. O. (2017) 'Decolonizing the spaces of European foreign policy: views from the Maghreb', *Interventions*, 19(6), 797–817. https://doi.org/10.1080/1369801X.2017.1348242.

Doharty, N. (2020) 'The "angry Black woman" as intellectual bondage: being strategically emotional on the academic plantation', *Race Ethnicity and Education*, 23(4), 548–62. https://doi.org/10.1080/13613324.2019.1679751.

EC. (1985) 'Resolution of the ministers responsible for cultural affairs, meeting within the council, of 13 june 1985 concerning the annual event "European City of Culture"', *Official Journal C*, 153.

European Cultural Foundation (2014) *Drawing Citizenship: Towards the European Elections through Drawings and Cartoons*. Amsterdam: European Cultural Foundation. https://culturalfoundation.eu/events/drawing-citizenship (accessed 29 February 2024).

Fadil, N. (2019) 'The anthropology of Islam in Europe: a double epistemological impasse', *Annual Review of Anthropology*, 48, 117–32. https://doi.org/10.1146/ANNUREV-ANTHRO-102218-011353.

Fadil, N. (2022) 'The pain of history: reflections on Charles Hirschkind's "The Feeling of History. Islam, Romanticism and Andalusia"', *Political Theology*, 24(1), 123–27. https://doi.org/10.1080/1462317X.2022.2107355.

Fernández Parrilla, G. (2018) 'Disoriented postcolonialities: with Edward Said in (the labyrinth of) Al-Andalus', *Interventions*, 20(2), 229–42. https://doi.org/10.1080/1369801X.2017.1403347.

Fryer, T. C. (2023) 'Heritage as liberation', *American Anthropologist*, 125(2), 420–34. https://doi.org/https://doi.org/10.1111/aman.13844.

Głowacka-Grajper, M. (2018) 'Internal colonization', *Keywords|ECHOES: European Colonial Heritage Modalities in Entangled Cities*. http://keywordsechoes.com/internal-colonisation (accessed 29 February 2024).

González-Ruibal, A. (2015) 'Heritage and violence', in Meskell, L. (ed.) *Global Heritage: A Reader*. London: Routledge, 150–70.

Halauniova, A. (2021) 'Getting the right shade of ochre: valuation of a building's historicity', *Space and Culture*, 24(3), 421–36. https://doi.org/10.1177/1206331221997656.

Hansen, P. (2002) 'European integration, European identity and the colonial connection', *European Journal of Social Theory*, 5(4), 483–98. https://doi.org/10.1177/136843102760513875.

Hansen, P. and Jonsson, S. (2011) 'Bringing Africa as a "dowry to Europe"', *Interventions*, 13(3), 443–63. https://doi.org/10.1080/1369801X.2011.597600.

Hansen, P. and Jonsson, S. (2014) *Eurafrica: The Untold History of European Integration and Colonialism*. London: Bloomsbury.

Kayikci, M. (2020) 'The politics of display: Islam European national museums, then and now', Conference Presentation & Working Paper. Lisbon: EASA2020.

Khosravi, S. (2021) 'To "study up" (social media post)', in *Critical Border Studies: Facebook Group*. www.facebook.com/groups/1799570010339722.

Kirshenblatt-Gimblett, B. (2004) 'Intangible heritage as metacultural production', *Museum International*, 56(1–2), 52–65.

Krivonos, D. and Diatlova, A. (2020) 'What to wear for whiteness?', *Intersections: East European Journal of Society and Politics*, 6(3), 116–32. https://doi.org/10.17356/IEEJSP.V6I3.660.

Kuus, M. (2004) 'Europe's Eastern expansion and the reinscription of otherness in East-Central Europe', *Progress in Human Geography*, 28(4), 472–89. https://doi.org/10.1191/0309132504ph498oa.

Kuus, M. (2014) *Geopolitics and Expertise: Knowledge and Authority in European Diplomacy*. Oxford: John Wiley & Sons.

Lähdesmäki, T. (2011) 'Rhetoric of unity and cultural diversity in the making of European cultural identity', *International Journal of Cultural Policy*, 18(1), 59–75. https://doi.org/10.1080/10286632.2011.561335.

Lähdesmäki, T. (2012) 'Discourses of Europeanness in the reception of the European capital of culture events: the case of Pécs2010', *European Urban and Regional Studies*, 21(2), 191–205. https://doi.org/10.1177/0969776412448092.

Lambrechts, M. (2019) 'Why Budapest, Warsaw, and Lithuania split themselves in two'. https://pudding.cool/2019/04/eu-regions (accessed 29 February 2024).

Levy, J. (1977) *Europe, Une Géographie, La Fabrique d'un Continent*. Paris: Hachette.

Macdonald, S. (2009) *Difficult Heritage: Negotiating the Nazi Past in Nuremberg and Beyond*. London: Routledge.

Mogherini, F. (2018) 'Remarks by High Representative/Vice-President Federica Mogherini at the Frankfurt Book Fair Opening Ceremony', Frankfurt: European External Action Service. www.eeas.europa.eu/node/51895_en (accessed 15 November 2019).

Nicolaïdis, K., Berny S. and Maas G. (2015) *Echoes of Empire: Memory, Identity and Colonial Legacies*. London: I. B. Tauris.

Oancă, A. (2010) *Governing the European Capital of Culture and Urban Regimes in Sibiu*. Budapest: Central European University.

Oancă, A. (2015) 'Europe is not elsewhere: the mobilization of an immobile policy in the lobbying by Perm (Russia) for the European capital of culture title'. *European Urban and Regional Studies*, 22(2), 179–90. https://doi.org/10.1177/0969776414535419.

Pack, S. D. (2006) *Tourism and Dictatorship: Europe's Peaceful Invasion of Franco's Spain*. New York: Palgrave Macmillan US. https://doi.org/10.1057/9780230601161.

Parvulescu, A. and Boatcă M. (2022) *Creolizing the Modern: Transylvania across Empires*. Ithaca, NY: Cornell University Press.

Said, E. W. (1978) *Orientalism*. New York: Vintage.

Sassatelli, M. (2009) *Becoming Europeans: Cultural Identity and Cultural Policies*. Basingstoke: Palgrave Macmillan.

Schalk, S. (2018) *Bodyminds Reimagined: (Dis)Ability, Race, and Gender in Black Women's Speculative Fiction*. Durham, NC: Duke University Press.

Sezneva, O. (2000) 'Historical representation and the politics of memory in Kaliningrad, former Königsberg', *Polish Sociological Review*, 131, 323–38. www.jstor.org/stable/41274763.

Sezneva, O. (2012) 'Architecture of descent: historical reconstructions and the politics of belonging in Kaliningrad, the former Königsberg', *Journal of Urban History*, 39(4), 767–87. https://doi.org/10.1177/0096144212470095.

Shore, C. (2000) *Building Europe: The Cultural Politics of European Integration*. London: Routledge.

Tunbridge, J. E. and Ashworth G. J. (1996) *Dissonant Heritage: The Management of the Past as a Resource in Conflict*. New York: Wiley.

Tzifakis, N. (2007) 'EU's region-building and boundary-drawing policies: the European approach to the Southern Mediterranean and the Western Balkans', *Journal of Southern Europe and the Balkans Online*, 9(1), 47–64. https://doi.org/10.1080/14613190701217001.

Velickovic, V. (2012) 'Belated alliances? Tracing the intersections between postcolonialism and postcommunism', *Journal of Postcolonial Writing*, 48(2), 164–75. https://doi.org/10.1080/17449855.2012.658247.

Venegas, J. L. (2018) *The Sublime South: Andalusia, Orientalism, and the Making of Modern Spain*. Evanston, IL: Northwestern University Press.

Vos, C. (2011) 'Negotiating Serbia's Europeanness: on the formation and appropriation of European heritage policy in Serbia', *History and Anthropology*, 22(2), 221–42. https://doi.org/10.1080/02757206.2011.558584.

Vos, C. (2017) 'European integration through "soft conditionality": the contribution of culture to EU enlargement in Southeast Europe', *International Journal of Cultural Policy*, 23(6), 675–89. https://doi.org/10.1080/10286632.2016.1276577.

Weheliye, A. G. (2014) *Habeas Viscus: Racializing Assemblages, Biopolitics, and Black Feminist Theories of the Human*. Durham, NC: Duke University Press.

Wolf, E. (1999) *Envisioning Power: Ideologies of Dominance and Crisis*. Berkeley, CA: University of California Press.

Yildiz, A. (2020) *'Why Don't You Talk to Refugees Instead?' Working on Whiteness in Europe as an 'Outsider'*, Conference Presentation, Lisbon: EASA2020.

7

The good, the bad and the ugly European: racial Eastern Europeanisation and stratified (sub)alter(n)ities

Ana Ivasiuc

I depart from David Theo Goldberg's (2009) conceptualisation of racial Europeanisation as a set of material, demographic, conceptual and historical ways in which 'race' acts to produce difference in Europe. In his account, the exclusive focus lies on the colonial histories of 'Europe' and the moment of the Holocaust. Eastern Europe, however, remains relegated to a secondary place far from the source of theorisation. Similarly, the Roma and their protracted racialisation as inferior to other Europeans is but sparsely mentioned. I address these two resounding absences by complexifying racial constructions in Europe. I propose a conceptualisation of racial *Eastern* Europeanisation at the confluence of several positional and conceptual entanglements.

Over the last two decades, a corpus of literature that is growing – both in size and in sophistication – has approached the construction of differentiated European identities in relation to Europe's Eastern margins. Using Edward Said's concept of Orientalism, this literature deconstructs the way in which Eastern and Central European subjects are perceived as inferior in relation to Western Europeans (Wolff, 1994; Böröcz, 2001; Boatcă, 2006, 2007; Kovács and Kabachnik, 2001; Melegh, 2006; Todorova, 2009). Empirically, the literature largely following these early works focuses predominantly on two phenomena: the so-called European integration, or the constitutive process of an EU that progressively incorporated its Eastern margins in a renewed formation of empire (Böröcz and Kovács, 2001; Arfire, 2011; Stubbs and Lendvai, 2016), and the dynamics and perceptions of the westward migration of Eastern Europeans (Fox et al., 2012; Böröcz and Sarkar, 2017; Ivasiuc, 2017; Böröcz, 2021; Tulbure, 2022). The differential kinds of whiteness involved in constructions of Europeanness have been conceptualised as processes of racialisation: the production of categories of difference and their stratification in hierarchies of value that cast Eastern Europe as failed, improper, not-quite-white Europeanness (Dzenovska, 2016; Rzepnikowska, 2018; Gressgård and Husakouskaya, 2020; Kalmar, 2022). A more recent strand of literature brings together the two empirical fields above under the conceptual umbrella of racial capitalism, where core European countries rely on cheap labour from the East while reinforcing violent hierarchies (Kalmar, 2023; Krivonos, 2022, 2023; Lewicki, 2023; Narkowicz, 2023; Rexhepi, 2023; Rzepnikowska, 2023). Another rich corpus of literature explores the postcolonial and decolonial potentialities of scholarship from and about (South) East Europeanness (Chari and Verdery, 2009; Cervinkova, 2012; Pârvulescu, 2015; Tlostanova, 2018; Kušić, Lottholz and Manolova, 2019; Majstorovič, 2019; Müller, 2020).

One of the dynamics of ascribing Eastern Europe as a subaltern, violent and uncivilised other revolves around the Roma in the social and moral landscapes of Eastern Europe. During the pre-accession negotiations, the 'integration' of the Roma was high on the conditionalities agenda, and Eastern Europeans were shunned for their poor human rights record regarding the treatment of this 'quintessentially' European minority (Goldston, 2002; Tesser, 2003). Yet EU accession occurred mostly without any marked progress on the treatment of the Roma: the need for a market in – and for cheap labour force from – Eastern Europe relegated the human rights framing of EU integration and the social inclusion of the Roma to a secondary place. Similarly, Southern Europe has long been produced as inferior to Northern Europe. The vernacular distinction between South and North is quintessential in Italy, where the far-right, anti-immigration Lega Nord started its political trajectory in the 1990s around the criminalisation and inferiorisation of the Southerners – *terroni*[1] – in distinctly racialising terms (Cole, 1997). In addition to the anti-Southerner narrative, Lega Nord openly harboured anti-Roma positions, at times its leaders advocating for mass deportations of Roma, considered essentially alien to Italy. The Easts and Souths of Europe thus share dynamics of producing subalterns with regards to a putatively superior centre situated in Northern/Western Europe that upholds a perpetually unattainable standard of civilisation (Boatcă, 2010), but also in relation to multiple dynamics of alterity production where Roma subjects would inevitably find themselves at the bottom of social hierarchies.

In this chapter, I conceptualise racial East Europeanisation from a position of East–South–North entanglement. I show how three racialised figures emerged simultaneously to the postsocialist labour migration of Romanians to Western Europe, and explore their relationality. Building on previous work on the securitisation of Eastern European identities in the relational construction of (sub)alter(n)ity in Western Europe (Ivasiuc, 2017), I show how the figure of the Good Western European emerged alongside the Bad Eastern European and the Ugly Roma, constituting stratified sub-alternities relationally in connection with racialising imaginaries of Easts and Souths. While the way I term these identities may suggest clearcut boundaries between coherent categories, they are, in fact, ambivalent positions enmeshed in a multiplicity of relational struggles within the landscape of European identities.

I rely on an ethnography of formal and informal policing of migrant Roma in the peripheries of Rome undertaken between 2014 and 2017, partly constituted by observation with a special police unit established in 2010 to police the Roma settled in *campi nomadi* and support the evictions of informal settlements of migrant Roma ordered by the municipality of Rome.[2] Initially called 'Operative coordinating unit for *nomad* settlements' (my emphasis), the unit contained a racial term in its very title, betraying the intent of racial policing inherent to the structure. Moreover, the unit was set up by far-right mayor Gianni Alemanno using the provisions of the 'nomad emergency' law of 2008. The declaration of a state of emergency allocated resources and power to local municipalities to combat the urban insecurity perceived to stem from informal settlements of Roma migrants from Eastern Europe. In 2011, the name of the unit changed to Public Security and Emergency-Related Unit (*Sicurezza Pubblica Emergenziale*), occulting its initial function of racial policing. Even though the declaration of the state of emergency was cancelled as anti-constitutional in 2011, the police unit is still operating in the peripheries of Rome. Within this unit, I spent three months intermittently, consulted reports of police activity in camps between 2010 and 2015, carried out formal interviews and informal discussions with various police, then accompanied officers on patrol, witnessing various acts of policing the Roma and observing interactions within these encounters.

My own positionality as a Romanian woman, based in a Northern European academic institution, and doing research in a Southern European context where being Romanian is saturated with meaning in contradictory ways, interacts in its own way with the subject at hand. My research inhabits the intersection between 'the east of the west' and 'the south of the north' (Mignolo, 2021), a privileged position from which to observe the relationality of racialising constructions in the multiple gradations of Europeanness, and, implicitly, ideas of 'civilisation'. At the same time, this privileged location is not one of external observation. It is itself enmeshed with such constructions, which reverberate with my lived experience as a precarious Romanian 'knowledge migrant' (see Aparna, Krivonos and Pascucci, this volume) in German academia, and as a researcher institutionally from the North *and* culturally from the East in Italy, researching the policing of racialised Eastern European Roma. The complexity of this position allows me to grasp nuances and contradictions that complexify the concept of racial East Europeanisation. Because this positionality is so central in my research, I will start there.

Souths and Easts as a method

What does it mean to take Souths and Easts seriously – and non-metaphorically – as a method? In their introduction to this volume, Kolar Aparna, Daria Krivonos and Elisa Pascucci emphasise the materiality of our geohistories as researchers. Souths and Easts as a method, they write, is 'an invitation for diasporic scholars speaking from exilic relations with territories and their elsewheres' to engage with inter-referencing (Chen, 2010) as 'a call to locate violence at points of reference across, between and against empires'.

As a knowledge migrant from Romania, residing in Germany at the time of my research and carrying out ethnography in Italy, I inhabited an intersection of imaginaries around East, South and North, where the latter was inevitably posed as prototype of European superiority pitched against the uncivilisedness, criminality and brutality of Eastern Europe, and against the chaos and moral corruption of the South. My research interlocutors, police officers, often drew comparisons between the Italian context and elsewhere – an elsewhere that varied between Romania and Germany. In their imaginary – as well as that of many Italians I spoke with – Germany constituted a heaven of order and discipline, worthy of being emulated, were it not that cultural differences would make that project always impossible to reach in practice. Germany – a location that I take to be synecdochical for North Europe – embodied the centre, the positively marked, in relation to which both East and South constituted faulty peripheries.

Taking a cue from Anca Pârvulescu's 'Eastern Europe as method' (2019), I use Souths and Easts as a method to decentre the North as umbilical centre on the imaginary map of civilisation, grasping the violence that the construction of (sub)alter(n)ity of the Souths and Easts in relation to this imaginary location produces, sustains and legitimises. I use the term (sub)alter(n)ity to suggest the simultaneity and processuality of constructions of alterity that amount to stratified subalternities in the differential imagined moral landscapes of Europe. The acts of observation and theorisation of these subalternities proceed from shifting positions of peripherality that attuned me, the diasporic knowledge migrant, to the multiplicity of violence exerted on the margins. This position of peripherality is not only a cognitive situatedness with regards to theory-making 'from the margins'. It contains affective strata of experience that make violence recognisable, not only against particular figures of alterity but also against the observer herself, touching a raw place of painful awareness of how power and violence work to order the world. The cognitive and the affective are indissociable here, rendering Souths and Easts as productive loci from where to theorise Europeanness as violence on multiple levels and registers. By focusing on this position of peripherality, I show how the coloniality of power works relationally between the Easts and Souths of Europe in everyday research encounters, as opposed to the macropolitical scale of coloniality in the context of the EU 'integration' of its Eastern hinterlands (Gagyi, 2016).

In what follows, I discuss the good, the bad and the ugly European as figures in relation to racial Eastern Europeanisation. They embody subject positions that are contradictory and ambivalent. Within each of them violence unfolds in specific ways towards a racialised other, while laying bare, at the same time, forms of violence that work along multiple axes of (sub)alter(n)ity.

The good: 'I was in Bosnia to protect your ass'

One evening in late autumn 2016, I joined two of the police officers preparing for a patrol around the camps. 'Let's go see what they are doing in the camp, check up on fires.'³ The fires – referred to as *roghi tossici* or toxic fires – is a phenomenon that intensified and became an object of great concern in the peripheries of Rome in the last fifteen years. The short story is that successive administrations in Rome have carried out a politics of eviction of Roma from long-established or more recent informal camps in the centre towards the peripheries, beyond the ring road (*il raccordo annulare*), in a process of gentrification that encompassed the city since the end of the nineties (Herzfeld, 2009). Evictions violently disrupted the social relations that the Roma had established with non-Roma for economic gain, and thinned out their livelihoods, forcing them to find sources of income elsewhere in the marginal economies of the Italian capital (Clough Marinaro, 2017). Some Roma turned towards the metal trade – spurred by a rise in demand for metals from China in the 2000s (Olivera, 2015) – and others towards the provision of a service in demand: the uptake of refuse, old furniture and house appliances from private individuals who preferred to call the Roma to pick up such objects rather than spend long hours filling out bureaucratic requirements to dispose of encumbering refuse in the facilities set up for the purpose. Companies also dumped their refuse near Roma camps, whose perimeters generally took the form of mountains of debris of various sizes, materials and shapes that kept piling up. While Romans blame the fires on the Roma on account of their practices of extraction of copper and other metals by burning plastics, Belli et al. (2015) show the complexity of the process by which mountains of waste piled up near *campi nomadi*. The fires happen for a multiplicity of reasons, too – from the extraction of metals to the necessity of dealing with garbage that the municipality does not regularly clear, and from youth literally playing with fire out of boredom to acts of rebellion by Roma in response to police actions – a 'pyropolitics' of resistance (Ivasiuc, 2024). When fires happen, they release dense columns of white or black smoke and sometimes pungent smells that anger the Romans, whose response is generally in a racist key: no matter the source of the fires, the Roma get the blame, and the inhabitants of the Roman peripheries demand more policing of *campi nomadi* and even military presence in camps (Ivasiuc, 2018, 2019). These demands were taken seriously by the Roman administration, who set up regular patrols around *campi nomadi* in a bid to spot and control the fires before they get out of hand.

That evening, Alessandro and Daniele[4] decided to show me how they operate to prevent fires. We arrived at dusk. They drove in the inner dirt alleys of the camp. When we reached the eastern edge of the camp, they stopped in front of a housing unit next to heaps of metal. Daniele asked about the whereabouts of the residents. A woman, who was finishing doing the laundry by hand on the right side of the housing unit, said she lived there.

'Where is your husband? Why are you gathering garbage here? Who does this shit belong to?' (*Di chi è 'sta merda?*)

The woman took the basin with dirty water and threw the contents on the ground, next to the housing unit. She avoided his look, but protested:

'This? This isn't "shit". This is our bread, our work'.

'I want it all gone by tomorrow. Tell your husband to move it elsewhere or you guys are in trouble when I come back to check. No garbage inside the camp!'

Daniele came back to the car, swearing under his breath. Alessandro made a U-turn and drove back towards the centre of the camp. He parked next to a group of men gathered around a metal barrel in which a fire burned. They were chatting around the fire, holding their hands out to warm them up, when Alessandro and Daniele irrupted out of the car, ordering the men to put out the fire immediately. The men protested: the fire was innocuous, they were burning some cardboard and bits of wooden furniture, not plastic and at any rate nothing toxic. Pleading with Alessandro and Daniele, however, was useless: they were intent on having the fire extinguished, and their commanding tone quickly escalated. One of the men threw some water on the fire, and white, dense smoke rose from the barrel.

'This is racism', said one of the men. 'You think we're burning plastics, but we're not. Why can't we just stand here and warm ourselves up?'

'Racism?' thundered Alessandro. 'What racism? Italians aren't racist.'

A heated conversation followed. The Roma man spoke about a recent visit to a doctor, who had shouted abuse at him, called him a dirty *zingaro* (Gypsy), and did not want to examine him because he was Roma. Alessandro stiffened up.

'No! Italians aren't racist! You can't tell me that I'm racist. I was in Bosnia protecting your ass!'

He went on to explain he had served in the army and was deployed with NATO troops in Sarajevo to protect the Bosnians from Serbian attacks, that there was a Roma community that was threatened by both sides, and his role was to protect them.

'Everyone wanted to kill you guys, and I was there to protect you. If I was a racist like you say, I would have let that happen, wouldn't I?'

Alessandro boasted about his service for a while. The authority to speak against the existence of racism in Italy was drawn from the 'goodness' of the position of protector in the hinterlands of Europe. The moral regulation (Arfire, 2011) that he engaged in enforced a social order that attempted to erase Italian racism and silence the voices of the Roma subaltern. In the subtext, the evocation of violence in Sarajevo pointed to a Balkanist imaginary (Todorova, 2009) where the victims were expected to cheer the arrival of white saviours like him, who took it upon themselves to save the locals from all-encompassing, irrational violence. Yet there was violence in the way the two police went around the camp in an attempt to 'order' things, people and their opinions on racism – *ordering* inhabiting here the double meaning of commanding and of establishing a particular order – while performing power in a spectacle where indisputable authority needed to be secured against resistance and defiance.

The bad: *Da voi* (where you're from), you wouldn't see such things

Earlier that day, at the start of the patrol, Alessandro and Daniele explained that they are the only police unit in Roma who take their work around *campi nomadi* seriously. They complained that whenever other units are tasked with the prevention of fires, they often do not act even as fires spread right next to them. The neighbourhood committee of Tor Sapienza – the most vocal about the fires in the eastern periphery of Rome – knew this well: on their Facebook page, they had posted a photograph of smoke rising up from the camp while a police car, encircled with a red frame on the photograph for rhetoric effect, was parked right next to it. As this image circulated on social media, it suggested the inaction of the police and ineffectiveness of patrols; it fed repeated requests for more policing and even for the presence of the military in *campi nomadi*; and it taunted the police, forcing it to strengthen their grip on camps. As we were approaching the camp of Salviati, Alessandro remarked the thin column of smoke rising from the camp:

'*Ecco* – there you go! Do you see that there's a fire there? Do you see the police just sitting there in their car doing nothing?'

Another police car, from one of the regular precincts of Polizia di Roma Capitale, was parked outside the camp. Alessandro stopped our car next to it and lowered his window. The woman in the other car's driver seat lowered hers.

'Hey, you might want to check on these Gypsies here. There's smoke coming up, they're burning something again. If you aren't careful, the whole camp could go up in flames.'

The woman looked at him, then turned her head to look at the thin column of smoke rising from the camp, then turned back at us and smiled at Alessandro, with a nearly imperceptible shrug:

'Oops. *Peccato*. What a pity.'

Both Alessandro and Daniele received the suggestion that it wouldn't be such a bad thing if the whole camp burned down with mild amusement, but they did not comment further on the woman's 'joke'. Instead, Daniele continued to complain about being the only ones doing their job and taking the blame for other units' inaction.

The imagery of *campi nomadi* burning down was not unfamiliar to me, or, for that matter, to anyone in Italy who remembers the 2008 mob attack and arson of the Ponticelli *campo nomadi* in Naples that contributed to the moral panic leading to the declaration of the 'nomad emergency' (Rivera, 2009; Ivasiuc, 2021). At the beginning of my research, I had accompanied a far-right neighbourhood patrol whose members openly talked about lynching a Roma or two 'to teach them a lesson'. The leader of the patrol had boasted that if he wanted to, he could mobilise two thousand people and burn down the *campo nomadi* of Salone, if the authorities did not eradicate camps in the capital. Small-scale arson attacks on *campi nomadi* happen recurrently in Rome and elsewhere, as the newspaper articles from the mid-1980s describing Romans' Not-In-My-Back-Yard politics of *campi nomadi* also attest (Ivasiuc, 2022).

Police officers often emphasised in our conversations that a general state of impunity rules in Italy, in particular regarding 'the Gypsies'. Italy has a real problem with 'Gypsy crime', they explained. There is no certainty of legal punishment, and consequently little deterrence to crime. One of the police once told the story of how a phone call from a judge's office suggested that they stop putting so many people in prison because there is no space. Impunity, they claimed, reigned supreme in Italy – and this opinion was recurrent among other people outside the police forces, too.

Often, my interlocutors would attempt comparisons with other contexts. *Da voi non è così*, they would say: 'where you're from, it isn't like that'. *Da voi* meant either Germany, or Romania, depending on their point of reference for the particular topic discussed. Some of them would refer to my country of residency, while some to my country of origin, and I would have to respond to questions like *Ma com'è da voi?* thinking about whether they meant one or the other. *Da voi*, they would say, 'there are no *campi*, it's sparkling clean everywhere, Gypsies are put in houses and whoever doesn't want to conform, boom, is sent away!' A sense of discipline and authority that reflected Italian stereotypes about Germans would suggest that *da voi*, in this case, meant in Germany. Or: 'Here, they're put in prison and next day they're out and start again. Nothing happens to them here. *Da voi*, when one steals a loaf of bread, that's it, they go to prison. They're beaten, they're taught a lesson, next time they think twice.' Distinct overtones of admiration for overt police brutality would betray that in this context, *da voi* meant in Romania. In any context other than this one, police brutality in Eastern Europe would be equated with barbarism and lack of civilisation. But, as one of my interlocutors added, 'here in Italy, we have this thing called "human rights", so we can't beat them senseless like the Romanian policemen do. That would solve the issue, wouldn't it?' If only they could act like the Romanian police! As officers were emphasising these differences, one could grasp, in the subtext, their approval and longing for harsher methods to deal with 'Gypsies'.

Moments like these make apparent the ambivalence of constructions of the Western European as 'good'. Whereas respect for human rights categorically ranks at the top of civilisational hierarchies where 'the West is the best', Italian police coveted the imagined freedom from human rights 'constraints' of Romanian police, which renders dynamic and relational the production of 'goodness'. Here, 'goodness', constructed according to the criterion of effectiveness in crime policing, contributes to a greater moral good where justice is legitimately imparted on the criminal. Goodness, then, is relayed to the putatively less civilised Eastern European hinterlands, where justice is thought to prevail against the criminalised figure of the 'Gypsy', albeit in unorthodox ways. In a time when Italy's anti-migrant policies criminalise acts of life saving at sea despite human rights principles (Basaran, 2015), constructions of 'goodness' are shifting from the moral 'good' to the effective 'good' that gets the job of protecting the country from criminalised migrants done. In the process, the 'bad' becomes the Italian state, paralysed by human rights imperatives that render it ineffective in imparting justice, as well as global actors like the EU, who is seen to impose the human rights paradigm to its members, rendering their justice systems ineffective.

The positioning of my interlocutors in relation to their German counterparts was highly ambivalent, too. Germans were admired both among the police officers and among my far-right interlocutors, but I heard the same discourse from other Italians. Germans, they claimed, followed rules flawlessly. Germany was a place of order and discipline, punctuality and respect for the law. In the eyes of many, Germany was an ideal version of what Italy should strive to become, although many claimed that Italy could never be Germany: too much chaos, too many people not following rules, not respecting the law. The way many Italians saw themselves and Italy in relation to Germany mirrored the way many Romanians thought of themselves and Romania in relation to 'Western Europe', in a self-colonising gaze that posited the self in opposition and inferiority to a more civilised other. The West, for Romanians (which included Italy), and the North, for Italians, represented a superior civilisation set as standard, but an ontologically unattainable one. Its unattainability kept producing the self as subaltern on imaginary hierarchies of civilisation that seemed set in stone for eternity – a self-orientalisation of sorts proving the enduring quality of orientalism and its effects on Eastern Europe (Boatcă, 2006; Böröcz, 2006).

In one of my informal conversations with a police officer, he made a remark on the striking contrast between Germany and Italy, and suggested that I must surely despise Italy in comparison to Germany. 'You come here and you see all this chaos, the dirt, the disorder … You must think to yourself "what am I doing here?"' When I replied that I actually prefer Italy and feel quite at home in Rome, which, to my sense, is chaotic in ways not unlike Bucharest, he laughed a tad uncomfortably at the comparison. 'Yeah, but come on, surely Italy is better, otherwise you people wouldn't come to live here in such big numbers.' Hierarchies needed to be put right: surely, in comparison to Germany, both Italy and Romania were at a civilisational disadvantage, but still, Romania could never be on a par with Italy. The reference to 'you people' reminded me of my own perceived place in the hierarchies of Europeanness: certainly, a mobile position – sometimes from Germany, sometimes from Romania – but in the end, a subaltern one in relation to Romanian migration to Italy. Simultaneously, I was in a position of whiteness, though unstable and contested (Böröcz, 2006, 2021).

This reminder of European hierarchies resonated with affective states produced by my own positionality and trajectory as diasporic knowledge worker. While doing research in Italy, I was sometimes able to negotiate my own position, as well as access to my field, by mobilising the capital that came with my affiliation with a German university. I knew that class distinctions would put me at a distance from the way other Romanian migrants are categorised in Italy, but my residence in Germany afforded me a residential kind of capital that proved useful, for instance, in gaining access to far-right interlocutors. And yet, this capital weighed heavy and felt ambivalent: in Germany, I only ever occupied a subaltern position in neoliberal academia, one that left indelible traces of hurt and inadequacy in a system that rejected me time and again. This, too, is a layer that adds complexity to adopting

Souths and Easts as a method: theorising from multiple unstable and contested positions of subalternity that leave affective marks on our trajectories inevitably shape the way we see, think and write. Occupying positions at the intersection between Souths and Easts attune us to dynamics of categorisation that would perhaps otherwise remain unseen.

The ugly: Europeanising slurs, or the travels of *țigan borât* across Europe

In my research, the migration of Romanians to Italy framed to a large extent the context in which constructions of Europeanness are constantly (re)produced, both by Romanian migrants and by Italians. A more granular hierarchisation coexisted: that between myself, as white Romanian, and Roma – many of whom came from Romania both before and after the country joined the EU. In my first conversation with one of the higher-ups in the police precinct, upon hearing that I was born in Romania, he said, with a smirk of knowingness aimed at suggesting cultural intimacy: 'Ah, so you're doing research on these – how do you people call them? – *țigan borât*.'

Țigan (Gypsy) is the slur that many Romanians prefer to use instead of the endonym Roma. They often make a point by correcting whoever uses the word Roma, and insist that *țigan* is the correct term. Many think that the claim to the term Roma is a new, distinctly European invention imposed to Romanians in the nineties in a bout of political correctness. Contrary to this claim, Roma organisations have been known to advocate for the use of Roma instead of the slur *țigan* as early as 1919. The term, many Romanians claim with conspiratorial overtones, is an attempt at placing Romania in an inferior position by facilitating the confusion between Romanians and Roma, suggesting that all Romanians are Gypsies, and that Romania is the land of Gypsies. Within this conspiratorial logic, they claim, the EU wants to erase Romanian identity and downplay Romanian culture and values. *Borât* – only rarely used with other nouns than *țigan* – is an adjective meaning 'ugly', bordering on the abject. The etymology of the word is telling of this connotation of abjectness: from the Latin *abhorrire*, to vomit, the word suggests disgust. The Romanian etymological dictionary explains that the meaning of disgust comes from the 'natural confusion of the reaction of vomiting with the idea of despising or hating something'.[5] It adds that the word was used in old Romanian, contradicting the idea pressed by some etymologists in the mid-1960s that *borât* would be a loanword from 'the Gypsy language' (Juilland et al., 1965). This surprising claim to a supposed Romani etymology of the word confirms that *țigan* and *borât* became nearly indissociable for Romanians, just like Roma and the abjection that many Romanians share for them.

This abjection and the vocabularies that carry it travel. Since the 1990s, an estimated four million Romanians left the country, looking for better opportunities elsewhere. This includes a high number of workers in formal or informal care-giving. Italy is a preferred destination for women from Romania and Moldova seeking employment in care-giving, because the similarities between languages make it easier for them to learn Italian. Many of the care-givers from these countries remained in subordinated positions in Italy, discriminated against, often exploited and perceived as inferior by virtue of their citizenship and the class categorisation of their employment. Romanians in Italy also mobilise the register of sameness to emphasise the cultural and linguistic similarities with Italians: after all, Romanians are the result of the Roman conquest of Dacia, and claim, through cultural and linguistic kinship, a place in the larger Romanic family. Romanian migrants devise strategies of 'precarity management' and 'adaptation' in their struggle to gain recognition (Anghel, 2013); they also enact practices of resistance to shaming grounded in class by mobilising strategies of reclassification (Mădroane, 2021). Among these strategies, one that is often put in motion to acquire the symbolic capital necessary for social ascension is the mobilisation of racial representations of the Roma (Moroşanu and Fox, 2013). Aware of their own subalternity in the West, Romanian immigrants in Italy and elsewhere obsessively fabricate distinction between themselves and the 'Gypsy', through discourses grounded in antigypsyism. Concerned not to be perceived as 'Gypsies' because of their Romanian citizenship, many migrants engage in purposefully representing the 'Gypsy' as lazy, deviant and essentially un-European, in contrast with their own efforts to 'integrate' and to be productive members of society (Kaneva and Popescu, 2014). As a consequence, many Italians learn from Romanians the distinction between the naturalised categories of ethnic Romanians and Romanian 'Gypsies', reproducing 'nesting Orientalisms' (Bakić-Hayden, 1995) that cast the Roma outside of the imaginary territories of Europeanness; here, often, the narrative of Roma's origin in India is emphasised as proof of their essential cultural and racial non-belongingness.

The idea that Romanian Roma bring bad fame to the country is a pervasive trope, and Romanians attentively police the boundary between themselves and Roma at home, too. As early as the 1990s, legislative proposals and petitions demanded that the ethnonym 'Roma' be banned, and that the exonym 'Gypsy' be used in official documents. Sometimes, such initiatives were supported – and even initiated – by various ministers of external affairs (Horváth and Nastasă, 2012). This is a perfect example of the coloniality of being. As Madina Tlostanova (2018: 22–3) put it, modernity/coloniality justifies violence and prompts those on precarious positions to turn against those standing on even lower rungs of social hierarchies. This 'insecure Europeanism' (Tlostanova, 2018: 24), and traces of the local, colonial histories in Eastern Europe, shape the ways in which its people claim their place anywhere else but in the lower rungs of Europeanness that the Roma often occupy. Rejecting their position as 'second-rate Europeans [or] as the new subalterns of the global coloniality' (26), Romanian migrants aim at carving for themselves a place on a par with 'Westerners'. They emphasise their shared civilisation and their propensity to work hard, to respect rules and thus, to fulfil their 'social duties'. In so doing, they stake claims to belonging that exclude and define as inferior others like the Roma, and that ultimately prove to be claims to whiteness and to goodness simultaneously (Böröcz and Sarkar, 2017). Here, racism works not so much as to police boundaries between homogeneities (Goldberg, 2009) but to displace downwards those class and ethnic boundaries experienced or perceived as oppressive. In short, Romanians painstakingly construct the boundary with Roma while aiming at dissolving the one between themselves and their Italian employers.

In the process, racisms circulate between East and West, reverberate and multiply. This happens as forms of everyday racism (Essed, 1991) shared in daily, casual conversations between Italian employers and their Romanian employees. But it also happens in institutional frameworks, as, for instance, Romanian and Italian police cooperate in combating 'Gypsy crime'. One of the police officers I met in the first days of my research at the precinct told me that he knows from Romanian staff at the embassy that the Roma are not Romanian, and that Romanians prefer for the *nomadi* this term *zingari* (Gypsies). The consul, so he claimed, had told them repeatedly to downplay the Roma's 'Romanianness' and emphasise their 'Gypsiness' instead in the police communications to the press. Italian police learned from their Romanian counterparts and from Romanian diplomats the politics of ethnic difference that refuse Roma from Romania their citizenship, even though their passports say otherwise.

Conclusion: The violence of racial Eastern Europeanisation

The three figures discussed above, as they emerged from my research – the good, the bad and the ugly – point at the relationality of racial constructions in Europe, along the East–West, North–South and core–periphery axes. The relationality of racism is also the tenet in how David Theo Goldberg (2009) conceptualised racial Europeanisation as regional racism (2009): a set of materially, demographically, historically and conceptually distinct ways in which 'race' acts in Europe. Goldberg focuses his conceptualisation on the colonial heritage of Western Europe and the post-war effacement of 'race' as an unfortunate accident of the Holocaust. In his book, the Roma, even though they also experienced persecution and genocide during the Holocaust, are mentioned sparsely and *en passant*. Eastern Europe, too, seems altogether erased from Europe. Inadvertently, this mirrors the violent effacement of Eastern Europe in conceptions of 'European history' (Davies, 2007), as well as of the crucial role that the Roma play in the construction of a racially stratified Europe. Conceptualising the racial violence towards Roma throughout Europe – North and South, East and West, putative core and periphery – is an inescapable multidimensionality along which to think racial Europeanisation, and erasing this violence is arguably in itself an act of epistemic violence.

Racial Eastern Europeanisation plays on a multiplicity of levels at which narratives of inferiority are entwined. It is always a nested construction in which Eastern Europeans compete for cultural, civilisational and social capital against others constructed as less deserving, inferior, the 'real' backwards subjects that bring bad reputation to Eastern Europe, be they Roma or Muslims – in short, those blamed for keeping the promise of European civilisation at bay. Treating the figures of the 'good', the 'bad' and the 'ugly' European relationally, and, more importantly, as situated within contrapuntal dynamics, avoids the pitfall of reifying difference across East/West, North/South and core/periphery axes, as well as that of suggesting representational agency solely on the part of the dominant Western European. Eastern Europeans construct racial inferiority just as much as their Western counterparts. Absolving them of the role they play in generating violence towards the Roma is akin to romanticising a subaltern subject position that is simplifying and misrepresenting. They exert symbolic violence by perceiving the figure of the Gypsy as uncivilised within unequal hierarchies of power in the West, but 'at home' in East Europe, the Roma are exposed to violence in more than symbolic terms. Police brutality results in deaths of Roma; the murder of Stanislav Tomáš in 2021 by Czech police, in a manner similar to the killing of George Floyd in the United States, is but one of the more recent cases that garnered media attention. The point of analyses such as this one is not to merely critique stereotypical representations, but to examine their effects within the knowledge/power assemblage that unites East and West and North and South in the reproduction of violent imperial categories. Unlearning imperialism, as Ariella Aïcha Azoulay (2019) recently argued, supposes denaturalising acts of representation and acknowledging their purported neutrality as an exercise of violence in itself.

Notes

1 *Terrone*, in Italian, signifies Southern Italian, with negative connotations of uncouthness, laziness, poor hygiene and mediocre education.
2 *Campi nomadi* are legally ambivalent housing options established by Italian authorities for the most destitute Roma groups in Italy (Clough Marinaro, 2014). They are often squalid and poorly serviced areas, segregated from residential neighbourhoods and situated in polluted or industrial peri-urban zones.
3 All translations from Italian are my own.
4 These are pseudonyms.
5 Romanian etymology dictionary, online version, www.dictionarroman.ro/?c=borat.

References

Anghel, R. G. (2013) *Romanians in Western Europe: Migration, Status Dilemmas, and Transnational Connections*. Lanham, MD: Lexington.
Arfire, R. (2011) 'The moral regulation of the Second Europe: transition, Europeanization and the Romanians', *Critical Sociology*, 37(6), 853–70.
Azoulay, A. A. (2019) *Potential History: Unlearning Imperialism*. London: Verso.
Bakić-Hayden, Milica. (1995) 'Nesting orientalisms', *Slavic Review*, 54(4), 917–31.
Basaran, T. (2015) 'The saved and the drowned: governing indifference in the name of security', *Security Dialogue*, 46(3), 205–20. doi: 10.1177/0967010614557512.
Belli, E., Granata, R., Risi, E. and Vivona, V. (2015) *A Ferro e Fuoco: Fumi tossici nella "città eterna"* [To Fire and Sword: Toxic smoke in the "eternal city"]. Rome: Kogoi.
Boatcă, M. (2006) 'No race to the swift: negotiating racial identity in past and present Eastern Europe', *Human Architecture: The Journal of the Sociology of Self-Knowledge*, 5(1), 91–104.
Boatcă, M. (2007) 'The eastern margins of empire', *Cultural Studies* 21(2–3), 368–84. http://dx.doi.org/10.1080/09502380601162571.
Boatcă, M. (2010) 'Multiple Europes and the politics of difference within', in Brunkhorst, H. and Grözinger, G. (eds) *The Study of Europe*. Baden-Baden: Nomos, pp. 51–66.
Böröcz, J. (2001) 'Introduction: empire and coloniality in the "Eastern Enlargement" of the European Union', in Böröcz, J. and Kovács, M. (eds) *Empire's New Clothes: Unveiling EU Enlargement*. Telford: Central Europe Review, pp. 4–50.
Böröcz, J. (2006) 'Goodness is elsewhere: the rule of European difference', *Comparative Studies in Society and History*, 48 (1), 110–138.
Böröcz, J. (2021) ' "Eurowhite" conceit, "dirty white" resentment: "race" in Europe', *Sociological Forum*, 36 (4), 1116–34. doi:10.1111/socf.12752.
Böröcz, J. and Kovács, M. (eds) (2001) *Empire's New Clothes: Unveiling EU Enlargement*. Telford: Central Europe Review.
Böröcz, J. and Sarkar, M. (2017) 'The unbearable whiteness of the Polish plumber and the Hungarian peacock dance around "race"', *Slavic Review*, 76(2), 307–14. doi:10.1017/slr.2017.79.
Buchowski, M. (2006) 'The specter of orientalism in Europe: from exotic other to stigmatized brother', *Anthropological Quarterly*, 79(3), 463–82.

Cervinkova, H. (2012) 'Postcolonialism, postsocialism and the anthropology of east-central Europe', *Journal of Postcolonial Writing*, 48(2), 155–63. doi: 10.1080/17449855.2012.658246.
Chari, S. and Verdery, K. (2009) 'Thinking between the posts: postcolonialism, post-socialism, and ethnography after the Cold War', *Comparative Studies in Society and History*, 51(1), 6–34. doi:10.1017/S0010417509000024.
Chen, K. H. (2010) *Asia as Method: Toward Deimperialization*. Durham, NC: Duke University Press.
Clough Marinaro, I. (2014) 'Rome's "legal" camps for Roma: the construction of new spaces of informality', *Journal of Modern Italian Studies*, 19(5), 541–55. doi: 10.1080/1354571X.2014.962254.
Clough Marinaro, I. (2017) 'The informal faces of the (neo-)ghetto: state confinement, formalization and multidimensional informalities in Italy's Roma camps', *International Sociology*, 32(4), 545–62. https://doi.org/10.1177/0268580917706629.
Cole, J. (1997) *The New Racism in Europe: A Sicilian Ethnography*. New York: Cambridge University Press.
Davies, N. (2007) *Europe East and West*. London: Pimlico.
Dzenovska, D. (2016) 'Eastern Europe, the moral subject of the migration/refugee crisis, and political futures', *Near Futures Online*, 1, 1–13. https://nearfuturesonline.org/wp-content/uploads/2016/01/Dzenovska_05.pdf.
Essed, P. (1991) *Understanding Everyday Racism: An Interdisciplinary Theory*. New York: Sage Publications, Inc.
Fox, J. E., Moroşanu, L. and Szilassy, E. (2012) 'The racialization of the new European migration to the UK', *Sociology*, 46(4), 680–95. https://doi.org/10.1177/0038038511425558.
Gagyi, A. (2016) '"Coloniality of power" in East Central Europe: external penetration as internal force in post-socialist Hungarian politics', *Journal of World-Systems Research*, 22(2), 349–72. https://doi.org/10.5195/jwsr.2016.626.
Goldberg, D. T. (2009) *The Threat of Race: Reflections on Racial Neoliberalism*. Oxford: Wiley-Blackwell.
Goldston, J. A. (2002) 'Roma rights, Roma wrongs', *Foreign Affairs*, 81(2), 146–62.
Gressgård, R. and Husakouskaya, N. (2020) 'Europeanization as civilizational transition from East to West: racial displacement and sexual modernity in Ukraine', *Intersections: East European Journal of Society and Politics*, 6(3), 74–96. doi: https://doi.org/10.17356/ieejsp.v6i3.634.
Herzfeld, M. (2009) *Evicted from Eternity: The Restructuring of Modern Rome*. Chicago: University of Chicago Press.
Horváth, I. and Nastasă, L. (eds) (2012) *Rom sau Ţigan: Dilemele unui etnonim în spaţiul românesc* [Roma or Gypsy: The Dilemmas of an Ethnonym in Romanian Space]. Cluj-Napoca: Editura Institutului pentru Studierea Problemelor Minorităţilor Naţionale.
Ivasiuc, A. (2017) 'Securitizations of identities and racial Eastern-Europeanization', *EuropeNow* 13, December 2017. www.europenowjournal.org/2017/12/05/securitizations-of-identities-and-racial-eastern-europeanization/ (accessed 29 February 2024).
Ivasiuc, A. (2018) 'Reassembling insecurity: the power of materiality', in Kreide, R. and Langenohl, A. (eds) *Conceptualizing Power in Dynamics of Securitization: Beyond State and International System*. Baden-Baden: Nomos, pp. 367–94.

Ivasiuc, A. (2019) 'Sharing the insecure sensible: the circulation of images of Roma in the social media', in van Baar, H., Ivasiuc, A. and Kreide, R. (eds) *The Securitization of the Roma in Europe*. London and New York: Palgrave Macmillan, pp. 233–59.

Ivasiuc, A. (2021) 'From folk devils to modern state devils: the securitization and racial policing of the Roma in Italy', in Fredriksen, M. D. and Knudsen, I. H. (eds) *Modern Folk Devils: The Construction of Evil in Contemporary Europe*, Helsinki: Helsinki University Press, pp. 157–77.

Ivasiuc, A. (2022) 'Spatial mobility as a threat to social mobility: Roma in the peripheries of Rome and the NIMBY politics of *campi nomadi*', in Hein-Kircher, H. and Distler, W. (eds) *The Mobility-Security Nexus and the Making of Order. An Interdisciplinary and Historicizing Intervention*. Abingdon: Routledge, pp. 142–60. doi: 10.4324/9781003246619–11.

Ivasiuc, A. (2024) 'Víc než zbraně slabých: Rezistence Romů vůči sekuritizační politice' (Beyond weapons of the weak: Roma Resistance to securitarian governance), *Romano džaniben*, 30(2), 41–63. https://doi.org/10.5281/zenodo.10495322.

Juilland, A., Edwards, P. M. H. and Juilland, I. (1965) *Frequency Dictionary of Rumanian Words*. The Hague: Mouton.

Kalmar, I. (2022) *White But Not Quite: Central Europe's Illiberal Revolt*. Bristol: Bristol University Press.

Kalmar, I. (2023) 'Race, racialisation, and the East of the European Union: an introduction', *Journal of Ethnic and Migration Studies*, 49(6), 1465–80. doi: 10.1080/1369183X.2022.2154909.

Kaneva, N. and Popescu, D. (2014) '"We are Romanian, not Roma"', *Communication, Culture and Critique*, 7, 506–23.

Kovács, M. and Kabachnik, P. (2001) 'Shedding light on the quantitative other', in Böröcz, J. and Kovács, M. (eds) *Empire's New Clothes: Unveiling EU Enlargement*. Telford: Central Europe Review, pp. 147–95.

Krivonos, D. (2022) 'Carrying Europe's "white burden", sustaining racial capitalism: young post-Soviet migrant workers in Helsinki and Warsaw', *Sociology*, 57(4), 865–81. https://doi.org/10.1177/00380385221122413.

Krivonos, D. (2023) 'Racial capitalism and the production of difference in Helsinki and Warsaw', *Journal of Ethnic and Migration Studies*, 49(6), 1500–16. doi: 10.1080/1369183X.2022.2154911.

Kušić, K., Lottholz, P. and Manolova, P. (2019) 'From dialogue to practice: pathways towards decoloniality in Southeast Europe', in Kušišić, K., Manolova, P. and Lottholz, P. (eds) *Decolonial Theory and Practice in Southeast Europe*. Sofia: dVersia, Special Issue 03.19: 7–30. Available at https://dversia.net/wp-content/uploads/delightful-downloads/2019/06/special-issue.pdf (accessed 12 August 2024).

Lewicki, A. (2023) 'East–west inequalities and the ambiguous racialisation of "Eastern Europeans"', *Journal of Ethnic and Migration Studies*, 49(6), 1481–99. doi: 10.1080/1369183X.2022.2154910.

Majstorović, D. (2019) 'Postcoloniality as peripherality in Bosnia and Herzegovina', in Kušišić, K., Manolova, P. and Lottholz, P. (eds) *Decolonial Theory and Practice in Southeast Europe*. Sofia: dVersia, Special Issue 03.19: 131–48. Available at https://dversia.net/wp-content/uploads/delightful-downloads/2019/06/special-issue.pdf (accessed 12 August 2024).

Mădroane, I. D. (2021) 'Shame, (dis)empowerment and resistance in diasporic media: Romanian transnational migrants' reclassification struggles', in Reifová, I.

and Hájek, M. (eds) *Mediated Shame of Class and Poverty across Europe*. London: Palgrave Macmillan, pp. 61–83.

Melegh, A. (2006) *On the East-West Slope: Globalization, Nationalism, Racism and Discourses on Eastern Europe*. Budapest: Central European University Press.

Mignolo, W. (2021) *The Politics of Decolonial Investigations*. Durham, NC: Duke University Press.

Moroşanu, L. and Fox, J. E. (2013) '"No smoke without fire": strategies of coping with stigmatised migrant identities', *Ethnicities*, 13(4), 438–56. doi: 10.1177/1468796813483730.

Müller, M. (2020) 'In search of the Global East: thinking between North and South', *Geopolitics*, 25(3), 734–55. doi: 10.1080/14650045.2018.1477757.

Narkowicz, K. (2023) 'White enough, not white enough: racism and racialisation among poles in the UK', *Journal of Ethnic and Migration Studies*, 49(6), 1534–51 doi: 10.1080/1369183X.2022.2154913.

Olivera, M. (2015) 'Insupportables pollueurs ou recycleurs de génie? Quelques réflexions sur les 'Roms' et les paradoxes de l'urbanité libérale', *Ethnologie française*, 45(3), 499–509.

Pârvulescu, A. (2015) 'European racial triangulation', in Ponzanesi, S. and Colpani, G. (eds) *Postcolonial Transitions in Europe*. London: Rowman and Littlefield, pp. 25–45.

Pârvulescu, A. (2019) 'Eastern Europe as method', *The Slavic and East European Journal*, 63(4), 470–81. www.jstor.org/stable/45408997.

Rexhepi, P. (2023) *White Enclosures: Racial Capitalism and Coloniality along the Balkan Route*. Durham, NC: Duke University Press.

Rivera, A. (2009) 'Il pogrom di Ponticelli', in Naletto, G. (ed.) *Rapporto sul razzismo in Italia*. Rome: Manifestolibri, pp. 69–71.

Rzepnikowska, A. (2018) 'Imagining and encountering the other in Manchester and Barcelona: the narratives of Polish migrant women', *EthnoAnthropoZoom/ЕтноАнтропоЗум*, 15(15), 55–105. https://doi.org/10.37620/EAZ16150055rp.

Rzepnikowska, A. (2023) 'Racialization of Polish migrants in the UK and in Spain (Catalonia)', *Journal of Ethnic and Migration Studies*, 49(6), 1517–33. doi: 10.1080/1369183X.2022.2154912.

Stubbs, P. and Lendvai, N. (2016) 'Re-assembling and disciplining social Europe: turbulent moments and fragile f(r)ictions', in Krajina, Z. and Blanuša, N. (eds) *EU, Europe, Unfinished: Mediating Europe and The Balkans in a Time of Crisis*. London: Rowman and Littlefield, pp. 31–56.

Tesser, L. M. (2003) 'The geopolitics of tolerance: minority rights under EU expansion in East-Central Europe', *East European Politics and Societies*, 17(3), 483–532.

Tlostanova, M. (2018) 'The postcolonial and the socialist: a deferred coalition? Brothers forever?', *Postcolonial Interventions: An Interdisciplinary Journal of Postcolonial Studies*, 3(1), 1–37.

Todorova, M. (2009) *Imagining the Balkans*. Updated edition. Oxford: Oxford University Press.

Tulbure, C. (2022) 'Mobility and post-socialism: cross-border shaming and unbelonging in a white Europe', *State Crime*, 11(1), 110–27. doi: 10.13169/statecrime.11.1.0110.

Wolff, L. (1994) *Inventing Eastern Europe*. Stanford, CA: Stanford University Press.

Part III

Europeanisation as epistemic dispossession

8

The trauma of the key beyond dominant narratives: navigating epistemic and structural violence in Yemen's historical landscape

Saba Hamzah

> Knowledge emerges only through invention and reinvention, through the restless, impatient, continuing, hopeful inquiry human beings pursue in the world, with the world and with each other.
>
> *Paulo Freire (1970: 72)*

It all began when I found the key – a key I believed unlocked countless tales [Figure 8.1]. Tales of an ancient narrative that dwelled within me. For years, I clung to the key and the hope of uncovering new stories, but ultimately, I had to let go.

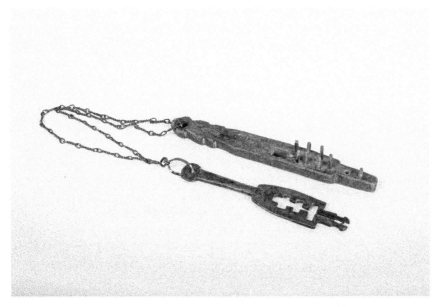

Figure 8.1 Wooden lock with keys, Tropen Museum/Wereld Museum, Amsterdam. Source: author. Yemeni, before 1956, circa 24.5 × 10 × 4.5 cm. Object Number: TM-2489–23a

My father insisted it was a lost history, one we could only know through the accounts others provided. Yet, how could we verify these stories? Do they require validation, or do they journey alone, like the people who lost them? Those who were silenced, stripped of their rights and whose lives ended without further explanation.

These people lost their stories to a larger one, not necessarily significant, but often an oppressive narrative that masquerades as triumph or resistance. Who is left to contradict such tales?

Now, I face a silent lock, haunted by the enigmatic past of the key. My memory holds both the key and the lock, while my body endures the violence of their memories. I lost the key when I was forced to flee, and now, the museum possesses the lock (Figure 8.2).

Can I assert that it's my lock? Can I claim this story as my own? I am unfamiliar with both, yet I yearn for them to open the unyielding walls that surround me.

Pages of silence: Deciphering Yemen's unrecorded chronicles

The history of Yemen is a complex tapestry, woven from various sources and narratives, ranging from the pre-Islamic era to the colonial period. What interests me the most, however, is the everyday life of ordinary people throughout these different historical periods. This curiosity began in my childhood, as I sought to learn about my grandparents' lives and my orphan parents through the stories of elderly villagers. In my quest for those stories and later for more knowledge, I realised that Yemen itself is an orphan land, with many of its people bearing the weight of inherited trauma.

I was born to parents who were both orphans, which unfortunately denied me the opportunity to forge relationships with my grandparents and hear their stories about their own and my parents' lives. My parents did not marry out of love; instead, their union was an arranged marriage intended to provide stability for two orphans of uncertain ages – my father, who was approximately 24 and my mother, who was around 12 years old at the time.

My mother ceased her literacy lessons to care for us, as she became overwhelmed with responsibilities. However, my father, who literally learned by engraving on stone, never stopped reading. Even though we lacked the presence of grandparents, we were fortunate to be enveloped by the love and care of other relatives. Our home was frequently visited by various women whom my parents respected, and it was filled with stories and tales that I would eagerly request whenever someone came by.

As I grew up, I found myself captivated by the stories that I could not find in the history books my father read and shared with me. These books

Figure 8.2 Wooden lock with keys, Tropen Museum/Wereld Museum, Amsterdam. Source: author. Yemeni, before 1956, circa 24.5 × 10 × 4.5 cm. Object Number: TM-2489–23a

Figure 8.3 An old notebook that I found in the notebooks section in a supermarket during my research stay in Doha. It was not for sale, but I convinced the manager to sell it to me. Source: author

felt distant and unrelated to my life, even if they appeared to be closer to the truth or, let's say, closer to reality. On the other hand, the grandmothers' stories were brimming with truth and life, despite sometimes seeming fantastical and removed from reality.

I became an attentive listener to the stories shared by these women, whether they were tales from our heritage or anecdotes from their daily lives and gatherings. Sometimes, I would seek more information about a story; if a woman stopped talking for any reason or if the story had concluded, I would approach her and insist that she continued. Frequently, my mother would intervene to explain that the story had ended or that it was inappropriate for me to inquire about 'adult' matters.

As I grew older, the stories from my childhood grew with me, and I found answers to many questions that had puzzled me. This is where, I believe, my interest in the silence in a story, rather than just the story itself, began.

In my first book (Hamzah, 2012), a collection of stories, I wrote about the tales that were either untold or whispered about in private gatherings. Often, the heroines of these stories were also the victims, and they typically bore the blame that society should have carried. In another research project, I collected extensive data on children who had experienced violence within their families. I visited overcrowded public schools filled with male and female students, as well as marginalised communities living on the edge of the city and history. The results of this research raised numerous questions for me, but for various reasons, including my mental well-being, I chose not to pursue it.

However, I never stopped pursuing what was not said in a story, and I carried this passion, if I may call it that, with me into academia, using artistic practices that allowed me to explore and navigate the world of the unknown or overlooked.

In my master's thesis (Hamzah, 2020), I sought to investigate Yemeni women writers throughout history. After conducting extensive readings, research and interviews with individuals knowledgeable about Yemeni history, it became apparent that this research would require significant effort, as I would not find many women in history books, let alone women writers. I was aware of some female poets, but they were the ones everyone seemed to know, and that was not enough for me. I desired to delve deeper into the reasons behind their absence from history books, whether those authored by Yemenis, Orientalists or travellers.

A historian friend told me that I was searching for a needle in a haystack. As a result, I shifted my focus during my studies to activating the silence in living archives that allowed me to reference women and engage with them directly. I postponed exploring the silence of historical archives for a later time.

About a year after graduating, I was invited to visit the Tropenmuseum in Amsterdam, Netherlands, to participate and make an artistic intervention. Upon arrival, I was informed that there was an item from Yemen on display. This item was an old lock that required a unique type of wooden key to open. I recognised the key, as it was the first artefact from my history that I received when I was seven years old. A woman gifted it to me in response to my curiosity and eagerness to learn more stories about my grandparents and the house we were visiting. The house belonged to my maternal grandfather but later became home to numerous heirs who eventually left it for another family to reside in. My paternal grandfather's house, which stood nearby, had fallen into disrepair and was uninhabited. The woman, noticing my dissatisfaction with the answers I received, decided to give me the key she had hidden in a nook of her room. She told me it had belonged to my grandfather.

As I stood facing the lock displayed in a glass case, a flood of memories washed over me. The lock appeared cold and pale, a stark contrast to the memories and stories it evoked within me, yet at least it had the opportunity to be exposed to the light in the exhibition hall. It served as a symbol and a connection to my past, my family and my heritage.

This was unlike the hundreds or even thousands of artefacts that remained hidden away in the basement of the museum, never to see or hear the light of day.

I was once again confronted with silence. I searched for stories about the objects and photographs in their collections, as a research associate at the cultural material centre of world museums, but there was little to be found. Despite this, I was thrilled to discover these objects because I knew they would evoke numerous stories and emotions, just as the key had done for me. I sought the knowledge that emerged from everyday life, as most of the objects and photos belonged to 'ordinary' people.

I came to understand that knowledge is not only found in written forms but also in practice. It was then that I embraced the voice I had denied for so long, allowing it to unearth and create a space for situated knowledges rooted in everyday life.

In response to the pain, anger and joy I founded the Yemeni Women Archive as a joyful act. I realised that if we did not have a space in the archive, then we are the archive. We embody the knowledge, the history and the future. By preserving and celebrating the now and then, we can create a living archive that honours the stories and experiences of everyday life. A space for knowledges emerging from women's experiences and histories in Yemen and the diaspora.

When I delved again on researching Yemeni women in history for the Yemeni Women Archive, I was overwhelmed and uncertain about where to begin. A friend assured me that my work held significance and that it would offer a new perspective on Yemeni history.

I had the opportunity to travel to Qatar and conduct research at the Qatar National Library, which houses an extensive collection of Arabic history books and manuscripts. The library was also in the process of digitising the British Museum archive that is related to the history of the Arabic and Islamic world, further expanding the resources available for my research.

As I immersed myself in literature and photographs, I realised that while my understanding was broadening, it was not necessarily transforming – it was akin to witnessing violence firsthand, then observing it through an amplified lens.

Perusing books and manuscripts in the library, I struggled to identify what I sought. Intrigued by how these materials reinforced my perception of Yemen as a subjugated and secluded nation, I still could not pinpoint the specific details I required. A library staff member assisted in translating additional documents, yet even then, I discovered scant information about women in Yemeni history.

In truth, I was hunting for a narrative that would likely remain unmentioned in those tomes and manuscripts – the tale of my grandfather, who never came back and the stories of innumerable generations that never found a space in the annals of time. I looked for the silences in those records but felt stifled and disconnected. The silence was ingrained within me – woven into my body and mind – and I grappled with finding a means to communicate with it (Figure 8.3).

Ghaiman: Home of stories and treasures

"غيمان محفوفة بالكروم لها بهجة ولها منظر قد قبر بها من مضى من آبائنا وبها نقبر

وإذا ما قبرنا بها حشونا مقابرنا الجوه"

Ghaiman laden with vineyards brings joy and presents a view where our ancestors were buried, and where we too shall be buried. And when we are buried there, our graves will be filled with precious jewels.[1]

The village of my upbringing has long been renowned as a site of historical significance (Figure 8.4), steeped in a rich tapestry of tales and legends. As a child, I was excited with captivating stories of hidden treasures that allegedly manifested themselves within the dreams of the villagers. It was commonly believed that any local inhabitants who discovered these treasures would see them transform into ashes. However, individuals hailing from outside the village were exempt from these stipulations and could

Figure 8.4 Ghaiman, the home. Photo © Abdulrahman Mohammed Alghabri

take the treasures if they were able to relinquish something of great personal value, such as a beloved son or daughter. In certain instances, the sacrifice of a lamb possessing a specific characteristic, such as being entirely white or black, would suffice to claim the treasure for themselves. Throughout my youth, I bore witness to numerous sites that had been excavated by unknown individuals under the veil of night (Figures 8.5 and 8.6).

This story, once a source of joy and pride for me, is now taking on a different form within me. It seems to be diving into unfamiliar depths within my genetic makeup, and burrowing into unknown chambers in my memory, making it difficult to recount with ease. The story is of the key that the woman who is named Atika gave me during my first visit to my grandparents' house in the old village. She told me then that it was for my grandfather. I visited there with my elder sister, cousins and friends who sought refuge in our house during the war in 1994. This war, between the South and North of Yemen, or between socialists and Islamists, or perhaps a conflict of interests, was something that I, as a seven-year-old, could not fully comprehend. However, I was content with the company of those around me, and happy that we were able to spend a few months in the village, where I made many new friends and learned a lot of stories.

Figure 8.5 Ghaiman, the old gate. Photo © Abdulrahman Mohammed Alghabri

The key became the reason I asked my father about his father, as I had no stories or knowledge about him. Although I had heard some stories about my grandmother from my father's step-brothers, there was nothing about his father. My father explained that he too knew very little about his own father, who had passed away when my father was only six years old. According to my father, a soldier of the Imam came to our village and claimed that my grandfather had passed away. The soldier took my grandfather's belongings, and they never saw his body or gave him a proper farewell.

I have asked my father to recount this story many times, hoping to gain new insights or details, but each time the story remains the same without any additional information as I had hoped. The story has become less about joy and more about a painful realisation of what little I know about the past that shaped us.

In the village, it was not only my father who did not know about his ancestry and their stories. Many people knew little or nothing about their ancestors, and their memories seemed limited. As I grew older and asked more villagers, I discovered that their stories were often legends about people who lived hundreds of years ago or tales of supernatural beings. When talking about family trees, one person, 'Sayyed'[2] Abbas, always came up. People said he was the only one who knew his family tree, but some believed his family line would soon end.

Figure 8.6 Asad Alkamel foot on a stone on a building in Ghaiman.
Photo © Abdulrahman Mohammed Alghabri

When I inquired further, some people explained that Assayyed was the only one who knew his family tree because he was from the Hashimite lineage, belonging to Al Albayet. As for the impending end of his lineage, they said it was because he refused to marry his daughters to anyone within the village, as he was the only Sayyed there.

History, as an area of knowledge, primarily focuses on the recorded past. However, when only the history of the privileged is studied, it often overlooks the experiences of the oppressed and underprivileged. Many people may not have had access to education or the means to record their lives and experiences, leaving their stories untold.

In our village, people knew more about the Imam and his stories than their own. Even in my father's story about his own father, the Imam's soldier took up a significant part of the narrative, and the Imam's violence was never addressed in that context.

I always knew that if I needed to know anything about the past and make the history of it, then I needed to document the stories of elderly people. It was 2015, and the anxiety of a potentially lost memory started to hit me. It was then when I called my sister who still lives in Sana'a and asked her to interview the few elderly people who were still alive about their life before the revolution in 1962 and after. My sister agreed to do so when in fact she was going along with me because she thought I was processing the trauma of war and exile.

Perhaps what I was processing was the death of my grandmother, my mother's aunt. She represented to me the past that I always wanted to learn about, the people I always wanted to meet, the lost memory of a whole generation that was not able to write or read anything or leave traces of who they were and what lives they led.

I saw her in January 2015 for the last time. We grew up calling her جدتنا الغربية, our Western grandmother (Figure 8.7). She was identified as such because she was living in the western part of the village. In our village, many women were named Atika, عتيقة, so people used different things to identify this Atika or that. The word Atika means ancient, and it was so widely used that even when the mother is named Atika, she calls her daughter Atika! It only shows how isolated people were in their environment because, after 1962, this name started to fade and vanish, allowing for a variety of other names that have always existed in the Arabic language.

Oral history: Intersecting narratives and perspectives

One particularly intriguing story revolves around a woman who temporarily resided in our village. It is said that, upon discovering a golden chicken laying golden eggs, she promptly vanished. It was later revealed that she

The trauma of the key beyond dominant narratives 173

Figure 8.7 My mother's aunt, my Western grandmother: Atika Hamdan. Photo by Anas Abbas. Copyright: author

had sold these valuable items to a city dweller, thus explaining her sudden disappearance. Another anecdote, which my aunt fervently asserts as truth, involves a farmer employed by my maternal grandfather. This farmer, known as Aljalal, reportedly discovered a statue accompanied by a sword. My grandfather entrusted Aljalal with the sword while retaining the statue for himself. When inquiring about the statue's whereabouts, my aunt recounted a harrowing tale of a moonless night when my grandparents were alerted by a mysterious noise originating from the lower level of their home. Venturing into the dimly lit corridor, they encountered the shadowy silhouette of an intruder. In a frantic act of self-defence, my grandfather wielded a nearby saw and struck the figure, only to realise he had inadvertently shattered the coveted statue.

As mentioned above, I grew up in a historical village, home to diverse people from different religions and castes. One day, my parents' cousin – also named Atika – told me about the Jews who lived in our village before they left in 1948 for Palestine. She recounted a story of a Jewish mother giving her son a cookie, telling him it was from Moses, only to take it later away, claiming that Muhammad, the Muslim prophet, had taken it from him. Aunt Atika attempted to convey the mutual hatred between Jews and Muslims, stemming from perceived deceit and religious differences.

However, I also heard a different perspective from another woman, Jumaa, جمعة who spoke fondly of her interactions with the Jews in the village. She was a Muslim woman of a lower caste, not from the tribes,[3] and she would visit Jewish families on Saturdays to celebrate and share meals since she was very poor. For her, it did not matter who provided the food. When she spoke about the Jews, her tone was filled with passion and compassion, in stark contrast to Atika's disdain.

These tales were far from mere fabrications; they held a profound significance within the historical narratives that permeated the daily lives of the villagers, as well as serving a central role in the governance of Yemen, spanning both the Imamate and Western imperial powers. As we delve into these stories, we must consider what they conceal and reveal within the context of historical narratives. Furthermore, we must examine the implications of their continued circulation in perpetuating the ongoing conflict in Yemen and the factors that contribute to maintaining the present state of affairs.

Oral history can offer valuable insights into the past, but it is essential to approach such accounts critically, considering what and how individuals choose to share and omit. Personal narratives may vary due to differing interpretations of events or cultural norms. Additionally, stories can be coloured by biases or even hatred, as illustrated by a village where Jewish children were taught to despise Islam. Nevertheless, untold stories of collaboration and love between Muslims and Jews may yet be discovered.

This discussion returns to the Imam's agreements with Israel to displace Jews to Palestine.[4] Although some Jews voluntarily relocated, others were reluctant to leave their homes, and many were persuaded or coerced to depart. Jews have been an integral part of the Yemeni community for centuries; however, since the establishment of Israel, their numbers have dwindled. Even when Imams were not in power, they continued to push Jews away from their villages in Saada. After the Houthis seized power, only one Jew remains in Yemen, imprisoned and accused by the Houthis of smuggling Hebrew manuscripts to Israel.

The right to narrate: Historical power dynamics, the caste system and social divisions in Yemen

Constructing a story often involves delving into libraries, archives, diaries and history books to establish a solid framework. Many challenges arise when these sources lack information about specific people or events. Black historians, for example, have pointed out that the history of slavery is limited due to the fact that colonial powers enslaved Black people and denied them the right to learn how to read or write.

Similarly, over many centuries, the Hashemite caste in Yemen monopolised education, making it nearly impossible for others to access their right to learn reading or writing, with only a few managing to challenge this control. Also, the continuous wars and conflicts fuelled by the Imamate confined people's concerns to life's essentials, a situation that continues today as the Houthis control most of North Yemen (Talib and Brehony, 2017).

My introduction to Yemen's caste system was a revelation. A high school friend belonging to the Hashemite caste told me of her 'superior' social standing. This was confirmed by my father, albeit with a hint of irony. He highlighted that the caste system's endorsement of Hashemite superiority was flawed and unjust.

The Imamate system divided people into distinct castes, with those descending from the Prophet's family occupying the highest echelon. Interestingly, even within this group, a hierarchy existed. Next in line were scholars, referred to in Arabic as Judges (Qodah قضاة), followed by tribes (Qabail). Then came the Mazaina, those who did not own land and worked in professions such as butchery, barbering or singing at weddings, among others. Following them were the Black people, believed to have African ancestry and known as Akhdam. The term Akhdam signifies both their colour as Black and their position as servants. At the bottom of the social hierarchy were the Jews (GarAllah, 2023).

I once encountered a saying about the Al-Mahdi family, the Imams, who claimed they were neither adept at governing people nor skilled in warfare, yet were shrewd enough to sustain ongoing conflict. This adage might encapsulate the enduring plight faced by a small country in southern Arabia for a millennium. Perpetual battle has left it no respite to rise from the ashes and flourish.

One of the Imams' methods, according to some historians, was to occupy people with each other and create animosity among them. This is evident in the relationships between different social classes and in the ignited conflicts among tribes. Yemeni history books and oral narratives are filled with stories of these conflicts.[5]

Two sides of the same coin: Colonial chessboard

When delving into the long-lasting conflicts and complex geopolitics of North and South Yemen, it is crucial to consider the question: Who is the coloniser?

Anti-colonial socialism was a common force uniting people from both sides of Yemen in their attempts to escape the Imamate system's tyranny in the North and British colonialism in the South. Their shared rebellion against

Figure 8.8 Excavated gold heads, gift from Yemen at the coronation of the British King. Sana'a, 1942. Source: author

internal and external colonialism culminated in the Yemeni Revolution of 1962, which freed the North after eight years of warfare from the Imamate system. Meanwhile, in South Yemen, socialists valiantly battled to establish an independent state.

Despite the significant efforts of young socialists aspiring to build a just state, the power struggles entrenched for centuries were not eradicated overnight. The primary focus of the Yemeni Revolution became the liberation of the oppressed. However, geopolitical interests led Russia, a socialist ally, to abandon South Yemen to secure its relationship with America.

This action, coupled with Saudi Arabia's and the West's shared interests, left the South unprotected and significantly influenced by the residual Imamate-era Zaidi state (Fawaz and Wedeen, 2021).[6]

The term 'colonisers' often refers to a group that exercises control or dominance over another group, often imposing their culture, values and systems. In the context of the Houthis, who originate from Saada in North Yemen and expanded to the capital in 2014, their actions have led to many people, both Muslims and Jews from various cities, to perceive them as colonisers.

The crucial question about colonialism is not easily answered, as the identity of a coloniser can vary depending on context and perspective. In the case of the Imams, both sides may exhibit supremacist attitudes, believing in their own superiority, erasing cultural identities and exploiting people. Furthermore, the Imamate of the past, now represented by the Houthis, isolates people in various ways, even amidst technological advancements. This isolation can be both external and internal, further contributing to the perception of them as colonisers.

Ultimately, the designation of a coloniser may be subjective and depend on the specific dynamics and power relations at play in any given situation.

The example of the Imamate represented today by Houthis demonstrates that colonialism is not solely the domain of foreign powers. It can also be enacted by those who share supremacist attitudes and seek to dominate other groups. Recognising and understanding these different forms of colonialism is essential for addressing their impacts and working towards a more just and inclusive society.

Albardoni (2002) provides a powerful lens through which to view the complex history and identity of Yemen and its people through his poetry. 'Invasion from Within' highlights the dual nature of colonialism in Yemen, emphasising that the Yemeni people were not only oppressed by Western colonisers but also by people from within. His work not only highlights the external colonisation by Western powers but also the internal colonisation perpetrated by the Imamate.

The impact of the Imamate on Yemeni identity cannot be understated. By erasing the culture and isolating the people, the Imamate created a new identity for Yemenis that was defined by their struggle for survival in the face of oppression. Albardoni's poetry serves as a reminder of this difficult past and the ongoing struggle to reclaim and redefine Yemeni identity in the face of internal and external forces.

The Imamate's rule not only led to the erasure of Yemeni culture but also the subjugation and isolation of its people, creating a new identity marked by isolation and fear.

The line from Albardoni's other poem, 'I knew him as Yemeni from the way he hesitatingly looks right and left', illustrates the effects of this subjugation and isolation on the Yemeni people. Their identity became characterised by a sense of hesitancy and wariness, as they were continuously subjected to both internal and external forces seeking to control and exploit them.

Colonial powers often employ strategies that seek to control the minds of the colonised before their bodies. By suppressing cultural expression, enforcing subjugation and inducing deprivation, colonisers aim to break the spirit and will of the people they dominate. This tactic helps ensure that the colonised population remains passive and less likely to revolt against their oppressors.

In addition, there are many instances in Yemeni history where the Imams had agreements with the West, particularly in relation to South Yemen (Naji, 1988). Qasimid Imams began in 1597 and thrived on profound collaborations with colonialism either by having agreements or by following the same brutal path that Imams have been using throughout history including genocides against indigenous people in Yemen (Mazariq and Matrafiah, for example).[7]

As the Imams aimed to consolidate their rule in North Yemen, they occasionally entered into agreements with the West to secure their interests or counter the influence of other regional powers. This complex relationship between the Imams and the Western empires led to numerous treaties, agreements and negotiations that shaped the political landscape of Yemen for centuries (Figure 8.8).[8]

These alliances suggest that the Imams were not strictly opposed to colonialism, contrary to some historians' claims, but rather were active collaborators. They did not necessarily share the same belief, but they shared the same supremacist ideology to justify their brutality and protect their interests. Colonialism is not only about invading the land but also colonising the mind by deliberately erasing cultural identity.

White laundering: Inter-imperial narratives and silenced narratives/narrators

In 'The Struggle Over Representation', Ella Shohat explicates the battle to articulate one's own experiences is deeply intertwined with a history of having others narrate your story, as well as the ongoing fight to express oneself and be genuinely acknowledged (Shohat and Stam, 2023).

Yemen has fascinated Westerners for centuries, attracting them for trade, military conquest and exploration of language and geography. These explorers fall into two categories: collective missions arranged by governments or scientific organisations, and individual travellers. Their experiences, documented through reports, studies or books, often benefited from institutional support (AlAmri, 2013). However, researching everyday Yemeni life from Western imperial archives is challenging due to dominant narratives.

I coined the term 'white laundering' to highlight the tactic employed by inter-imperialists to obscure colonial/anti-colonial intentions under benign pretexts, often leading to the marginalisation of indigenous perspectives.

White laundering serves as a term to describe the manipulation and concealment of colonial intentions and actions by European powers, often under the guise of scientific exploration or trade missions. Recognising these deceptive practices is crucial for understanding the complex and often hidden dimensions of colonialism and its enduring effects on the regions and people impacted by it.

The 'French mission' of 1708 and 1709 serves as an example of the complex and often deceptive nature of colonial endeavours. Though the mission was presented as an economic expedition focused on trading in coffee, the presence of 50 cannons on two ships raises questions about its true intentions.

The French justification for carrying such a significant amount of weaponry was to protect themselves against potential attacks from rival European powers, such as the Dutch and the British. This reasoning suggests that the French were well aware of the competitive nature of colonial interests in the region and sought to secure their own interests by arming themselves heavily (Omar, 2017).

However, the presence of the cannons could also be interpreted as a display of power and a means of exerting control over the local population and resources. In this sense, the French mission could be seen as an example of colonialism disguised as a trade mission. This tactic allowed the French to maintain a veneer of legitimacy while pursuing their colonial agenda.

In any case, the 'French mission' highlights the complicated dynamics of colonialism, where trade, competition and power struggles often coexisted and overlapped. Understanding these dynamics is crucial for gaining a more comprehensive view of the historical impact of colonialism on the regions it affected and the people who lived there.

The Royal Danish mission in the mid-eighteenth century, though claiming to be a scientific expedition to explore Yemen and learn about its biblical connections, had ulterior motives. At the time, Denmark was looking for potential colonies, but, apparently, the existence of different imperial powers in Yemen and the tragic loss of four out of the five scientists leading the mission during the journey changed their minds. The only survivor of this mission travelled back to Denmark with a great archive of this expedition but the mission remained inactive for over a century.

Subsequently, the British utilised the information from the Danish mission to establish their colonial presence in Yemen. These strategic acts of obscuring truths to further European imperial objectives exemplify what can be referred to as white laundering.

Another example of white laundering can be seen in the report of a French Jew who documented his mission to Yemen. In this report, he neglected to give any credit to Habshoosh, his Yemeni Jewish guide, who not only shared his knowledge but also looked after him throughout his stay. Habshoosh's absence in the report is conspicuous, and if other local people are mentioned at all, they are relegated to roles of 'servers', 'helpers' or those who were 'simply serving food'.

The French report, written for the French imperial government, highlights the struggles the author faced to acquire the knowledge he gathered, without acknowledging the invaluable contributions of local individuals like Habshoosh. Such omission of the key roles played by local people in these missions is another example of how European colonial powers manipulated and concealed the truth to further their imperial objectives.

By disregarding the contributions of local people and focusing only on the efforts of the European 'explorers', these reports perpetuate a narrative that diminishes the importance of indigenous knowledge and perspectives, further entrenching colonial ideologies and biases. Recognising and acknowledging these omissions is vital for a more accurate understanding of history and the impact of colonialism on the people and regions affected by it.

An anti-colonial politician from Syria visited Yemen around 1936. I was told that his narrative challenged the colonisers' dominant narrative about Yemen. However, when reading his book, all I found was praise for the Imam for not allowing European colonisers to totally occupy Yemen. According to the author, the Imam had 'saved Yemen'. He was reproducing the same supremacist narrative used by the Imams who claimed Yemen's isolation was because the people were 'poor' and 'ignorant'. He emphasised that the people were saved by the Imam from the colonial powers, without being able to analyse the epistemic and structural violence of Imamate rule to keep people in place and isolated.

Many historians tend to be drawn to the narratives of foreign explorers because of this tension in naming the violence of strategic isolation. I still remember the first book I read in my childhood about Yemen, it was written by a French doctor and anthropologist who worked in Yemen during the 1950s. Her book was translated into Arabic, albeit with modifications to emphasise the violence of Imamate rule. This book also highlighted the difficult lives of Yemeni women.

However, the anti-imperialist gaze continues to become blind to the violence of inter-imperial formations between and across ruling relations, in this case between the Imamate and European imperial powers.

Additionally, it is crucial to examine the types of stories found in archives and consider whose narratives are represented or excluded. Many history books tend to focus on politics and the nation, with only a few accounts of people's personal experiences. Diaries often belong to Yemeni politicians and concentrate on political events rather than their daily lives. In contrast, travelogues by visitors to Yemen in the past four centuries can provide valuable insights into public life during those times. Still, there are only a few stories regarding women. Which requires writing/rewriting history through a gender-sensitive lens.

Inter-imperial[9] narratives and isolation have characterised the history of Yemen. Despite the presence of explorers and agreements with foreign imperial powers, the Yemeni people have remained isolated in their minds, perpetuating a cycle of conflict and subjugation. Strategic ignorance and isolation have been used as tools of control by various ruling relations, including the Imamate and European imperial powers.

The lives and stories of ordinary Yemeni people, particularly women, are often absent from historical records. The few existing accounts often come from Western explorers or scholars with imperialist motives, which may distort or misrepresent their experiences. The selective documentation of Yemen's history has left silences and absences that must be acknowledged and explored.

Inter-imperial formations, such as the relationship between the Imamate and European colonial powers, have also played a role in perpetuating the narrative of Yemen as an isolated land. This narrative has been used by both sides to maintain power and control over the people. Socialist narratives have similarly perpetuated the image of Yemen as 'poor' and 'ignorant', without analysing the structural violence inherent in the Imamate rule.

In conclusion, the complexities of colonialism and inter-imperial narratives in Yemen cannot be reduced to a single story. Recognising the impact of internal and external forces on the country's history is crucial for understanding the present situation. The silences and absences in historical accounts must be addressed, and the stories of ordinary Yemeni people must be brought to light to reveal the true nature of the colonial experience in Yemen.

By acknowledging the limitations and biases of historical sources, researchers and storytellers can work to fill gaps and strive for a more comprehensive understanding of the past. This may involve seeking alternative sources, exploring oral histories or engaging in interdisciplinary research to uncover the stories that have remained hidden for generations.

While journeying through these stories, it is important to remember that the ones we encounter are just parts of a greater narrative. Each one is a testament to the enduring spirit of Yemen, an invitation to look beyond the dominant narratives, and an invitation to listen to the silence and whispers in the living, non-existent and historical archives.

While the aim of this chapter is to focus on the stories that are often overlooked, I acknowledge the limitations imposed by the scope of the book, its duration and the space allotted to it. Not every voice in Yemen's rich and complex history can find a place in these pages. Therefore, this chapter is just a humble beginning, an invitation and a starting point for further studies on challenging the dominant narratives and does not claim to be a definitive or all-encompassing account of Yemen's history.

Acknowledgements

The author would like to thank the staff of Qatar National Library for supporting her stay and research during the months of December 2021 to January 2022.

This chapter has been written during the author's position as Research Associate at the Wereld Museum, Amsterdam, between August 2021 and August 2023.

Notes

1 Asaad Tuba bin Maad Yakrib (أسعد تبع بن معد يكرب) from the book: الإكليل Al-Iklil: From the *History of Yemen and the Genealogy of the Himyar*, by Abu Muhammad al-Hasan bin Ahmad al-Hamdani, a Yemeni geographer and historian. This book comprises ten sections, ten books of which six are lost, that merge the fields of history, archaeology, genealogy and language. It is a well-known historical book in Yemen and the surrounding region, and scholars regard it as an encyclopaedia of Yemeni civilisation in the pre-Islamic era. Besides being a source of information on history, genealogy, provinces and antiquities, it is also a representation of Yemen's cultural and historical identity.
2 The term 'Sayyed' translates to 'Master' in English and is exclusively used for individuals who claim to be part of the Hashemite dynasty.
3 See the next section on caste.
4 It is true that Jews in Yemen had journeys to Palestine before the establishment of the Zionist entity, but they went there because it is the Holy Land in the Torah, and also some of them were fleeing the tyranny of the Imams and the persecution they were suffering as a religious minority and a group at the bottom of the social pyramid. So the goal was not always to settle. After the Yemeni Revolution, the Jews lived in their communities inside Yemen and despite the fact that their communities were still marginalised, they were not forced to leave, even though there were many attempts by America and Israel to encourage them to leave Yemen. Now, that Yemen is under the control of the Houthis since 2014, both Yemeni Jews and Muslims were displaced, but the focus here is on the Jews because they were a minority and today only one Jew remains, who is imprisoned in the Houthi jails on charges of smuggling some manuscripts to Israel.
5 The contrasting perspectives of a French Jew who visited Yemen in the nineteenth century and Yemeni Jew Habshosh shed light on the societal divisions that existed then and still persist today. While the French Jew emphasised the oppression of the Imamate against both Muslim tribes and Jews, Habshosh focused exclusively on the violence they experienced at the hands of the tribes.
6 It is important to note that the difference between the Zaidiyyah as a doctrine and the Hashemite Imamate. While the two agree on many points, there are

many who believe in Zaidiyyah. Those who believe that rule can be outside the scope of the Hashemite household, and the Matrifiyyah was the first to call for this. However, Abdullah bin Hamza, the Hashemite Imam, fought and eradicated the Matrifiyyah group for adopting a point of view that does not limit the Imamate to the Hashemite household. So, the Imamate was confined to those who are Hashemites only.

7 See Ibrahim Jalal: Century-old grievances continue to fester in Yemen's Tihama region, Middle East Institute, 2021 and Fathi Abo Alnassr, The Tragedy of Almatrafia, Al Modon, 2014.
8 See Amin Alrahabni, Kings of Arabs, Handawi Foundation.
9 See Aparna and Krivonos, this volume.

References

لإكليل Al-Iklil (n.d.) *From the History of Yemen and the Genealogy of the Himyar, Abu Muhammad al-Hasan bin Ahmad al-Hamdani.* Egypt: Al Salafia Publisher and its Libraries.
AlAmri, H. (2013) *Yemen and the West.* Damascus, Syria: Dar Alfekr.
Al-Bbaradoni, A. (2002) *The Complete Poetic Works Of Al-baradouni.* Sana'a: The General Book Commission.
Freire, P. (1970) *Pedagogy of the Oppressed.* New York: Continuum.
GarAllah, G. (2023) *The Horror of Adornment, What Does it Mean to Mozayn in Yemen.* Yemen: Almadania.
Hamzah, S. (2012) *Taratil Athra.* Yemen: Maktabat Khālid ibn al-Walīd.
Hamzah, S. (2020) *Stranded: Stories from the Abysmal Sea, Feminist Intersectional Politics of Death*, MA Thesis, Utrecht University.
Jalal, I. (2021) 'Century-old grievances continue to fester in Yemen's Tihama region', *Middle East Institute.* www.mei.edu/publications/century-old-grievances-continue-fester-yemens-tihama-region (accessed 6 August 2024).
Naji, Sultan A. (1988) *Military History of Yemen 1839–1967.* Beirut: Dar Aloudah.
Omar, H. (2017) *Yemen in French Memory.* Cairo: Dar Aladab.
Shohat, E. and Stam, R. (2003) *Unthinking Eurocentrism: Multiculturalism and the Media.* London: Routledge.
Talib, S. and Brehony, N. (2017) 'Hadhramaut in Yemeni Politics since the 1960s', in Brehony, N. (ed.) *Hadhramaut and Its Diaspora: Yemeni Politics, Identity and Migration.* London: I. B. Tauris, pp. 19–40.
Trabulsi, F. and Wedeen, L. (2021) *Memoirs of Jarallah Omar: The Struggle for Power and Wealth in Yemen.* Beirut: Almada.

9

From singular to plural: how to write the story of a Roma actress

Mihaela Drăgan

Translation: Viorica Stefania Cappello

In elementary school, I used to 'stage' Caragiale's plays by myself, rummaging through the whole house for masquerade ball costumes from my mother and aunt's youth for all sorts of items that I thought would be useful to me in the 'production', and bring them all to school. Then, I would select the cast from my class (of course, I would cast myself in lead roles, pretending to be the boss) and rehearse 'with intonation' along with the colleagues until we memorised the text. When I was ready, I notified the teachers to stop everything and invited my colleagues from other classes to see the 'Show'. In my mind, I truly believed that my show was more important than any other course. It didn't even cross my mind that I disrupted the classes and that, at my age of about ten, I did not sound credible when I said that 'I have a show'. Well, this repeated a few times a year, and everyone had got used to me.

I wrote this status on Facebook in August 2019, after performing in the show *Who Killed Szomna Grancsa?* in Cândești, the village where I grew up, right in my schoolyard.

All last summer, I performed alongside my theatre company, Giuvlipen, in villages for Roma communities that have no access to theatre. I returned from real theatre stages, after more than twenty years, to perform at the school where I studied, but this time as a professional with a degree in acting. It was so touching to see in the middle of the audience relatives that I barely knew anything about, or my grandpa, who dressed for this occasion to see me playing for the first time.

I've said many times before that I am exactly like in that cliché story: I wanted to be an actress ever since I was little, and that is what I've become. Many times, however, having this profession hasn't been the most beautiful thing in the world, as I imagined when I was a child. I remember I once read in *Libertatea* an article about me entitled 'The Fabulous Story of Mihaela

Drăgan: From a Roma girl from Cândești to the actress who broke the hearts of Italians'.[1] It said:

> Somehow, miracles do exist. It's just that it doesn't happen all of a sudden, overnight. Instead, it takes years of work, torment, humiliations and battles. These ingredients are a part of Mihaela Drăgan's story, a girl born in a mixed family (a Roma mother and a Romanian father), in a village of a forgotten world from Buzău county. Nothing could have foreseen the success story that was to follow.

I must admit that I felt confused rather than proud of this phrase about me. Indirectly, the article implies that it is a miracle that I, a Roma girl from Cândești village, am an actress. Although I've never mentioned to the reporter that I grew up in an impoverished family, the article suggests information that I didn't offer, content about which I had no say and no control before it was published: 'An actress [...] whose life story is worthy of a movie script. Because her life has not been worry-free, quite the contrary.'

The story of the 'poor Roma man or woman who educated/emancipated themselves' is about the only positive story about us that sells in the press. The dehumanised perception about Roma people as entities bound for failure is so internalised in the collective mentality that when we are presented with a success story of a Roma person, sensationalism doesn't take long to appear: success seems the result of a miracle. This way, a new stereotype is created: the Roma exception – a minority within our minority that attained the status of 'Roma who overcame their condition'. Every time I hear or read in the press this dehumanised utterance, it is obvious to me that it refers to Roma as belonging to a lower, inferior, subhuman condition.

The mentality that Roma are inferior to the white majority and that they cannot be equal to the Romanians stems from the shameful history of Roma slavery in the Romanian Principalities. When we get presented as exceptions, we are reminded that only some of us have overcome our historical condition of enslaved men and women. Thus, a modern vision of the relationship of power between the former boyars/slave owners and we Roma, still exists. By reinforcing and updating this power relationship, the violence against us is once again justified. To be portrayed in the press as 'exceptions' or as 'Roma people who overcame their condition' is a dangerous reverse psychology strategy to dehumanise the entire Roma minority.

We live in a neoliberal society that considers competition a defining feature of inter-human relationships and regards the fight for equality and social rights as counterproductive in forming a 'natural hierarchy' between those who succeed and those who lose the competition. Neoliberalism promotes the false idea that the successful are those who deserve it, while those who are not successful must be blamed for failure. Neoliberalism ignores class, ethnicity privilege or access to education, which contribute to the success of an individual, making it seem that success is solely based on merit while blaming the marginalised. People of colour fail exactly because the system and lack of privileges don't allow them to do anything to change their social standing.

Therefore, in a society based on neoliberal principles that maintains social hierarchies, my story can only be one of exception, in which I am a heroine who succeeded in the battle with all the hardships of life, defeated them on her *own*, and accomplished the great dream as in the American movies. Because the only stories the majority can hear and understand about us Roma are those in which we must strive for education with every ounce of strength, we must struggle, must humiliate ourselves but, in the end, we must succeed, otherwise, we don't deserve their respect. Their respect will be our ultimate medal, and this idea of respectability that is imposed upon us is, in fact, their own vision of the world we live in – not ours.

Their vision of respect is built arbitrarily following their experience as a dominant social group, and to gain the quality of being worthy of their respect, you must adopt the values that guide them and are imposed by them. We ought to recognise their power and cultural domination to be respected. They made us believe that the art and culture of white people represent a guiding landmark and that only their cultural creation and works are 'high and noble culture', while Roma art and culture is defined as inferior, traditional and folkloric. More often than not, as an actress, I've met other Roma actors who refused to be associated with the idea of Roma theatre and culture because it would have given them less personal dignity than their only alternative: to adhere to a white culture in which, most often, we are forced to accept stereotypical roles as Roma characters. Not sufficiently exposed to critical discourse, we internalise the idea that we need to aspire to this 'high white culture' instead of contributing to the development of a Roma culture that is still not acknowledged for the contribution and inspiration it instilled in the mainstream culture over time. We often crave the white artists' success without being aware of the fact that we don't have access to the same resources. In theatre and movie environments where we work, I often feel that they expect us to prove that we are professionals, that we are not some amateurs, that unlike other Roma, we have chosen education.

When 'successful Roma' talk about how education saved their life, *gadjes* weep with joy because they will once again, for the nth time, have the confirmation that Roma are the only ones responsible for their own education and the only culprits when they do not benefit from it. This is because society prefers to blame Roma for their lack of education instead of admitting that we live in an inequality-based system that doesn't offer them access to education. Even the Roma civic rights movement has often taken over this discourse of the need for education, forgetting that the educational environment in Romania discriminates against and segregates Roma children.

Therefore, when the exception of the 'successful Roma' is celebrated, what is, in fact, being celebrated is an oppressive system that does not offer equality of opportunity in education and, after graduation, in the workforce, to everyone.

In my case, according to the mainstream press, the success story was about overcoming my primary condition of 'a Roma girl from Cândești village' and turning into 'the actress who broke the hearts of Italians'. I should point out that I only played once in Italy, in Rome, on tour with the show *Roma Armee*, a production by Berlin Maxim Gorki Theater. But 'to break the hearts of the Italians' meant that I received recognition from the West, and if the 'superior West' of the Romanian mentality validated the work of a Roma artist, then their self-colonising need is to imitate the West. I received recognition in Romania only after I've won theatre prizes abroad. My work was especially appreciated only after I performed and worked in cities such as Berlin, London or New York. Although I enjoyed every artistic experience I had with Western cultural institutions and I satisfied my need to bring the Roma art into the mainstream spaces ignorant of our culture, it was obvious to me, every time, that the work we do at Giuvlipen is much more important and valuable. And that an autonomous Roma theatre collective can truly generate a change in the marginal status of Roma artists.

It hasn't been easy at all to form a collective. As in the press, our voice was listened to only if our speech did not contain too much social and political criticism or was completely devoid thereof. The public seemed to get excited only if we exposed our personal life, intimate and humiliating experiences we and our close ones went through. However, if we have a critical speech directed to the unjust society in which we live, if we speak too much about slavery, Roma Holocaust or our rights, we are rebuked for spreading 'Roma propaganda' or for being too radical. The mainstream public wants to hear stories in which we victimise ourselves, to give them the opportunity to get emotional and thus prove that they are 'tolerant of the Roma' because being tolerant means nothing more than restoring the relationship of supremacy over us. In racist logic, only they are tolerant of us, only we are wrong. Using this psychological defence mechanism, they wash their hands of any responsibility they would have towards us as an oppressed ethnic group and towards our anti-racist battle. They will not become our allies; instead, they will find solace in the tears they were able to shed for our exceptional story that again engrains in their subconscious the feeling that we are the 'other'.

In movies, things are even worse because fictional films don't depict us beyond the known stereotypes. There is only a one-dimensional narrative about what it means to be Roma, which is usually closely related to poverty, lack of education and the traditional community life. Roma women are represented only through the maternal role; Roma men are associated with violence. And what consistently goes unmentioned is the non-Roma audience and their own contribution to the history of racism against us. Nothing from these one-dimensional narratives gives them the possibility of questioning the stereotypes about Roma people; on the contrary, it gives them the occasion to strengthen them through the exoticism that these movies maintain. Thus, from the 'white gaze' that exoticises Roma culture, to the abuse against us, is only one step. An exceptional, individual story can gain the respect of *gajdes,* but more of the same will arouse their contempt. Society doesn't want us all to be successful; it wants the social hierarchisation to continue. It doesn't want us, Roma actors, to perform on the stage of a famous theatre, occupying spaces not built for us, but it wants us to remain where we belong, at the bottom of society, to struggle to perform in theatres without budgets, and without having a building to call the Roma theatre.

This is why, even in 2024, there is no plan to establish a state Roma theatre in Romania. This is why we don't even have a cultural institution to represent us.

Because the idea of a strong collective and ethnic group would represent a shift from perceiving the group as inferior to perceiving us as on equal footing. And society wants the opposite: to maintain the stereotypes about us. History taught us so many times how profitable it is for the governments of the countries we live in to present us as enemies and scapegoats to divert attention away from real problems such as discrimination and abuse against us. The racist and neoliberal society we live in wants us to believe that, with a lot of work and ambition, anyone can be famous, rich and in a position of power. But this is a lie because we don't live in a meritocratic society but in one based on privileges and the lack thereof. Individual success is never gained individually; rather it is the result of class, ethnic and gender privileges. Thus, with much regret, I have to tell the future Roma girl from Cândeşti who wants to be an actress that her chances of success in such a society are minimal.

If she reads the sensationalist material about me in *Libertatea,* I don't want her to feel guilty at the end of the battle for fulfilling her dream that she failed to become an actress while I succeeded.

She deserves my honesty that I wouldn't have succeeded only through work, talent or determination. That there is something else that we are not told about when we build our dreams in childhood, and that something is called social injustice. And if that village girl who dreams of becoming an actress still wants to know what the superpower of the few Roma who succeeded is, I will tell her that they have almost always benefited from affirmative action measures, but they are no superheroes. I hope that many contexts of reparative measures will also be created for her for all the injustices she suffered from the moment she was born into a Roma family and missed the start in the race for success.

The support I received to become an actress adds up to this:

1. I have a family who supported me financially, including the third time when I failed the university admission exam. I am not going into details about the sacrifices that made it possible, but no family should ever have to fight for their children's education.
2. When my theatre teacher insulted me for my dark-coloured skin, I had the support of the diction teacher who had the same skin colour as me. For three years, I had her moral support. I didn't believe in myself for a long time but having someone who believed in me made me fight for the graduation diploma.
3. After graduation, when I wanted to have my one-woman show, a feminist NGO paid part of the costs of production. I received the support of a Roma and non-Roma feminist community that promoted me, supported me financially, encouraged and inspired me to do the work I trained for: to be an actress and much more.

That was the moment when I realised that solidarity and social justice could only be built beyond neoliberal values such as individualism. So I've created a collective. It seemed more important to create a Roma theatre collective in which we can represent ourselves than to fight for individual careers in a theatrical and cinematographic environment that reduces us to some stereotypical roles about our ethnic identity. Unquestionably, some still naively think that acting is a universal profession and that any actor, if talented, can play any character.

However, for the Roma actors, the reality is that if they have dark skin, they will not get cast in lead roles that were, in fact, written for white actors, but in roles of Roma characters, rendered as caricatures or prejudicially. As an alternative to the roles we would have received in a dominant white culture, we preferred to create other new Roma characters to restore the dignity of the Roma image in the artistic discourse. Nine years after the founding of Giuvlipen together with the actress Zita Moldovan, we have in our repertoire ten shows: Giuvlipen has become a platform for promoting Roma actors and actresses from Romania. We have created representation for Roma in the local theatre, and we have produced a new artistic discourse in Romania: Roma, queer and feminist. Although we didn't overcome the precarious condition of underfunded independent theatre status, I believe that this is the moment when I could tell the Roma girl who dreams of becoming an actress that now she has a bit more of a chance than we had nine years ago when we set off, and that our theatre is meant exactly for people like her.

I have faith in the power of the collective and the example created by a group of Roma actresses who refuse to have an exceptional, individual story but rather prefer to create an artistic movement around them. In all these years, we've learned that we generate change when we adopt an intersectional and critical artistic discourse, without compromises. Instead of capitalising interest through our personal stories as Roma people or by exposing our victimisation that, as I explained above, do nothing more than reinforcing the stereotypes, we prefer to develop our artistic practice creatively and create diverse narratives about what it means to be Roma. Instead of the 'white tears' from our non-Roma audience, we choose to place our non-Roma spectators face to face with a critical discourse because we want them to question their own biases against Roma men and women and LGBTQI+ people when they leave our shows. You cannot expect to create a revolutionary theatre when you use a tempered discourse that satisfies everyone, but you have to take on brave and provocative topics in your shows.

If you use this 'recipe', you will not achieve the success of a 'Roma exception' that appeals to the mainstream, but you will definitely make history for your collective and Roma community. Focus on how to increase resistance and empower your Roma community through your art, rather than on changing the racist mentality of your non-Roma spectators. Tell stories of resistance, not of victimisation. After all, we have a history full of abuse and violence that we bravely survived. The *gadjes* have to learn how to regard us as people able to fight for their rights, not as vulnerable entities, lacking any kind of power.

I often think of the new generations of Roma actresses that will come after Giuvlipen, and I care about leaving them this artistic legacy. When we founded the collective, there were no theatre shows in Romania talking about us from a queer feminist perspective. We had to learn from our mistakes to refine our artistic discourse and bring the Roma theatre to the next creative level. I've written and produced contemporary theatre pieces such as *Gadjo Dildo*, *Who Killed Szomna Grancsa?*, *Corp Urban*, or *Trauma Kink*, historical-themed shows: *Kali Traš* – the first theatre show about the Roma Holocaust, and I developed *Roma futurism* (an artistic movement that places at an intersection the Roma culture with the technology of the future and witchcraft) so we can talk about a future of the Roma in which we have a say, in shows such as *The Age of The Witch*.

I do not know what the future of Roma theatre will look like, all the more so now as an independent theatre troupe. However, we are proud to have written history so far for the (Roma) theatre in Romania, and we wouldn't have succeeded without real solidarity, collective support and the queer feminist unity we have benefited from in the last years. Together we are strong but as 'Roma exceptions' we will not change the racist imaginary. I imagine and dream that ten, twenty years from now, the collective artistic practice will be embraced by new generations of Roma actresses who will find and reinvent themselves as artists, just as we feel we are doing in our collective.

Note

1 Available at: www.libertatea.ro/stiri/povestea-fabuloasa-a-mihaelei-dragan-de-la-fata-de-romi-din-candesti-la-actrita-care-a-rupt-inimile-italienilor-2095095 (accessed 1 March 2024).

Part IV

Border epistemologies of Europeanisation

10

Patterns of coloniality within the innovation economy: talent attraction and the converging racialising processes of migration administration

Olivia Maury

The channelling and facilitation of student-migrants to European countries relies on complex webs of colonial power and underlying (post)colonial trajectories (Ploner and Nada, 2020). Studying in Europe, and more broadly in the Global North, is often perceived as a stepping stone to living in the 'West' (Ginnerskov-Dahlberg, 2019). The recruitment of students generates income for 'Western' universities at the same time as it forges colonial power/knowledge structures, while branches of 'Western' universities in newly industrialised countries appear as forms of neo-colonialism (Ploner and Nada, 2020). New knowledge hubs emerging in the Asia-Pacific region however challenge and compete with the 'Western' centres of education and knowledge (Börjesson, 2017). From this perspective, the competition for talent articulated in multiple governmental strategy reports can be seen as an effort to retain the 'West' as the cradle of knowledge and to reproduce the systems of knowledge and modern education as disciplinary practice, which has been foundational in creating a self-understanding of the 'West' ever since the sixteenth century.

The efforts to attract international talent go hand in hand with the innovation economy. In the Finnish context, it is claimed that companies need greater numbers of talented workers than Finland has to offer and that greater diversity in society and at workplaces will make Finland more attractive to international talent (Andersson et al., 2020). A government report entitled *Innovaatiotalouden maahanmuuttopolitiikka* (Migration policy of the innovation economy) explicitly calls for migration policies to spur value accumulation out of migrants' talent and produce societal wealth (Raunio, 2015: 9) while others state that in the global innovation economy 'skills, knowledge and know-how of individuals form a central engine of value creation' (Rilla et al., 2018: 4). The recently published *Talent Boost Cookbook 2.0* (Andersson et al., 2020: 52) emphasises the attraction of international students and start-up talent to resonate with 'Helsinki's desire to be an edgy, creative hotspot for tech and start-ups'.

The innovation economy is not a neutral description of the current phase of capitalism, but points to the globally dominant idea of progress (Tarvainen, 2022). A critical reading of innovations suggests that successful innovations are part of the constructions through which the West knows itself as 'modern' or 'advanced' (Fougère and Harding, 2012: 22) and that beneath the supposed novelty of innovation economy lies the unfinished history of Eurocentrism and colonialism. From this perspective, the 'coloniality of innovation' further spurs the capitalist system, incorporating mythic images such as the start-up entrepreneur, who as a white male hero figure embodies reason, creativity and future-making capacity (Tarvainen, 2022).

In this chapter, I contribute to the critical analysis of the governmental aims of 'channelling of the expertise and talent of international graduates' in the 'innovation economy'. Attracting international students necessitates movement within the global border regime, itself inextricable from global capitalism and the histories 'Western' colonialism (De Genova et al., 2021; Sharma, 2020). Although the racial logic of the state has gained research attention (e.g. Goldberg, 2002), the complex workings of bordering practices in reproducing racialisation and global coloniality is an under-researched area. Drawing on the lived experiences of persons from the Global South and East who have obtained a student residence permit in an EU country, Finland, I demonstrate how this 'international talent' in the making is firmly entangled in the coloniality of power reproduced in a world of nation states founded on a naturalised spatial separation of national subjects from migrants (Sharma, 2020: 4). Thereby, I address how colonial asymmetries materialised 'outside' Europe, for example, in the Mediterranean (Ould Moctar, this volume) travel to the 'inside' via positively framed talent-seeking, accompanied nonetheless by the filtering of migratory subjects.

While colonial power relations permeate most social relations, in this chapter I focus on non-EU students' encounters with migration administration, which on multiple levels generate a pattern of coloniality in the present. I focus on the lived experiences of student permit-holders to grasp the mutable colonial power relations dispersed in and constantly reinvented in the national and supra-national administrative-legal context. I propose to analyse this from the perspective of converging processes of racialisation that reproduce a colonial pattern in the present. Thus, my method is relational and reaches beyond a monocausal approach to racialisation and coloniality. I draw theoretical inspiration from Antonio Gramsci (1971) and Stuart Hall (2021 [1980]) to grasp the complex 'relations of force' stemming from political, administrative and legal procedures, which in their intersection produce the conjuncture of a racial-colonial present of the innovation economy. The argument is that racialised graded differentiation is generated as an assembled process of convergence produced in a specific socio-historical time and place. I use Souths and Easts as method to analyse how, in interaction, the administrative and political migration procedures categorise people as 'international students', 'migrant-workers' or 'asylum-seekers' in relation to their embodied trajectories from post-Soviet contexts and former colonies under European rule to Finland and the EU. Through these categories, which are historically uneven in terms of their imagined and material conditions of proximity and distance to Europe and Europeanisation, I address the structural and administrative violence of the border regime.

Rather than talent attraction in the innovation economy advancing a teleological narrative of historicist progress, the material structures of migration administration reproduce a spectrum of racialised subject positions situated at various distances from the 'Eurocentric' power core of liberal humanity. This generates situations in which rather than know-how constituting 'a central engine of value creation' (Rilla et al., 2018), the socially and legally differentiated labour of the migratory subjects exhausted in the low-paid service sector contributes to value accumulation. The theoretical crux of this argument is that the complex 'relations of force' articulate a structure of global coloniality in the context of international talent attraction materialised through national migration administration. Thereby, in this chapter I contribute to research that resists static binaries and the temptation to trace global coloniality back to one single source or spatially delimit coloniality to certain parts of the globe (e.g. Krivonos, 2019; Krivonos and Diatlova, 2020). This approach goes against the grain of relegating coloniality to the past by underscoring how graded differentiations occur on an everyday basis and how the coloniality of power constantly reshapes itself in novel constellations.

I begin by discussing border and migration administration in relation to theoretical perspectives of race, after which I methodologically set the scene. Then, in four analytical sections, I analyse four student-migrants' experiences of migration administration and racialisation. I devote the conclusion to discussing administrative violence in the context of Europeanisation, innovation economy and talent attraction.

Borders, migration administration and race

Racialising features of border and migration management are seldom straightforward. Explicit racial nomenclature has been erased from European migration policies and replaced with neutralised and technical language (e.g. Bashi, 2004; Heller, 2021). Racialisation may work through any dimension of social personhood such as class, ethnicity and generation, which come to be essentialised, naturalised or biologised (Wodak and Reisigl, 1999: 180). Moreover, 'the social meaning ascribed to both somatic difference and cultural Otherness is grounded in material conditions' (Calavita, 2007: 105), suggesting that economic otherness often translates into or coincides with racialisation.

The versatility of racialisation processes can be grasped by accounting for how material-administrative assemblages produce multiple hierarchical differences between human beings (Tazzioli, 2021). Thus, racialisation is an outcome of 'interlocking policies at both EU inter-governmental and national levels' (Garner, 2007: 78), and policies put to practice in administrative processes. This account brings to the fore the administrative violence of the migration and border regime, woven into the technical and neutralised language utilised and unevenly dispersed in the assemblage of racialising practices.

To demonstrate how racialisation occurs at many different levels simultaneously and targets subjects in different ways, I take from the work of Stuart Hall, himself inspired by the work of Antonio Gramsci. Hall (2021 [1986]) writes that even if Gramsci (1971) did not specifically analyse racism, his concepts may be helpful for such analysis. Gramsci opposes a purely economistic reading of the social formation and the relationships between its different levels of articulation because it fails to address the political and the ideological levels, such as social differentiation based on gender, race, ethnicity and nationality. Approaching the historical conjuncture beyond a reductionist economistic approach, Gramsci's thinking permits a more complex reading of the 'relations of force' able to identify the 'various moment or levels' in a conjuncture. Hall contends that different levels of articulation – such as economic, political and ideological – generate different configurations of social forces. From this combined theoretical and methodological point of departure, I trace moments in student-migrants' experiences, which articulate complex relations of force stemming from political, administrative and legal procedures. In their intersection, these relations produce the conjuncture of a racial-colonial present.

Setting the scene: Student migration and global coloniality

In this chapter, I draw on interviews with thirty-eight people coming from Asian, Eastern European and African countries who work in Finland while holding a student residence permit, and follow-up interviews with twelve of them, to explore evolvement and subjective reflection on the experiences of hierarchisation and struggle. For many, Finland appeared a suitable second or third option for studying in the 'West', after the more desired destinations of the UK and the US (Maury, 2021). For many non-EU/EEA citizens, Finland was an economically feasible destination, offering various higher education programmes in English free of charge before tuition fees for non-EU/EEA students were introduced in 2017.

To arrive for the purpose of studying, a non-EU/EEA citizen needs to apply for the residence permit for studies in the closest Finnish embassy or consulate, which often may be located at far distance perhaps in another country, and make sure to meet the requirements of demonstrating savings of 6,720 euros, private health insurance and a study place. The holder of a student permit has the right to work 25 hours weekly and due to the strict economic requirements of the student residence permit, many non-EU/EEA students become dependent on low-paid wage work in Finland (Maury, 2020). The residence permit system is a constitutive part of the global border regime which hierarchically reduces migrants' opportunities of choosing where and how to work, study, live and settle. Therefore I employ a critical use of the term migrant as 'a person who, in order to move to or stay in a desired place, has to struggle against bordering practices and processes of boundary-making that are implicated by the national order of things' (Scheel and Tazzioli, 2022: 3).

By way of qualitative content analysis, I suggest a reading of global coloniality through the research participants' diverse experiences of administrative bordering (Könönen, 2018; Maury, 2022a) and associated instances of racialisation and othering. Since legal text and administrative practices are presented as natural and neutral, it is only through the subjective encounters with these administrative-legal structures that we can perceive the racial-colonial power relations ingrained in them. The diverse experiences among the interviewed student-migrants of different backgrounds allows me to methodologically take stock of the particular 'relations across differences' (Lowe, 2015: 5). As far as possible, I attempt to seize hold of the research participants' own analysis of the situations and place these analytical considerations in a wider research context in order to point to the occurrence of racialisation and discrimination beyond an individual level and reveal the structures which enable such othering and racism. However, this presents apparent variations of experience and hierarchy in the current setting of me as a researcher, EU citizen and white passing in most Nordic spaces, doing research with non-EU citizens who in different ways become subject to racialisation. During the research, I have attempted to make use of the collective and versatile knowledge of the practices of migration administration acquired via more than ten years of no-border activism in Helsinki, to critically bring the varying individual experiences together into an analytical context.

In the following analytical sections, I trace the converging processes of racialisation beginning from the most evident legal divisions, then slowly entering into more complex relations of force that articulate a racial–colonial present within the system of nation states, via the narrated experiences of four research participants of different geographical and social background.

The hierarchical border regime

Irina had come to Finland from Russia to study sales and marketing. As common for many student-migrants, her hopes for the future had been high when arriving but soon turned gloomier after realising the difficulties of finding work reflecting her expertise. Business students were offered start-up and freelance work framed by insecurity over income and continuity. During our first meeting in 2017 Irina commented on the fact that many non-EU students undertake work in an unrelated field such as cleaning: 'Just having a Finnish degree won't take me where I want.'

Irina knew that taking the easy road through low-paid manual work would make future job-seeking challenging. Therefore, she was decisive about finding work corresponding to her field of study. Irina found some jobs somewhat related to her field, but often on zero-hour contracts. We met again a couple of years later when Irina was graduating and seeking full-time work instead of accepting clearly exploitative freelance work.

> When you are employed as a freelancer but expected to do things as if you were on a pay roll it is worse, and undertaking tasks that are not written in your contract. You want to do this new thing and it is fine, I developed a lot of new skills but, another way to look at it is, well, being exploited as a freelancer. (Irina, 23, Russian citizen, interview in 2019)

Although Irina initially had the idea of applying for a business residence permit, using her acquired skill and starting her own firm – perfectly in line with policies of talent boost trying to 'attract start-up talent' (Andersson et al., 2020: 5) – she was now leaning toward applying for a residence permit based on regular employment. Full-time work, through which she would apply for the residence permit, appeared to be the least 'bumpy road', Irina told me. In this way she would get the opportunity to apply for a continuous residence permit in Finland to have time to think and dream: 'I have been planning my life just to get the visa, not thinking what I would like to do. That's the life of the third-country people' (Irina, interview in 2019).

Irina described the non-EU citizens' ongoing concern to reside in Finland after graduation as a legally and administratively shaped life. The hierarchical division between non-EU citizens and EU citizens, built into the administrative framework of the EU and reinforced particularly since 1985 with the introduction of the Schengen Agreement on freedom of movement, hierarchises non-EU citizens in numerical order as third after the EU's own first and second citizens.[1] This administrative-legal grouping intimately orients 'the life of the third-country people', to use Irina's expression, as they need to navigate the residence permit system and find a suitable legal basis for staying in the country. Thus, non-EU citizens' lives become organised in relation to the hierarchical system of borders placing the EU centre stage, and thereby, constructing barriers to hinder so-called third-country nationals reaching their subjective goals. Border management is highly flexible as it quickly reacts to political developments such as war, by introducing stricter border controls, as in the current conjuncture towards Russian citizens aspiring to move across the border to Finland. The relation between Finland and Russia has evolved over the centuries, with Finland being part of the Russian empire (1809–1917). Specifically, the fall of the Soviet Union led to a significant increase in migration to Finland, intensifying discrimination against and racialisation of Russian speakers in Finland (Krivonos, 2019). Thus, despite political discourses claiming the need for foreign talent for the innovation economy, the residence permit system intertwined with racialisation often channels non-EU citizens into low-paid work or pushes graduates to leave Finland.

Racialising administrative practices

The EU border regime enforces hierarchical divisions, as illustrated in Irina's experiences. However, third-country nationals are further differentiated in legal-administrative practices, backed up by societal and political discourses. Isra had moved from Turkey to Finland to do a master's degree in communication. Isra experienced the visa process with its requirements as 'a big deal' since it generated financial load combined with logistical challenges to reach the embassy, located in another country, and obtain the right travel documents – a task she failed on the first attempt. The trouble of reaching Finland followed, according to Isra, a dominant political logic of welcoming non-EU migrants from the Global North while assembling people from the Global South into a less desired category.

> There is a very loud group who would want certain types of immigrants to make it here. And that doesn't unfortunately include the Global South, so welcome to I mean Australians and Canadians and US. I feel like they are very accepted here and then people coming from Sudan or Morocco or Lebanon it's like, even though we come as students it's so easy for people to group us into the asylum-seeker box. (Isra, 25, Turkish citizen, interview in 2018)

Elsewhere (Maury, 2022b) I have argued that the hierarchical management of migrants becomes particularly salient in relation to the EU's list of the third countries whose nationals must be in possession of visas when crossing its external borders and those whose nationals are exempt from that requirement (Council Regulation (EC) No. 539/2001). This listing enforces a division between nationalities that find easier access to short-term mobility (three months) and those who do not and are categorised into the 'negative' list, formerly known as the 'blacklist' (van Houtum, 2010). The positive/negative divide not only impacts on one-time entry to the EU but also affects how people of different nationalities are able to move and how intimately they experience being governed by the temporal border regime (Maury, 2022b).

Defining certain nationalities as negative, that is, as less desirable and consequently othered, points to how EU policies attempt to protect and reproduce a 'Western identity' and to act as a shield against the 'global poor' (van Houtum, 2010: 96). This can be viewed as part of the process of European integration which has bolstered structures of global inequality set in place by colonialism (El-Enany, 2020: 196). Gutiérrez Rodriguez (2018: 205) maintains that while contemporary EU migration policies do not explicitly operate within a matrix of racial or ethnic difference, the connection between nationality and the rights of migrants produces hierarchies of nationalities founded on racialised notions of the other. Similarly, the EU's positive/negative list accords people different mobility rights depending on nationality, which points to the preference for white migration placed at the top of the intersecting hierarchies of the racial system and the hierarchy of nations (Bashi, 2004; El-Enany, 2020).

The legal hierarchisation is intermingled with racialised imaginaries of the so-called negative group and reverberates not only in everyday contexts such as media and personal relations, but also in the encounters with institutions of migration administration. Isra pointed out that despite people's different reasons for migration, those suffering from minimised opportunities to mobility are also more easily racialised into 'the asylum-seeker box'. Isra raised this after describing being given 'a hard time' by migration officials who asked her to supplement her application for extended residence permit. Isra found her stay in Finland threatened as migration officials stated that according to the regulations, she had not been studying enough. To solve the problem Isra needed to contact her supervisor to get her a certificate of her study development.

Isra claimed that because of her nationality and ostensible characteristics – her dark hair in particular – she was easily grouped into what she called 'the asylum-seeker box'. Thus, in the context of administrative bordering both processes of official criteria (study development) and racialising processes (asylum box) merged. It is notable that Isra herself uses the 'asylum-seeker box' to claim distance from the racialised figure of the asylum-seeker. Nevertheless, a migration system where applications are handled on a 'case-by-case' basis (Maury, 2021) certain applications and applicant profiles may demand excessive scrutiny – a procedure that often is directed toward those racialised as non-Western. Such administrative processes backed up by supposedly neutral law generates racialised effects through which people are governed as 'objects' within the entanglement of the white national citizen and the racially different other (Gutiérrez Rodriguez, 2018). This making of migrants also overlaps with the blurring of perceived categories of migrants and non-white EU nationals, who may be visually identified as 'asylum-seekers' (Garner, 2007: 69). In relation to Irina's trajectory that administratively was met with official criteria developed through proximate but asymmetrical relations to Russia, specifically after Finland's entrance into the EU as an aspiration to become a nation of the West rather than the East (Paasi, 1999), Isra's case points to forms of racialisation in administrative bordering practices converging with existing differentiations produced by the formal regulations of the border regime.

Syncopated movement across borders

Arvin, who I met in 2017, came from the Philippines and studied information technology. In addition to studying, his weeks consisted of cleaning a corporate building while listening to audio books. Arvin had initially tried to find work in business but said that 'most is unpaid, so it is impossible, I will not have any income'. In his little free time, he was not interested in joining student activities, which were mostly in Finnish and circulated around drinking alcohol, thus appearing to exclude for most of the Asian community, Arvin said.

Arvin's landing in Finland had caused frictions within the border regime as he had first applied for a tourist visa to come to Finland to meet his cousin. He recounted this instance both in 2017 and later in 2019:

> They [at the embassy] saw my application, and I am single, so they denied it after two days. It was 200 euros for that application. The decision is very clear, 'we cannot grant you a tourist visa and we don't consider cousin a direct relative [in order to be a sponsor for the visa]'. (Arvin, 24, Filipino citizen, interview in 2019)

Arvin explained that the assumptions about his marital status – single – and gender – male – influenced the negative decision on his tourist visa, not dissimilar to the logic presented in the documents of the European Border and

Coast Guard Agency (Frontex) viewing risks emanating from 'single men' of different 'backgrounds and nationalities' (Stachowitsch and Sachseder, 2019: 11). Additionally, the officials noted that his cousin could not be considered a sponsor due to a nuclear-based notion of family mobilised within the Finnish migration system. Arvin managed to pass an online exam for a Finnish university of applied sciences, which allowed him to apply for a residence permit for studies, issued at the Norwegian embassy in Manila.

While studying in Finland, Arvin was to do a study exchange in the UK. Already residing in the EU, he was not prepared to face difficulties of crossing borders. Nevertheless, on vague grounds, Arvin explained, he was denied a visa to the UK:

> My guess is that it is my nationality, Philippines is in the 'yellow line' for Western countries. We call it that when the visa got expired and they will stay. That is my theory, because I had all [that was required]. They [border officials] stated in my [negative] decision that I might stay. I thought it would be really easy 'cause I am in Finland. What I hate is that you devote everything of yourself, you give up your privacy. (interview with Arvin, 2019)

The discussions with Arvin levered an embodied reservation, expressing a sentiment of being always beforehand judged as less worthy of the right to mobility (Sayad, 1999). The rejected visa application made clear that the bordering institution suspected he would overstay his visa. These suspicions were according to Arvin often directed at Filipinos, which points to racialisation here appearing as a process by which nationality, presumably in combination with other aspects visible in the application such as gender and marital status, is essentialised and ascribed a social meaning of risk and undesirability among migration and border officials.

Arvin's narration pictures a syncopated form of movement where the rhythm is characterised by displaced accentuations and interruptions. The constant delay of non-EU/EEA citizens' cross-border movement, such as Arvin's failed attempts at moving from one country to another, demonstrates how third-country nationals are on ongoing basis 'pushed back in time' as another student-migrant once phrased it (Maury, 2021: 82). This temporal push back is directed toward certain subjects defined as less desired according to a Eurocentric logic of the global power dynamics. Thus, in combination with EU migration regulations, temporal borders produce racialisation resulting in a push away from the imagined centre toward 'the edge of the world' (Mbembe, 2000) and temporally reaffirms graded divisions between Europe and its varying 'others'.

In conclusion, the border regime temporally and spatially syncopates migrants' movement based on national, racialised and gendered criteria, so a Filipino IT student finds himself cleaning office buildings despite the 'talent gap in tech' identified in policy documents (Andersson et al., 2020: 6).

This case demonstrates that the hierarchical global order not only consists of categories of people subject to varying rules (such as visa regulations) but how these regulations produce effects that are unevenly distributed, racialised and continue to impact people's everyday lives, thereby reproducing a pattern of coloniality in the present. Compared to Irina migrating from Russia, and Isra from Turkey, Arvin's trajectory discloses encounters with bordering institutions along the way converging with national, racialised and gendered categorisations. With a history of the Philippines encompassing 300 years of Spanish rule, US colonial rule (1899–1946) accompanied by assimilationist aspirations of modernising and civilising the Filipinos resulting in a contemporary 'neocolonial polity' (Eder, 2016: 454) associated with the production of the 'globally competitive Filipino nurse' (Vaittinen et al., 2022: 187), Arvin's way forward may be seen as a form of resistance to being placed in a predefined postcolonial global order of labour and channelled towards nursing, as was the case with his (male) cousin with whom he lived in Finland. Thus, Arvin's experiences demonstrate how in addition to the legal differentiations generated by the border regime intensified by layers of racialisation in legal-administrative practices, further converge with temporal borders that causes interruptions of movement and temporally distances non-EU citizens and thereby reproduces patterns of global coloniality.

Dispersed anti-Black racism

I met Justin from Cameroon in 2017, when he had reached his eighth year of residence in Finland. During his stay he had faced difficulties, especially in the labour market and he had the impression that his and many other foreigners' knowledge and potential was not recognised. He explained the need to get used to the education and migration system that presented additional demands:

> It's not an easy thing when you come to Finland and the school, you have to know the environment. There is pressure from the environment, from the school from the immigration [service]. You need a minimum of 45 credits to renew [the permit], and the school is a whole new system, it takes time to adapt. Even though I have a previous degree from my country, but here it was a whole new approach adapting to this and this, and meeting all the requirements, it was just ... some people just gave up. Some returned, some switched fields. And I have a degree in banking law from my country. (Justin, 40, Cameroonian citizenship, interview in 2017)

The conversation with Justin deployed a range of obstacles in his transition from student to educated employee in Finland and a multiplicity of racialising encounters. He posed me a question: 'Why would you educate someone and at the end there are requirements that he can't meet, and he is useless?' His question referred in particular to the demand for 'native Finnish' language skills to enter the job market, which in itself has proven to imply a search for non-migrant or white workers (Näre, 2013; Krivonos, 2020; Maury, 2021). As time passed, racist encounters multiplied.

We met again in 2019 as Justin counted his tenth year in Finland. He had finally been granted a permanent residence permit after years of struggle with extending and switching permits, managing to get a mobile phone subscription instead of just prepaid ones, opening a bank account, buying lousy health insurance without actual cover and recording friends being deported. Ten years of struggle to stabilise one's residence points again to the temporariness produced and the temporal pushback by the border regime. Moreover, in a similar fashion as every single research participant I interviewed, Justin recounted the challenges non-EU citizens face to have enough money to show to the authorities to extend a temporary student permit. During the first interview he described a harsh example:

> One friend got rejected the first year as she borrowed [the money]. She was so unfortunate that her application was handled by this *very* bad ass person, one of the officers. When she had returned the money to her friend, they [the officials] asked for those again. (Justin, interview in 2017)

Administrative personnel use their discretion to choose who to check and when, demonstrating how the seemingly neutral processes of the administrative-legal nexus (re)produce forms of racialisation. Justin summarised his experience of living on a student permit: 'the life of a foreign student here is hell, in every aspect'.

According to Justin, the climate in Finland had become explicitly racist. He described several everyday racist incidents in the street and racial profiling by the police. Justin pictured racism as firmly ingrained in social structures: 'all of this is institutionalised, it is at work, in school, in families'. He gave an example of working in a care facility where a child below elementary-school age asked him how many times he had been in prison. Justin continued: 'I mean, where do children learn that Black people go to prison?' These contentions articulate his position not only as a foreign student, but as a person coming from a Central African country and being racialised as Black in one of the most anti-Black countries in the EU (FRA, 2018). As the EU report 'Being Black in the EU' showed, 63 pe cent of people of African descent in Finland had experienced racist harassment within the past five years, thus placing Finland at the most negative extreme in the survey comprising participants primarily of first- or second-generation immigrants from sub-Saharan African countries residing across twelve EU member states (FRA, 2018). The enduring racism intertwined with trouble with migration administration, Justin (2019) described, provoked feelings of being 'you against the world'. Justin continued analysing his own position: 'We are victims of colonisation, and one of the worst things colonisation did to us was that we learned to hit ourselves'.

Justin contemplated his internalised world view shaped through the history of various colonisers, among them the French until Cameroon's independence in 1960. This internalised world view incorporated the perception that 'everything good is related to white', as Justin phrased it. Thus, it appears that in the context of talent attraction to the innovation economy, the white male figure who embodies reason, creativity and future-making capacity (Tarvainen, 2022: 10) is reflected in the subjective experiences of the student–migrants as explicitly as in Justin linking the notion of 'good' with 'white'. This experience also highlights that being perceived as white and having European citizenship continue to be symbols of status, often interpreted as signalling the possession of specific or sought-after 'skills' (Liu Farrer et al., 2020).

Compared to the legal divisions between EU and non-EU citizens articulated in Irina's case, continuously converging with forms of racialisation in the administrative context as in Isra's case, and the deferral of migrants' movement across borders as in the Arvin's case, the complex relations of force converge from a variety of perspectives in Justin's case. Justin's experiences of pressure and racism are generated via legal-administrative requirements concerning his education and residence permit combined with institutional and everyday racism, which cumulate and generate a converging effect of racialisation that situates him at the very edge of the white core of the EU, that is, him positioned 'against the (white) world'.

Conclusion

This chapter has examined the hierarchical differentiations produced between student-migrants – a group politically framed as one of the 'engines' of the innovation economy. The analysis in this chapter has allowed me to contend that the intersecting 'relations of force' (Gramsci, 1971) articulate converging processes of racialisation in the practices of migration administration that differentially constrain student-migrants' possibilities to decide where to work, how to study, when and where to travel and do internships.

Rather than approaching global coloniality through an imaginary of fixed spatial blocks of coloniality of power, which runs the risk of distancing colonial power relations from the everyday lived experiences, the multimodal analysis of individual experiences articulates interrelated relations of force, which produce an archive in the making of a colonial pattern in the present. This perspective adds to the analysis of a graded (post)colonial formation of the European space beyond a white/other binary (Krivonos and Diatlova, 2020) by grasping how hierarchical relations emerge between different non-EU citizens, and how these relations spatially and temporally position student-migrants at various distances from the European centre. These graded differentiations reproduce the proximity between EU citizenship and whiteness and the preference for white migration, which is placed at the top of the intersecting hierarchies of the racial system and nations (El-Enany, 2020). Importantly, I have demonstrated that the EU core and the preference for white migration is produced not only as a discursive or symbolic construction but as a material structure of law, regulations and administration which forge hierarchical divisions.

The examined legal structures and the administrative power of institutions of border and migration control generate structural violence. In contrast to direct violence understood as episodic with an identifiable perpetrator and disrupting people's understanding of their social worlds, structural violence is constant, not caused by a single agent and clearly shapes the social worlds of people by providing them with a situated knowledge with its own epistemic certainties (Gupta, 2012: 21–2). For non-EU student–migrants, structural violence manifests in their experiences of otherness and incompleteness emerging out of seemingly neutral procedures, which produces a sensibility and a certain way of conduct when faced with such institutions. Europeanisation imbued with the aim to retain a global power position through talent attraction in the innovation economy thus appears to ossify what it means to produce 'crime without a criminal' (Gupta, 2012: 21). That is, when approached from a juridic–social outside, the EU and the innovation economy lose their sheen, rather appearing as a violent exploitative structure and revealing the 'coloniality of innovation' (Tarvainen, 2022).

This analysis has demonstrated the strength of Souths and Easts as method in grasping the relational forms of violence produced in encounters with administrative borders among bodies racialised unevenly across categories and placed at various distances to Finnish citizenship and belonging. While attempting to filter migration to include only 'the good ones', the contemporary conditions of the EU migration regime simultaneously suggest a decline of Western hegemony (Ould Moctar, this volume) with its lamentable effort to repair the regime while struggling to keep it alive against the forceful decisiveness, drive and struggle of people departing from the South and East of the globe.

In conclusion, student migration is complex: managed migration of highly skilled individuals is encouraged, but mobility is restricted for the 'global poor' (Garner, 2007; van Houtum, 2010) and student mobilities may take many forms, from providing low-paid service labour to integrating into the metropolitan 'talent hubs'. I have demonstrated that despite political discourses claiming the need for foreign talent for the innovation economy, the current border and residence permit system often channels non-EU citizens into low-paid work, and thereby into raced labour markets (Aparna et al., this volume; Țîștea this volume) or pushes graduates to leave Finland for other destinations (Maury, 2021).

This examination of the racialising features of administrative-legal migration practices has provided a better understanding of the material foundations of the innovation economy. The labour of the student-migrants, homogenously framed in political discourses, becomes hierarchically fragmented from a subjective perspective and thus reproduces the imaginations of white spaces, knowledge and subjectivities as more promising than others in the innovation economy (Tarvainen, 2022). Lastly, the positively framed efforts to invite foreign talent nevertheless appears to be based on selection and discarding of non-desired subjects primarily from the Global South and East, thus purporting 'European values' as the cause of – not the solution to – the epistemic and structural violence of the current border and migration system.

Note

1 Third country: A country that is not a member of the European Union as well as a country or territory whose citizens ('third-country nationals') do not enjoy the European Union right to free movement. 'Regulation (EU) 2016/399 on a Union Code on the rules governing the movement of persons across borders (Schengen Borders Code), Art. 2(5) *Official Journal of the European Union L 327/1*, p. 7. Available at: https://eur-lex.europa.eu/legal-content/EN/TXT/?uri=celex:32016R0399

References

Andersson, M., Pärtel-Peeter, P., Vanhanen, L. and King-Grubert, M. (2020) *Talent Boost Cookbook Finland 2.0*. Helsinki: Ministry of Economic Affairs and Employment and Business Finland.

Bashi, V. (2004) 'Globalized anti-blackness: transnationalizing Western immigration law, policy, and practice', *Ethnic and Racial Studies*, 27(4), 584–606.

Börjesson, M. (2017) 'The global space of international students in 2010', *Journal of Ethnic and Migration Studies*, 43(8), 1256–75.

Calavita, K. (2007) 'Law, immigration and exclusion in Italy and Spain', *Papers: revista de sociologia*, (85), 95–108. https://raco.cat/index.php/Papers/article/view/74163

Council Regulation (EC) No. 539/2001 of 15 March 2001 listing the third countries whose nationals must be in possession of visas when crossing the external borders and those whose nationals are exempt from that requirement. *Official Journal of the European Communities* L 81/1. https://eur-lex.europa.eu/legal-content/EN/TXT/?uri=CELEX:32018R1806 (accessed 9 February 2024).

De Genova, N. and Tazzioli, M. (2021) 'Minor keywords of political theory: migration as a critical standpoint A collaborative project of collective writing', *Environment and Planning C: Politics and Space*, 40(4), 781–875. doi: 10.1177/2399654420988563.

El-Enany, N. (2020) *Bordering Britain: Law, Race and Empire*. Manchester: Manchester University Press.

European Union Agency for Fundamental Rights (FRA, 2018) *Second European Union Minorities and Discrimination Survey: Being Black in the EU*. Luxembourg: Publications Office of the European Union.

Eder, R. (2016) 'I am where I think I will work: higher education and labor migration regime in the Philippines', *Educational Studies*, 52(5), 452–68.

Fougère, M. and Harding, N. (2012) 'On the limits of what can be said about "innovation": inter-play and contrasts between academic and policy discourses', in Sveiby, K.-E., Gripenberg, P. and Segercrantz, B. (eds) *Challenging the Innovation Paradigm*, New York: Routledge, pp. 29–50.

Garner, S. (2007) 'The European Union and the racialization of immigration, 1985–2006', *Race/Ethnicity: Multidisciplinary Global Contexts*, 1(1), 61–87.

Ginnerskov-Dahlberg, M. (2019) *'I Guess That Things Can Work in the West'. Unravelling the Narratives of Eastern European Master's Students in Denmark*. PhD dissertation, Aarhus University.

Goldberg, D. T. (2002) *The Racial State*. Oxford: Blackwell.

Gupta, A. (2012) *Red Tape: Bureaucracy, Structural Violence and Poverty in India*. New Delhi: Orient Blackswan.

Gutiérrez Rodríguez, E. (2018) 'The coloniality of migration and the "refugee crisis": on the asylum-migration nexus, the transatlantic white European settler colonialism-migration and racial capitalism', *Refuge: Canada's Journal on Refugees*, 34(1), 16–28.

Gramsci, A. (1971) *Selections from the Prison Notebooks*, ed. and trans. Nowell-Smith, G. and Hoare, Q. London: Lawrence & Wishart.

Hall, S. (2021 [1980]) 'Race, articulation and societies structured in dominance', in Gilroy, P. and Gilmore, R. W. (eds) *Selected Writings on Race and Difference*. Durham, NC: Duke University Press, pp. 195–245.

Heller, C. (2021) 'De-confining borders: towards a politics of freedom of movement in the time of the pandemic', *Mobilities*, 16(1), 113–33.

Krivonos, D. (2019) *Migrations on the Edge of Whiteness: Young Russian-speaking Migrants in Helsinki, Finland*. PhD dissertation, University of Helsinki.

Krivonos, D. (2020) 'Swedish surnames, British accents: passing among post-Soviet migrants in Helsinki', *Ethnic and Racial Studies*, 43(16), 388–406.

Krivonos, D. and Diatlova, A. (2020) 'What to wear for whiteness? "Whore" stigma and the East/West politics of race, sexuality and gender', *Intersections*, 6(3), 116–32.

Könönen, J. (2018) 'Border struggles within the state: administrative bordering of non-citizens in Finland'. *Nordic Journal of Migration Research*, 8(3), 143–50.

Liu-Farrer, G., Yeoh, B. and Baas, M. (2020) 'Social construction of skill: an analytical approach toward the question of skill in cross-border labour mobilities', *Journal of Ethnic and Migration Studies*, 47(10), 2237–51. https://doi.org/10.1080/1369183X.2020.1731983.

Lowe, L. (2015) *The Intimacies of Four Continents*. Durham, NC: Duke University Press.

Maury, O. (2022a) 'Ambivalent strategies: student-migrant-workers' efforts at challenging administrative bordering', *Sociology*, 56(2), 369–85.

Maury, O. (2022b) 'Punctuated temporalities: Temporal borders in student-migrants' everyday lives', *Current Sociology*, 70(1), 100–117.

Maury, O. (2021) *Punctuated Lives: Student-Migrant-Workers' Encounters with the Temporal Border Regime*. PhD dissertation, Faculty of Social Sciences, University of Helsinki.

Maury, O. (2020) 'Between a promise and a salary: student-migrant-workers' experiences of precarious labour markets', *Work, Employment and Society*, 34(5), 809–25.

Mbembe, A. (2000) 'At the edge of the world: boundaries, territoriality, and sovereignty in Africa', *Public Culture*, 12(1), 259–84.

Näre, L. (2013) 'Ideal workers and suspects: employers' politics of recognition and the migration division of care labour in Finland', *Nordic Journal of Migration Research*, 3(2), 72–81.

Paasi, A. (1999) 'Boundaries as social practice and discourse: The Finnish–Russian Border', *Regional Studies*, 33(7), 669–80.

Ploner, J. and Nada, C. (2020) 'International student migration and the postcolonial heritage of European higher education: perspectives from Portugal and the UK', *Higher Education*, 80(2), 373–89.

Raunio, M. (2015) 'Innovaatiotalouden maahanmuuttopolitiikka. Kansainvälinen muuttoliike, maahanmuuttajat ja innovaatiopolitiikka', *Työ- ja elinkeinoministeriön julkaisuja*, (33), 1–80. https://urn.fi/URN:ISBN:978-952-227-994-1.

Rilla, N., Deschryvere, M., Oksanen, J., Raunio, M. and van der Have, R. (2018) 'Immigrants in the innovation economy: lessons from Austria, Canada, Denmark and the Netherlands', *Publications of the Government's Analysis, Assessment and Research Activities*, (1), 1–53. http://urn.fi/URN:ISBN:978-952-287-503-7.

Stachowitsch, S. and Sachseder, J. (2019) 'The gendered and racialized politics of risk analysis: the case of Frontex', *Critical Studies on Security*, 7(2), 107–23.

Sayad, A. (1999) 'Immigration et "pensée d'État"'. *Actes de la Recherche en Sciences Sociales*, 129(1), 5–14.

Scheel, S. and Tazzioli, M. (2022) 'Who is a migrant? Abandoning the nation-state point of view in the study of migration', *Migration Politics*, 1(1), 1–23.

Sharma, N. (2020) *Home Rule. National Sovereignty and the Separation of Natives and Migrants*. Durham, NC: Duke University Press.

Tarvainen, A. (2022) 'The modern/colonial hell of innovation economy: future as a return to colonial mythologies', *Globalizations* (latest articles). https://doi.org/10.1080/14747731.2022.2048460.

Tazzioli, M. (2021) 'The making of racialized subjects: practices, history, struggles'. *Security Dialogue*, 52(1), 107–14.

Vaittinen, T., Sakilayan-Latvala, M. and Vartiainen, P. (2022) 'Filipino nurses as enablers of the future welfare state: the global commodity chains of producing racialized care labour for ageing Finland', in Kettunen, P., Pellander, S. and Tervonen, M. (eds) *Nationalism and Democracy in the Welfare State*. Cheltenham: Edward Elgar Publishing, pp. 184–208.

van Houtum, H. (2010) 'Human blacklisting: the global apartheid of the EU's external border regime', *Environment and Planning D: Society and Space*, 28(6), 957–76.

Wodak, R. and Reisigl, M. (1999) 'Discourse and racism: European perspectives', *Annual Review of Anthropology*, 28, 175–99.

11

'Keep your clients because I quit': An ethnodrama of creolising research with Roma women

Ioana Țâștea

In 2021 I worked for a project that trained and hired Romanian and Bulgarian Roma women in Finland, who had little or no formal schooling or language skills, to do cleaning work. Romanian and Bulgarian migrant women from privileged racial and socio-economic positions, myself included, were hired as translators/interpreters and mediators, and white Finnish women were hired to promote the project's cleaning services to potential Finnish clients. Moreover, the project was mainly run and sponsored by Finnish women who constituted the majority in the decision-making board. None of the Roma women were part of the board and they never took part in board meetings. Occasional tensions arose over claiming ownership over the project. Roma women saw how the existence of the project depended on them and their hard labour and wanted more participation in decision-making. Romanian and Bulgarian women working as mediators made paternalistic claims to ownership based on their intimate knowledge of the Roma women's needs and on the perceived centrality of their translation services to the project. Finnish women claimed ownership based on financially sponsoring the project or on bringing financial resources from the clients they sought, through a logic of incorporation into the racial capitalist order. The project offered me a part-time one-year contract with a fixed monthly income and an office, to recruit Roma women as potential cleaners, to create and implement with the women personal work and training plans, to supervise and check the quality of their work, and to offer mediation and translation services whenever needed. The Roma women were hired as cleaners with zero-hour contracts, meaning they could have between 0 and 40 work hours per week and get paid a certain hourly fee, and it was up to me and other project coordinators to decide how many hours to give to each worker based on experience and seniority. The project thus exerted power hierarchies in opportunities afforded to Roma and non-Roma women, relied on non-Roma 'experts' claiming authority over Roma-related issues and made decisions for the Roma without their input as decision-makers.

In this chapter, I address the reproduction of epistemic violence in using non-Roma mediators in Roma-related projects, taking as a point of departure my role as a mediator in the cleaning project, while foregrounding plural alternative, resistant, creative and divergent forms of Roma agency. Thus I align with emerging approaches in Romani studies that highlight the requirement for researchers, especially non-Roma researchers who conduct most Roma-related research, to reflect on their epistemological and methodological underpinnings and to reassess the way they work with Roma participants towards disrupting the reproduction of epistemic violence (Brooks, 2015; Matache, 2016, 2017; Fremlova, 2019; Silverman, 2019). These approaches in Romani studies are further brought into dialogue with theories of creolisation emerging from the Caribbean, theatre-based methods and the Roma coresearchers' vernacular viewpoints. Through fusing vernacular language in the shape of a theatre play script with what is considered to be 'academic' language, I stay with the frictions and tensions of entangling these unequal discourses, to see whether it is possible for the vernacular to 'absorb imported practices, distort them and invent new expressions' (Vergès, 2015: 41–6). While questioning academic norms and practices, including my own reproduction of those practices and their hierarchisations, in this chapter I reflect on the limitations of the academic writing format and genre.

Ethnodrama as method

Ethnodrama (short for ethnographic drama) is a written script with dramatised narratives which can be selected from interview transcripts, observation notes, journal entries, memory stories, secondary print/digital sources, etc. (Saldaña, 2018: 662). Researchers use it for its theatrical immersivity to evoke deep reflections in readers/audiences. Ethnodrama comes with the responsibility to create an 'entertainingly informative, aesthetically sound, intellectually rich, and emotionally evocative' experience (Saldaña, 2018: 664). By bringing together the aesthetic demands of performance and theoretical ambitions of research, ethnodrama is not only an emerging or critical methodology, but also a way of writing that unsettles dry, unemotional and objectivised discourses that tend to uphold dominant voices (Țîștea, 2021). The ethnodrama enacted in this chapter is a vehicle for scripting daily social performances. Social performances of daily interactions may or may not involve a self-conscious awareness that those interactions are socially scripted, while the ethnodrama involves self-conscious scripted acts set within certain cultural, political or aesthetic conventions (Sughrua, 2020: 6). By turning social performances into theatrical representations, the ethnodrama subverts multiple complicities with neo/colonial relations of exploitation, as well as disrupting those complicities through alternative, resistant and creative agencies.

I wrote initial versions of the script based on memories of my experience of working as a mediator in the cleaning project during 2021, and on informal conversations I had with the Roma women who worked with me in the project. For the adaptation of memories into a script, I transformed the 'in-my-head' reflective narratives into engaging performances and added plausible conversation exchanges between characters.[1] I then considered how the resulting dialogues might be performed on stage and inserted italicised stage directions in brackets, like movements, gestures, acting recommendations and interactions with other characters or with objects (Saldaña, 2018: 677). I wrote the script in Romanian and read it to the Roma women who expressed dis/agreements, criticisms and recommendations for improvement. The women challenged my mis/representations and mis/readings of events, and at times problematic tendencies of giving voice, empowering or speaking on behalf of the characters, and they proposed new lines to add to the characters representing them, lines through which they theorised the drama's content. After applying their suggested changes, I read the script again to them for further checks and changes. Emerging from our discussions, we agreed that the main purpose of the ethnodrama is to reveal the violence of 'empowering' and 'liberating' less privileged 'others' in the benefactors' own terms. Finally, I translated the ethnodrama to English.

An ethnodrama of complicities and disruptions

Act 1. Don't be their friend
Three office desks with chairs lined up on the stage, facing the audience. Seated at the desks are, from left to right: Ioana, Anja and Bogdan. A tall reception desk is on the right side of the stage, facing the office desks, with Claudia standing behind it. Lavinia and Andrada are mopping the floor.

    Bogdan: Ioana, can you come to my office, please?
    Ioana walks over to Bogdan's desk and addresses him: Yes, you wanted to see me.
    Bogdan: What is this thing about a training here? You think you can have trainings here at the centre[2] whenever you want? What is it about?
    Ioana: It's about discrimination in the workplace. Anja has informed you about it quite some time ago; I thought you knew.
    Bogdan: Is the training also for Claudia?

Ioana:	It's actually for Roma people, so for Lavinia and Andrada. But Claudia could also come, if she is being discriminated against in the workplace.
Bogdan:	Ha, ha … she would say she is discriminated against by me … I want to join this training. Send me a calendar invitation, I have so many things going on, hard to keep track of everything.
Ioana:	Alright ….
Bogdan:	By the way, you have to be more authoritative with the cleaners. When you come to work, they have to fear you. Don't be their friend. That will not work with them. They will get lazy if you are too friendly with them.
Ioana:	Right … [*sighs and rolls her eyes*]. I will go now.

Ioana walks over to Anja's desk and addresses her: Did you hear how Bogdan just talked to me? He instructed me on how to do my job. He is not my boss.

Anja:	Jesus! He NEVER does that with me! I guess he does it depending on your cultural background, given that both of you are from the Balkans and I'm Finnish. He is an important client for our project with Roma cleaners, but that does not mean he can be disrespectful to you. I will talk to him. Don't feel discouraged by this.
Ioana:	Thanks! I don't feel discouraged. [*she walks back to her desk and sits down*].

Lavinia leaves the mop on the floor, walks over to Claudia's reception desk and addresses her: I have not been feeling well the past couple of days. I have back pains. I need to go see the doctor. Can you come with me to translate?

Claudia [*addresses Lavinia*]:	Go with your husband, he speaks some Finnish, doesn't he?
Lavinia:	But wait a minute, he only knows a little bit how to speak, he doesn't speak well [*sighs*]. He doesn't know how to explain my medical problems.
Claudia [*arrogantly*]:	Ah, there's always something with you. We have many other residents here. I cannot come to translate for you all the time.
Lavinia [*raises her voice while gesticulating to emphasise her words*]:	You know what? I don't need you anymore, nothing from you! I don't need you to come with me anywhere! I will pay my person and go by myself! You would not even have that job if it wasn't for us Roma! [*she walks to Ioana's desk and addresses her*]: You have to talk to Claudia. She's doing it again.
Ioana:	Alright, I'll talk to her and see what I can do [*sighs*].

Lavinia [*with a slightly raised yet firm voice*]: I'm sure there's a lot you can do. What, you sit there on that chair in the office for nothing? All of you would not have these jobs if it wasn't for our hard work. Do you think only people like yourself work? Us Roma, we also work. We are maybe 1,000 times more hard-working than Romanians because I can carry a bag of cement, but Romanian girls will not do that kind of work. But whenever you have your meetings, you never invite us.

Ioana: I'll raise these issues in the next board meeting. I'll do my best, I promise. Now, where is Andrada? She's late for her next shift.

Lavinia goes back where she had left the mop and resumes cleaning the floor. Andrada leaves the mop and walks over to Ioana's desk. A chair is placed next to the desk, slightly turned toward it and also facing the audience. Andrada sits on the other chair.

Ioana [*addresses Andrada enthusiastically*]: We will visit a nice client's home today. If things go well, she will remain your permanent weekly client.

Andrada [*addresses Ioana with doubt and cynicism*]: Go there for what? For two hours? 20 euros? I can make that much in a few minutes selling magazines on the street. [*continues with increased confidence*] How can I live with two hours? And if I go today, who knows if you will call me tomorrow? Like this, you are wasting my time.

Ioana [*visibly intimidated, trying to maintain her calm*]: Look, I explained this to you from the beginning. For the time being, that is all we can offer. But we are looking for new clients and with time the situation will improve. Have some patience, please. Also, the number of hours is divided according to seniority. Those who have worked with us longer receive more hours. With time your number of hours will also increase.

Andrada [*with a slightly raised and determined voice*]: Look, I am struggling a lot. Everyone is ahead of me. There are others who have only been here for two or three months, and they already have stable work and I have been here for so many years, ten years! [*continues with a strong energy while raising her voice higher*] Ten years and you won't give me a more stable position!? So, I can have a future, so my children will not suffer. Three-four hours one week, five hours the next ... How can I survive on that? I don't have time, I have to sell magazines or beg every day from morning to night, otherwise I waste my time, there is nobody to feed my children back in Romania, they rely on the money I send them.

Ioana [*visibly frustrated*]: Please, Andrada, like I said, have more patience. Things will improve. Now with the pandemic clients are more sceptical, but in a few months, it will no longer be like this. Please, we have to work together on this, for the sake of everyone involved. Now we really must go, the client is waiting for us. You know we cannot afford to lose clients.

Ioana attempts to stand up. Andrada remains seated with disappointment in her eyes. Ioana takes Andrada's hand in hers and gently squeezes it while looking with pleading eyes into Andrada's eyes. Ioana stands up. Andrada joins reluctantly. They leave the stage. Curtain.

* * *

Act 2. Keep your clients because I quit

A sofa centre-stage. A bed on its side. Next to it a closet. A desk on the other side of the sofa. Anne is sitting at the desk, working on a laptop, facing the audience. A door next to the desk. Andrada and Ioana enter the stage, walking toward the door from the other side. Ioana knocks on the door. Anne slowly stands up from her desk and walks to open the door with some difficulty.

Ioana [*after Anne opens the door, addresses her*]: Hello! My name is Ioana, and this is Andrada. [*points towards Andrada*]. We are from the cleaning company. I am here to translate any cleaning related requests from you to Andrada.

Anne: Yes, come in. [*As Andrada and Ioana enter, she addresses them*]: I will show you where the cleaning products are and explain what I need for each room. [*Anne guides Andrada and Ioana to the closet. She opens it and addresses Ioana*]: Can you please tell Andrada to take out the vacuum cleaner and that bucket from the closet? I would take them out myself, but I've had brain surgery and my movement is a bit impaired.

Ioana [*addresses Anne*]: No worries, that's why we are here. [*Addresses Andrada*]: Can you please take out the vacuum cleaner and that bucket? And please be extra nice with Anne, she's had brain surgery.

Andrada has a blank facial expression, her eyes gazing through Ioana and Anne, seemingly inattentive to what is going on. She gives no reaction to Ioana's request.

Ioana [*addresses Andrada impatiently as she takes out the things from the closet herself*]: Could you please be more cooperative? This is important.

Andrada [addresses Ioana calmly and detached]: This place is already clean and tidy. It seems like my services here are not *really* needed. I will go. You are wasting my time. [*She walks toward the door. Ioana remains shocked, unable to move. Anne is watching confused the interactions between Andrada and Ioana. Andrada addresses Ioana as she reaches the door.*]: Are you going to walk me out? Come on.

Anne [addresses Ioana]: Is everything alright?

Ioana [addresses Anne nervously, shaking with discomfort, her voice trembling]: I am so sorry, but Andrada is feeling unwell today and has to leave. She is new and has not accommodated to the working pace yet. I am so, so sorry, this has never happened before. Please forgive this recklessness. I will send one of our other cleaners to do the job later today or whenever it is most suitable for you.

Anne [addresses Ioana with pity, slightly annoyed]: Um ... Alright ... Send someone tomorrow please, same time. Please make sure she can do the job, this place really needs some cleaning, and I am unable to do it myself.

Ioana [addresses Anne]: I will. Thank you so much for your understanding. [*Rushes toward Andrada. They both walk through the door. Ioana then snaps at Andrada angrily*]: Why did you do that!? What did that woman do to you? She even has brain damage, for God's sake. What if she cancels our services? We cannot afford that!

Andrada [addresses Ioana firmly and decisively]: Don't worry, you can safely keep your clients because I quit.

Andrada and Ioana leave the stage. Anne slowly sits down back at her desk. Curtain.

***

Act 3. Im/mobilities

A tall desk centre-stage facing the audience. A man standing behind the desk. Five chairs are lined up on the side of the desk, at some distance from it. Ioana is sitting on one of the chairs. Four other characters are sitting on the other chairs. The man behind the desk addresses the audience.

Airport worker: The gate for flight number 786 to Helsinki is now open for boarding.

The passengers stand up from the chairs and stop in front of the desk, queuing.

Airport worker [addresses one of the passengers, the third in line]: You there, come here in front! Do you have all the travel documents?

Cătălina, the passenger targeted by the airport worker, is wearing a long colourful skirt and a kerchief. She is the only 'visibly' Roma person queuing at the boarding gate. She walks to the airport worker. The other characters stare at her visibly annoyed with her presence. Ioana, the last to queue, looks down at the floor.

Airport worker [addresses Cătălina authoritatively]: Show me all your travel documents. You know we are in the midst of a pandemic and additional travel documents are required? [*Cătălina hands her documents to the airport worker. He addresses Cătălina, same authoritative tone*]: What is the purpose of your travel?

Cătălina [addresses the airport worker calmly and politely]: I am visiting my son and my daughter-in-law who is eight months pregnant. I will help them with taking care of the baby and with house chores during the first couple of months after the baby is born.

Airport worker: Where is the letter of invitation?

Cătălina [with a slightly worried tone]: All the documents are there, their permanent residence, their income situation because they will support me while I am there.

Airport worker [less authoritatively]: I see that but they need to send you a signed invitation letter. Call them and ask them to write it now and send it to you on WhatsApp.

Cătălina [perplexed]: But … I do not have a smartphone …

Airport worker [annoyed, raises his voice]: Really!? How can you travel like that?

One of the other passengers, indignant, shouts: Come on, already, we will miss the flight because of her!

Ioana [addresses Cătălina with a friendly tone]: You can use my phone to call your son.

The other passengers turn to Ioana bewildered. They stare resentfully as Cătălina walks towards her.

Cătălina [addresses Ioana]: You must have been sent from heaven.
Curtain.

***

Epilogue. Un/learning with Gabriela
Gabriela and Lili are standing centre-stage, watching Cătălina and Ioana as the two approach them from the side of the stage. Lili is visibly pregnant.

Gabriela gives a small shout of surprise and joy and runs towards Cătălina and Ioana, not knowing which one to hug first. They all hug together laughing and Lili joins them.

>Gabriela [*addresses Ioana, radiating with joy*]: It's you! I told Lili it was you on the phone! I recognised your voice.
>
>Ioana [*addresses Gabriela with a big smile on her face*]: So good to see you! I wasn't expecting you here. Truly a nice surprise.
>
>Lili [*addresses Ioana*]: Thank you for helping our mother-in-law. Let us buy you coffee or tea at that café. [*She points to the other side of the stage, where there is a table with four chairs around it.*]
>
>Cătălina [*addresses Ioana*]: Yes, let us treat you.

The women sit down at the table, Gabriela facing Ioana closer to the audience, and Cătălina facing Lili more to the back. Small white cups on the table in front of them.

>Gabriela [*approaches Ioana*]: Have you found a replacement for Andrada?
>
>Ioana [*addresses Gabriela*]: Not yet.
>
>Gabriela [*confidently*]: Hire me, doll.
>
>Ioana [*doubtfully*]: But what if it goes terribly wrong again?
>
>Gabriela [*calmly and slowly*]: It won't. I am friends with the other women. They have invited me to their homes, they trust me. And we will both discuss this with them before you hire me.
>
>Ioana [*inquisitively*]: Why did Andrada quit like that?
>
>Gabriela [*lowers her voice, close to whispering*]: She got intimidated by the other women. They refused to accept her. They said she got the job behind their backs. Which is partly true. When you hired her, neither of you discussed it with the other women. So, they took it out on Andrada. She could not sleep at night, all the time thinking and worrying about what the other women told her. Andrada told me once, 'How do I make all these thoughts stop? They just go on and on in my head and I have no peace. I don't know whom to trust anymore.' I tried to help her, but in the end, she also turned against me. She noticed that the other women like me and started getting envious.
>
>Ioana [*with shame and guilt in her voice*]: So, Andrada had a very hard time because of me. I should have known better. What happened to her is terrible. I feel so guilty! Andrada came to me. I did not have any legitimate reason to tell her no at the time. I had a good opinion of her based on the interview I did with her. I should have known better.

Gabriela [matter-of-factly]: You see, there are many different types of Roma people. Many different types of languages, families, clothing. There are those who wear the kerchief in the front, those who wear it in the back. Andrada and I are Bădărani, those with the kerchief in the back are Bănăţani, others are Ursari, others are Căldărari, others are more Romanianised and maybe they don't even speak Romanes. We have our own hierarchies and structures. Us Bădărani are seen more as 'Gypsies' because we hold tightly to our old customs. So, we are usually at the bottom of the hierarchy. We have it harder. But I've always found my way, I am resilient like that, and am a good people person, people like me. But Andrada is more closed and for her it was difficult to become accepted ...

Ioana [shyly, her voice still trembling]: Yes, I noticed that you always wear 'traditional' dresses and the kerchief, and the other women also wear gadji dresses and don't wear the kerchief. So, I noticed the internal diversity among you. And I thought it would be good to have someone represent your group as well. But I didn't suspect there would be these strong barriers. So ignorant of me ...

Gabriela [with confidence and optimism]: We all make mistakes. What's important is that we learn from them. You are new, you still have many things to learn. There are other gadje who have worked with us Roma for many years. You could have asked them. Or you could have asked us Roma.

To be continued ...

Inter-relating Romani studies and creolisation

During the past couple of decades, both Roma and non-Roma researchers have been discussing and applying ethical, theoretical and methodological tools and insights for decolonising research and engaging critically with racialisation and racism (Tidrick, 2010; Gay y Blasco and Hernández, 2012; Brooks, 2012, 2015; Ryder et al., 2015; Mirga-Kruszelnicka, 2015, 2018; Costache, 2018). A few directions came out of these debates, such as the emerging critical Romani studies (Bogdan et al., 2018) and the growing call for reflexive, participatory and collaborative research practices (Brooks, 2015; Matache, 2016, 2017; Fremlova, 2019; Silverman, 2019; Gay y Blasco and Hernández, 2020; Ţîştea, 2020; Dunajeva and Vajda, 2021). For instance, Matache (2016: 2, 2017: 8) and Brooks (2015: 58) encourage scholars in Romani studies to use reflexivity in exploring historic and present-day dynamics of power, their own and the Roma participants' positionalities in social and epistemic hierarchies, disciplinary limitations manipulating their inquiries, investments in 'truth' production in their research, and how they involve people from the researched community not only to validate findings but also to participate equally and substantively in all stages of studies. I respond to these calls drawing on creolisation.

Creolisation helps explore historic and present-day dynamics of power. As a theoretical and methodological tool, creolisation emerged from the specific historical context of the Caribbean marked by colonialism, slavery, racial classification, forced displacement, loss of social identity and a double consciousness based on experiences of oppression and struggles for liberation (Glissant, 1997; Du Bois, 2005). Roma people's diasporic histories and subjectivities present a few parallels with the contexts of the African diaspora in the Caribbean and the Americas (Chang and Rucker-Chang, 2020). These include Roma people's historical displacement in relation to India, movements in multiple directions, historical enslavement on the territory of what is now Romania, current exile in relation to countries of residence either as citizens or as migrants, and a double consciousness based on experiences of oppression and creative forms of resistance (Le Bas, 2010; Matache and Bhabha, 2021; Parvulescu and Boatcă, 2023: 124–25). Creolisation thus resonates with the plea by Costache (2018: 39) to creolise Roma subjectivities through pluritopic, multifarious Romani counter-histories that engage with other subaltern counter-histories.

To address disciplinary limitations and investments in 'truth' production, creolisation decentres dominant disciplines that act as powerful academic 'centres'. Dominant disciplines validate theoretical 'truths' and prevent communication between marginalised, subaltern or emergent paradigms of knowledge; it is particularly important to connect 'minor to minor' fields of study to transgress hegemonic disciplines (Constable, 2011: 138), as I do here through dialogues between Romani studies, creolisation and ethnodrama. In the chapter, I challenge social and epistemic hierarchies and enact collaborations with coresearchers beyond the validation of findings, through dialogues between plural ways of knowing and of doing research. These enact a multi-directional, reciprocal and mutually constituting knowledge production process that nonetheless entails 'inequality, hierarchisation, issues of mastery and servitude, control and resistance' (Hall, 2015: 15). By keeping these contradictory factors together, the coresearchers and I creolise research through creative expressions and practices, while highlighting and challenging issues of domination, hegemony and subalternity (Hall, 2015: 16). Our cocreated ethnodrama makes this possible; it blurs distinctions between theatre and research, data and analysis (Petersen, 2013: 297).

The script entangles multiple analytical interpretations of our lived experiences made by Lavinia, Andrada and Gabriela. Lavinia and Andrada challenge the racialised, classed and gendered hierarchies reproduced by the cleaning project. Lavinia severely criticises the exploitative working conditions that they endure and the white workers' ignorance of their dependency on the Roma women's hard labour. She further reveals the absurdity of situations where they are present in the office cleaning but deprived of access to unfolding conversations between Bogdan, Anja and I, conversations that draw boundaries and make decisions regarding the Roma women's livelihoods. Andrada is required to be more patient, to wait until her employability will eventually improve. Yet she breaks the status quo through the act of refusal to perform cleaning services, thus refusing to invest in her subordination and her precarious incorporation into the Finnish cleaning sector. Gabriela teaches me about the limitations of white activist scholarship, about how some of my decisions at the workplace ignored the plurality and agencies of Roma women, thus un/learning how to collaborate with Romani communities. Gabriela's analysis echoes certain calls for more reflexivity in Romani studies regarding scholars' assessment of the place of academia in struggles over social justice, the need to engage in advocacy or not, and what advocacy and action might accomplish or by whom (Fotta and Gay y Blasco, 2024: 7). This resonates with the research by Solimene (2024) who refuses to speak on behalf of Roma participants, a refusal through which he explores silence as a way for non-Roma researchers to defer to Roma knowledges. On a similar note, and in dialogue with creolisation theories, the Roma women's relational, dynamic and radically subversive vernacular viewpoints provide not just the material for the ethnodrama but indeed theoretical narratives through which they criticise socio-economic and epistemic hierarchies (Constable, 2011: 120). Ultimately, they teach me when to remain silent and defer to their knowledges.

Through the Roma women's analyses, the ethnodrama becomes a creolising research practice that disrupts the reproduction of whiteness as the norm against which to explore Romani experiences, and the paternalistic intent to 'help' or 'rescue' Roma, by shifting the focus from Roma marginalisation, exoticisation or victimisation to multiple creative agencies of Roma as free thinking and acting subjects (Matache, 2016: 2; 2017: 1). In addition to creative and disruptive practices, the ethnodrama also keeps visible issues of domination (Hall, 2015: 16), challenging how the epistemic violence of the white academic agenda and dominance of non-Roma researchers in Romani studies intersect with the hierarchies of knowledge production in which an Eastern European non-Roma researcher, adviser, mentor and interpreter – who is usually side-lined from the discussion – is elevated as a knowing subject while silencing the resistant, divergent and creative agencies of Roma women. This intersects with Roma scholars' calls to be taken seriously as knowledge producers beyond the validating approval of their non-Roma peers. For instance, Lee (2000: 132) has documented how Roma-related research historically and presently has been dominated by non-Roma academics from privileged positionings and marked by Gypsylorism, a specific form of epistemic violence, which is an equivalent of orientalism in studying Europe's internal 'others'. Matache (2016: 3) has highlighted how non-Roma scholars have been invested with power to validate or reject Romani scholarship as a legitimate form of knowledge production based on claims like lack of objectivity due to emotional and political investments.

Within the Finnish context, some scholars conducting Roma-related migration research have used reflexivity to challenge essentialising approaches that focus on nation state and ethnicity, East/South–West/North migration patterns, and biased understanding of Roma migration as predominantly a socio-economic issue, through approaches that show the heterogeneity and divergent agencies of Roma people, such as entangled mobilities (Roman, 2014, 2018; Enache, 2018; Markkanen, 2018). For instance, Roman (2018) entangled Finnish Roma missionaries' North–South transnational mobility to engage in humanitarian work with Roma communities in Romania, and Romanian Roma representatives' South–North mobility when invited to participate in planning meetings in Finland and express the views and needs of their communities. She thus illustrates a web of engagements, collaborations and reciprocal relationships, along with the politicised and differential positions of authority and power within which such entanglements occur between non/believers, non/Roma, missionaries, missionised, pastors, members of local communities, research participants, and herself as researcher, translator and mediator accompanying the missionaries in their journeys (Roman, 2018: 49).

The entangled mobilities approach answers calls for more reflexivity in Romani studies, particularly in Roma-related migration research, by broadening understandings of Roma agency and mobility, and by inter-relating multiple Roma and non-Roma agencies and mobilities (Roman, 2018: 52). By inter-relating plural and unequal lived experiences of im/mobility, entangled mobilities can also creolise migration research (Gutiérrez Rodríguez, 2021; Boatcă and Santos, 2023). The ethnodrama enacts several entangled im/mobilities. First, it explores the interdependence between privileged and underprivileged mobilities (Wyss and Dahinden, 2022: 10) through the co-dependency between non-Roma and Roma South East European migrants in Finnish work contexts. Roma migrant workers, because they are exposed to a racialised migration regime that marginalises them, are pushed to provide cheap labour and become economically dependent on the mobility of more privileged migrants who translate and mediate their access to the labour market. Yet, as Lavinia has analysed above, the more privileged migrants' jobs also depend on the presence of Roma migrants to whom they offer mediation and translation services.

Second, the ethnodrama explores how and which people become or do not become 'migratised' or racialised, and what role class, gender and other categories of difference play, in two small localities rather than a nation-state container (Tudor, 2018; Wyss and Dahinden, 2022: 7). At the airport, Cătălina's mobility is dependent on my privileged positioning as a mobile person. Cătălina is racialised and migratised and her right to migrate is questioned through bordering apparatuses. On the other hand, my mobility is not migratised and subjected to additional immigration controls, but taken for granted. In the emergency accommodation centre, Roma migrants sleep, Roma workers clean, white Finnish workers lead and non-Roma Romanian and Bulgarian workers supervise, mediate and offer social assistance. The exploitation of Roma migrant workers thus unfolds in the context of multiple other power asymmetries based on race, gender, class and nationality, in which some people are seen more as migrants than others based on their proximity to or distance from Finnish whiteness. Both the interdependence between non-Roma and Roma privileged and underprivileged mobilities, and the interconnections between how people become or do not become migratised or racialised, reflect creolisation processes where unequal power relations are constantly renegotiated in unexpected ways (Boatcă and Santos, 2023: 8). Centring Romani lived experiences to theories of both mobility *and* reflexivity ultimately creolises research, by thinking through and with minoritised formations that have been ignored or rendered invisible, to become theories in themselves (Lionnet and Shih, 2011: 21; Boatcă and Santos, 2023: 11).

Closing reflections

By inter-relating Romani studies, creolisation and ethnodrama, in this chapter I have rethought social hierarchies, inequalities and epistemologies, by exploring the multiple points of entanglement characterising both migration narratives *and* research practices (Lionnet and Shih, 2011; Gutiérrez Rodríguez, 2015). In creating the ethnodrama, I engaged with the Roma women as active producers of knowledge who related their own knowledges to the drama and took part in analyses of the script (Petersen, 2013: 297). Yet why am I the sole author of this publication?

Gabriela,[3] one of the coresearchers experimented with collaborative storytelling and coauthored a book chapter with me (Țîștea and Băncuță, 2023). For the chapter coauthored with Gabriela, we jointly developed a method designed to enable people without so-called 'literacy' skills to author written papers. For that chapter, we cowrote everything. We dedicated most of the space to the stories we shared with one another and a very small amount of space to the introduction and summary. Gabriela is fully aware of everything that is written in that piece. I translated and discussed everything with her, including the literature review. This piece, however, is more theoretical and includes a lot of my own views derived from the literature I have read but which is inaccessible to Gabriela and the other women. The women have other ongoing life projects and their time did not allow them to dedicate as much effort to this piece as Gabriela did with the other text. Furthermore, they did not see the benefit of being named as coauthors of a text that is largely inaccessible to them due to containing extensive parts written in an alienating academic genre. We therefore considered that mentioning them as coauthors on such terms would merely tokenise them. Thus the best option was to acknowledge their contributions.

Like other researchers who have attempted coauthorial collaborations with participants, I see the women's arguments as triggers to question the value of using academic publications as a venue for collaborative knowledge production and dissemination (Mainsah and Rafiki, 2022: 14). The ethnodrama indeed questions normative academic writing, yet the overall text does not completely depart from such writing and thus deters more meaningful participation from the women. By staying with these tensions and im/possibilities to reconcile different agendas and expectations, the text is thus a contribution to ongoing debates on how research could be carried out otherwise. Through the entanglement of multiple im/mobilities, of disciplines that are not usually brought together, and of abstract theories and concepts with dramatised stories rooted in the vernacular and the embodied and affective everyday, certain paths may open towards imagining alternative possible futures.

Notes

1 All the characters in the script have pseudonyms, except for myself, as well as Gabriela at her request.
2 Emergency accommodation centre for Roma migrants, one of the main clients for the cleaning project.
3 While Gabriela chose to have her identity revealed, the other women chose to stay anonymous and be named by pseudonyms.

References

Boatcă, M. and Santos, F. (2023) 'Of rags and riches in the Caribbean: creolizing migration studies', *Journal of Immigrant & Refugee Studies*, 21, 132–45. doi: 10.1080/15562948.2022.2129896.

Bogdan, M., Dunajeva, J., Junghaus, T., Kóczé, A., Rostas, I., Rovid, M. and Szilvasi, M. (2018) 'Introducing the new journal *Critical Romani Studies*', *Critical Romani Studies*, 1(1), 2–7. https://dx.doi.org/10.29098/crs.v1i1.19.

Brooks, E. (2012) 'Comparative perspectives symposium: Romani feminisms', *Signs: Journal of Women in Society*, 38(1), 1–46.

Brooks, E. (2015) 'The importance of feminists and "halfies" in Romani Studies: new epistemological possibilities', *Roma Rights*, 2, 57–61.

Chang, F. B. and Rucker-Chang, S. T. (2020) *Roma Rights and Civil Rights: A Transatlantic Comparison*. Cambridge: Cambridge University Press. https://doi.org/10.1017/9781316663813.

Constable, L. (2011) 'Material histories of transcolonial loss: creolizing psychoanalytic theories of melancholia?', in Lionnet, F. and Shih, S. (eds) *The Creolization of Theory*, Durham, NC: Duke University Press, pp. 112–41.

Costache, I. (2018) 'Reclaiming Romani-ness', *Critical Romani Studies*, 1(1), 30–43. https://dx.doi.org/10.29098/crs.v1i1.11.

Du Bois, W. E. B. (2005/1906) *The Soul of Black Folk*. New York: Pocket Books.

Dunajeva, J. and Vajda, V. (2021) 'Positionality, academic research and cooperative inquiry: lessons from participatory research with Roma', in Burns, D., Howard, J. and Ospina, S. M. (eds) *The SAGE Handbook of Participatory Research and Inquiry*, London: SAGE Publications, pp. 224–37.

Enache, A. (2018) 'Children's agency in translocal Roma families', in Laura Assmuth, L., Hakkarainen', M., Lulle, A. and Siim, P. M. (eds) *Translocal Childhoods and Family Mobility in East and North Europe*. Cham: Palgrave Macmillan, pp. 193–215.

Fotta, M. and Gay y Blasco, P. (2024) 'Introduction: emerging trends in Gypsy, Roma and Traveller Research', in Fotta, M. and Gay y Blasco, P. (eds) *Ethnographic Methods in Gypsy, Roma and Traveller Research: Lessons from a Time of Crisis*. Bristol: Bristol University Press, pp. 1–11. https://doi.org/10.51952/9781529231878.

Fremlova, L. (2019) 'Non-Romani researcher positionality and reflexivity', *Critical Romani Studies*, 1(2), 98–123. https://dx.doi.org/10.29098/crs.v1i2.25.

Gay y Blasco, P. and Hernández, L. (2012) 'Friendship, anthropology', *Anthropology and Humanism*, 31(1), 1–14.

Gay y Blasco, P. and Hernández, L. (2020) *Writing Friendship: A Reciprocal Ethnography*, Cham: Palgrave Macmillan.

Glissant, É. (1997) *Poetics of Relation*, trans. and ed. Wing, B. Ann Arbor, MI: University of Michigan Press.

Gutiérrez Rodríguez, E. (2015) 'Archipelago Europe: on creolizing conviviality', in Gutiérrez Rodrérrez, E. and Tate, S. A. (eds) *Creolizing Europe: Legacies and Transformations*. Liverpool: Liverpool University Press, pp. 80–99.

Gutiérrez Rodríguez, E. (2021) 'Entangled migrations: the coloniality of migration and creolizing conviviality', *Mecila Working Papers*, 35.

Hall, S. (2015) 'Creolité and the process of creolization', in Gutiérrez Rodríguez, E. and Tate, S. A. (eds) *Creolizing Europe: Legacies and Transformations*. Liverpool: Liverpool University Press, pp. 12–26.

Le Bas, D. (2010) 'The possible implications of diasporic consciousness for Romani identity', in Le Bas, D. and Acton, T. A. (eds) *All Change! Romani Studies through Romani Eyes*. Hatfield: University of Hertfordshire Press, pp. 61–9.

Lee, K. (2000) 'Orientalism and Gypsylorism', *Social Analysis: The International Journal of Social and Cultural Practice*, 44(2), 129–56.

Lionnet, F. and Shih, S. (2011) *The creolization of theory*. Durham, NC: Duke University Press.

Mainsah, H. and Rafiki, N. (2022) 'Methodological reflections on curating an artistic event with African youth in a Norwegian city', *Qualitative Research*, 0(0). https://doi.org/10.1177/14687941221096599.

Markkanen, A. (2018) 'Sensitive Ethnography: a researcher's journey with translocal Roma families', in Assmuth, L., Hakkarainen, M., Lulle, A. and Siim, P. M. (eds) *Translocal Childhoods and Family Mobility in East and North Europe*. Cham: Palgrave Macmillan, pp. 87–112.

Matache, M. (2016) *The Legacy of Gypsy Studies in Modern Romani Scholarship*. FXB Center for Health & Human Rights, Harvard University. https://fxb.harvard.edu/the-legacy-of-gypsy-studies-in-modern-romani-scholarship (accessed 1 April 2022).

Matache, M. (2017) *Dear Gadje (non-Romani) Scholars* ... FXB Center for Health & Human Rights, Harvard University. https://fxb.harvard.edu/2017/06/19/dear-gadje-non-romani-scholars/ (accessed 1 April 2022).

Matache, M. and Bhabha, J. (2021) 'The Roma case for reparations', in Bhabha, J., Matache, M. and Elkins, C. (eds) *Time for Reparation? Addressing State Responsibility for Collective Injustice*. Philadelphia, PA: University of Pennsylvania Press, pp. 253–71. https://doi.org/10.2307/j.ctv1f45q96.19.

Mirga-Kruszelnicka, A. (2015) 'Romani studies and emerging Romani scholarship', *Roma Rights*, 2, 39–46.

Mirga-Kruszelnicka, A. (2018) 'Challenging anti-gypsyism in academia', *Critical Romani Studies*, 1(1), 8–28. https://dx.doi.org/10.29098/crs.v1i1.5.

Parvulescu, A. and Boatcă, M. (2023) 'Creolization as method', *Cambridge Journal of Postcolonial Literary Inquiry*, 10(1), 121–7. doi:10.1017/pli.2022.34.

Petersen, E. B. (2013) 'Cutting edge(s): an ethnographic drama in three acts', *Cultural Studies ↔ Critical Methodologies*, 13(4), 293–98. https://doi.org/10.1177/1532708613487876.

Roman, R. B. (2014) 'Trans-national migration and the issue of "ethnic" solidarity: Finnish Roma elite and Eastern European Roma migrants in Finland', *Ethnicities*, 14(6), 793–810. https://doi.org/10.1177/1468796814542179.

Roman, R. B. (2018) 'Roma mobility, beyond migration: religious humanitarianism and transnational Roma missionary work as de-constructions of migration. Intersections', *East European Journal of Society and Politics*, 4, 2. https://doi.org/10.17356/ieejsp.v4i2.380.

Ryder, A., Kóczé, A., Rostas, I., Dunajeva, J., Bogdan, M., Taba, M., Rövid, M. and Junghaus, T. (2015) 'Nothing about us without us? Roma participation in policy making and knowledge production', *Roma Rights Journal 2*. www.errc.org/uploads/upload_en/file/roma-rights-2-2015-nothing-about-us-without-us.pdf.

Saldaña, J. (2018) 'Ethnodrama and ethnotheatre: research as performance', in Denzin, N. K. and Lincoln, Y. S. (eds) *The SAGE Handbook of Qualitative Research*. 5th edition. Thousand Oaks, CA: SAGE Publications, pp. 662–91.

Silverman, C. (2019) 'From reflexivity to collaboration', *Critical Romani Studies*, 1(2), 76–97.

Solimene, M. (2024) 'The anthropologist's engagement: lessons from a digital ethnography of a nomad camp in times of COVID-19', in Fotta, M. and Gay y Blasco, P. (eds) *Ethnographic Methods in Gypsy, Roma and Traveller Research: Lessons from a Time of Crisis*. Bristol: Bristol University Press, pp. 61–76. https://doi.org/10.51952/9781529231878.ch005.

Sughrua, W. M. (2020) 'The core of critical performative autoethnography', *Qualitative Inquiry*, 26(6), 602–32. https://doi.org/10.1177/1077800419830132.
Tidrick, H. (2010) '"Gadžology" as activism: what I would have ethnography do for East European Roma', *Collaborative Anthropologies*, 3, 121–31. https://doi.org/10.1353/cla.2010.0012.
Țîștea, I. (2020) '"Reflexivity of reflexivity" with Roma-related Nordic educational research', *Nordic Journal of Comparative and International Education (NJCIE)*, 4(1), 26–42. https://doi.org/10.7577/njcie.3579.
Țîștea, I. (2021) '*"Ain't I also a migrant?"* An ethnodrama of weaving knowledges otherwise in Finnish migration research', *Nordic Journal of Studies in Educational Policy*, 7(3), 136–47. http://dx.doi.org/10.1080/20020317.2021.2009102.
Țîștea, I. and Băncuță, G. (2023) 'Creolizing subjectivities and relationalities within Roma-gadje research collaborations', in Suárez Krabbe, J. and Groglopo, A. (eds) *Coloniality and Decolonization in the Nordic Countries*. Abingdon: Routledge, pp. 126–44. http://dx.doi.org/10.4324/9781003293323-8.
Tudor, A. (2018) 'Cross-fadings of racialisation and migratisation: the postcolonial turn in Western European gender and migration studies', *Gender, Place & Culture*, 25(7), 1–16. https://doi.org/10.1080/0966369x.2018.1441141.
Vergès, Françoise (2015) 'Creolization and Resistance', Gutiérrez Rodríguez, E. and Tate, S. A. (eds) *Creolizing Europe: Legacies and Transformations*. Liverpool: Liverpool University Press, pp. 38–56.
Wyss, A. and Dahinden, J. (2022) 'Disentangling entangled mobilities: reflections on forms of knowledge production within migration studies', *Comparative Migration Studies*, 10(1), 33. https://doi.org/10.1186/s40878-022-00309-w.

12

Swimming with the coelacanth into the black holes of Breslau/Wrocław, the Eastern Polish Kresy and Madagascar

Olivier Kramsch

My Papa and his mother ('Mutti') survived the massive Soviet bombing of Breslau[1] by living for three years in the basement of their destroyed apartment block (1942–45). After an artillery mortar cratered the wall of their living room, Mutti, with typical, wry Silesian humour, is said to have responded, '*Ich wollte immer ein Fenster da*'.[2] At the end of the war, due to efforts to 'Polonise' formerly German settlements in Lower Silesia, both she and Papa were forcibly deported in packed trains to the West, towards what was soon to become the new West German Federal Republic (Bundesrepublik), landing in the Rhineland, not far from the provincial city of Krefeld. Little remarked upon because its victims were on the 'wrong' side of history, the post-war deportation of Germans constitutes one of the most significant cases of ethnic cleansing on European soil in the twentieth century. Although raised in the United States, I am a son and grandson of that ethnic cleansing, its associated violence, silence and ongoing trauma. I speak now with my ninety-two-year-old Papa, ensconced in his Berlin senior home; the images of Soviet artillery attacks on Ukrainian cities and of Ukrainian women and children huddled in basements seventy-seven years after his own identical experience as a teenager in Breslau rips open the wound of that trauma anew.

It is commonplace now among scholars exploring the intersections of post-socialism and post-colonialism to foreground their positionality, the better so as to reveal a perspective sensitive to the historical entanglement of Easts and Souths (Koobak et al., 2021; Aparna et al., this volume). In this chapter, I join this chorus, speaking from a situated family knowledge embracing myriad Easts and Souths across the long twentieth century. Rather than bundled into a short paragraph, however, as is oft found in the literature, I distribute my family positionalities across key junctures in the narrative, each serving as an entry point into realms connecting disparate Eastern and Southern bordered geographies of the present. What I attempt in this exercise is no claim to unique, regionalised knowledge reproducing an imperial gaze on my subject matter. Rather, in the manner of Ryszard Kapuściński's inter-continental travelogues (2007), I seek to combine the intimately biographical with a sensuously analogical and allegorical attitude capable of piecing together worldly experience on the basis of the inherently limited and fractured self. For it is precisely due to the partiality of vision conferred upon the biographical self, not on the basis of a universalising 'gaze from nowhere', that surprising and distinctive connections can be forged between East(s) and South(s). In other words, I propose that the spatial accidents of biography can become a 'method' for discovering surprising connections at the joints of the post-socialist and post-colonial in ways that offer more productively imaginative openings to the impoverished, ressentiment-laced and strategic essentialist framings of Central and Eastern Europe currently on display in what passes for Continental European critical geography (Müller, 2020). The silences over past violences and resulting 'holes' in my family history serve as a pivot from which to narrate wider geographies linking today's global Souths and Easts, here and there, now and then.

The geographies I attempt to stitch together via this method are the post-war 'Recovered Territories' of Western Poland retrieved after the mass expulsion of ethnic Germans from the region; the so-called Kresy encompassing Eastern Poland and Western Belarus and Ukraine; and finally, the South Indian Ocean island of Madagascar. In the mid-twentieth century these territories were infused with a very specific Polish post-socialist and post-colonial 'mythology'. Whereas the Eastern Polish Borderlands were conceived either as a site of nostalgic longing for a lost arcadia, a territory of benevolent colonisation towards the less-developed Belarussian and Ukrainian 'other', and/or the space of catastrophe, the Western 'Recovered Territories' and Madagascar entered the Polish public and political imagination as sites capable of 'Polonising' its urban peripheries while once and for all solving Poland's 'Jewish Question'. Through the simultaneous interplay of these three inter-war Polish myths, I trace the emergence of a nationalising border and external frontier dynamic whose subterranean rumblings continue to inform our lived post-socialist and post-colonial present, as witnessed most recently in the so-called 'migrant crisis' at the Polish–Belarussian border. To make sense of these hybrid crossings, I argue we need to 'swim with the coelacanth', that half-fish, half-mammal, once thought extinct, only to be rediscovered in the mid-twentieth century off the coast of Madagascar.

My German grandfather ('Vati') fought as a machine-gunner in the First World War. According to family lore, in the trenches of Verdun and the Somme, facing oncoming waves of Senegalese tirailleurs literally armed to the teeth with knives, he had to tear out the machine-gunner's insignia from his uniform, knowing well how they were singled out for particularly cruel punishment. Vati later fought under von Paulus' Sixth Army at Stalingrad, then was interned in a Soviet prisoner of war camp. Fatally ill, he was transported back to Germany, where he is buried in a mass grave together with 7,500 other Wehrmacht soldiers in a cemetery in Frankfurt an der Oder. Sitting by his plaque at that mass grave with my father and my teenage son a few years ago, I remarked to Papa that his deportation in 1945 made him a refugee not unlike today's refugees attempting to enter Europe across the Mediterranean. At this, he bristles, telling me he has nothing in common with 'them'. Unlike today's refugees from Africa and the Middle East, '*Wir sind geflüchtet innerhalb des Deutschen Reiches*'.³ Startlingly, sitting there at the grave of my son's great-grandfather in Frankfurt an der Oder, my father says the words 'Deutschen Reiches' as if he still inhabited it.

Much later, I would learn that the term Deutsches Reich was the constitutional name for the German nation that existed from 1871 to 1945. Its sovereignty was grounded entirely from a continuing unitary German 'national people', whose authority was exercised over a unitary German 'state territory with variable reach and boundaries' (Willoweit, 2013; see Figure 12.1).

Figure 12.1 The German Reich, 1920–37. Source: https://de.wikipedia.org/wiki/Deutsches_Reich#/media/Datei:Karte_des_Deutschen_Reiches,_Weimarer_Republik-Drittes_Reich_1919–1937.svg (accessed 20 May 2022)

As a result of decisions taken by the victorious Allies at the Potsdam Conference on 17 July and 2 August 1945, the territory to the east of the Oder–Neisse line was assigned to Polish and Soviet administration pending the final peace treaty. All Germans had their property confiscated and were placed under restrictive jurisdiction. The remaining population faced theft and looting, also in some instances rape and murder, crimes that were rarely prevented nor prosecuted by the Polish Militia Forces and newly installed communist judicial system (Urban, 2006). Between 1944 and 1950 approximately 12 million ethnic Germans (Volksdeutsche) and German citizens (Reichsdeutsche), including my Papa and Mutti, were permanently moved from into Allied-occupied Germany and Austria, representing the largest movement of any single ethnic population in European history, and the largest among the post-war expulsions in Central and Eastern Europe (Kacowicz and Lutomski, 2007; Wasserstein, 2007). The largest outflow stemmed from the former German eastern territories ceded to the People's Republic of Poland and the Soviet Union, as well as from Czechoslovakia. Deported from Breslau on cattle trains, my Papa and Mutti belonged to the former group.

The expulsion of Germans from the Silesian territories of the former Reich, now turned over to Poland, was integral to the broader goal of the Allies and the Soviet Union to carve out ethnically homogeneous nation states from the formerly mixed landscapes of Central and Eastern Europe (Prauser and Rees, 2004). As early as 9 September 1944, Stalin and Polish communist Edward Osóbka-Morawski of the Polish Committee of National Liberation signed a treaty in Lublin on population exchanges of Ukrainians and Poles living on the 'wrong' side of the Curzon Line. As a result, many of the 2.1 million Poles expelled from the Soviet-annexed Kresy, so-called 'repatriants', were resettled to formerly German populated 'Recovered Territories', including Breslau, now renamed Wrocław – bringing Poland much-desired industry, coalfields, as well as a long Baltic coastline. For the Polish communist regime, the 'Polonisation' of the Oder–Neisse border landscape and corollary policy of 'de-Germanisation' constituted a form of 'internal colonisation' which received wide support among Polish society. Polish colonisation would be matched by a Soviet political and military colonisation which sought to extend Communism as far west as possible under the guise of Polish national self-determination. Both considered themselves in pursuit of a 'Manifest Destiny' to rebuild the war-torn region, bring 'Germanised' Poles back into the Polish fold, and use the Recovered Territories as a bulwark against the eastward spread of capitalism (McNamara, 2014).

But who was to be effectively defined as 'German', and therefore expellable? Within the context of Polish 'verification programmes', ethnic lines were not clear cut, made all the more difficult by the notorious 'national indifference' of the Silesian populace, as well as the presence of large regional indigenous groups with mixed Polish and German identities, such as the Cashubians, Warmians and Masurians (Madajczyk and Rocznik Polsko-Niemiecki, 1992; Bjork, 2008). The Polish government defined Germans as either Reichsdeutsche or those who held German citizenship. Neither of these categories fully applied to these indigenous groups; as a result, despite having lived in the region for centuries, they found themselves in the position of having to constantly prove their identity to different external authorities (McNamara, 2014). Approximately 1,165,000 German citizens of Slavic descent were verified as 'autochthonous' Poles. Of these, most were not expelled. However, many chose to migrate to East Germany in 1951–82, including most of the Masurians of East Prussia, who were resentful at being perceived as Germans willing to work for free under the newly arrived Polish settlers.

A further motivation of the Potsdam Agreement pushing for the mass expulsions was to punish the Germans, as the Allies declared them collectively guilty of German war crimes (Brunnbauer et al., 2006). Guilt was not uppermost in the minds of Papa and Mutti at the war's ending. At the time of his expulsion, Papa was fourteen years old. In the final days of the war, Mutti cut his hair and made him wear short trousers so that he would look younger and avoid his being sent to the trenches surrounding Breslau to fight the oncoming Soviet army, where he would have surely perished. As he and Mutti came out of their basement shelter, Breslau lay in ruins. Decomposing bodies lay in the streets. This experience damaged Papa, producing an emotional numbness that would haunt him his entire life. In the 1950s, he went on to study medicine in Munich, then married my mother (a French woman from Versailles), the two of them moving in the early 1960s with the author of this chapter, escaping a Europe that had traumatised them, seeking to escape memory and the necessity of working through the trauma of that memory, to the United States, that *Land der Unbegrenzten Möglichkeiten* (the 'Land of Limitless Opportunities'). From that initial displacement, flight would follow flight, through alcohol, drugs and 'free love', from the US East Coast to its West Coast, landing Papa late in life in a Berlin senior home, scant hours by train from his place of birth, in a 'foreign' city. I now seek to make sense of the space of that ongoing displacement from Eastern Europe, across the Atlantic and back, including its accompanying silences, as one of my family's black 'voids' (Tlostanova, 2017). I now belatedly work through that void, in English, from a neighbourhood café in Cleves, Niederrhein, Germany.

> Time evidently is more stretchable when we are young, and with appropriately focused effort it can be expanded to make additional room, like the pockets of my school uniform, in which [...] I carried more than their prosaic dimensions allowed. Or can it be that space itself favors children? (Lem, 1966: 93)

> The 'Borderlands' surround us on all sides; I would even go so far as to say that their multiplication and hyperbolization in a country the size of Poland are an expression of collective experiences functioning for mythologizing rather than for genuine geographical, political or ethnic reasons. (Bakuła, 2007: 97)

Chances are high that once Papa's neighbourhood was rebuilt after the war, in the newly baptised Polish city of Wrocław, its deserted houses and streets and shops were repopulated by former inhabitants of the 'Kresy', or Eastern Polish Borderlands, who were forcibly deported to Silesia so as to 'Polonise' the formerly German 'Recovered Territories'.[4] We must now pause for a moment to take in the vastness of this enterprise: the emptying out of an entire city-region of 620,000 German inhabitants and full replacement by a Polish community also recently subject to mass removal and expulsion. An entire city, we might say, twice deported. What ghosts remain of the departing German populace? What phantasms did the forcibly removed Eastern Polish Borderlanders bring with them to their new, Western home? As I sit with Papa in a small regional train station café with my son after visiting Vati's grave in Frankfurt an der Oder, I haphazardly remark how strikingly 'Slavic' I find the faces of the passengers hustling about the station. Again, he explodes in a barely suppressed rage. The pain is there, always was there, tender to the bone, just beneath the outer surface of apparent strength and calm. How can the void of that pain be laid to rest? Can it be worked through by going down into the black hole of silenced family memory, recognising its palimpsest of layered shadows, hovering over the phantom limbs inhabiting this zone in the lived post-socialist and post-colonial present, picking up, literally, where Papa 'left off'?

The Polish settlers arriving suitcase in hand in Wrocław and other cities of the Recovered Territories stepped into a landscape whose Polish sovereignty and administration were kept fragile and unstable by Soviet authorities in order to make them permanently in need of the Soviet Union's protection (Allen, 2003). As a result, widespread crime and political instability due to the settlers' perception of the impermanence of Poland's new borders pervaded the post-war urban atmosphere of the territories (McNamara, 2014). 'In practice', writes Paul McNamara (2014: 217), 'many so-called settlers behaved more like squatters, occupying farms and houses but neither maintaining nor rebuilding them, while living in constant expectation of a Third World war among the "Big Three"'. The resulting feeling of impermanence and nostalgia for their lost Eastern homeland produced in many émigrés a particular geographical imaginary of the Kresy from which they had been forcibly expelled, one that they would nurture for generations in their transplanted Silesian home. The Eastern Borderlands (in Polish Kresy Wschodnie, the plural form of the word 'kres' meaning 'edge') referred specifically to the eastern part of the Second Polish Republic during the inter-war period

Figure 12.2 Kresy. Source: https://en.wikipedia.org/wiki/Kresy (accessed 22 May 2022)

(1918–39). Mostly agricultural and profoundly multi-ethnic, it amounted to nearly half of the territory of pre-war Poland (see Figure 12.2). Historically situated in the eastern Polish–Lithuanian Commonwealth, following the eighteenth-century external partitions, it was annexed by Russia and partly by the Habsburg monarchy (Galicia) and finally ceded to Poland in 1921 after the Peace of Riga.[5] As a result of border reconfigurations after the Second World War, almost none of the Kresy remains in Poland today.[6]

Even though the Kresy are no longer part of Poland, the provinces are still home to a Polish minority and the memory of Eastern Borderlands, particularly among the deported émigrés, is cultivated among many of them (Zarycki, 2014). Indeed, for Bogusław Bakuła (2007: 97) the very term 'Borderlands' is to be associated with wider structure of feeling 'possessing a specific magical-mythical nature', one which continues to exert a 'considerable influence on the social and political attitudes of the Polish community'. In this view, just as Silesia was perceived by German National Socialism as a frontier meant to preserve the essence of 'Germanness':

> The 'Borderlands' were a place of specific political confrontation and struggles for Polishness, which means that they were de facto about maintaining the Polish possession. In the word 'Borderlands' there lies the unconcealed great power of local patriotism (transferred in the twenty inter-war years as well as today to the official patriotism of the Polish state), exoticism, otherness, colorfulness, and uncommonness, which are attractive not only to Poles. On the other hand, there is also in this word the hint of a lowering of status, a specific message indicating the peripheral nature of the 'Borderlands' as a world far from the Polish centres and, of course, not exclusively Polish (for both reasons the term 'Borderlands' was and still is attacked in Ukraine and rejected as absurd in Lithuania) [...] The 'Borderlands' seen in this perspective become after all that which is most Polish, although – and precisely because – they have been lost, that which ennobles *ex definitione* everyone who talks about them. And conversely – any criticism encounters a sharp reaction and even the accusation of betraying the nation. (Bakuła, 2007: 97, 100)

For authors such as Bakuła, since at least a century the overarching discourse supplying knowledge of the 'Borderlands' to Polish public opinion is literary fiction. Such fictions 'mythologized reality, drove out any rational historical assessment, particularly at the time of the Partitions and then again during the communist isolation, and created the mythology of a lost homeland, suffering and sacrifice' (Bakuła, 2007: 98; see also Mick, 2014).[7] According to the Polish border scholar, under the literary influence of these myths, particularly émigré Poles believe 'every claim for restitution is possible [...] while they entertain no thoughts about its colonial nature' (Bakuła, 2007: 98). Although the properly 'colonial' nature of this mythology is subject to debate among leading Polish scholars, there exists a growing agreement that the very term 'Borderlands' has become politically incorrect. Bakuła writes:

> The former 'Borderlands' react negatively after all to their continual 'Borderlands-ization' [...] No one in Poland asks whether the Lithuanians, Belarusians, or Ukrainians want to be, metonymically, the 'Borderlands' of Poland within either its historical or its present borders, or what they think about it. The 'Borderlands' discourse loudly proclaimed as a form of dialogue and above all of multiculturalism reveals its emptiness already at the outset. In this discourse there is no discussion. 'Borderlands-ness' and 'Borderlands studies' are in any case reserved for Poles and only rarely can we find any active Lithuanians, Belarusians, Jews, or Ukrainians here. (Bakuła, 2007: 99)

Rather than reproduce a power discourse in borderlands studies that 'relies on solidifying myths and presiding through them' in order to 'dominate, restructure and retain our lost power in the "Borderlands"' (2007: 115),

Bakuła (2007: 123) invites us to develop a 'new scientific language' rooted in a post-colonial sensibility attuned to comparative study, democratic accountability, 'parallel thinking' and an intellectual framework 'devoid of national solipsism':

> We will not change our post-Soviet world [...] if we continue to live in a zone contaminated by colonial ideology and with a feeling of distrust and fear in the face of the Other [...] [O]nly a common reading of the Borderlands makes sense – without mutual exclusions and treated as the recognition of a common heritage ... in which the contradictory experiences of all the subjects of the history of the Borderlands will not turn away from one another but will be enabled to reach understanding. (Bakuła, 2007: 123)

In January 2022, a decade and a half after Bakuła's plaidoyer for an Eastern Polish borderland whose inhabitants 'will be enabled to reach understanding', Poland began to build a border fence cutting through pristine forest and a world heritage site, extending half the length of Poland's border with Belarus at a cost estimated to be ten times higher than the Polish migration ministry's annual budget (Andersson, 2022). For the Polish government, the rationale for the fence was a response to the actions of Belarusian president Alexander Lukashenko, who the previous autumn had bused hundreds of migrants from war-torn and impoverished countries of the so-called Global South to the Polish border in a move European Union officials considered an attempt to 'weaponise' migrants and refugees as a revenge for sanctions imposed on the Lukashenko regime after the bloc accused him of stealing the 2020 elections and ordering human rights violations (NPR, 2021; Pszczółkowska, 2022). Adding misery to the unlawful pushbacks exerted by the Polish border patrol on migrants halted at the country's 250–mile-long border with Belarus, the new wall across the forest is consistent with the ruling Polish Law and Justice Party's discriminatory policy from 2016 to 2023 of denying applications for international protection to people crossing its border from Belarus, thus failing to meet Poland's Geneva Convention and European Convention of Human Rights obligations (Pszczółkowska, 2022).

Such a policy stands in stark contrast with the preferential treatment offered by Poland to Ukrainian refugees fleeing war around the time the forest wall was being built:

> Poles headed to the border and train stations to offer newcomers housing, transportation and food. Hundreds of thousands joined social media help groups; friends, former classmates, neighbours, fitness club members spontaneously organized to provide whatever was necessary, from humanitarian aid for cities in Ukraine, 'free shops' in Poland (where Ukrainians could pick up clothes, cosmetics and other items), to the transportation of two Kharkiv cats from the Polish border to Israel (an authentic request from one group, executed within 23h). (Pszczółkowska, 2022: 221)

This 'unprecedented' rise of Polish civil society dovetailed with government policy, which passed an emergency law guaranteeing Ukrainians access to the labour market, education, health care and benefits, while offering financial support to locals hosting Ukrainians for 60 days (subsequently extended to 120 days). In this current borderscape, it would appear as if 'two borders' have emerged (Pszczółkowska, 2022: 221), each vindicating a face of the historicised Kresy border myth dissected by Bakuła: one facing oncoming waves of Ukrainian refugees, an Arcadian space 'without mutual exclusions and treated as the recognition of a common heritage'; the other facing migrants from the Global South, a 'zone contaminated by colonial ideology and with a feeling of distrust and fear in the face of the Other' (Bakuła, 2007: 123). In a very real sense, then, Bakuła's 'post-Soviet world' remains a fraught, degraded achievement. But the two borders of the Kresy also refract a globally racialised border regime implicating not just Bakuła's 'post-Soviet world' but a fully post-colonial constellation. To understand the proper imbrication of these 'worlds', it would be helpful at this juncture to dive into the Pacific Ocean and swim with the coelacanth.

> It is not stated anywhere, after all, that a colonized community cannot display colonizing features. That is why Poles know very well what the world both of the colonized and of the colonizing looks like. They know, but they are not interested in thinking in the categories of responsibility for this dichotomy. (Bakuła, 2007: 103)

In 1947, three years after my Papa and Mutti were expelled from Breslau to the Rhineland, and in the period when hundreds of thousands of Poles were forcibly being moved from the Kresy into the newly minted Wrocław, my great-uncle, the French naturalist Jacques Millot, found himself on the South Indian Ocean island of Madagascar. In this period, he founded the Institut de Recherche Scientifique de Madagascar at Antananarivo, surrounding himself with young scientists and researchers from around the world, and created an oceanographic research centre at Nosy-Bé (Dorst, 1980). Inspired by the knowledge of accidental discoveries of the fish specimen known under the name *Latimeria chalumnae* brought to South Africa in 1938, Millot suspected this same species to inhabit the waters surrounding the nearby French-controlled Comores Islands. On 24 September 1953, with the help of local fishermen, Millot's research team discovered the coelacanth off the coast of the island of Anjouan, near the village of Mutsamudu (Dorst, 1980; see Figure 12.3). Millot transported it immediately to Paris to be dissected under his direct supervision. On the basis of his path-breaking research findings on this specimen – half-fish, half-mammal, the purported 'missing link' between the species, ostensibly extinct since 70 million years – Millot later became director of the Musée de l'Homme

Figure 12.3 Reconstruction of a West Indian Ocean coelacanth: 'archaique, lourd, gras et gluant' (Millot, cited in Coppens, 1988: 122–23). Source: *Citron* https://en.wikipedia.org/wiki/Coelacanth (accessed 15 May 2022)

in Paris, precursor to today's Musée Quai-Branly, which showcases objects and artefacts received (and/or stolen) from the entire French imperial world (Millot, 1954; Laurière, 2019).

Situated at the crossroads of animal species, continents and millennia, how can we think with the coelacanth to forge further connections between the Eastern European borderlands and post-colonial worlds located in today's Global South? I argue we may do so by observing that a decade before Jacques Millot's arrival on *la Grande Isle*, the regime of the Second Polish Republic seriously considered deporting its Jewish population to Madagascar (Trębacz, 2021). From the mid-1930s on, the Polish government saw in the resettlement of Jews a means to reduce unemployment and 'Polonise' cities, as masses of landless peasants could replace Jewish workers, especially in trade and craft-related professions (Modras, 2004; Miedziński, 2010).[8] Given Palestine's perceived low absorption rate for émigré Jews and Polish Catholic concerns regarding their impact on Christian holy sites, the Polish government issued new proposals for alternative locations for Jewish colonisation, the most popular being Liberia, Kenya, Rhodesia, Angola, Belgian Congo and Madagascar (on the Polish 'mission' to Liberia, see Puchalski, 2017; on Madagascar, see Ormicki, 1937 and Fiedler, 2006). As Piotr Puchalski has argued, through the establishment of a Liga Morska I Kolonialna (LMiK, Maritime and Colonial League) in 1930, Poland developed a colonial discourse that both saw itself as morally superior to its British, French and German colonial counterparts and appealed to an alleged Polish–African brotherhood that could serve as a unique bridge between Europe and Africa (Puchalski, 2017). In this vein, while some Polish politicians understood that the colonial conditions experienced by Black Africans resonated with their own fate under the partitioning powers, others grappling with the legacy of partitions viewed themselves superior to their supposed African 'brethren' as a way to shore up their own whiteness, viewed as synonymous with culture and civilisation (Ureña Valerio, 2019; Zaremba, 2022).

Against this wider Polish colonial backdrop, and building on earlier, nineteenth-century French, Dutch and German calls to settle Europe's Jews on the island, Polish authorities formulated the 'Madagascar Plan', conceived as an attempt to solve once and for all the demographic, national and social problems associated with the 'Jewish question' (Yahil, 1974; Korzec, 1980). Despite French scepticism that there was very little terrain in Madagascar with a climate that would allow Europeans to work, as well as concerns that absorbing large numbers of Jews would provoke political instability on the island, the issue of making Madagascar open for Polish emigration came to a head in autumn 1936, during discussions between the Polish minister of foreign affairs Józef Beck and French prime minister Léon Blum, with Marius Moutet, French minister of colonies, who were favourably disposed to the idea (Trębacz, 2021: 14). On 16 January 1937, Moutet expressed carefully formulated consent to the Madagascar Plan in the Parisian journal *Le Petit Parisien*. In it he also showed support for additional Jewish emigration to the French colonies of New Caledonia, New Hebrides and French Guyana. He made it clear that Polish Jewish emigration to Madagascar would only be acceptable as a way to help victims of political and religious persecution, and it would be dependent on receiving financial help and support from important Jewish organisations after a careful vetting of potential settlers.

In May 1937, France allowed the Polish government to send a special Commission to Madagascar to study the climate and working conditions on the island. Led by major Mieczysław Bohdan Lepecki, the commission was tasked with the 'objective possibility of settling on the island for "white man"' (Trębacz, 2021: 14). The Polish commission spent approximately thirteen weeks on Madagascar, in which its members visited different parts of the island (Drymmer, 1968). Relying on the testimonies of French experts in the fields of geology, climatology, agriculture and demography, complemented with his own observations, Lepecki and his team indicated three areas suitable for potential resettlement: Betroka, Itasy and Ankaizina (the latter on the northern portion of the high central plateau). Although Lepecki drew his locational conclusions from the opinions of French experts regarding the areas' rich soil and supposed beneficent influence of Madagascar's climate on human health, he ignored the fact that only a small percentage of the Jewish community in Poland made their living as farmers (Trębacz, 2021: 14). In addition, the commission's members underestimated the fear among the Malagasy of losing their employment due to the influx of white Europeans.

Sensing a weakening of colonial control over their territory, the Polish colonisation of Madagascar was attacked in the media across the French political spectrum, from the socialist *Le Populaire*, the radical *La République* to the monarchist *L'Action Francaise*. The heightened aversion of the new French government that assumed power in April 1938, combined with the unfavourable opinion of Jewish communities led to a gradual fading of support for the Madagascar Plan of stimulating Polish Jewish emigration to the South Indian Ocean territory. Reflecting on this failed experiment in Jewish resettlement, Zofia Trębacz asks:

> What was the intention behind the efforts of the special commission? Did the representatives of the Polish government indeed see in Madagascar a chance to acquire an overseas colony? Did they believe that it was possible to gain their own settling territory? Or were they drawn by an unbridled desire to expel Jews from the country? Or maybe Madagascar could really become a new Promised Land for escapees persecuted in their current homelands? (Trębacz, 2021: 21)

If, as Trębacz argues, '[t]his exotic island clearly stirred the collective imagination in the years before the Second World War' (2021: 21), I would add that 'this island' was part of a broader, global Polish imaginary encompassing an ethnically cleansed, Western 'Polonising' frontier situated in its formerly German 'Recovered Territories', including a powerful mythology – nourished by generations of displaced Poles forced to inhabit those same territories, often against their will – of an Arcadian, Eastern Polish borderland living in a supposed multicultural but ultimately illusory harmony with its Lithuanian, Belarussian and Ukrainian brethren.[9] These imaginaries interlaced and concatenated, producing internal European borders as well as external, Southern colonial frontiers whose racial logics were often transposed from the latter to the former. That the Polish colonising mission in Madagsacar (as well as Liberia, Brazil and other tropical settings) drew on cultural tropes of the 'white man's burden' later projected onto the civilising mission of Poland's Eastern Belarussian and Ukrainian peripheries (Ureña Valerio, 2019).

To the extent that, as Nandita Sharma has recently argued, the nation state has globalised, thus unsettling its territorial borders (Sharma, 2022), the violence and exclusionary effects of these historically entangled borderlands resonate into our day. This is reflected in Poland's ongoing efforts to prevent the in-migration of displaced persons from Africa and the Middle East fleeing war by building a wall through the forest, while benevolently opening its Eastern border wide to Ukrainians fleeing war. Following Hassan Ould Moctar (this volume), we may press this point by stating that the 'histories of each of these regions indeed engulf and enfold one another, in a manner similar to the ritual advance and retreat of waves and dunes that are so fundamental to the basic ecological rhythm of each zone'. 'Waves', the Yemeni feminist poet-scholar Saba Hamzah writes:

> is a metaphor to help me understand the power relations that are in control of a stranded life and its conditions. I use waves because they can depict the challenges, oppression, and boundaries a stranded is confronted by. No matter how brilliant a swimmer you are, if you are left alone in the middle of the ocean, waves can push you away from your goal, set you upside down, cause you to lose orientation and/or kill you. When I use the waves metaphor to illustrate how stranded lives live their life, on the one hand, it reminds me of the many times someone who is stranded fights alone, thrives, loses, suffocates, survives, and struggles, again and again, trying to reach what could be a safe mode or a safe place. (Aparna and Hamzah, 2023)

Swimming with the coelacanth through such waves into the black holes of collective family memory has allowed us to forge surprising 'sub-continental analogies' (Kapuściński, 2007) that would otherwise have remained hidden to an eye that can only perceive Central and Eastern Europe through the lens of an impoverished, ressentiment-laced, nation-centric 'strategic essentialism' (Müller, 2020: 734). In our struggle to safely explore such analogous modes of enquiry, it is time to set the coelacanth free to swim in the wide, wide ocean, to found new connectivities between the many Easts and Souths that inhabit our post-socialist and post-colonial worlds.

Acknowledgements: I wish to thank the editors of this volume for pointing me to invaluable recent scholarship, strengthening the overall argument of this chapter.

Notes

1 'In this chapter, I use the place name used by the administration at the time described, e.g. Breslau under German administration, then Wrocław under Polish administration.'
2 My translation: 'I always wanted a window there'.
3 My translation: 'We were refugees internal to the German Reich'.
4 Altogether, in 1944–46, more than a million Poles from the Kresy were moved to the Recovered Territories. Poles from the southern Kresy (now Ukraine) were forcibly resettled mainly in Silesia, while those from the north (Belarus and Lithuania) moved to Pomerania and Masuria. Polish residents of Lwów settled not only in Wrocław but also in Gliwice and Bytom, which had not been destroyed during the war. The latter cities were relatively closer to the new

eastern border of Poland, which could become significant in case of a sudden hoped-for return to the East.

5 Kresy was also largely coterminous with the northern area of the 'Pale of Settlement', a territory devised by Catherine the Great to limit Jews from settling in the homogenously Christian Orthodox core of the Russian empire, such as Moscow and St Petersburg. The Pale lasted until 1917, when the Russian Empire ceased to exist (Wegner, 1997).

6 In terms of major urban-administrative regions, the Eastern Borderlands were composed of Lwów, Nowogródek, Polesie, Stanisławów, Tarnopol, Wilno, Wołyn and Białystok provinces. Today, all these regions are divided between Western Ukraine, Western Belarus and Southeastern Lithuania.

7 Bakuła (2007) situates the rise of Eastern Polish 'Borderlands-mania' in post-1989 Poland, the fall of the Berlin Wall and the implosion of the Soviet Union. It is perhaps not a coincidence that this is precisely the period during which Western border scholars have signalled a 'renaissance' in border studies, after being relegated to a relative academic backwater (Newman and Paasi, 1998). The beauty of Bakuła's intervention is that – from an ostensibly Eastern 'backwater' location in global circuits of academic knowledge production – he reveals what three decades of so-called critical borderlands studies has not had the courage to admit. Rather than liberate the field, the celebration of 'border studies' and its associated fashionable terminology (boundary 'spatial socialisation', 'b/ordering', 'borderscapes', 'border poetics'), has only served to reinforce processes of colonial 'othering' by intensifying the framing of the world into fundamentally exclusionary Us/Them relations (Kramsch, 2020). In this very specific sense the so-called 'bordering turn' of the early millennium, like Bakuła's 'Borderlands', can be said to have 'lost its geographical sense a long time ago, gaining mostly an ideological status' (Bakuła, 2007: 116); see also Aparna and Hamzah, in press.

8 Polish antisemitism responding to a perceived over-representation of Jews in the liberal professions of course stoked much of this policy (Puchalski, 2022). In the 'Recovered Territories' of Upper and Lower Silesia this was overlaid onto a robust German antisemitism. Late in his life, Papa would tell me '80 per cent of lawyers in Breslau were Jews', his tone suggesting that this number was unacceptable. When I asked him as a young college student what he knew of Jews being deported to Auschwitz and other concentration death camps, he replied, 'All we knew is that they were going to labour camps, and we thought, "good, now they will know what real work is"'. Thus spoke the unreflective, working-class Breslau milieu my father was raised in.

9 In an important recent intervention decoupling the notion of 'territory' from 'homeland' so prominent in contemporary border studies, LA-based geographer John Agnew proposes a conceptual distinction between borders for 'dwelling spaces' and for 'geopolitical spaces': the former implies that the 'pursuit of basic life purposes and the possibility of living a "satisfactory" life trump the inheritance of a given territorial address' (Agnew 2020: 57). The late, great Gloria Anzaldúa would surely concur. But for the neologism to gain historical

traction in Eastern Europe, borders as 'dwelling spaces' must confront the traumatic void of forced expulsion, ethnic cleansing and the rehabitation of populations who then cling to an ideal of 'lost homelands' that destabilise any notion of Heimat ('homeland') forged from post-war geopolitical dispensations (see Grass, 2002).

References

Agnew, J. (2020) 'Taking back control? The myth of territorial sovereignty and the Brexit fiasco', *Territory, Politics, Governance*, 8(2), 259–72.
Allen, D. J. (2003) *The Oder-Neisse line: the United States, Poland and Germany in the Cold War*. Westport, CT: Praeger.
Andersson, R. (2022) 'Border walls, irregular migration and the co-optation of the border security playbook', *International Migration*, 60, 226–30.
Aparna, K. and Hamzah, S. (2023) 'Languaging as refusal', *Fennia*, 201(2), 215–28 https://doi.org/10.11143/fennia.122372
Bakuła, B. (2007) 'Colonial and postcolonial aspects of Polish borderlands studies: an outline', *Teksty Drugie*, 1, 96–123.
Bjork, J. (2008) *Neither German nor Pole: Catholicism and National Indifference in a Central European Borderland*. Ann Arbor, MI: University of Michigan Press.
Brunnbauer, U., Esch, M. G. and Sundhaussen, H. (eds) (2006) *Definitionsmacht, Utopie, Vergeltung: 'Ethnische Säuberungen' im östlichen Europa des 20.Jahrhunderts*. Berlin: LIT Verlag.
Coppens, Y. (1988) *Pré-ambules: les premiers pas de l'homme*. Paris: Odile Jacob.
Dorst, J. (1980) 'Notices nécrologiques sur Jacques Millot, Membre de la Section de Biologie animale et végétale', *Comptes Rendus de l'Académie des Sciences, t.291* (29 September), 14–21.
Drymmer, W. T. (1968) 'Zagadnienie żydowskie w Polsce w latach 1935–1939', *Zeszyty Historyczne*, 13, 55–75.
Fiedler, A. (2006) *Madagaskar: Gorąca wieś Ambinanitelo*. Warsaw: Pelplin.
Grass, G. (2002) *Crabwalk*. London: Faber and Faber.
Kacowicz, A. M. and Lutomski, P. (eds) (2007) *Population Resettlement in International Conflicts: A Comparative Study*. Washington, DC: Lexington Books.
Kapuściński, R. (2007) *Travels with Herodotus*. New York: Vintage.
Koobak, R., Tlostanova, M. and Thapar-Björkert, S. (eds) (2021) *Postcolonial and Postsocialist Dialogues: Intersections, Opacities, Challenges in Feminist Theorizing and Practice*. London: Routledge.
Korzec, P. (1980) *Juifs en Pologne: La question juive pendant l'entre-deux-gerres*. Paris: Sciences Po.
Kramsch, O. (2020) 'Remembering Chris Rumford (1958–2016)', *Journal of Borderlands Studies*, 35(5), 819–27.
Laurière, C. (2019) 'Un lieu de synthèse de la science anthropologique: histoire du musée de l'Homme', in *Bérose: encyclopédie internationale des histoires de l'anthropologie*. Paris: CNRS, pp. 319–24.
Lem, S. (1966) *Highcastle: A Remembrance* [transl Michael Kandel]. Cambridge, MA: MIT Press.
McNamara, P. (2014) 'Layered colonialism: colonization and Sovietisation in Poland's recovered territories', in Healey, Róisín and Dal Lago, Enrico (eds)

The Shadow of Colonialism on Europe's Modern Past. Basingstoke: Palgrave Macmillan, pp. 211–27.

Madajczyk, P. and Polsko-Niemiecki, T. I. R. (1992) *Mniejszość niemiecka w Polsce w polityce wewnętrznej w Polsce i w RFN oraz w stosunkach między obydwu państwami*. Warsaw.

Majewska, E. (2011) 'La mestiza from Ukraine? border crossing with Gloria Anzaldúa', *Signs: Journal of Women in Culture and Society*, 37(1), 34–41.

Mick, C. (2014) 'Colonialism in the Polish Eastern borderlands, 1919–1939', in Healey, Róisín, and Dal Lago, Enrico (eds) *The Shadow of Colonialism on Europe's Modern Past*. Basingstoke: Palgrave Macmillan, pp. 126–41.

Millot, J. (1954) *Le troisième coelacanthe: historique, éléments d'écologie, morphologie externe, documents divers*. Paris: Let Naturaliste Malgache.

Modras, R. (2004) 'Obyż jak najprędzej! Osadnictwo Żydów w koloniach francuskich. Madagaskar, Nowa Kaledonia, Guyana', *Warszawski Dziennik Narodowy*, (17 Jan 1937), 17, 2.

Müller, M. (2020) 'In search of the Global East: thinking between North and South', *Geopolitics*, 25(3), 734–55.

Newman, D. and Paasi, A. (1998) 'Fences and neighbours in the postmodern world: boundary narratives in political geography', *Progress in Human Geography*, 22(2), 186–207.

NPR (2021) 'The EU accuses Belarus of luring global migrants into other European countries'. www.npr.org/2021/10/12/1045345417/poland-belarus-lukashenko-eu-migrants-asylum (accessed 27 October 2021).

PleOrmicki, W. (1921) *Warunki i możliwości emigracji żydowskiej*. Warsaw: Nakładem Instytutu Badań Spraw Narodowościowych.

Prauser, S. and Rees, A. (2004) *The Expulsion of 'German' Communities from Eastern Europe at the End of the Second World War*. Florence: European University Institute. HEC No. 2004/1.

Pszczółkowska, D. (2022) 'Poland: what does it take for a public opinion coup to be reversed?', *International Migration*, 60, 221–25.

Puchalski, P. (2022) *Poland in a Colonial World Order: Adjustments and Aspirations, 1918–1939*. Abingdon: Routledge.

Puchalski, P. (2017) 'The Polish mission to Liberia, 1934–1938: constructing Poland's colonial identity', *The Historical Journal*, 60(4), 1071–96.

Sharma, N. (2022) 'National citizenship and the institutionalization of postcolonial racisms', Unpublished presentation at the international workshop *Souths and Easts as Method: Europeanisation as Violence*, University of Helsinki, Finland.

Tlostanova, M. (2017) *Postcolonialism and Postsocialism in Fiction and Art: Resistance and Re-existence*. Cham: Palgrave Macmillan.

Trębacz, Z. (2021) '"Jews to Madagascar": Poland in the face of ethnical problems in the 1930s', *European Spatial Research and Policy*, 28, 9–24.

Urban, T. (2006) *Der Verlust: Die Vertreibung der Deutschen und Polen im 20. Jahrhundert*. Berlin: C. H. Beck.

Ureña Valerio, L. A. (2019) *Colonial Fantasies, Imperial Realities: Race Science and the Making of Polishness on the Fringes of the German Empire, 1840–1920*. Athens, OH: Ohio University Press.

Wasserstein, B. (2007) *Barbarism and Civilization: A History of Europe in Our Time*. Oxford: Oxford University Press.

Wegner, B. (1997) *From Peace to War: Germany, Soviet Russia, and the World, 1939–1941*. Oxford: Berghahn.

Willoweit, D. (2013) *Reich und Staat. Eine kleine deutsche Verfassungsgeschichte.* Munich: C. H. Beck.

Yahil, L. (1974) 'Madagascar: phantom of a solution for the Jewish Question', in Vago, Bela and Mosse, George L. (eds) *Jews and Non-Jews in Eastern Europe, 1918–1945.* New York: John Wiley & Sons, pp. 217–34.

Zaremba, Ł. (2022) 'Slavic blackface: from the archive of the visual colonial complex of the inter-war period', *Konteksty*, 3, 44–63.

Zarycki, T. (2014) *Ideologies of Eastness in Central and Eastern Europe.* Abingdon: Routledge.

Afterword: Souths, Easts and the politics of dissent at this colonial conjuncture

Prem Kumar Rajaram

Europe has increasingly been riven by colonial and imperial violences. The full-scale invasion of Ukraine showed us, not for the first time in recent years, the fissures in Europe, its demarcations between those to be welcomed and those outside of solidarity. To be sure, the dichotomy is false, solidarity towards Ukrainian refugees is 'false' and limited temporally, socially and spatially, as Ruslana Koziienko (2023) has succinctly argued and the editors have also noted. As I write this afterword, the Israeli attacks on Gaza remind us of Europe's persistent coloniality. Israel's disproportionate and brutal attacks in Gaza are pussy-footed around by governments in the North and West. Cultural institutions and universities do the same (Srećko et al., 2023). In Austria, we have the unedifying sight of a major antifa network condemning pro-Palestine protests. At this conjuncture, historical guilt is weaponised against criticism as Europe shores up its cultural and political borders and histories. The university in Austria where I work is publicly accused of antisemitism (Weidinger, 2023), bizarrely given its history, largely because of a refusal by brave colleagues to call off a teach-in on Palestine and by students protesting a talk on 'terrorism'. As history is weaponised, so too is culture deployed to quell critique and make dissent, the very stuff of democracy, unlawful on cultural, and not political, grounds. We are, indeed, at the razor's edge where the sharpness of demarcations making illegible the lives and indeed humanity of a multitude becomes apparent. This is of course not new in itself. The striking undemocratic Western response to the war, making impermissible and indeed illegible the representation of Palestinian death as unacceptable tragedy, shows the multiple weapons and weaponising strategies at the heart of Europe. A persistent coloniality is at the heart of the North and the West, and the dependency on it for the maintenance and reproduction of its ways of life and for justifying or making illegible its inequalities and violences becomes ever clearer.

How has this been forgotten? How has the longue-durée violence at the core of our contemporary situation become illegible? What has happened so that the West and the North can allow, justify, support or make invisible the unspeakable actions on which our common prosperity rests?

The Souths and Easts method can provide us with analytical tools to understand the violences that wrack our time. This important book presents us with ways of seeing that potentially allow us to read both the stark and the mundane violences of the contemporary order. This means that the patterns of violence become legible, and as they do so the mythologies behind them are shown up for what they are – constructs, whose perpetuation speaks to the continuation of an unequal and exploitative order.

What ways of seeing do Souths and Easts as method generate? And what patterns do they make legible? Thinking with the book has been productive, pushing me to consider and reconsider positions and practices based on my own concerns about the closures and violences of persistent coloniality as they play out in the Third World (a term I prefer to 'Global South' as it is historically situated in struggles) and in Eastern Europe. In this short reflection, my thoughts are organised around five situations where, as far as I see it, Souths and Easts entangle. In other words, I will reflect on critique, thoughts and ideas of the authors in this book in relation to situations of our time that bump up against my own concerns, to use John Clarke's phrasing (Clarke, 2022). These are to do with my struggles to understand (1) the persistent coloniality of our time, (2) the cultural and economic cheapening of subaltern populations, (3) the disconnecting of people from publics, (4) the weaponisation of culture and (5) the limiting of dissent through cultural claims and expert interventions particularly in our universities. I will engage with the Souths and Easts method as the authors do, and with reference to their ideas, to think through these situations which are all core concerns of the book as a whole

Antonio Gramsci (1971) argued that we should analyse 'situations' by thinking about the relations of force that bring them into being. He distinguishes between organic and conjunctural forces operating in and patterning these situations. Building on Gramsci, Stuart Hall developed 'conjunctural analysis', which analyses how different elements come together in the making of any given situation (Hall, 1988; Clarke, 2019). Different levels of society and ways of thinking and seeing, each with their different and contradictory histories and struggles, comprise a situation. Their contradictions can be brought to light in crisis when the explicit or latent alliance and relations between different forces collapse under the weight of their own contradictions. Souths and Easts as method seems to me to be conjunctural analysis. The method parses out the relations of force and the forgotten or concealed relations and contradictions that make up situations. Maury (this volume) and the editors (its Introduction) are most explicit in demonstrating the racial-colonial conjuncture of the present, and I think this Gramscian analysis of conjunctures is central to the method and to the chapters in the book.

The persistent coloniality of our time

Accounts of contemporary colonialism tend to shore up different histories. Rather than a multiply constituted and even contradictory idea of coloniality, a consistent and transferable idea of the colonial present tends to be sounded by activists and by academics. The contradictions of such positions can be sparked by paying attention to their inconsistency. Such contradictions include: the support by leftist scholars and commentators of Bashar al Assad's murderous regime in Syria in recognition of his father Hafez's old anti-imperial work (Mrie, 2018), a similarly confused ideologically induced myopia about Vladimir Putin's Russia and the previously mentioned dispiriting sight of antifa in Austria condemning pro-Palestine rallies.

There is by contrast a sense of movement in the critique of the colonial present in this book. As the editors show in their Introduction, coloniality remains a persistent operating force in the imaginations of Europe and in the active attempts to realise this imagination through bordering strategies that code Europeanness with whiteness, leading to cultural, political and security justifications for the exclusion or marginalisation of people from the Third World. Maury (this volume) shows us how as migrant labour is sorted it is positioned in relation to Finland and Finnish citizenship, serving as a way of Europe knowing itself. Maury's argument resonates with Edward Said's insight that Orientalism was a way of clarifying the fullness of Europe, a way of knowing founded on fixing the Orient in a regressive time, by which European knowledge, progress and modernity was realised (Said, 1977).

The production of difference is often taken as the abiding feature of colonialism in the past and present. Krivonos and Aparna show how projects of imperial extraction, Western or Soviet, are premised on ideas of progress and modernity, which can function via the homogenisation of a population. Difference is perhaps a product of a deeper ideological and political process – extraction and dispossession – and not the basis of colonialism. This forces attention to deeper histories and conjunctures that allow us to move away from the foreground of colonialism, to its deeper background.

The *Guardian* (2023) reported on unmarked graves of migrants that pepper Europe's borders on 8 December 2023. On a map in this report, graves outline Europe. The red dots are concentrated in areas where the idea of Europe seems especially weak: the borders between Spain and North Africa, the Italian and Greek islands with their diverse and complicated Mediterranean histories and cultures, and along the 'Balkan route'. Neuman Stanivuković (this volume) argues that the European Union's attempt to control its borders is contingent on making both South East Europe and migrants abject. 'The Balkans' become a space of multiply constituted deviance, where backwardness of not-quite Europeans intermingle in chaotic ways with troublesome irregular migrants. South East Europe is then a space of encounter, not simply a border, and in that encounter the Europeans who meet migrants are unreliable, requiring the coding and organising of Frontex and of European infrastructure projects. In a similar vein, Krivonos and Aparna start their chapter on encounters between Afghans and Ukrainians by striving to build cognition of common histories in places where the – fake – solidarity accorded to Ukrainians leads to 'competitive victimhoods' and a breakdown of solidarity between displaced people in the local histories of the borderlands (Kramsch, this volume). All this points to the complex conjunctures of coloniality in the present, not simply of a border regime (re)producing difference but rather encounters and relations where the messy commonality of marginalisations before an idea of a pristine Europe are apparent.

Cheapening and asymmetries that maintain the European order of things

The war in Gaza, like the war in Ukraine, shows us starkly the relative value of different human lives. The unmarked graves peppering the European border is another reminder of the cheapening of human life on which contemporary value regimes rest. This is another actively forgotten aspect of European modernity – other worlds must end, their endings must be possible, for the European world to persevere and to dominate. Such endings can be epistemic and they can be visceral and existential. Drăgan's chapter shows us the condition of being cheapened, of existing as Roma in Romania in a world where value is only accorded to the exception who successfully leaves community to be judged by white audiences.

Cheapened conditions are actively made, they are part of the toolkit of Europe, and the idea of Europe cannot exist without it. Oancă argues sharply that the making of European heritage through common and celebratory endeavours, notably the European Capital of Culture initiative, produces 'stratified subalternities, various rankings of non-Europeanness and non-Westernness, and affective registers of stratified longings and belongings'. The stratification – or layering – of identity points to the reliance of authorised European worlds on ending other possibilities, histories and worlds. This is cheapening: the cultural and political derogation of other ways of living culturally, socially, politically and economically. In essence what is being done is controlling the social reproduction of others, so that they may serve the reproduction of European worlds. There is also the by-product of Europe becoming a project to be aspired to by those admitted to its ideas of heritage and identity, minimising class and other stratifications within, and also effectively depoliticising the European public sphere in the weaponisation of culture. Ivasiuc shows how the social reproduction of the good European labourer is contingent on the production of the 'Bad Eastern European and Ugly Roma'.

But it is not enough of course to imagine cheapness; its hierarchical layering in Europe is made durable and reproducible over time by a multitude of practices. Such practices – legal, infrastructural and cultural – add uneven weight to the relations that constitute Europe. There is a colonial asymmetry (Moctar's words in this volume) at the heart of Europe and reproduced through migration policies, where violence in northern Africa and elsewhere is integral to the maintenance of the liberal peace in Europe (and its capitalist economy). Competing imperialism, as Manatouma shows, embeds and normalises asymmetrical temporalities that further entrenches the European and imperial order.

Disconnecting publics

I have been a citizen of Europe for more than two years. I became a Hungarian citizen in May 2021, thirteen months after sitting for and passing an academic exam on the law, constitution, culture, arts, history and geography of the country. The exam is based on a slim text, written in dense academic Hungarian. I could pass because I could afford to hire a tutor, the excellent Orsolya, and because, while my Hungarian is certainly not at an academic level, I am familiar enough with the convolutions of academic writing, even in another language. In the exam there were sixteen or seventeen of us, and five of us passed. All five were people who could afford a tutor, and had the leisure time afforded by our middle-class jobs to study. It took me thirteen months after passing the exam to be granted citizenship, during which period, apparently, the president of the country reviewed my (and everyone else's) application. The process is not transparent; I do not know what was reviewed, or why my publications critiquing the Hungarian illiberal state, my employment at the Central European University (CEU) – institution non grata in the country – and my leadership of an education programme for refugees did not stand in the way. Most likely they were inconsequential – I had been a tax payer in Hungary for some fifteen years and have three Hungarian children. In any case, the time I spent 'waiting' was not consequential, except for more middle-class concerns about the difficulty of being a third-country national trying to buy an apartment in Budapest.

I did not have to wait, not in any real sense of waiting. I was not caught in a temporal limbo and had a pretty good sense of what the eventual outcome would be. Friends of mine with refugee status had a different sense of waiting, with outcomes uncertain. Citizenship is set up as a goal for people who have been displaced. It promises an end to a general uncertainty that characterises refugee statuses in Hungary, which now have to be renewed every year or two (though the immigration bureaucracy is not often up to that task). This casts a pall over education and work, with employers often unsure if people can be hired despite a clear legal entitlement. At the Open Learning Initiative (OLIve), the education programme for displaced people at CEU, we often employed our graduates. In 2021, CEU refused to pay out contracts unless further proof of the right to work was provided – a bizarre requirement, but one that seemed justifiable to conservative employers like CEU in the face of hostility towards migrants and refugees. At one point, CEU refused to pay unless highly confidential court documents about employees' refugee status, which contain reasons for their flight, were shared. CEU has its own story here, the deep and traumatic loss to the Hungarian government ended with the core of our programmes being relocated to Vienna. Another less tangible loss has been a fear of dissent, and an anxious reliance on regulations to fill an empty space where there was once an *attitude*.

People with refugee statuses in Hungary find that their planning for the future is obstructed by the anxiety of remaining in a situation where future plans are delayed, where time is stolen, waiting on citizenship, or the renewal of protection, or moving in ceaseless circulation from employer to immigration ministry to get surplus, unnecessary documents. The colonial tactic of keeping people waiting is 'a tactic of domination' (Khosravi, 2019: 418), a way of leveraging Europeanness and a way of disconnecting people from a desirable public. There are no statistics as far as I am aware, but people with refugee statuses whom I know have their citizenship statuses turned down regularly. No reasons are given.

Since becoming a Hungarian citizen, I have participated in one election and will choose not to participate in the latest of a series of 'national consultations' by which the Hungarian state clarifies its public (Magyarország Kormánya, 2023). The general election of 2022 was accompanied by a national referendum, essentially a scare tactic directed against the LGTBQI+ community and their 'gender ideology'. At the voting booth, citizens had to fill out a form asking a series of questions if they would support children learning about sexual orientation or gender reassignment in schools (many of us spoiled the form instead of filling it out). In the latest national consultation – titled 'On the Protection of Our Sovereignty' – the ostensible target is 'Brussels', but the consultation finds its way to target the usual – migrants

(Brussels wants to create a 'migrant ghetto' in Hungary); migrant terrorists, specifically Palestinians (Brussels supports Hamas financially); and the LGBTQI+ community (Brussels wants to overturn the child protection law that forbids discussion on sexuality and so on in classrooms, in the face of 'aggressive LGBTQI+ propaganda').

The discourses that are used to cohere a public, by making them angry at Brussels in this case, also clarify its borders. In the colonial fashion, disconnecting people clarifies the boundaries of virtuous citizenship. There is cultural capital to be gained from disconnections. The Hungarian government has over the last decade been a pioneer of the 'organised abandonment' that the editors write about with reference to Gilmour (see Introduction). The Hungarian government is on the other side of Europeanisation. Ostensibly, the disconnection is formulated in opposition to 'Brussels', figured as the liberal integrative force encroaching on Hungary's 'sovereignty'. But there has always been a dark underbelly to Europe's liberalism, as just about all the authors in this volume show. Viktor Orbán's Hungary has been strategic in speaking to this underbelly, and has cultivated a European alliance along his illiberal and populist politics. The European Commission has picked up on this, with the Hungarian response to migration in 2015 once condemned, now par for the course and replicated in strategies of detention and obstruction continent-wide. The Commission's office for the Promotion of Our European Way of Life speaks most explicitly to the illiberal shoring up of the boundaries of Europeanness and the cultural pall given to Europeanisation. As Deiana and Kušić point out, the only way possible is Europe, but this Europe is contradictory and its shadowy violences intertwine with its liberalisations, leading to occlusions and abandonment, and their justification in terms of Europeanisation.

The weaponisation of culture

Positioning ourselves in our political and academic interventions are fundamental. As the editors say, embodied writing, where the scars of history and politics remain material, is a way to move beyond rarefied academic and policy approaches that can erase, or fade into the background, the violences of Europe. Embodied stories are connected; we are rarely, I think, separate or distinguish between bodies. We bear the scars of people like us – people who are said to be like us – and awareness of the mutual scarring that policies of connection and disconnection produce is integral. As the European body shores itself up, it is scarred; histories that connect Europe to what is now its 'other' are removed only with a force that leaves an imprint. Writing that imprint is important. Someone said to me the other day that she cannot believe how, and to what extent, the North and the West are so much on the wrong side of history. She was speaking, of course, of the war in Gaza, and the readiness of governments in Europe and the United States to try to somehow look away from the violence that the Israeli state is systematically inflicting on a civilian population. Part of the answer lies in the rationalisations of history, where documents of progress and civilisation restrict the shape of our concerns and our solidarities.

Stories of embodied scarring are of course intergenerational. We are formed in historical association, including with relatives who share our social and personal histories. I have three part 'Hungarian' children, which means that their ancestry contains Roma, German, French and Tatar connections, as well as family rumours of a hidden Jewishness. All this is shored up in the common identity, 'Hungarian'. Multiple histories speaking to the passages and sojourns over time in this part of the world are rendered invisible or reduced to the minor role of a past before the Hungarian nation was built. In Orbán's manufacture of a virtuous public, a distinct Hungarian culture is imputed, '*we* have a right to decide with whom *we* live', (Magyaroszág Kormánya, 2023, my emphasis). In this weaponisation of culture, the other is demarcated and excluded (in ways useful to accumulating cultural capital), and there is a drift towards a bare and brutal racialism. Orbán drew censure across Europe for his statements in 2022 that Hungary was not and did not want to be a 'mixed race' nation (his choice of Hungarian *kevert fajú* is problematic, its most literal translation is 'mixed species'). My children, in this sensibility, are *kevert fajú*, and while many would recoil at such terms, Orbán is clever in speaking to a general taken-as-neutral commonsense of who is Hungarian.

The weaponisation of culture, for example in the office for the Promotion of Our European Way of Life, disconnects people from publics. Such disconnecting allows for the reproduction of 'Europe' and its culture, but it also has the side effect of depoliticising European public spheres. This has been particularly apparent in the trope of 'active citizenship' which is used, Biesta (2009) charges, to limit the fundamentally political acts of dissent and disagreement in favour of the cultivation of European values. European populists, like Orbán, see through this and recognise it as the culturalisation of a public sphere: important questions about whom we should live with and how become cultural ones, not political, and much is left to experts to design ever more sophisticated border technologies to keep the other, ripped from common histories with Europe, out.

Limiting dissent

Srećko Horvat, Paul Stubbs and Dubravka Sekulić, Croatian scholars, disinvited themselves recently from a talk they were asked to give in Berlin's Maxim Gorki Theatre on Yugoslavia and the Non-Aligned Movement. They did so because the theatre followed hard on the heels of other German cultural institutions, notably the Frankfurt Book Fair, in disinviting or postponing Palestine-focused events or people. In an opinion piece in Al Jazeera, the scholars note that as people who remember the Yugoslav wars of secession, they fundamentally disagreed with the theatre's statement that 'war is a great simplifier' that 'demands a simple division into friend and foe' (cited in Horvat et al., 2023). They call their piece, 'Against the "Denkverbot": If you cancel Palestine, cancel us'. *Denkverbot* means 'prohibition to think'.

The Souths and Easts method promulgated by the authors in this book is an explicit refusal of *Denkverbot*. The authors think creatively, forcefully and politically against the violences of our time, and provide us tools to understand how thinking about some things and some events has become beyond the pale – prohibited explicitly or by commonsense. Hamzah, Dragana, Ivasiuc and Țîștea in particular show us how academic knowledge can obscure the complications of whiteness attributed to Eastern Europeans. Hamzah's poetic language uncovers hidden histories. Țîștea's ethnodrama sheds light on the dissenting positions of Roma women working as cheapened labour in Finland.

The prohibition of dissent when it comes to Palestine certainly speaks to European historical guilt and to the complex geopolitical questions. The forcefulness of that dissent here in Austria took me, naively, by surprise (despite my European citizenship, I am still an outsider, constantly surprised by the forces of history in this part of the world). In an online article in the flagship Austrian newspaper *Der Standard* (2023, my translation here), I am called out, without being named, as a supervisor of a thesis which questioned and critiqued 'Zionism' and, the author charges, furthered antisemitism. The author of the piece, Bernhard Weidinger, is 'a right-wing extremism researcher'. Weidinger says he is 'not naming any names in this article because I am not interested in shaming individual people'. The student and her two supervisors, myself included, seem to be taken as effects of a structure, unthinking automatons:

> CEU serves as an illustration of a phenomenon that is widespread internationally and is also gaining importance in the academic milieu in this country: talk about Israel/Palestine that rests on the self-image of absolute moral

superiority and fundamentally brings out the heaviest possible rhetorical guns against others and conversely objections are defamed as a priori amoral; a self-immunising judgement that unmovedly brushes nuances and complexity off the table and proudly carries this Manichaeism in front of it.

Arguing against this is not simple, it is a charge that could be made too easily by 'us' against 'the other side'. In taking Weidinger's claims seriously, we can see the operating effects of polarisation, where separation into entrenched positions is at least partly based on not recognising our own polarising. This is where Souths and Easts as method is important. It asks, to my mind, what has happened so that this violence, this abandonment, this marginalisation has come about, has been legitimised and is barely noticed? The book is an avowedly political one of course, but its dissent and disagreement is based on a social and historical reading of the genealogy of situations, and not on taking up simple positions. I am not a fan of polarisation. I prefer to talk with people with whom I disagree, and to understand how our political positions have emerged. This does not prevent condemnation of retrograde and violent positions, but allows for dissent and disagreement to be rooted in the historicity of situations.

The urgency of dissent and disagreement in this moment of course goes far beyond the concerns of a small American university in central Europe. But we can think from there. The prohibition to think comes out with such force now with regards Gaza due to a variety of factors. One is almost certainly the various culturalisations that have led to European histories and positions becoming disconnected from its colonial histories. This disconnection leads to a rarefied space of confidence and security, where the project of Europeanisation gains moral grounding born perhaps from security of its successful culturalisations. This type of security and confidence seems somewhat new, a revival of a colonial position. To my mind it is an effect of the new European and North American populism, where that which for decades could not be said are now – since Trump, Johnson, Orbán, Le Pen and others – a normalised part of everyday discourse. The Gorki Theatre's and Weidinger's willingness to polarise positions, to declare who to stand with and who not, is akin to Orbán's strange national consultations and his parsing out of who belongs to the Hungarian public and who simply cannot. Orbán was always clear that for his vision of Hungary and Europe to exist, other people's worlds must end. The Gorki Theatre and Weidinger speak to the same position. To demand the ending of other worlds, and to pursue this through limiting dissent, speaks to a colonial sensibility, an authority to disregard other claims, and to enact violence.

References

Biesta, G. (2009) 'What kind of citizenship for European higher education? Beyond the competent active citizen', *European Educational Research Journal*, 8(2), 146–58.

Clarke, J. (2019) 'A sense of loss? Unsettled attachments in the current conjuncture', *New Formations*, 96–7, 132–46.

Clarke, J. (2022) 'Afterword: privilege, plurality, paradox, prefiguration – the challenges of opening up', in Cantat, C., Cook, I. M. and Rajaram, P. K. (eds) *Opening Up the University: Teaching and Learning with Refugees*. New York: Berghahn, pp. 293–306.

Gramsci, A. (1971) *Selections from the Prison Notebooks*. New York: International Publishers.

Guardian (2023) 'Revealed: More than 1,000 unmarked graves discovered along EU migration routes'. www.theguardian.com/world/ng-interactive/2023/dec/08/revealed-more-than-1000–unmarked-graves-discovered-along-eu-migration-routes (accessed 11 December 2023).

Hall, S. (1988) *The Hard Road to Renewal: Thatcherism and the Crisis of the Left*. London: Verso.

Horvat, S., Stubbs, P and Sekulić, D. (2023) 'Against the "Denkverbot": if you cancel Palestine, cancel us'. Al Jazeera, 1 November 2023. www.aljazeera.com/opinions/2023/11/1/against-the-denkverbot-if-you-cancel-palestine-cancel-us (accessed 11 December 2023).

Khosravi, S. (2019) 'What do we see if we look at the border from the other side?', *Social Anthropology/Anthropologie Sociale*, 27(3), 409–24.

Koziienko, R. (2023) 'Against false solidarity: a call for true solidarity among people with experiences of displacement', March, Allegra Lab. https://allegralaboratory.net/against-false-solidarity-a-call-for-true-solidarity-among-people-with-experiences-of-displacement (accessed 11 December 2023).

Magyarország Kormánya (2023) 'Nemzeti konzultáció szuverenitásunk védelméről'. Hungarian Government. https://kormany.hu/konzultacioaszuverenitasvedelmerol (accessed 11 December 2023).

Mrie, L. (2018) 'The problem with leftist myths about Syria'. Al Jazeera, 4 March. www.aljazeera.com/opinions/2018/3/4/the-problem-with-leftist-myths-about-syria (accessed 11 December 2023).

Said, E. (1977) *Orientalism*. London: Verso.

Weidinger, B. (2023) '"Antizionismus" und Academia: Das Beispiel Central European University', *Der Standard*, 7 December. www.derstandard.at/story/3000000198609/antizionismus-und-academia-das-beispiel-central-european-university?ref=rss (accessed 11 December 2023).

Index

Andalusia 19, 122–137
   Córdoba 122–137

Balkans 11, 17, 36–38, 40–41, 44–45, 103–116
   Bosnia-Herzegovina 33–34, 44, 47, 146, 153–154
   Croatia 33, 46–47, 107, 109
border xii–iii, 1–4, 11–13, 15–16, 18–21, 55–57, 61, 204
   externalisation 44, 54, 57, 111, 122

Cesaire, Aimée viii, 6, 87
Chad 18, 55, 62, 68–80
colonialism viii–x, 4, 6–7, 9–10, 12, 14–15, 19, 21–22, 58, 68, 70, 80, 86–87, 93, 95, 127–130, 132, 134, 137, 175–180, 195–196, 202, 222, 230, 250
   coloniality x, xii, 11–12, 20, 102, 105–108, 111, 146, 195–199, 205, 207–208
COVID-19 xiii, 54, 85
counterinsurgency 54–57
creolisation 213, 221–223, 225

doubt 6–8, 16, 37, 39–40, 53–54, 123, 216

ethnodrama 213
Eastern Europe xii–xiii, 6–7, 92, 142–143, 231–234
   Blackness 106, 241
   Eastern Europeanisation 142, 154–155
   labour xiii, 5, 85, 96, 212, 224
   internationalism 6, 14
   Lebensraum 92

European Union ix, 3, 51, 92, 130, 209, 238, 250
Europeanisation ix–x, xiii xv, 1–4, 7–10, 13–22, 34–43, 47, 52, 86, 101, 103–105, 107–116, 120–130, 133–137, 142–144, 146, 154, 156, 197, 208, 254, 257
Eurafrica ix, 17

Fanon, Franz viii, 4, 15, 52
feminism 3–4, 7
Frontex 44–46, 57, 63, 204, 251

Gaza 1, 248, 251, 255, 257
genocide 1, 9, 89, 129, 155, 178
Gramsci, Antonio 52, 196, 198, 207, 249

heritage 15, 19, 120–122, 126, 129–137, 238–239, 251
   colonial 73, 93, 130, 155
Holocaust xi, 8, 142, 155, 187, 190

imperialism 2, 6, 12, 68–70, 86, 127, 155
India xi, 3, 5, 110, 153, 222
   British India Office 93
   Dutch East India Company 82–83
   Indian Ocean ix, 21, 231, 242
   United East India Company 93
   West Indian 74, 240
infrastructure 1, 13, 15–17, 34–39, 42–47, 73
   infrastructural violence 16–17, 35–38, 43, 45, 91
   projects 9, 114, 251
innovation 195–197, 207–209

inter-imperiality x, 36–37, 85–86, 95, 127–128, 137, 178, 181
inter-referencing 2, 7, 14, 16–18, 20, 145
   violence 8, 145

Jews 12, 130, 135, 173–174, 240–241

Madagascar 231, 239–241
Mamdani, Mahmoud 10
Mauritania 54–55, 63
Mediterranean 42, 54, 57–59, 68, 92, 127, 232
   crossing 51
migration 44, 51–52, 54, 61
   governance 11, 55, 57
   labour 5, 83, 95–96, 209, 223, 250
muticulturalism 19, 131–132, 134–135, 242
   multicultural monoculturalism 134
Muslims xi–xii, 12, 106, 121, 133–135
   Islamophobia 106

Orientalism 18, 124, 128, 132, 137, 142, 151, 153, 224, 250

Palestine xiii, 1, 6, 9, 10, 21, 110, 173–174, 182, 240
   nakba 9
   occupation 9–10
   pro-Palestine 248, 250
Poland 11, 12, 21, 82, 84, 231, 233, 235–236
   Belarus border 11, 238
   borderlands 236, 237

race 6, 7, 10, 13, 21–22, 106, 116, 142, 155, 197, 198, 225, 255
   racialisation ix, 7, 11, 18, 85, 87, 102, 106, 121, 142, 196–201, 203–208
      racism xi, 2, 4–6, 9–11, 20–21, 87, 95, 105, 124, 147–148, 154, 188, 198, 199, 205–207, 221
representation 22, 36, 103
   policy representations 46
   violence 16, 53
Roma 134, 143, 146, 154, 185–188, 212, 221–224
   Roma futurism 190
   Romani 133

Romania 122, 150–151, 190
Rome 19, 144, 146, 148–149, 151, 187
   Treaty of 10
Russia 74–78, 84, 176, 201, 236, 250
   Russian Empire 6–7, 92, 201
   Wagner group 75–76

Sahel 18, 34, 51, 53–57, 61
   Sahelian periphery 61–62
   Sahelo-Sahara 18, 51, 53–55, 58, 62
   Sahelo-Saharan interior 61
Said, Edward viii, 1–2, 121–123, 142, 250
socialism 6–8, 14, 37, 68, 87–88, 101–102, 105–106, 110, 124, 128, 132, 135, 176
   anti-colonialism 175
   internationalism 70, 112
   modernisation 87
   primitive socialist accumulation 88
solidarity 2, 7, 12, 14, 21, 82–83, 94
   fatigue 1
Soviet Union 3, 6, 9, 17, 68, 70, 74, 78, 82, 85, 88, 91–92, 201, 233, 235
subalternities ix, 2, 96, 145
   stratified 13, 95, 121–122, 125, 134, 143, 145, 251

Tlostanova, Madina 13, 87, 143, 153–154, 234

Ukraine xiii, 1, 5, 10–11, 76, 84–86, 92–93, 231

violence ix, xi, 1, 15–20, 34–38, 43–44, 47, 52–53, 58, 70, 83, 86–87, 101, 111–115, 120–122, 145, 180–181, 190, 208, 248–249, 257
   administrative 197–198
   boomerang viii
   civilising xi
   developmentalism 9
   epistemic 155, 213, 223–224
   military 15, 57, 255
   racial 7, 9, 155
   slow violence 101
   starvation 88, 91, 93
   waiting 1, 17, 37–40, 46

welfare state 3
Whiteness 52, 91
   ignorance 223
   White laundering 178

Wynter, Sylvia 11

Yemen 164, 174–178
Yugoslavia 6, 43, 106, 112, 256

EU authorised representative for GPSR:
Easy Access System Europe, Mustamäe tee 50,
10621 Tallinn, Estonia
gpsr.requests@easproject.com

www.ingramcontent.com/pod-product-compliance
Ingram Content Group UK Ltd.
Pitfield, Milton Keynes, MK11 3LW, UK
UKHW051407100425
5429UKWH00004B/64